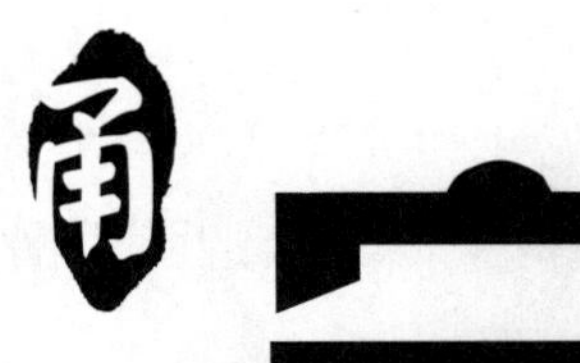

宁波 2023 统计年鉴

NINGBO STATISTICAL YEARBOOK

宁 波 市 统 计 局
Ningbo Municipal Bureau of Statistics
国家统计局宁波调查队
Survey Office of the National Bureau of statistics in Ningbo
编

中国统计出版社
China Statistics Press

图书在版编目（CIP）数据

宁波统计年鉴. 2023 = Ningbo Statistical Yearbook 2023 : 汉英对照 / 宁波市统计局, 国家统计局宁波调查队编. -- 北京 : 中国统计出版社, 2023.12

ISBN 978-7-5230-0346-6

Ⅰ. ①宁… Ⅱ. ①宁… ②国… Ⅲ. ①统计资料 - 宁波 - 2023 - 年鉴 - 汉、英 Ⅳ. ①C832.553-54

中国国家版本馆CIP数据核字(2023)第223699号

宁波统计年鉴 2023

作　　者/ 宁波市统计局 国家统计局宁波调查队
责任编辑/ 钟钰
装帧设计/ 汪培云
出版发行/ 中国统计出版社有限公司
地　　址/ 北京市丰台区西三环南路甲6号
邮政编码/ 100073
电　　话/ 邮购（010）63376909 书店（010）68783171
网　　址/ http://www.zgtjcbs.com
印　　刷/ 宁波鄞州启鸣印务有限公司
经　　销/ 新华书店
开　　本/ 890mm × 1240mm 1/16
字　　数/ 470千字
印　　张/ 26.5
版　　别/ 2023年12月第1版
版　　次/ 2023年12月第1次印刷
定　　价/ 368.00元 Price: 368.00yuan(RMB)

本书附同版本CD-ROM一张，光盘内容以书面文字为准。
如有印装差错，由本社发行部调换。

编者说明

一、《宁波统计年鉴2023》以大量统计数据，全面、系统地反映了2022年宁波经济、科技、社会各方面的发展情况，是一本信息密集的资料性年刊和工具书。本年鉴采用中英文排版方式。

二、《宁波统计年鉴2023》在内容编排顺序上做了调整，本年鉴内容包括：1.2022年宁波市国民经济和社会发展概况；2.综合；3.人口与劳动力；4.国民经济核算；5.财政、金融、保险、证券；6.物价指数和人民生活；7.农业；8.工业、能源消费和电力；9.固定资产投资和建筑业；10.港口、交通、运输、邮电；11.国内贸易、餐饮业；12.对外经济、旅游；13.文化、教育、卫生、体育、科学技术；14. 市政、环保、民政、政法及其他等十四个部分。为方便读者使用，各篇章前设有《主要统计指标》，篇末附有《主要统计指标解释》。

三、《宁波统计年鉴2023》辑入的统计数据，2018年及以前年份数据已根据第四次经济普查结果进行了数据调整，凡以往发表过的统计数据与本年鉴有出入的，均以本年鉴为准。

四、《宁波统计年鉴2023》在编辑中作如下规定，以使读者在使用时明了：

1.凡有注解均注在第一张表的下方。

2.凡在表内显示“空格”的，表示有数据但不足计量单位中的最小数，或表示该项统计数据不详或无该项统计数据；显示“#”表示其中的主要项。

五、《宁波统计年鉴2023》辑入的统计数据，对来自非政府统计部门的，注明数据来源。

六、《宁波统计年鉴》出版以来，受到社会各界的关心、支持，不少读者对于年鉴的内容和编辑工作提出了许多宝贵的意见，对此，我们采纳修正。并欢迎读者一如既往地对年鉴的不足之处给予批评指正，以进一步提高编辑水平。

I. *Ningbo Statistical Yearbook 2023* is an annual publication which provides comprehensive and systematic data covering the economic, technological and social development in Ningbo Municipality in 2022. This yearbook uses the Chinese and English mix typesetting the way.

II. This yearbook has made the adjustment in the content arrangement order. This yearbook is comprised of 14 parts including: 1.Brief Introduction of 2022 Ningbo National Economy and Social Development; 2.General Survey; 3.Population and labor force; 4.National Economic Accounting; 5.Finance, Banking, Insurance and Securities; 6.Price Index and People's Livelihood; 7.Agriculture; 8.Industry, Energy Consumption and Electricity; 9.Investment in Fixed Assets and Construction; 10.Port, Transportation, Post and Telecommunication; 11.Domestic Trade and Catering Trade; 12.Foreign Trade and Tourism; 13.Education, Culture, Public Health and Sports, Science and Technology; 14.Civil Facilities, Environmental Protection, Civil Affairs, Judicature and Others. Major statistical indicators at the beginning of each chapter, Explanatory Notes on Main Statistical Indicators are provided at the end of each chapter.

III. The content of this yearbook , the data of 2018 and previous years have been adjusted according to the data of the fourth economic census.
In case of any discrepancy between the previously published statistical data and the Yearbook, please refer to this yearbook as accurate and final.

IV. This yearbook makes following stipulation in the edition, in order to make it clear for readers to use this book:

1.The footnotes are placed at the first page.

2.Explanations on symbols used in this yearbook:"space"indicates that the data are not large enough to be rounded into the minimal unit, or unknown or indicates the data not available; "#"indicates major item in a category.

V. In this yearbook, data from non- statistical departments', we dedicate the data origin.

VI. Since the publication of the Ningbo Statistical Yearbook, it has received attention and support from various sectors of society. Many readers have put forward valuable opinions on the content and editing work of the yearbook, and we have adopted revisions accordingly. We welcome readers to continue to criticize and correct the shortcomings of the yearbook, in order to further improve their editing skills.

目　录
CONTENTS

第一篇　综　合　CHAPTER 1 GENERAL SURVEY

第三篇 国民经济核算 CHAPTER 3 NATIONAL ECONOMIC ACCCOUNTING

第四篇 财政、金融、保险、证券 CHAPTER 4 FINANCE,BANKING,INSURANCE AND SECURITIES

第五篇 物价指数和人民生活 CHAPTER 5 PRICES INDEX AND PEOPL'S LIVELIHOOD

第六篇 农 业 CHAPTER 6 AGRICULTURE

第七篇　工业、能源消费和电力　CHAPTER 7 INDUSTRY, ENERGY CONSUMPTION AND ELECTRICITY

第八篇 固定资产投资和建筑业 CHAPTER 8 INVESTMENT IN FIXED ASSETS AND CONSTRUCTION

第九篇　港口、交通、运输、邮电　CHAPTER 9 PORT,TRANSPORTATION,POST AND TELECOMMUNICATION SERVICE

第十篇　国内贸易、餐饮业　　CHAPTER 10 DOMESTIC TRADE AND CATERING TRADE

第十一篇 对外经济、旅游 CHAPTER 11 FOREIGN TRADE AND TOURISM

第十二篇　文化、教育、卫生、体育、科学技术　CHAPTER 12 CULTURE,EDUCATION,PUBLIC HEALTH AND SPORTS,SCIENCE & TECHNOLOGY

第十三篇 市政、环保、民政、政法及其他 CHAPTER 13 CIVIL FACILITIES,ENVITONMENT, CIVIL AFFAIRS,JUDICATURE AND OTHERS

2022年宁波市国民经济和社会发展统计公报

宁波市统计局 国家统计局宁波调查队

2023年2月28日

2022年，面对异常复杂严峻的外部环境和超预期因素叠加冲击，全市上下坚决贯彻习近平总书记“疫情要防住、经济要稳住、发展要安全”重要指示，全面落实国家、省、市稳住经济大盘的系列决策部署，以超常规力度推进经济稳进提质，携手各类市场主体共度时艰，全市经济呈现承压回稳向好态势，主要指标好于全国全省，彰显经济大市勇挑大梁的政治责任和使命担当。三次产业逐步恢复，三大需求协同发力，新动能持续增强，新发展格局加快构建，市场活力提振复苏，社会民生保障有力，共富先行稳步推进，实现现代化滨海大都市建设良好开局。

一、综合

地区生产总值。全年全市实现地区生产总值15704.3亿元，按可比价格计算，比上年增长3.5%。分产业看，第一产业实现增加值382.0亿元，增长4.1%；第二产业实现增加值7413.5亿元，增长3.2%；第三产业实现增加值7908.8亿元，增长3.8%。三次产业之比为2.4：47.2：50.4。按常住人口计算，全市人均地区生产总值为163911元（按年平均汇率折合24369美元）。

表1 2022年宁波市分行业增加值情况

	实绩（亿元）	增长（%）
按行业分		
农林牧渔业	400.4	4.2
工业	6681.7	3.3
建筑业	742.7	3.3
批发和零售业	1870.6	3.3
交通运输、仓储和邮政业	656.1	0.4
住宿餐饮业	177.1	3.5
金融业	1266.8	6.8
房地产业	1035.8	-4.8
其他服务业	2873.1	6.9
营利性服务业	1796.7	9.6
非营利性服务业	1076.3	2.7

财政收支。全年全市完成财政总收入3358.6亿元，比上年增长2.9%，其中一般公共预算收入1680.2亿元，下降2.5%，扣除留抵退税因素后增长5.1%。全年全市完成一般公共预算支出2187.8亿元，增长12.5%，其中卫生健康支出、节能环保支出、社会保障和就业支出分别增长38.4%、27.3%和22.3%。

就业和再就业。全年全市新增城镇就业人员24.4万人，13.8万名城镇失业人员完成再就业，其中困难人员2.6万人。年末全市城镇登记失业率为1.77%。

市场价格。全年市区居民消费价格比上年上涨2.3%，其中食品类价格上涨3.7%。商品零售价格上涨4.1%。工业生产者出厂价格上涨5.3%，工业生产者购进价格上涨10.8%。12月全市新建商品住宅销售价格同比上涨1.8%，涨幅在全国70个大中城市中排第9位。

图1 2022年宁波市区居民消费价格月度涨跌幅度（单位：%）

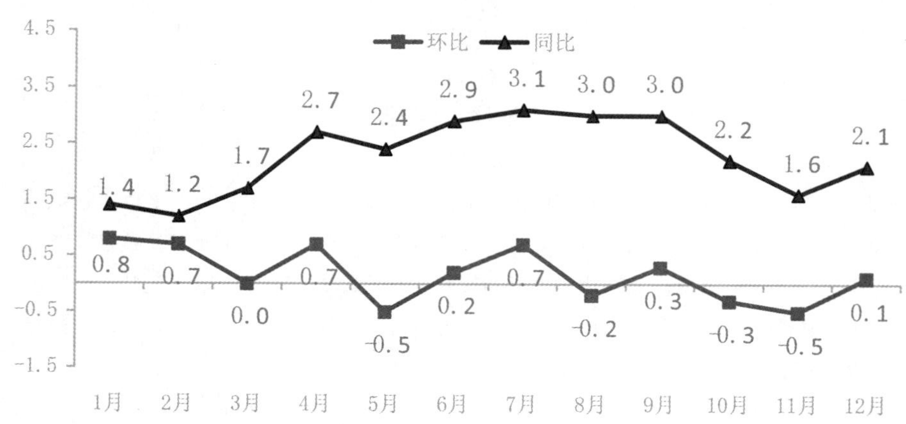

表2 2022年宁波市区CPI同浙江、全国比较（上年=100）

指标	宁波	浙江	全国
居民消费价格指数	102.3	102.2	102.0
一、食品烟酒	103.1	102.6	102.4
二、衣着	99.7	100.4	100.5
三、居住	100.4	100.7	100.7
四、生活用品及服务	101.0	101.8	101.2
五、交通通信	105.8	105.1	105.2
六、教育文化娱乐	102.2	103.1	101.8
七、医疗保健	101.8	100.3	100.6
八、其他用品及服务	101.5	101.8	101.6

二、农业、美丽乡村建设

农业生产。全年全市完成农林牧渔业增加值400.4亿元，比上年增长4.2%。粮食播种面积172.4万亩，增长1.9%,粮食产量71.6万吨，增长5.6%；肉类总产量9.3万吨，增长9.1%；禽蛋产量3.5万吨，下降5.4%；牛奶产量4.3万吨，增长2.4%；水产品总产量114.0万吨，增长6.2%。全年新增市级农业龙头企业20家，截至年末累计达342家，其中省级骨干农业龙头企业52家、农业产业化国家重点龙头企业11家。

美丽乡村建设。全年全市新增慈溪、宁海2个省级新时代美丽乡村示范县，累计达到3个；新增示范镇乡（街道）11个、特色精品村38个，截至年末累计分别达到78个和231个。新增省级高标准农村生活垃圾分类处理示范村40个、历史文化村落保护利用重点村3个，累计分别达119 个和32个。完成农村公厕改造439座，农村生活污水治理和农村公厕规范化管理实现行政村全覆盖。

三、工业、建筑

工业经济。全年全市实现工业增加值6681.7亿元，比上年增长3.3%。规模以上工业增加值增长3.8%，其中民营企业增长5.4%。分行业看，在35个行业大类中，15个行业增加值实现正增长；增加值比重前十大行业呈“五正五负”，其中化学原料、计算机通信和汽车制造业分别增长24.8%、15.1%和14.5%。分经济类型看，国有控股企业增加值增长6.9%，股份有限公司增长0.2%，有限责任公司增长12.2%，私营企业增长4.4%，外商投资企业下降3.1%，港澳台投资企业下降1.3%。全年全市规模以上工业企业完成销售产值23694.2亿元，增长6.6%，其中出口交货值4133.8亿元，下降0.1%。规模以上工业企业完成利税总额2308.9亿元，下降10.4%，其中利润总额1413.7亿元，下降18.2%。

工业转型升级。全年全市规模以上工业新产品产值增长6.9%，新产品产值率达到33.3%。年末全市“246”万千亿级产业集群拥有规模以上工业企业7621家，全年实现增加值4359.5亿元，增长5.3%。新增国家级制造业单项冠军企业（产品）20家，截至年末累计达83家，稳居全国城市首位。新增国家级专精特新“小巨人”101家，累计283家，居全国城市第四位。

图2：2022年宁波市规模以上工业分产业增加值增长情况（单位：%）

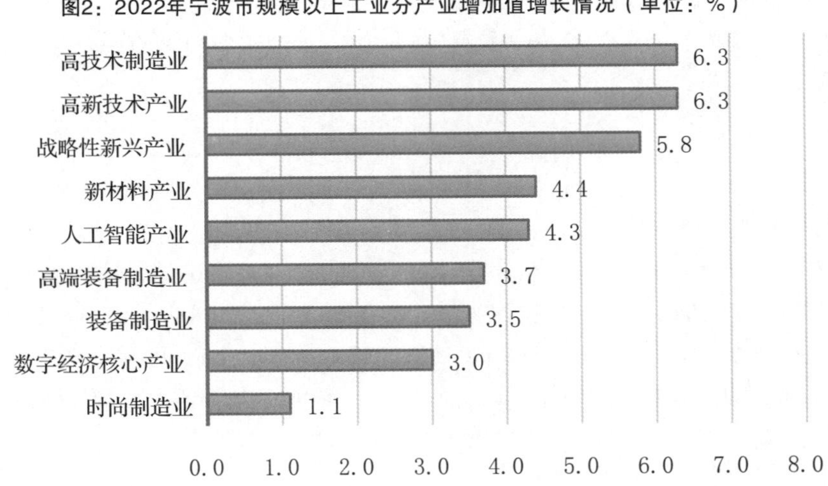

建筑业。全年全市建筑业实现增加值742.7亿元，比上年增长3.3%。截至年末，全市共有资质建筑业企业1520家，其中特级17家，一级250家，二级458家，三级及以下795家。

四、固定资产投资、城市建设

固定资产投资。全年全市固定资产投资比上年增长10.4%。全年全市完成商品房销售面积1128.8万平方米，下降29.7%。

表3：2022年宁波市固定资产投资主要领域增速

领域名称	增长（%）
工业投资	14.5
制造业投资	14.8
房地产投资	2.7
基础设施投资	14.1
高新技术产业投资	17.6
民间投资	4.6

城市建设。环城南路西延（环镇北路-秋实路）、鄞州大道-福庆路（东钱湖段）一期建成通车，快速路总里程已达142.1公里,中心城区形成“中”字型快速交通格局。新典桥、西洪大桥建成，中心城区过江通道达30座，有力助推“拥江”发展。市六区新增停车位18660个。新建（改造）绿道471公里，实现576公里省级绿道主线基本贯通，镇海九龙湖绿道入选省级最美绿道。全年全市完成“三改”建筑面积1404万平方米，拆除违法建筑面积1468万平方米。新增省级垃圾分类示范小区195个、片区12个。

五、贸易、旅游、会展

贸易业。全年全市完成社会消费品零售总额4896.7亿元，比上年增长5.3%，其中限额以上社会消费品零售总额1966.2亿元，增长9.0%。从限额以上主要商品类别看，汽车类零售额增长9.7%，其中新能源汽车增长80.3%；文化办公、粮油食品、家用电器和音像器材、石油及其制品分别增长46.2%、27.4%、24.2%和14.6%。年末全市限额以上贸易法人企业达9504家，全年完成营业收入40431.4亿元，利润总额501.5亿元。

电子商务。全年全市完成网络零售额2999.1亿元，比上年增长6.6%。实现跨境电商进出口额2005.6亿元，增长12.3%。

旅游业。全年全市完成旅游总收入776.3亿元，按同口径计算，比上年下降5.3%。接待国内游客5083.6万人次，下降1.4%；完成国内旅游收入775.6亿元，下降5.3%。接待入境游客3.2万人次，完成入境旅游收入990.2万美元。年末全市共有星级酒店75家，其中五星级21家；共有4A级以上景区37处，其中5A级2处；共有省级以上旅游度假区9处，其中国家级1处。

会展业。全年全市举办各类会展项目18个，其中举办展览13个，展览总面积37.3万平方米。展览面积2万平方米以上的大型展会10个。全市共举办市场化会议超过1000场，参会总人数超过10万人次，其中800人以上大型会议6场。获2021-2022年度“中国会展品牌城市”等荣誉称号。

六、对外经济、合作交流

货物贸易。全年宁波口岸完成进出口总额24950.1亿元，比上年增长21.6%。全市完成自营进出口总额12671.3亿元，增长6.3%，其中出口总额8230.6亿元，增长8.0%；进口总额4440.7亿元，增长3.4%。进出口总额占全国比重为3.01%。全年全市新增对外贸易经营备案登记企业4896家，截至年末累计达61751家；全年有进出口实绩的企业25903家。民营企业（包括私营企业和集体企业）进出口额9237.5亿元，增长10.1%，占同期进出口总额的72.9%。直接与我市开展贸易往来的国家和地区达222个。

表4 2022年宁波市自营进出口主要分类情况

指标	实绩（亿元）	增长（%）
进出口总额	12671.3	6.3
出口总额	8230.6	8.0
其中：一般贸易	7558.1	10.2
加工贸易	545.2	-13.8
其中：机电产品	4602.3	4.6
高新技术产品	610.1	10.1
进口总额	4440.7	3.4
其中：一般贸易	3814.3	1.9
加工贸易	200.0	-29.7
其中：机电产品	548.7	-14.9
高新技术产品	322.6	-23.5

表5 2022年宁波市对主要市场货物进出口情况

国家和地区	实绩（亿元）	增长（%）
欧盟	2292.1	7.8
美国	2162.5	3.8
东盟	1494.8	19.6
“一带一路”沿线国家	3891.2	16.8
其中：中东欧国家	450.4	17.8
RCEP其他成员国	3266.5	4.7

利用外资。全年全市批准外商投资项目数410个；合同利用外资57.5亿美元；实际利用外资37.3亿美元，增长13.8%，累计实际利用外资达679.4亿美元。第三产业新批项目356个，实际利用外资26.2亿美元，增长17.1%。截至年末，累计有72家境外世界500强企业来甬投资156个项目（分支机构），投资总额254.2亿美元。

对外合作。全年全市新批境外投资企业和机构191家，比上年增长2.7%；核准备案中方投资额39.6亿美元，增长63.2%。全年完成境外承包工程劳务合作营业额19.2亿美元，增长2.2%。

服务贸易。全年全市完成国际服务贸易进出口额1717.5亿元，其中出口额1148.7亿元，进口额568.9亿元，比上年分别增长22.5%、21.3%和25.1%。全年承接服务外包执行额650.8亿元，增长23.7%，其中承接离岸服务外包执行额363.3亿元，增长26.4%。

国内合作。全年全市国内招商实际到位资金1851.7亿元，比上年增长3.0%。上缴省财政东西部协作帮扶资金68772万元，追加拨付凉山财政资金3500万元，安排帮扶项目183个；落实财政对口支援资金5.02亿元，实施援助项目70个。

七、港口、交通、邮电

港口生产。全年宁波舟山港完成货物吞吐量12.6亿吨，比上年增长3.0%，连续14年蝉联世界首位，其中宁波港域完成吞吐量6.4亿吨，增长2.2%。全年宁波港域完成铁矿石吞吐量10468.9万吨，增长9.1%；煤炭吞吐量6380.5万吨，增长0.7%；原油吞吐量

6293.1万吨，增长0.3%。全年宁波舟山港完成集装箱吞吐量3335.1万标箱，增长7.3%，全球第三大集装箱港的地位进一步巩固，其中宁波港域完成集装箱吞吐量3077.8万标箱，增长4.8%。年末宁波舟山港共有集装箱航线300条，其中远洋干线144条，近洋支线104条。全年宁波港域完成海铁联运145.2万标箱，增长20.6%

交通基础设施。年末全市公路总里程达11480.2公里，其中高速公路583.9公里。宁波港域建成万吨级以上泊位4个，累计达118个，码头前沿最大水深27.5米。

综合运输。全年完成全社会货运量8.0亿吨，比上年增长1.7%，货物周转量4739亿吨公里，增长7.8%。全年完成全社会客运量0.5亿人次，下降32.7%。其中，公路客运量1105.1万人次，下降22.6%；铁路客运量2964.3万人次，下降35.8%；民航客运量616.6万人次，下降34.8%。

表6 2022年宁波市交通货运情况。

指标	单位	实绩	增长（%）
货运量	万吨	80100.4	1.7
其中：铁路	万吨	3502.9	6.2
水路	万吨	31279.0	–0.7
公路	万吨	45310.0	3.2
民航	万吨	8.5	–24.3
货物周转量	亿吨公里	4739.0	7.8
其中：水路	亿吨公里	4025.6	7.7
公路	亿吨公里	713.4	8.5

公共交通体系。年末全市共有公交标准运营车辆9936标台，比上年增长0.8%；运营线路1226条，增长1.2%。轨道交通流量相对平稳，全年轨道交通完成客运量25656.3万人次，下降0.6%。年末共有公共自行车网点1278个，公共自行车26650辆，全年租车总量1534.8万辆次。年末共有出租车6135辆。

邮电业。全年全市邮政行业完成寄递业务量17.8亿件，比上年下降5.0%，其中快递业务量14.4亿件，下降5.9%。年末全市拥有固定电话用户207.8万户，移动电话用户1385.4万户，其中5G移动电话用户499.4万户；固定互联网宽带接入用户518.1万户。

八、银行、证券、保险

银行业。年末全市拥有银行业金融机构67家，其中政策性银行3家，大型银行6家，股份制商业银行12家，城市商业银行13家，外资银行7家，农村合作金融机构9家，新型农村金融机构12家，非银行金融机构5家。年末本外币存款余额31303亿元，比上年末增长15.0%；本外币贷款余额32986亿元，增长13.6%。

表7 2022年末宁波市金融机构存贷款情况

指标	实绩（亿元）	比上年末增长（%）
本外币存款余额	31303	15.0
其中：住户存款	11842	25.0
非金融企业存款	11844	13.5
人民币存款余额	30204	15.3
本外币贷款余额	32986	13.6
其中：住户贷款	11538	4.8
企（事）业单位贷款	21100	18.3
人民币贷款余额	32377	13.6

证券业。全年全市完成证券成交总额12.0万亿元，比上年下降2.7%，其中股票和基金成交额6.5万亿元，下降14.1%。年末客户证券资产总额12900.9亿元，增长7.0%。全年期货代理交易量11154.0万手，下降1.3%；代理交易额7.3万亿元，下降2.2%。年末证券投资者开户数286.0万户，增长10.2%。年末全市共有1家证券公司、32家证券分公司、167家证券营业部、1家证券投资咨询公司、1家期货公司、13家期货分公司和40家期货营业部。继续推进“凤凰行动”宁波计划，全年新增境内上市公司8家，完成首发（IPO）融资69.6亿元，年末境内上市公司总数达114家。全年各类公司通过定向增发、公司债券等工具再融资972.7亿元。

保险业。年末全市共有市级及以上产险机构31家、寿险机构26家、专业中介机构87家。全年完成保费收入416.1亿元，比上年增长10.9%。其中财产险保费收入190.7亿元，增长8.5%；人身险保费收入225.4亿元，增长13.1%。全年提供风险保障45.5万亿元，下降6.0%。全年赔付支出163.4亿元，其中财产险赔付支出117.7亿元，人身险赔付支出45.7亿元。

九、科技、教育、人才

科技创新。全年全市规模以上工业企业研发费用599.3亿元，比上年增长16.7%。完成财政科技支出151.0亿元，增长15.1%。完成专利授权7.6万件，其中发明专利9611件。全年新认定高新技术企业1514家，年末有效高新技术企业5337家。新认定国家科技型中小企业5702家、省级科技型中小企业3092家；新增省科技领军企业6家、省科技小巨人企业26家；新认定省技术创新中心2个；新增省级新型研发机构7个，累计19个；新增省部级重点实验室3个，累计45个；新增省级科技企业孵化器7家，累计23家；新增省级众创空间13家，累计53家。全年全市共认定登记技术合同3962项，增长3.6%；完成技术交易额515.8亿元，增长61.4%。

教育事业。年末全市共有各级各类学校1802所，在校学生总数148.1万人。其中，在甬高校16所，全日制在校学生19.1万人；普通高中85所，在校学生10.3万人；中职学校32所，在校学生6.1万人；初中243所，在校学生22.8万人；小学388所，在校学生55.5万人；幼儿园1028所，在校学生28.5万人。年末全市共有全日制民办中小学（幼儿园）698所，在校（园）生18.7万人，占全市全日制中小学（幼儿园）在校（园）生数的15.3%。义务段有28.9万名随迁子女就学问题得到妥善解决。

人才开发。全年全市新引进大学生22.7万人，新增博士1130人，新增硕士10324人，均创历史新高。新增省级以上博士后工作站68家，累计345家。新增高技能人才7.2万人，累计达70.4万人，高技能人才占技能人才比重达33.6%；新建技能大师工作室15家，累计130家；全年全市完成技能人才培训38万人。

十、文化、卫生、体育

文化建设。年末全市共有国家级非物质文化遗产代表性项目28项，省、市级非物质文化遗产代表性项目478项。新增1家国有博物馆——周尧昆虫博物馆，年末全市累计国有博物馆17家。奉化方桥顾家庄遗址入选“浙江考古重要发现”。奉化区博物馆选送的《山海交响——奉化历史文明展》获评全国博物馆十大陈列展览精品。建成“15分钟品质文化生活圈”860个，城市书房20家、文化驿站10家和乡村博物馆46家。年末全市共有全国重点文物保护单位33处。

卫生事业。年末全市共有医疗卫生机构4916家，医院204家，其中三级甲等医院8家，三级乙等医院11家；社区卫生服务中心和乡镇卫生院157家。年末全市实有病床4.7万张，拥有各类专业卫生人员10.3万人，卫生技术人员8.8万人，其中执业医师（含助理）3.6万人，注册护士3.8万人。按户籍人口统计，每千人床位数、卫技人员数、执业医师（含助理）数和注册护士数分别达到7.5张、14.1人、5.8人和6.1人，每万人全科医生数6.9人。全市适龄儿童免疫规划疫苗接种率95.0%。

体育事业。全年全市共举办全国性以上赛事22项。组队参加第十七届省运会，共获得金牌386.75枚、奖牌792.75枚和总分8218.75分，均居全省第二。年末全市共有体育场地设施28231个，总面积达2714.3万平方米。全年体育彩票销售额达30.7亿元，比上年增长36%。

十一、人口、居民生活、社会保障

人口规模。年末全市拥有户籍人口621.1万人，比上年末增加2.7万人，其中市区314.2万人。全年全市出生34556人，其中男性18062人，男女性别比为109.5　100。人口出生率为5.58‰，死亡率为6.83‰，自然增长率为-1.25‰；人口净迁入35157人，净迁移率为5.67‰。年末全市常住人口为961.8万人，比上年末增加7.4万人，城镇人口占总人口的比重（即城镇化率）为78.9%，提高0.5个百分点。

居民收支。全年全市居民人均可支配收入68348元，比上年增长4.5%,扣除价格因素影响，实际增长2.2%。按城乡分，城镇居民人均可支配收入76690元，增长3.8%，实际增长1.5%；农村居民人均可支配收入45487元，增长5.9%，实际增长3.5%。城乡居民人均收入倍差为1.69。全市居民人均生活消费支出42997元，增长6.2%。按城乡分，城镇居民人均生活消费支出47916元，增长5.6%；农村居民人均生活消费支出29514元，增长7.5%。

表8 2022年宁波市居民人均收支主要指标

指标	全体居民		城镇常住居民		农村常住居民	
	实绩（元）	增长（%）	实绩（元）	增长（%）	实绩（元）	增长（%）
人均可支配收入	68348	4.5	76690	3.8	45487	5.9
1. 工资性收入	38016	1.8	42390	1.4	26031	2.2
2. 经营净收入	12028	1.0	13019	0.5	9313	1.9
3. 财产净收入	7332	5.0	9385	3.9	1705	12.8
4. 转移净收入	10972	19.5	11896	18.1	8438	23.8
人均生活消费支出	42997	6.2	47916	5.6	29514	7.5

社会保险。年末全市企业职工基本养老、医疗、失业、工伤和生育保险参保人数分别为526.7万人、501.6万人、341.6万人、451.5万人和377.0万人，城乡居民基本养老保险、城乡居民医疗保险参保人数分别为99.4万人和296.2万人。截至年末全市累计发行社保卡1003.3万张，社保卡金融账户激活率达71.2%。

民生保障。年末全市共有养老机构258个，床位数5.1万张。年末全市共有最低生活保障对象5.7万人，全年低保资金实际发放6.3亿元。全市最低生活保障标准提高到1181元/月。企业职工最低工资标准为2280元/月、2070元/月两档。全市低收入农户人均可支配收入为21869元，比上年增长13.8%。全年有4.1万名困难残疾人享受生活补贴，9.1万名重度残疾人享受护理补贴。全市2.9万名有康复服务需求的残疾人全部得到康复服务。年末全市特困对象集中供养2352人。

保障性安居工程。全年建设筹集保障性租赁住房7.4万套（间），完成老旧小区改造项目159个、建筑面积827万平方米。累计筹集租赁住房15万套，培育专业化住房租赁企业22家。新市民住房保障改革入选省共同富裕首批试点并获五星评价。出台《公租房保障管理办法》，全市公租房在保家庭5.53万户。共有产权房试点启动，开工建设1438套共有产权住房。

慈善事业。全年市县两级慈善机构募集善款9.2亿元，救助支出7.5亿元，帮扶困难群众56.8万人次；截至年末市县两级慈善机构累计募集善款达107.4亿元，救助支出87.6亿元，帮扶困难群众619.6万人次。全年市慈善总会共开展志愿服务活动876场次，参加服务的义工4万余人次，服务时长达4.5万小时。

十二、生态建设、社会安全

生态建设。全年中心城区空气质量优良天数比率为89%，在全国168个重点城市排名第17，比上年上升3位；$PM_{2.5}$浓度为22微克/立方米。全年全市新增排污权交易138笔，交易金额5222.1万元；新增有偿使用1032笔，金额1.94亿元。全年全市污水处理量8.4亿吨，污水处理率为99%，COD减排总量16.9万吨。全市地表水市控以上断面水质优良率为93.6%，提高5.4个百分点；水环境功能区达标率为100%，提高1.2个百分点。县级及以上饮用水源地水质常年保持100%达标率。年末全市共有国家级生态文明建设示范县（区）5个、省级生态文明建设示范县（区）9个、国家级“两山”实践创新基地2个。

“平安宁波”建设。连续第16次获“省平安市”称号。全年全市共发生各类生产安全事故114起，死亡81人，比上年分别下降32.9%、36.2%。全年全市共立案查处食品安全各类违法案件5659件，其中大要案9件，罚没款2586.3万元，移送公安机关涉嫌犯罪案件45件。全年人民调解组织共调处各类民事纠纷11.5万件，调解成功11.4万件，成功率达99.7%。

注：（1）本公报所列2022年的各项数据均为初步统计数。

（2）全市地区生产总值、各产业增加值绝对数按当年价格计算，增长速度按可比价格计算。

（3）规模以上工业：年主营业务收入2000万元及以上的工业法人单位。

限额以上批发、零售、住宿、餐饮企业指：

批发业：年主营业务收入2000万元及以上；

零售业：年主营业务收入500万元及以上；

住宿业：年主营业务收入200万元及以上；

餐饮业：年主营业务收入200万元及以上。

（4）表格中“增长”均指“比上年增长”。

（5）因部分保险机构目前处于风险处置阶段，保费收入相关数据口径暂不包含这部分机构。

2022 Statistics Bulletin of National Economy and Social Development of Ningbo

Ningbo Municipal Statistics Bureau
State Statistical Bureau Ningbo Investigation Team
February 28, 2023

In 2022, facing the extremely complex and severe external environment and the superimposed impact of unexpected factors, provincial and municipal governmentsresolutely implemented the important instructi ons,which was made by president Xi Jinping, to prevent the epidemic, stabilize the economy, and ensure safe development,comprehensively implemented a series of national, provincial and municipal decisions and deployments to sustain stable macroeconomic performance, promoted steady progress and quality improvement of economy with extraordinary efforts, and joined hands with various market players to tide over the difficulties.Ningbo's economy showed a satisfying trend of stabilization under pressure, and had a better performance in major indicators than that of the whole country and the province, demonstrating the political responsibilites and mission commitment as an economically prosperous city. The three industries have gradually recovered, the three major demands have exerted concerted efforts, new kinetic energy continued to strengthen, the construction of a new development pattern has been accelerated, the market vitality has been revived, the social livelihood has been ensured, and common prosperity has made steady advances, thus achieving a good start in the construction of a modern coastal metropolis.

I. Overview

General GDP:The GDP in Ningbo in 2022 achieved to ¥1.57043 trillion. Calculating on comparable prices, up by 3.5% fromthe last year, among which, the increase in primary industry was ¥38.20 billion, up by 4.1%; the increase in secondary industry was ¥741.35 billion, up by 3.2%; and the increase in tertiary industry was ¥790.88 billion, up by 3.8%. The ration of the increase of the three industries was 2.4:47.2:50.4.Calculated by permanent population, the per capita GDP of Ningbo is ¥163,911 ($24,369 at the average annual exchange rate).

Table 1: Value added of Ningbo by industry in 2022

	Actual (100 million)	Year–on–yeaincrease (%)
By industry		
Agriculture, forestry, animal husbandry and fishery	400. 4	4. 2
Industry	6681. 7	3. 3
Construction	742. 7	3. 3
Wholesale and retail trade	1870. 6	3. 3
Transportation, warehousing and postal services	656. 1	0. 4
Accommodation and catering industry	177. 1	3. 5
Finance	1266. 8	6. 8
Real estate industry	1035. 8	-4. 8
Other service industries	2873. 1	6. 9
For–profit service industry	1796. 7	9. 6
Non–profit service sector	1076. 3	2. 7

Fiscal Revenue and Expenditure: The general public fiscal revenue in Ningbo in 2022 was ¥335.86 billion, up by 2.9% compared with that of last year. The general public fiscal budget revenue was ¥168.02 billion, down by 2.5%, and up by 5.1% after deducting the factor of tax credit refund. The general public fiscal budget expenditure was ¥218.78 billion, up by 12.5%, among which that the input in health, energy conservation and environmental protection and social security and employment, had a growth in 38.4%,27.3% and 22.3%, respectively in which the general public fiscal budget expenditure.

Employment and Re-employment: Number of employees newly created in urban areas and towns in Ningbo was 244,000 in 2022 and 138,000 laid-off workers were re-employed, 26,000 of which were the workers in trouble. The registered unemployment rate of city and towns was 1.77% at the end of the year.

Market Price: In 2022, the consumer prices of urban residents in Ningbo increased by 2.3% over the same period last year, among which,the price of food rose by 3.7%. The retail price of commodities rose by 4.1%. The industrial producers leaving the factory price rose by5.3% from a year earlier, while the purchase price rose by 10.8%. In December, the sales price of newly built residential buildings in Ningbo rose 1.8% year-on-year, ranking 9th in 70 large and medium-sized cities in the whole country.

Graph 1: The Consumer Price Increase and Decrease of Consumer Prices in Ningbo Monthly in 2022 (%)

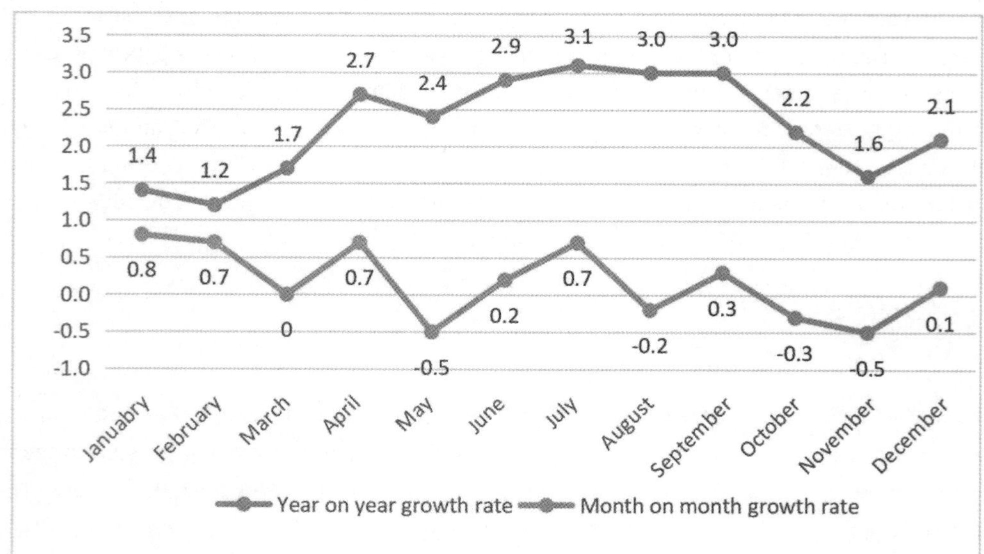

Table 2: Comparison of Ningbo CPI with Zhejiang province and the whole country in 2022(previous year=100)

Index	Ningbo	Zhejiang province	whole country
Consumer Price Index	102. 3	102. 2	102. 0
Food, tobacco and alcohol	103. 1	102. 6	102. 4
Clothes	99. 7	100. 4	100. 5
Residence	100. 4	100. 7	100. 7
Daily necessities and services	101. 0	101. 8	101. 2
Traffic and communication	105. 8	105. 1	105. 2
Education culture and entertainment	102. 2	103. 1	101. 8
Medical insurance	101. 8	100. 3	100. 6
Other supplies and services	101. 5	101. 8	101. 6

II. Agriculture and Beautiful Rural Construction

Agricultural Production: The gross output value of farming, forestry, husbandry and fishing in Ningbo reached ¥ 40.04 billion, up by 4.2% than that of last year. The acreage sown to grain was 1,724,000 mu, up by 1.9%, the grain output was 716,000 tons, up by 5.6%; The total output of meat was 93,000 tons, *up* by 9.1%; the output of poultry eggs is 35,000 tons, *down by* 5.4%; the output of milk is 43,000 tons, *up by* 2.4%; the total output of aquatic products was 1.14 million tons, up by 6.2%. During the year, 20 municipal agricultural leading enterprises were added, with a cumulative total of 342, of which52 are provincial backbone agricultural leading enterprises and 11 are national key leading enterprises of agricultural industrialization.

Beautiful Countryside Construction:2 provincial beautiful village demonstration county,Cixi and Ninghai, with a cumulative total of 3; 11 beautiful rural demonstration towns, 38 characteristic fine quality villages were added in the whole year, with a cumulative total of 78 and 231 respectively. 40 provincial-level high-standard rural domestic waste classification and treatment demonstration villages and 3 provincial historical and cultural villages protection and utilization key villages were added, with a cumulative total of 119 and 32respectively. Completed the renovation of 439 rural public toilets, and all administrative villages were covered by the treatment of domestic sewage and the standardized management of rural public toilets.

Ⅲ. Industry and Construction

Industrial Economy: The total industrial added value for industrial above designated size was ¥668.17 billion, up by 3.3% compared to last year. Among all the industries above scale, there is 3.8%increase in investment; and there is 5.4% increase among which the private enterprise. In the perspective of 35 categories under the industry trade, 15 categories undergo a positive increment in the added value under the same ratio; The proportion of added value in the top ten industries shows "five positive and five negative", with the chemical raw materials, computer communications and automobile manufacturing industry growing by 24.8%,15.1% and14.5%,respectively.An analysis by types of ownership showed that state-owned and state-holding enterprises achieved growth of 6.9% year on year; that of shareholding enterprises was up by 0.2%; that of companies with limited liability was up by 12.2%; that of private enterprises was increased by 4.4%; that of enterprises funded by foreign investors was downby 3.1%; and that of enterprises funded by investors from Hong Kong, Macao and Taiwan decrease1.3%. The sales value of industries above designated size reached ¥2.36942trillion, up by 6.6%, among which the delivery value of exports was ¥413.38 billion,down by 0.1%. The total pre-tax profits of industries above designated size were ¥230.89billion,down by 10.4%, among which the total profits reached ¥141.37billion with a decrease of 18.2%.

Industrial Transformation and Promotion: The output of industrial new products above the scale was up to6.9%,the output ration of new products hit 33.3%. Atthe end of year, there have been 7621enterprises of industries above designated size in the “246” trillion-levelindustrialcluster with an industrial added value of ¥435.95 billion, up by 5.3% from last year.There were 20 new National–Level manufacturing single–sport champion enterprises (products) which was totally 83 enterprises in the city, and ranking first among the cities in China. A total of 101 state-level "little giants" have been added, totaling 283, ranking the forth among cities in China.

Graph 2: Growth of Top 10 Industrial Categories in Total Industrial Added Value of Industries above the Designated Size in 2022 (%)

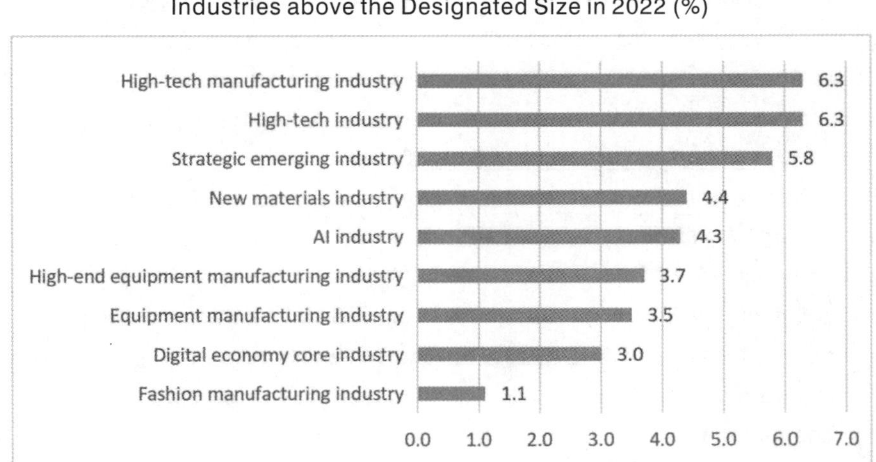

Construction Industry: The output value of construction industry in Ningbo increased by ¥74.27 billion, up by 3.3% compared with that of last year.Atthe end of year, there have been1,520 qualified construction enterprises in the city, including 17 special grade, 250 first grade, 458 second grade, and 795 third grade and below.

IV. Investment in Fixed Asset and Urban Construction

Investment in Fixed Asset: Investment in fixed asset in Ningbo was up by 10.4% compared with the last year. The sales area of commercial housing was 11.288 million square meters, down by 29.7%.

Table 3: Ningbo fixed assets investments main categories rate of increase in 2022

Category name	Rate of increase (%)
Investment in industry	14. 5
Investment in manufacturing	14. 8
Investment in real estates	2. 7
Investment in infrastructure	14. 1
High Technology investments	17. 6
Civilian investments	4. 6

Urban Construction:The west extension of South Ring Road (Huanzhen North Road - Qiushi Road) and the first phase of Yinzhou Avenue-Fuqing Road (the section of Dongqian Lake) completed and opened to traffic, and the total length of expressways has reached 142.1 kilometers, forming a "medium" shaped rapid transportation pattern in downtown area. The constructions ofXindian Bridge and Xihong Bridge have been completed, and 30 river crossings have been built in the central urban area, vigorously boosting the developmentgathering around the river.18,660 parking spaces have been added in the six districts of Ningbo. A total of471 kilometers ofgreenways have been built, and 576 kilometers of provincial greenway main lines were basically connected, and Zhenhai Jiulong Lake Greenway was selected as the most beautiful provincial greenway. 14.04million square meters "Three Renovations" were completed, and 14.68 million square meters of illegal buildings were demolished.195 provincial-levelhigh-standardgarbage classification demonstration communities and 12 districts were added.

V. Trade, Tourism and Exhibition

Trade: Wholesale and retail sales added up to ¥489.67billion in 2022, up by 5.3% over the previous year,of which the total retail sales of consumer goods above designated size reached 196.62 billion, an increase of 9.0%.In terms of the main categories of goods above designated size, the retail sales of automobile products increased by 9.7%, among which new energy vehicles increased by 80.3%; office supplies, grain, oil and foodstuff, household appliances and audio-visual equipment, and petroleum and its products increased by46.2%, 27.4%, 24.2% and 14.6% respectively. By the end of 2022, there have been 9504 trading corporate enterprises above designated size, making revenues of ¥4.04314 trillion and profits of ¥50.15billion.

E-commerce: In 2022, the whole city completed the network retail sales of ¥299.91billion, with an increasing of 6.6% over the previous year. In the whole year, the import and export volume of cross-border e-commerce reached 200.56 billion, with an increasing of12.3%.

Tourism: In 2022, Ningbo's tourism income totaled ¥77.63 billion, down by 5.3% over the previous year. This sector received 50.836million domestic tourists throughout the year with an decrease of 1.4% and earned ¥77.56 billion in domestic tourism income with an decrease of 5.3%. Accommodations hosted 32,000 oversea tourists and earned $9.902 million in oversea tourism income. By the end of the year, there have been 75 starred hotels, including 21 provincial level, including 1 national tourist resort.

Exhibition Industry: More than 18 conventions and exhibitions of all kinds were held in 2022, among them, there were 13 exhibitions with the exhibition areas of 0.373 million square meters, 10 of which owned an area of more than 20,000 square meters.

More than 1000 market-oriented conferenceswere held with more than 0.1millionparticipants, among them, there were6 large-scale conferences with more than 800 participants. In 2022, Ningbo has won the honorary titles of "China's Convention and Exhibition Brand City" in 2021-2022.

VI. International Trade,Cooperation & Exchange

Foreign Trade:Ningbo accomplished the total volume of export and import for ¥2.49501 trillion, up by 21.6% compared to last year. The total volume of self-employed imports and exports was ¥1.26713 trillion, up by 6.3%, of which, the volume of exported reached ¥823.06 billion, increased by 8.0%, and the volume of imported reached ¥ 444.07 billion, increased by 3.4%. Total import and export accounted for 3.01% of the country. During the year, 4,896 new foreign trade enterprises were registered, with a cumulative total of 61,751, and there were 25,903 import and export enterprises. The import and export volume of private enterprises (including private enterprises and collective enterprises) reached 923.75 billion, up by10.1%, accounting for 72.9% of the total import and export volume in the same period. And 222 countries and regions have directly engaged in trade with our city.

Table 4: Main classification of Ningbo's self-operated import and export in 2022

Indicator	Value (100 million)	Growth Rate (%)
Total Imports and Exports	12671. 3	6. 3
Total Exports	8230. 6	8. 0
General Trade	7558. 1	10. 2
Processing Trade	545. 2	-13. 8
Mechatronic products	4602. 3	4. 6
High-tech products	610. 1	10. 1
Total Imports	4440. 7	3. 4
General Trade	3814. 3	1. 9
Processing Trade	200. 0	-29. 7
Mechatronic products	548. 7	-14. 9
High-tech products	322. 6	-23. 5

Table 5: Import and export of goods from Ningbo to major markets in 2022

Country and region	Value (100 million)	Growth Rate (%)
European Union	2292. 1	7. 8
the United States	2162. 5	3. 8
ASEAN (Association of Southeast Asian Nations)	1494. 8	19. 6
Countries along the "Belt and Road" route	3891. 2	16. 8
Central and EasternEuropean countries	450. 4	17. 8
Other RCEP countries	3266. 5	4. 7

Foreign Investment Utilization:410 foreign-invested projects were approved in 2022. The contractual foreign investment utilized was $5.75 billion; the actually utilized foreign investment was $3.73 billion, up by13.8%, with a cumulative total of $67.94 billion.356 tertiary industry projects were newly approved, actually utilizing $2.62 billion of foreign investment, up by 17.1%. By the end of the year, there has been 72 enterprises of Fortune Global 500 investing 156 projects in Ningbo (Branch office), with a total investment of $25.42 billion.

Foreign Cooperation: In 2022,191 new overseas investment enterprises and institutions were newly approved, up by 2.7%. China's investment was $3.96 billion, up by 63.2% over the previous year. The turnover of labor cooperation for overseas contracting projects was $1.92 billion, up by 2.2%.

Service Trade: The total value of international service foreign trade was ¥171.75billion, among which, that of exports was ¥114.87 billion, that of imports was ¥56.89 billion, up by 22.5%, 21.3%, and 25.1% respectively. The execution value of undertaking service outsourcing reached ¥65.08 billion with a growth of 23.7%, of which that of undertaking offshore service outsourcing was ¥36.33billion, up by 26.4%.

Domestic Cooperation: In 2022, the domestic investment funds actually amounted to ¥185.17 billion, up by 3.0%. ¥687.72 million was handed over to the eastern and western cooperation and assistance fund of the provincial finance, ¥35 million was allocated to Liangshan, and 183 assistance projects were arranged. A total of ¥502 million of matching funds were provided, and 70 projects were implemented.

VII. Port Traffic, Transportation& Post and telecommunications

Port Production: In 2022, the cargo handling capacity of Ningbo Zhoushan Port reached 1.26billion tons, up by 3.0% on the previous year, ranking the first in the world for 14 consecutive years. Of this total, Ningbo Port completed throughput of 640 million tons, up by 2.2%. Ningbo Port completed 104.689 million tons of iron ore throughput in the whole year, increased by 9.1%, coal throughput of 63.805 million tons, up by 0.7%, and crude oil throughput of 62.931 million tons, up by 0.3%. Throughout the year, the container handling capacity of Ningbo Zhoushan Port reached 33.351 million, up by 7.3%, further consolidating its position of the world's third biggest container port. 30.778 million of total were accomplished by Ningbo Port, up by 4.8%. By the end of the year, Ningbo Zhoushan Port has owned 300 container shipping routes, among which there have been 144 ocean trunk lines, 104 offshore branch lines. 1.452 million TEUs were completed by sea-rail transport throughout the year, increased by 20.6%.

Transport Infrastructure: The length of road reached 11480.2 kilometers,including 583.9 kilometers of expressways. Ningbo Port area has built 4 berths of 10,000-ton class and above, and has 118 berths of 10,000-ton class and above. The maximum water depth at the front of the terminal was 27.5 meters.

Integrated Transportation: The total volume of the goods transported reached 800 million tons this year, achieving a year-on-year growth of 1.7%, and the volume of cargo turnover was 473.9 billion tons, increase by 7.8%.The overall visitors flow was50 million, decrease by 32.7%. Of these, the visitors flow of road was 11.051 million persons, down by 22.6%; that of railway was 29.643 million persons, down by 35.8%; that of civil aviation was 6.166 million persons, down by 34.8%.

Table 6: 2022 Ningbo freight transportation

Index	Absolute Value	Growth Rate (%)
Goods Transported(10,000 tons)	80100.4	1.7
Railway	3502.9	6.2
Waterway	31279.0	-0.7
Road	45310.0	3.2
Civil Aviation	8.5	-24.3
Freight (10,000 ton-km)	4739.0	7.8
Waterway	4025.6	7.7
Road	713.4	8.5

Public Transportation Systems: The city had 9,936 standard public transport vehicles,up by 0.8% on the previous year. 1,226 lines in operation, up by 1.2%. The flow of rail transportation was relatively stable,and the annual passenger traffic reached256.563 million, down 0.6%.By the end of the year, there have been 1,278 public bicycle outlets and 26,650 public bicycles, which were rented for 15.348 million times in total. And there have been 6,135 taxis in Ningbo.

Post and Telecommunications Industry:In the whole year, the total volume of mail delivery business completed by the city was 1.78 billion pieces, down by 5.0% over the previous year. Among them, the volume of express delivery was 1.44 billion, down 5.9%. At the end of the year,Ningbo had2.078 million fixed-line telephone users and 13.854 million mobile phone users,including 4.994 million 5G mobile phone users;5.181 million fixed Internet broadband access users.

Ⅷ. Banking, Securities and Insurance

Banking: At the end of the year, there were 67 banking institutions in the city, including 3 policy banks, 6 large banks, 12 joint-stock commercial banks, 13 urban commercial banks, 7 foreign-funded banks, 9 rural cooperative financial institutions, 12 new rural financial institutions and 5 non-bank financial institutions.At the end of the year, the balance of domestic and foreign currency deposits amounted to ¥3,130.3 billion, up by 15.0% over the end of the previous year. And the balance of domestic and foreign currency loans amounted to ¥3,298.6 billion, up by 13.6%.

Table 7: Deposits and Loans of Financial Institutions in Ningbo in the end of 2022

Indicator	Actuals (100million)	Growth Rate (%)
Domestic & Foreign Currency Deposit Balance	31303	15. 0
Household Deposits	11842	25. 0
Deposits of Non-financial Enterprises	11844	13.5
RMB deposit balance	30204	15. 3
Domestic & Foreign Currency Loan Balance	32986	13. 6
Household Loans	11538	4. 8
Loans of Non-financial Enterprises & Government Organizations	21100	18. 3
RMB deposit balance	32377	13.6

Securities: The total trade volume of securities transactions was 12.0trillion, down by 2.7% over the previous year, of which the transaction volume of stocks and funds was 6.5 trillion, down by 14.1%. At the end of the year, the total amount of client securities assets was 1,290.09 billion, up by 7.0%. Futures agency trading volume was 111.54 million, decreased by 1.3%; agent trading volume was ¥7.3 trillion, decrease by 2.2%.At the end of the year, the opened accounts of securities investors have reached 2.86million, up by 10.2%; there has been 1 securities company, 32 branch securities companies, 167 securities exchanges, 1 securities investment consulting company, 1 futures company, 13 branch futures companies and 40 futures exchanges. To continue to promote the "Operation Phoenix" Ningbo Program, 8 companies were newly listed, achieving an IPO financing of ¥6.96 billion; by the end of 2022, there have been 114 domestic listed companies in total. Throughout the year, the refinancing of companies of all categories reached ¥97.27 billion, by using financing tools such as private placements and corporate bonds.

Insurance: By the end of 2022, there were 31 property insurance institutions at the municipal level and above, 26 life insurance agencies and 87 specialized agencies. The city realized a premium income of ¥41.61 billion, up by 10.9% over the previous year, among which, the premium income of property insurance was ¥19.07 billion, up by 8.5%;

those of life insurance was ¥22.54 billion, up by 13.1%. The risk insurance provided reached ¥45.5 trillion in total during the year, down by 6.0%. The claims expense reached to ¥16.34billion, among which the expense of property insurance were ¥11.77 billion and those of life insurance were ¥4.57 billion.

Ⅸ.Science & Technology, Education and Talents

Scientific and Technical Innovation: Over the year, theR&D expenses of industrial enterprises above designated size was¥59.93 billion, up by 16.7% over the previous year. The fiscal expenditure on science and technology reached to¥15.10 billion, up by 15.1%. 76,000 patents were granted, including 9,611 invention patents. There was a net increase of 1,514 high-tech enterprises, and the effective number of high-tech enterprises reached 5,337. 5702 and 3092 small and medium-sized science and technology enterprises were newly identified at the national and provincial level respectively;6 provincial-level technology leading enterprises and 26 provincial-level technology giant enterprises were added; 2 technology innovation center at the provincial level were newly identified; 7 provincial-level R&D institutions were added, with a total of 19; 3 key laboratories, with the total number of 45; 7 scientific and technological enterprises incubators, 23 of total; 13provincial maker spaces, with the total number of 53;A total of 3,962 technical contracts were approved and registered in the whole city, up 3.6% over the previous year. The total amount of technology turnover was ¥51.58 billion, up by61.4%.

Education: At the end of the year, there were 1,802 schools of all kinds in the city, with a total of 1.481 million students. Among those schools, there were 16 colleges and universities with 191,000 students, 85 ordinary high schools with 103,000 students, 32 secondary vocational schools with 61,000 students, 243 junior high schools with 228,000 students, 388 primary schools with 555,000 students, and 1,028 kindergartens with 285,000 students.There have been 698 full-time private secondary and primary schools (kindergartens) in Ningbo by the end of 2022, with 187,000 students on campus, 15.3% of the students in full-time secondary and primary schools (kindergartens). 289,000 migrant children's schooling problems in the obligatory section have been properly resolved.

Intellectual Resources:In 2022, 227,000 college students, 1,130 doctors and 10,324 masters were newly employed, all hit a record high.A total of 68 post-doctoral stations were added, totaling 345.The number of highly skilled personnel increased by 72,000, totaling 704,000, and highly skilled personnel accounted for 33.6% of skilled personnel; 15 new skill master studios, 130 in total; In the whole year, 380,000 skilled personnel were trained in Ningbo.

Ⅹ. Culture, Health and Sports

Cultural Construction: By the end of 2022, there has been 28 national representative projects of intangible cultural heritage and 478 provincial and municipal ones.1 state-owned museum, Zhou Yao Insect Museum, was added, totaling 17. FenghuaGujiazhuangsite was selected as "Important Discovery of Zhejiang Archaeology". The"Symphony of Mountains and Seas - Fenghua's History and Civilization Exhibition" selected by Fenghua Museum was awarded as one of the top ten national museum exhibitions. 860 "15-minute quality cultural life circles", 20 urban bookstores, 10 cultural stations and 46 rural museum have been built. At the end of the year, there were 33 National Priority Cultural Relic Protection Sites.

Public Health: By the end of 2022, there have been 4,916 medical institutions and 204 hospitals, including 8Grade III Level A hospitals, 11 Grade III Level B hospitals, and 157 community health centers and township health centers. There have been 47,000 hospital beds, 103,000 professional health workers, 88,000 health technical workers, 36,000 practicing doctors and assistants and 38,000 registered nurses. According to the census population statistics, the number of beds, health workers, medical practitioners (including assistants) and registered nurses per thousand people reached 7.5, 14.1, 5.8 and 6.1 respectively, and 6.9 general practitioners per 10,000 population. The immunization coverage rate of children of school age in the city was 95.0%.

Sports: 22 national events were held in Ningbo in 2022. The team participated in the 17th Games of Zhejiang Province, winning 386.75 gold medals, 792.75 medals and a total score of 8218.75 points, all ranking second in the province. By the end of the year, the city has a total of 28,231sports venues and facilities, the total area of 27.143 million square meters. In 2022, the sales of sports lottery in Ningbo reached ¥3.07 billion, an increase of 36% over the previous year.

XI. Population, Livelihood and Social Insurance

Population:By the end of 2022, the registeredpopulation of Ningbo has reached 6.211 million, an increase of 27,000 from the end of the previous year, with the3.142million of urban residents. The year 2022 saw 34,556 births, 18,062 males out of the total, with a sex ratio (male to female) of 109.5:100. It represented a birth rate of 5.58‰, a death rate of 6.83‰ and a natural growth rate of -1.25‰.The net migration was 35,157, and the net migration rate was 5.67‰.At the end of the year, the city's permanent resident population was 9.618 million, an increase of 74,000, and the proportion of urban population in the total population (namely the urbanization rate) was 78.9%, up by 0.5% over the previous year.

Residents' Incomes & Expenditures: Ningbo's disposable income per urban resident in 2022 was ¥ 68,348, up by 4.5% over the previous year and a real growth of 2.2% after deducting the price factor.In terms of urban and rural areas, the per capita disposable income of urban residents achieved ¥76,690, with a growth of 3.8% and a real growth of 1.5% ; that of rural residents achieved ¥45,487, with a growth of 5.9% and a real growth of 3.5%. The income multiplier between urban and rural areas was 1.69. In 2022, the per capita living expenditure of Ningbo residents was 42,997, up by 6.2%. Dividing by urban and rural areas, the per capita living expenditure of urban residents was 47,916, up by 5.6%, while that of rural residents per capital was 29,514, up by 7.5%.

Table 8:Main Indicators of Per Capita Income and Expenditure of Ningbo Residents in 2022

Index	All Residents		Urban Residents		Rural Residents	
	Actuals (%)	Increase over last year (%)	Actuals (%)	Increase over last year (%)	Actuals (%)	Increase over last year (%)
Disposable Income Per Capita	68348	4.5	76690	3.8	45487	5.9
1.Wage income	38016	1.8	42390	1.4	26031	2.2
2.Net operating income	12028	1.0	13019	0.5	9313	1.9
3.Net property income	7332	5.0	9385	3.9	1705	12.8
4.Transfer net income	10972	19.5	11896	18.1	8438	23.8
Per Capita Living Consumption Expenditure	42997	6.2	47916	5.6	29514	7.5

Social Insurance: At the end of 2022, the number of workers and staff in the city participating in basic old-age pension, basic medical treatment, unemployment& work-related injury and maternity insurance were 5.267million, 5.016 million, 3.416 million, 4.515 million and 3.77 million respectively; while the numbers of insured of basic pension insurance for urban and rural residents and basic medical care for urban and rural residents have achieved 994,000 and 2.962 million. The social security cards issued have reached 10.033 million, while the activation rate of financial accounts for the social security cards have reached 71.2%.

Livelihood Security: By the end of the year, there have been 258 nursing faculties with 51,000 beds. 57,000 people have received minimum living security, receiving 630 million of financial assistance. The minimum standard of living increased to ¥1,181 per month. The standard of minimum salary for enterprise staffs has two levels, which demonstrated as ¥2,280 and ¥2,070. The per capita disposable income of low-income farmers in the city was 21,869, an increase of 13.8% over the previous year. There were 41,000 difficult disabilities enjoyed the living allowance and 91,000 severe disabled persons enjoyed nursing subsidies in the year. There were 29,000 disabled persons who need rehabilitation services and have all received rehabilitation services. At the end of 2022, the city's destitute objects provided centralized support for 2,352 people.

Government-subsidized Housing Projects: Throughout the year, 74,000 units (rooms) of affordable rental housing were built and raised, completed 159 old community renovation projects with a construction area of 8.27 million square meters. A total of 150,000 units rental housing have been raised, and 22 specialized housing rental enterprises have been fostered.The housing security reform for new citizens was selected as one of the first pilot projects of the provincial Common Wealth and was awarded a five-star rating. The Measures for the Administration of Public Rental Housing Guarantee were issued, and there were 55,300 public rental housing households under guarantee. The pilot of co-ownership housing has been launched and the construction of 1,438 units co-ownership housingbegan.

Charity: In 2022, the charity funds raised by charity organizations of municipal and county-level reached ¥920 million, spent ¥750 million on relief, benefiting 568,000 people, and raised a total of ¥10.74 billionover the years,spent ¥8.76 billionon aid, benefiting 6.196 million people. Throughout the year, the Municipal Charity Federation carried out a total of 876 volunteer service activities, with more than 40,000 volunteers participating in the service and 45,000 hours of service.

Ⅻ. Ecological Construction and Social Safety

Ecological Construction: The rate that the number of days the air quality was excellent to good was 89% in the city's central urban area, ranking 17th among 168 key cities in China, up 3 places from the previous year; the concentration of $PM_{2.5}$ was 22micrograms per cubic meter. In the year, the number of new emissions transactions was 138 and the transaction amount was ¥52.221 million; the number of new paid uses was 1,032, and the amount was ¥194 million. The city's sewage treatment capacity is 840 million tons throughout the year, the sewage treatment rate is 99%, and the total COD emission reduction was 169,000 tons. The excellent and good water quality rate of the sections above municipal control was 93.6%, an increase of 5.4% points over the previous year; the water environment functional zone compliance rate is 100%, up by 1.2%. The water quality of drinking water sources at county level and above maintains a 100% compliance rate throughout the year. At the end of 2022, the city had 5 National-Level ecological civilization construction demonstration counties (districts), 9Provincial-Level ecological civilization construction demonstration counties (districts), and 2 national "Two Mountains" practice and innovation bases.

"Safety Ningbo" Construction:In 2022,Ningbo was awarded the title of "Provincial Peaceful City" for the 16th consecutive time. By the end of the year, 114 accidents and 81 deaths occurred in the city, down by 32.9% and 36.2% respectively over the previous year. Throughout 2022, 5,659 cases concerning food safety were put on record and settled. In all the cases, there were 9 major cases with the total fine and confiscated money of ¥25.863 million, and 45 suspected criminal cases referred to the police. Throughout 2022, the people's mediation organizations mediated a total of 115,000 civil disputes of various kinds and successfully mediated 114,000, with a success rate of 99.7%.

Notes:

(1)All the statistics of 2022 listed in the bulletin are preliminary statistics.

(2)The regional GDP and the absolute value of industries are calculated at current prices while the growth rates are calculated at comparable prices.

(3)The industrial enterprises above designated size refers to those enterprises with their main business income of ¥20 million and above.

The enterprises of wholesale, retail sales, accommodations and public catering above designated size refer to those with their main business income of ¥20 million and above, ¥5 million and above, ¥2 million and above, ¥2 million and above respectively.

(4)In the tables,"growth" refers to "growth over the previous year".

(5)As some insurance institutions are currently in the risk disposal stage, the relevant data caliber of premium income does not include these institutions.

NINGBO 2023 Statistical Yearbook

CHAPTER 1

第一篇

综合

GENERAL SURVEY

综合
General Survey

宁波的经济发展
Economic Development of Ningbo

		2022	比上年增长（%）Increase Over Last Year
国内生产总值（亿元）	Gross Domestic Product(100 million yuan)	15704.30	3.5
第一产业	Primary Industry	381.99	4.1
第二产业	Secondary Industry	7413.47	3.2
第三产业	Tertiary Industry	7908.84	3.8
规模以上工业总产值	Gross Output Value of Above Designated Sized Industry	24205.17	7.3
社会消费品零售总额	Total Retail Sales of Consumer Goods	4896.70	5.3
财政总收入	Total Financial Revenue	3358.50	2.9
宁波港域货物吞吐量（万吨）	Cargo Handled at Ningbo Port (10000 tons)	63721.50	2.2
宁波港域集装箱吞吐量（万标箱）	Container Handled at Ningbo Port (10000 TEU)	3077.80	4.8
自营进出口额（亿美元）	Directive Import and Export (USD 100 million)	1905.00	6.3
出口额（亿美元）	Export (USD 100 million)	1237.40	8.0
实际利用外资（亿美元）	Amount of Foreign Capital Actually Used (USD 100 million)	37.27	13.8

宁波的一天
One Day in Ningbo

国内生产总值	Gross Domestic Product	1430255	万元	10000 yuan
第一产业	Value - added of Primary Industry	10466	万元	10000 yuan
工业增加值	Value - added of Industry	183061	万元	10000 yuan
第三产业增加值	Value - added of Tertiary Industry	216680	万元	10000 yuan
社会消费品零售额	Retail of Consumer Goods	134157	万元	10000 yuan
财政总收入	Total Financial Revenue	92014	万元	10000 yuan
宁波港域货物吞吐量	Cargo Handled at Ningbo Port	174.58	万吨	10000 tons
宁波港域集装箱吞吐量	Container Handled at Ningbo Port	84323	标箱	TEU
自营出口额	Directive Export	33901	万美元	USD 10000
全社会用电量	Electricity Consumption	26648	万千瓦时	10000 kW·h

表1-1 行政区划和陆域面积（2022年）
Administrative Division and Land Area(2022)

单位：个（unit ）

地区	Region	镇 Town	乡 Township	街道办事处 Subdistrict Offices	居民委员会 Neighborhood Committee	村民委员会 Villages Committee	陆域面积（平方公里） Land Area(sq.km)
全市	**Whole Municipality**	**73**	**10**	**73**	**791**	**2154**	**9816**
市区	**Urban Area**	**24**	**1**	**55**	**544**	**912**	**3730**
海曙	Haishu	7	1	9	110	164	595
江北	Jiangbei	1		7	72	65	208
镇海	Zhenhai	2		5	51	43	246
北仑	Beilun			11	72	154	599
鄞州	Yinzhou	10		15	196	203	814
奉化	Fenghua	4		8	43	283	1268
县级市	**County**	**49**	**9**	**18**	**247**	**1247**	**6087**
余姚	Yuyao	14	1	6	61	261	1501
慈溪	Cixi	14		5	93	294	1361
宁海	Ninghai	11	3	4	43	332	1843
象山	Xiangshan	10	5	3	50	355	1382

注：本表数据来自宁波市民政局与宁波市自然资源和规划局。
Note：Data in this table are obtained from Ningbo Civil Affairs Bureau and Ningbo Bureau of Natural Resources and Planning .

表1-2 各月主要气象指标（2022年）
Main Climate Indicators(2022)

时间 Time	平均气温（℃） Average Temperature（℃）	降水量（毫米） Precipitation (millimeters)	相对湿度(%) Relative Humidity (%)	日照时数（小时） Sunshine Hours (hours)
1月 Jan.	7. 1	92. 0	78. 7	82. 4
2月 Feb.	6. 0	118. 9	78. 1	73. 7
3月 Mar.	13. 8	160. 9	76. 3	136. 1
4月 Apr.	17. 2	93. 7	71. 3	150. 6
5月 May	19. 5	128. 9	76. 5	123. 2
6月 June	25. 5	162. 2	81. 6	122. 8
7月 July	30. 6	77. 7	73. 4	256. 1
8月 Aug.	30. 6	72. 6	72. 3	263. 4
9月 Sept.	24. 4	435. 4	77. 7	150. 3
10月 Oct.	19. 1	43. 6	74. 3	118. 9
11月 Nov.	16. 6	87. 1	82. 7	70. 6
12月 Dec.	6. 6	79. 5	68. 9	122. 7

注：本表数据来自宁波市气象局。
Note: Date in this table are obtained from Ningbo Meteorological Bureau.

表1-3 部分年份国民经济主要指标
Main Indicators of National Economy in Partial Years

指标	单位	Indicators	Unit
人口		**Population**	
年末总人口	万人	Year-end Population	10000persons
地区生产总值	**亿元**	**Gross Domestic Product**	**100 million yuan**
第一产业增加值	亿元	Added Value of Primary Industry	100million yuan
第二产业增加值	亿元	Added Value of Secondary Industry	100million yuan
第三产业增加值	亿元	Added Value of Tertiary Industry	100million yuan
人均生产总值(户籍人口)	**元**	**Per Capital GDP (by Registered Population)**	**yuan**
人均生产总值(常住人口)	**元**	**Per Capital GDP (by Permanent Population)**	**yuan**
农业		**Agriculture**	
粮食产量	万吨	Yield of Grain Crops	10000tons
工业		**Industry**	
全部工业增加值	亿元	Added Value of Industry	100 million yuan
运输、邮电和通信		**Transportation. Post and Telecommunications Services**	
宁波港域货物吞吐量	万吨	Cargo Handled at Ports	10000 tons
宁波港域集装箱吞吐量	万标箱	Container Handled at Ports	10000 TEU
旅客运输量	万人	Passenger Traffic	10000 persons
货物运输量	万吨	Freight Traffic	10000 tons
固定电话用户	万户	Number of Local Telephone Subscribers	10000 subscribers
移动电话用户	万户	Number of Subscribers of Mobile Telephone	10000 subscribers
全社会用电量	**亿千瓦时**	**Total Consumption of Electricity**	**100 million kW·h**
#工业用电	亿千瓦时	Electricity Consumption for Industry Use	100million kW·h
生活用电	亿千瓦时	Electricity Consumption for Urban and Rural Residents	100million kW·h
财政金融		**Finance and Banking**	
财政总收入	亿元	Financial Budgetary Revenue	100million yuan

注:（1）本表价值量指标按当年价格计算，发展速度按可比价格计算。
（2）2014年起为城乡住户一体化新口径,2013年(含)之前城镇均为市区口径，2013年(含)之前农村居民可支配收入指人均纯收入口径。
（3）2018年及以前年份生产总值相关数据已根据四经普数据修订，表1-5至表1-11同。

Notes:（1）Figures in value terms are calculated at current prices, While the indices growth rates are calculated at comparable prices.
（2）2014 for the integration of new urban and rural households, 2013 (inclusive) before the towns are urban caliber, 2013 (inclusive) before the disposable income of rural residents refers to the per capita net income caliber.
（3）The GDP related data of 2018 and previous years have been adjusted according to the data of the 4th economic census, the same as Table 1-5 to Table 1-11.

1978	2000	2010	2015	2020	2021	2022	指数(2022年为以下各年%) Index (2022 As Percentage of the Following Years) 1978	2000	2010	年平均增长(%) Average Annual Growth Rate(%) 1978–2022	2000–2022
457.70	540.94	574.08	586.57	613.66	618.33	621.10	135.7	114.8	108.2	0.7	0.6
20.17	**1144.57**	**5264.70**	**8295.35**	**12599.22**	**14594.92**	**15704.30**	**16566.5**	**769.9**	**221.9**	**12.3**	**9.7**
6.52	94.24	216.66	275.13	338.52	356.16	382.00	556.5	188.0	125.4	4.0	2.9
9.69	635.83	2915.09	4210.91	5793.11	6997.17	7413.50	26957.0	755.0	219.0	13.6	9.6
3.96	414.50	2132.95	3809.31	6467.59	7241.59	7908.80	22959.5	918.5	248.8	13.2	10.6
437	**21208**	**91952**	**141758**	**206186**	**236933**	**252847**	**57859.6**	**1192.2**	**275.0**	**15.6**	**11.9**
		70734	**97604**	**134650**	**153922**	**163911**			**231.7**		
180.51	132.51	87.13	79.05	67.44	67.79	71.60	39.7	54.0	82.2	-2.1	-2.8
8.62	578.30	2613.74	3717.89	5147.04	6297.53	6681.70	77513.9	1155.4	255.6	16.3	11.8
214	11547	41217	51005	60098	62340	63722	29776.4	551.8	154.6	13.8	8.1
	90.20	1300.35	1982.40	2705.40	2937.30	3077.80		3412.2	236.7		17.4
2966	22736	33911	14230	7513	7169	4822	162.6	21.2	14.2	1.1	-6.8
1385	10819	30553	42083	71898	78747	80100	5783.4	740.4	262.2	9.7	9.5
1.07	130	317	269	242	218	208	19420.6	159.7	65.5	12.7	2.1
	118	846	1257	1336	1375	1385		1174.9	163.9		11.8
7.09	**113.48**	**459.04**	**585.07**	**832.15**	**938.41**	**972.66**	**13718.8**	**857.1**	**211.9**	**11.8**	**10.3**
4.37	84.01	354.27	434.90	603.17	674.67	674.67	15438.6	803.1	190.4	12.1	9.9
0.43	15.13	49.83	64.73	101.33	110.64	134.21	31211.6	887.0	269.3	13.9	10.4
4.97	143.15	1171.75	2072.73	2835.60	3264.39	3358.50	67575.5	2346.1	286.6	16.0	15.4

表 1－3 续表 Continued

指标	单位	Indicators	Unit
#一般公共预算收入	亿元	General Public Budget Revenue	100 million yuan
一般公共预算支出	亿元	General Public Fiscal Budget Expenditure	100 million yuan
年末金融机构存款余额	亿元	Balance of Deposits of Financial Institutions	100 million yuan
#住户存款	亿元	Saving Deposits of Urban and Rural Residents	100 million yuan
年末金融机构贷款余额	亿元	Balance of Loans of Financial Institutions	100 million yuan
社会消费品零售总额	**亿元**	**Total Retail Sales of Consumer Goods**	**100 million yuan**
对外经济		**Foreign Trade**	
进出口总额	亿美元	Total Exports and Imports Value	USD100 million
#出口总额	亿美元	Total Exports Value	USD100 million
进口总额	亿美元	Total Imports Value	USD100 million
合同利用外资	亿美元	Foreign Investment Contracted	USD100 million
实际利用外资	亿美元	Foreign Investments Actually Use	USD100 million
城乡居民生活		**Living Standard**	
城镇居民人均可支配收入	元	Per Capital Disposable Income of Urban Households	yuan
城镇居民人均生活消费支出	元	Per Capital Annual Expenditure for Consumption of Urban Households	yuan
农村居民人均可支配收入	元	Per Capital Annual Disposable Income of Rural Residents	yuan
农村居民人均生活消费支出	元	Per Capita Annual Living Expenditure of Rural Residents	yuan
教育		**Education**	
高等学校在校学生数	万人	Students Enrollment in Institutions of Higher Education	10000 persons
中等专业学校在校学生数	万人	Students Enrollment in Technical Secondary Schools	10000 persons
中学在校学生数	万人	Students Enrollment in Secondary Schools	10000 persons
小学在校学生数	万人	Students Enrollment in Primary Schools	10000 persons
专任教师数	万人	Number of Full－times Teachers	10000 persons
卫生事业		**Health Care**	
卫生技术人员数	万人	Number of Medical Technical Personnel	10000 persons
#医生	万人	Doctor	10000 persons
卫生机构床位数	张	Number of Beds in Health Institutions	bed

1978	2000	2010	2015	2020	2021	2022	指数(2022年为以下各年%) Index (2022 As Percentage of the Following Years)			年平均增长(%) Average Annual Growth Rate(%)	
							1978	2000	2010	1978–2022	2000–2022
	64.35	530.93	1006.41	1510.80	1723.14	1680.10		2610.9	316.4		16.0
	83.91	600.75	1252.64	1742.10	1944.42	2187.70		2607.2	364.2		16.0
4.84	1172.94	9552.03	15400.24	23166.68	26187.66	30203.75	624044.3	2575.0	316.2	22.0	15.9
1.52	586.06	3282.26	5302.84	8522.07	9387.31	11749.75	773009.7	2004.9	358.0	22.6	14.6
6.50	883.12	9000.62	14966.92	25051.98	28513.16	32377.28	498111.9	3666.2	359.7	21.3	17.8
7.09	**383.86**	**1617.68**	**3050.18**	**4238.30**	**4649.10**	**4896.70**	**69064.9**	**1275.6**	**302.7**	**16.0**	**12.3**
	75.41	829.04	1004.66	1412.77	1845.28	1905.00		2526.2	229.8		15.8
	51.68	519.67	714.30	924.46	1179.71	1237.40		2394.3	238.1		15.5
	23.73	309.37	290.36	488.32	665.56	667.60		2813.3	215.8		16.4
	9.52	40.46	76.54	47.00	86.41	57.50		604.0	142.1		8.5
	6.22	23.23	42.34	24.68	32.74	37.27		599.7	160.5		8.5
306	10921	30166	47852	68008	73869	76690	25062.1	702.2	254.2	13.4	9.3
299	7997	19420	29645	38702	45362	47916	16025.4	599.2	246.7	12.2	8.5
	5069	14261	26469	39132	42946	45487		897.4	319.0		10.5
	3929	9794	17800	23481	27451	29514		751.2	301.3		9.6
0.10	2.59	14.08	15.58	17.67	18.41	17.93	17931.3	692.3	127.3	12.5	9.2
0.29	2.51	8.07	6.90	6.92	6.05	6.09	2101.0	242.7	75.5	7.2	4.1
27.16	27.98	32.54	27.39	31.01	32.16	33.16	122.1	118.5	101.9	0.5	0.8
59.11	42.40	46.19	48.02	51.73	53.79	55.51	93.9	130.9	120.2	-0.1	1.2
3.55	5.17	7.29	8.20	9.11	9.51	9.70	273.4	187.7	133.1	2.3	2.9
0.93	1.92	4.31	5.67	7.95	8.32	8.75	940.7	455.7	203.0	5.2	7.1
0.36	0.95	1.72	2.19	3.19	3.43	3.59	998.3	378.3	208.9	5.4	6.2
5989	14535	26097	32871	44447	45181	46804	781.5	322.0	179.3	4.8	5.5

表1-4 各区（县、市）社会经济基本情况(2022年)
Main Indicators of Society and Economy by Region(2022)

指标	单位	Indicators	Unit	全市 Total
人口、劳动力及土地面积		**Population, Employment and Land Areas**		
年末户籍总人口	万人	Year-end Population	10000 persons	621.07
年户籍平均人口	万人	Annual Average Population	10000 persons	619.70
年末户籍总户数	万户	Total Households of Year-end	10000 households	245.20
常住人口	万人	Permanent Population	10000 persons	961.80
全社会从业人员	万人	Total Employment Personnel	10000 persons	599.02
行政区域面积	平方公里	Land Area of Districts	sq.km	9816
#建成区面积	平方公里	Developed Areas	sq.km	582
综合经济		**General Economy**		
生产总值(当年价格)	万元	Gross Domestic Product (at Current Price)	10000 yuan	157042963
第一产业增加值	万元	Value-added of Primary Industry	10000 yuan	3819926
第二产业增加值	万元	Value-added of Secondary Industry	10000 yuan	74134665
第三产业增加值	万元	Value-added of Tertiary Industry	10000 yuan	79088372
工业增加值	万元	Value-added of Industry	10000 yuan	66817224
人均生产总值（常住）	元	Per Capital GDP (by Permanent Population)	yuan	163911
生产总值增长率	%	Increase Rate of GDP	%	3.5
一般公共预算收入	万元	General public budget revenue	10000 yuan	16802309
一般公共预算支出	万元	General public budget expenditure	10000 yuan	21878133
#一般性公共服务支出	万元	Expenditure for General Public Services	10000 yuan	1791137
科学技术支出	万元	Expenditure for Science and Technology Promotion	10000 yuan	1509955
教育支出	万元	Expenditure for Education	10000 yuan	2987893
文化体育与传媒支出	万元	Expenditure for Culture, Sports & Media Services	10000 yuan	399116
卫生健康支出	万元	Expenditure for Medical and Health	10000 yuan	1925322
节能保护支出	万元	Expenditure for Energy Saving and Environmental Protection	10000 yuan	312371
城乡社区事务支出	万元	Expenditure for Urban and Rural Community Services	10000 yuan	3032076
交通运输支出	万元	Expenditure for Transportation	10000 yuan	1164113
社会保障和就业支出	万元	Expenditure for Social Security & Employment	10000 yuan	2375970
住房保障支出	万元	Expenditure for Housing Security	10000 yuan	682642
年末金融机构人民币存款余额	万元	Balance of RMB Deposits of Financial Institutions	10000 yuan	302037454
#住户存款余额	万元	Balance of Household Deposits	10000 yuan	117497481

注：本表非年报数据。
Note: Data in this table are not reported data.

各区 by Districts						余姚市 Yuyao	慈溪市 Cixi	宁海县 Ninghai	象山县 Xiangshan
海曙区 Haishu	江北区 Jiangbei	镇海区 Zhenhai	北仑区 Beilun	鄞州区 Yinzhou	奉化区 Fenghua				
64.33	28.33	30.17	44.95	98.77	47.66	83.09	106.91	62.98	53.88
64.25	28.07	29.82	44.69	98.17	47.72	83.19	106.70	63.06	54.02
26.13	11.94	12.34	18.20	39.54	18.44	33.12	42.61	24.50	18.37
105.80	50.30	51.60	87.90	166.20	58.60	126.40	186.50	70.90	57.60
63.30	34.02	33.83	60.78	108.97	34.31	73.41	112.51	40.00	37.90
595	208	246	599	814	1268	1501	1361	1843	1382
						54	51	44	35
15012748	8603155	13742923	26308414	27347839	9072828	15135928	25215815	9007216	7200357
171793	89439	73187	89240	307279	359780	537583	660105	545151	984459
4258353	2710647	9549213	13001273	7511622	5473704	8982721	15313453	4364870	2737481
10582602	5803069	4120523	13217901	19528938	3239344	5615624	9242256	4097195	3478418
3378825	2254734	9001851	12335518	6063404	4928526	8442891	14244732	3865601	2057083
142234	172408	267372	304319	165244	155091	119889	135423	127131	125224
2.7	4.9	5.9	4.2	3.0	2.4	1.9	2.3	4.3	5.2
1170566	1019419	744025	4241297	2795978	692970	1207431	2047306	624665	608166
1383524	945557	1075739	3718022	2697215	1073185	1489567	2508550	1024918	1016696
227611	93076	93732	182200	224881	156137	123870	204527	94840	128625
62806	49545	49180	362004	212085	57281	83886	385492	31178	56513
231406	130532	162807	233990	379663	162851	272115	450000	181312	157498
16146	10759	14689	57700	39662	24292	24505	36092	18893	24705
129845	71021	99884	178642	301351	74648	176401	229893	129226	93634
6678	6920	6964	172777	21454	4912	20465	11716	4196	5251
177375	123064	241664	415265	435012	76830	77789	234581	65537	42165
19502	4702	15896	54030	57750	39044	38411	33475	57495	24406
150312	104806	139781	250804	347980	189253	246801	245596	175852	191257
85341	56406	40833	49129	114948	32406	25562	82192	34912	30014
						26182098	39506954	10651522	9414715
						15250007	22344662	5220180	5163054

表 1－4 续表 1 Continued 1

指标	单位	Indicators	Unit	全市 Total
年末金融机构人民币贷款余额	万元	Balance of RMB Loans of Financial Institutions	10000 yuan	323772756
规模以上工业企业		**Industry Enterprises Above Designated Size**		
工业企业数	个	Number of Industrial Enterprises	unit	10342
从业人员年平均人数	万人	Annual Average Employees	10000 persons	167. 0
工业总产值（当年价）	万元	Gross Output Value of Industry (at current price)	10000 yuan	242051716
营业收入	万元	Operating Revenue	10000 yuan	254064101
本年应交增值税	万元	Value－added Taxes Payable in This Year	10000 yuan	4236988
利润总额	万元	Total Profits	10000 yuan	14180052
交通运输、邮电通信、能源电力		**Transport, Post & Telecommunications,Energy and Electricity**		
铁路客运量	万人	Railway Passenger Traffic	10000 persons	2988. 8
铁路货运量	万吨	Railway Freight Traffic	10000 tons	3502. 7
公路客运量	万人	Highways Passenger Traffic	10000 persons	1104. 4
公路货运量	万吨	Highways Freight Traffic	10000 tons	45310. 0
水运客运量	万人	Waterways Passenger Traffic	10000 persons	135. 7
水运货运量	万吨	Waterways Freight Traffic	10000 tons	31279. 0
民用航空客运量	万人	Civil Aviation Passenger Traffic	10000 persons	616. 6
民用航空货邮运量	万吨	Civil Aviation Freight Traffic	10000 ton	8. 5
民用汽车拥有量	辆	Number of Civil Motor Vehicles	unit	3357053
#私人汽车拥有量	辆	Number of Private Car	unit	2723231
公路里程	公里	Length of Highways	km	11470. 5
邮政业务收入	万元	Business Value of Post	10000 yuan	1504613
电信业务收入	万元	Business Value of Telecommunications	10000 yuan	1539864
本地电话用户数	万户	Number of Subscribers of Local Telephone	10000 subscribers	207. 77
年末移动电话用户数	万户	Number of Mobile Telephone Subscribers at Year－end	10000 subscribers	1385. 40
国际互联网用户数	万户	User of International Computer Network	10000 subscribers	518. 13
全年用电量	万千瓦时	Electricity Consumption	10000 kW·h	9726637
国内贸易、对外经济		**Domestic Trade, Foreign Trade**		
社会消费品零售额	万元	Total Retail Sales of Consumer Goods	10000 yuan	48967201
当年新签合同项目数	个	New Signed Constract	unit	410
当年实际使用外资金额	万美元	Amount of Foreign Capital Actually Used	USD10000	372658
进口额	万元	Total Import	USD10000	44406691

各区 by Districts						余姚市 Yuyao	慈溪市 Cixi	宁海县 Ninghai	象山县 Xiangshan
海曙区 Haishu	江北区 Jiangbei	镇海区 Zhenhai	北仑区 Beilun	鄞州区 Yinzhou	奉化区 Fenghua				
						22185111	36412497	15584235	13220003
836	380	668	1039	1473	753	1581	2167	755	690
11.9	6.5	10.1	24.2	19.3	10.1	24.9	40.3	12.1	7.5
14452875	11042016	38038425	54704355	21490439	9511213	23963352	47637782	12864034	8347226
14919031	12321740	41016529	56895965	22685042	10900702	24063644	48792113	14402056	8067279
273106	148739	414881	803029	411033	410519	351312	985131	276170	163067
488671	612591	1058372	3811892	1549341	678523	1365924	3503835	591144	519759
1999.4	6.8				44.8	734.6		203.2	
	497.9	534.3	2287.5	5.3		177.7			
145.5	198.8		55.8	376.6	29.9	40.8	73.0	18.3	165.6
1262.7	5174.5	2623.3	22205.5	6573.9	3530.8	1417.7	1441.1	734.6	345.9
		7.1		6.8		1.3		1.4	119.0
77.1	11168.3	3843.1	9036.7	1638.4	691.6	7.8		562.6	4253.4
616.6									
8.5									
381947	217190	170027	367689	632145	188240	424135	585794	210401	179485
306366	168280	134913	278987	504882	154829	345170	498415	174975	156414
997.0	348.8	337.6	515.1	1013.8	1386.7	2028.1	1639.6	1649.0	1554.6
455656	153514	30649	69763	344983	80869	163227	140791	47726	17438
611167	391308	1418670	1796813	1134806	471974	1246323	1876017	469449	342515
8793988	4497062	1919699	4133886	10379102	1706647	4544693	7336471	3206625	2449031
28	52	19	91	102	23	28	34	8	25
25705	22931	22040	132936	53123	12016	9607	52328	12920	14252
970796	2770501	3806285	25203478	6738187	357443	2676899	1334466	278976	269659

表 1－4 续表 2 Continued 2

指标	单位	Indicators	Unit	全市 Total
出口额	万元	Total Export	USD 10000	82305891
商品房销售		**Commercial Building Sales**		
商品房屋销售面积	万平方米	Floor Space of Building Sold	10000 sq.m	1128. 80
#住宅	万平方米	Residential Buildings	10000 sq.m	835. 15
商品房屋销售额	万元	Total Actually Sales of Commercial Buildings	10000 yuan	19375751
#住宅	万元	Residential Buildings	10000 yuan	15981551
待售面积	万平方米	Floor Space of Sale Building	10000 sq.m	419. 96
文教、卫生、科技		**Culture, Education, Public Health, Science**		
全日制学校数	所	Number of Full－time Schools	unit	1790
各类学校专任教师数	人	Teachers	person	97049
各类学校在校学生数	人	Students in School	person	1412376
专利申请授权量	项	Number of Patent Certified	piece	76127
#发明专利	项	Inventions	piece	9611
体育场地数	个	Number of Public Stadiums and Gymnasiums	unit	28231
公共图书馆图书藏量	万册	Collection of Public Libraries	10000 copies	1400. 97
医院、卫生院数	个	Number of Health Institutions	unit	290
卫生机构床位数	张	Number of Beds in Health Institutions	bed	46804
医生数	人	Number of Doctors	person	35939
注册护士	人	Number of Register Nurses	person	37657
人民生活		**People's Livelihood**		
城镇居民人均可支配收入	元	Per Capital Annual Disposable Income of Urban Residents	yuan	76690
城镇居民人均消费支出	元	Per Capital Annual Expenditure for Consumption of Urban Residents	yuan	47916
农村居民人均可支配收入	元	Per Capital Annual Net Income of Rural Residents	yuan	45487
农村居民人均消费性支出	元	Per Capital Annual Expenditure for Consumption of Rural Residents	yuan	29514
居民消费价格指数（上年=100）	%	Consumer Price Index (Preceding Year=100)	%	102. 3
基本养老保险参保人数	人	Number of Personnel Engaged Basic Endowment Insurance	person	6559257
基本医疗保险参保人数	人	Number of Personnel Engaged Basic Medical Insurance	person	7978684
#职工基本医疗保险	人	Basic Medical Insurance for Employees	person	5016301

各区 by Districts						余姚市 Yuyao	慈溪市 Cixi	宁海县 Ninghai	象山县 Xiangshan
海曙区 Haishu	江北区 Jiangbei	镇海区 Zhenhai	北仑区 Beilun	鄞州区 Yinzhou	奉化区 Fenghua				
7775528	5777748	3340462	19982445	19271799	2509489	8290631	9907280	3397948	2045035
125.29	109.00	34.47	88.36	231.26	117.86	157.82	151.15	59.72	53.86
110.64	48.68	23.03	71.05	159.84	97.04	126.70	103.30	51.55	43.34
2908856	2104314	524117	1486218	5721125	1431357	1943915	1981401	704354	570094
2724570	1080535	421827	1326346	4778282	1287163	1694678	1537772	643240	487138
22.13	39.67	29.70	40.06	66.76	31.90	47.20	46.41	50.79	45.35
198	100	91	128	230	123	271	315	167	115
7682	4336	4686	6984	13078	4978	11401	15505	7578	5610
116497	59832	70485	98898	189127	69904	162317	220915	107734	79086
5561	4434	3923	6664	14487	3332	11093	18969	5717	1888
589	1016	847	761	2409	346	1147	1992	262	236
2121	1237	1892	1913	3968	2179	3380	6057	2693	2791
124.42	51.77	67.78	101.33	301.67	77.49	83.39	102.27	57.45	71.08
42	18	13	18	52	17	29	40	31	30
9049	3581	2541	2877	9650	2726	3842	7098	3038	2402
6438	2191	1908	2421	7251	2022	3815	5318	2580	1995
7367	2534	1906	2332	8140	2099	3625	5076	2755	1823
81600	79480	81078	78474	84630	67490	73749	73385	72549	69478
50842	46179	51369	46790	58949	47896	46729	48163	47601	40378
46504	48088	47027	47397	50333	41007	45665	47142	42165	41578
30736	34834	31346	30355	34115	25649	31338	31793	32491	27524
607393	304409	306396	659702	1027829	436494	873084	1108360	483980	425229
744525	369022	386281	766963	1271291	498053	997563	1288299	609179	517175
530301	281151	277524	582372	928656	260369	600014	716376	252840	232533

表 1－4 续表 3 Continued 3

指标	单位	Indicators	Unit	全市 Total
#城乡居民医疗保险	人	Urban and Rural (town) Residents Medical Insurance	person	2962383
失业保险参保人数	人	Number of Personnel Engaged Unemployment Insurance	person	3415878
养老服务机构床位数	张	Number of Beds in Social Welfare Institutions	bed	51448
社会治安		**Social Security**		
交通事故死亡人数	人	Death of Traffic Accidents	person	382
交通事故损失额	万元	Losses Converted into Cash of Traffic Accidents	10000yuan	345. 60
刑事案件立案数	件	Number of Criminal Cases Registered	case	9068
犯罪人数	人	Number of People of the Crime	person	12748
市政公用事业		**Civil Facilities, Environment Protection**		
年末实有城市道路面积	万平方米	Area of City Roads(Year－end)	10000sq.m	11263. 79
排水管道总长度	公里	Length of Sewage Pipes	km	10938
供水综合生产能力(含自备水源)	万吨/日	General Productive Capacity of Tap Water Supply	10000tons/day	435. 5
全年售水总量	万吨	Annual Volume of Tap Water Sale	10000tons	78375
#居民家庭用水量	万吨	Water Consumption for Residents Use	10000tons	35434
液化石油气供气总量	吨	Total Volume of Liquefied Petroleum Gas	ton	201879
#家庭用量	吨	For Residents Use	ton	159867
年末实有公共汽(电)车营运车辆数	辆	Number of Public Transportations Vehicles under Operation	unit	9073
全年公共汽(电)车客运总量	万人次	Number of Passengers Carried with Public Transportations Vehicles	10000 person-time	29685
年末实有出租汽车数	辆	Operating Taxes at Year － end	unit	6135
绿地面积	公顷	Green Areas	hectare	38963
#公园绿地面积	公顷	Public Green Areas	hectare	7557
建成区绿化覆盖面积	公顷	Coverage Area of Green Area in Developed Area	hectare	25306
环境保护		**Environment Protect**		
工业废水排放量	万吨	Volume of Industrial Waste Water Discharged	10000tons	14331. 84
工业二氧化硫排放量	吨	Volume of Industrial Sulphur Dioxide Emission	ton	8016. 32
工业烟（粉)尘排放量	吨	Volume of Industrial Soot Emission	ton	11524. 31
一般工业固体废物综合利用率	%	Rate of General Industrial Solid Waste Treated and Utilized	%	99. 71
污水处理厂集中处理率	%	Rate of Disposal Living Waste Water in Sewage Treatment Plant	%	93. 37
生活垃圾无害化处理率	%	Rate of Living Garbage Harmless Treatment	%	100

各区 by Districts						余姚市 Yuyao	慈溪市 Cixi	宁海县 Ninghai	象山县 Xiangshan
海曙区 Haishu	江北区 Jiangbei	镇海区 Zhenhai	北仑区 Beilun	鄞州区 Yinzhou	奉化区 Fenghua				
214224	87871	108757	184591	342635	237684	397549	571923	356339	284642
371276	209030	465870	198278	579854	165358	371720	464527	158786	134086
4319	1045	3191	3068	6278	4969	7025	3654	6955	7527
39	16	22	39	47	36	61	66	27	21
33.60	20.40	10.10	77.40	20.00	45.40	23.70	41.70	17.20	52.40
1052	642	549	603	1314	647	1083	1804	657	567
1342	978	743	782	1739	1034	1470	2546	1003	706
						1185.01	1736.53	793.19	929.10
						882	539	1057	509
						40.5	49.0	23.0	30.5
						5580	3560	3421	3326
						2802	2016	2110	1508
						6028	52843	18049	8447
						4691	51851	13490	4950
			729		755	712	866	716	649
			2456		1903	1730	1885	2511	1430
1771	623	60	161	2000	140	286	605	278	211
						14967	2384	1771	1690
						604	766	370	362
						2418	2279	1894	1457
171.60	122.60	3493.29	6180.06	394.92	386.88	1117.57	1082.39	428.31	954.22
12.93	4.78	1107.50	2999.14	130.02	67.41	576.86	575.50	1313.78	1228.40
11.71	62.53	496.46	7400.17	186.24	218.78	825.40	544.27	768.43	1010.34
99.81	100.00	99.39	99.84	99.91	99.99	100.00	100.00	99.95	99.20
						98.50	97.99	99.01	98.19
100	100	100	100	100	100	100	100	100	100

表1-5 部分年份经济社会结构指标
Structural Indicators of Society and Economy in Partial Years

单位：%

指标	Indicators	2010	2015	2020	2021	2022
生产总值产业结构	**Industrial Structure of GDP**					
第一产业	Primary Industry	4.1	3.3	2.7	2.4	2.4
第二产业	Secondary Industry	55.4	50.8	46.0	48.0	47.2
第三产业	Tertiary Industry	40.5	45.9	51.3	49.6	50.4
农林牧渔业产值结构	**Structure of Agricultural Gross Output Value**					
农业	Farming	49.3	48.1	45.7	47.1	46.5
林业	Forestry	2.9	3.0	3.3	2.9	3.0
牧业	Animal Husbandry	15.2	11.0	9.7	7.3	7.1
渔业	Fishery	31.1	36.3	37.3	38.2	38.9
农林牧渔服务业	Services	1.4	1.6	4.0	4.4	4.6
规模以上工业总产值比例	**Structure of Gross Industrial Output Value**					
轻工业	Light Industry	31.4	28.1	26.4	24.6	22.1
重工业	Heavy Industry	75.4	71.9	73.6	75.4	77.9
全社会固定资产投资产业结构	**Industrial Structure of Fixed Assets Investment**					
第一产业	Primary Industry	0.5	1.1	0.2	0.1	0.1
第二产业	Secondary Industry	31.8	33.3	23.36	25.4	26.2
第三产业	Tertiary Industry	67.7	65.6	76.45	74.5	73.7
自营进出口结构	**Structure of Directive Import and Export**					
出口	Exports	62.7	71.1	65.4	63.9	57.0
进口	Imports	37.3	28.9	34.6	36.1	43.0
社会消费品零售额结构	**Structure of Retail Sales of Consumer Goods**					
批发和零售贸易业	Wholesale and Retail Sale Trades	90.7	91.6	92.5	90.9	90.9
餐饮业	Catering Trade	9.3	8.4	7.5	9.1	9.1
城镇人口与农村人口比例	**The Proportion of Urban Population and Rural Population**					
城镇人口	Urban Population	64.3	64.6	65.8	67.7	68.5
农村人口	Rural Population	35.7	35.4	34.2	32.3	31.5

注：2015年及以前人口划分口径为农业人口与非农业人口，自2016年起人口划分口径为城镇人口与乡村人口。
Note: In 2015 and before, the population size was divided into: agricultural population and non-agricultural population. From 2016, the population size was divided into: urban population and village population.

表1-6 部分年份平均每天主要社会经济活动
Indicators on Average Daily Social and Economic Activities in Partial Years

指标	单位	Indicators	Unit	2010	2015	2020	2021	2022
平均每天创造财富		**Daily Production**						
生产总值	万元	Gross Domestic Product	10000 yuan	144238	227270	344241	399861	430255
第一产业	万元	Primary Industry	10000 yuan	5936	7538	9249	9758	10466
第二产业	万元	Secondary Industry	10000 yuan	79865	115367	158282	191703	203109
第三产业	万元	Tertiary Industry	10000 yuan	58437	104365	176710	198400	216680
工业增加值	万元	Added-value of Industry	10000 yuan	71609	101860	140629	172535	183061
财政总收入	万元	Financial Revenue	10000 yuan	32103	56787	77475	89435	92014
一般公共预算收入	万元	General Public Budget Revenue		14546	27573	41280	47209	46034
每天其他经济活动		**Other Daily Economic Activities**						
社会消费品零售总额	万元	Total Retail Sales of Consumer Goods	10000 yuan	44320	83567	115800	127373	134157
宁波港域货物吞吐量	万吨	Cargo Throughput	10000 tons	112. 92	139. 74	164. 20	170. 79	174. 58
宁波港域集装箱吞吐量	标箱	Container Throughput	TEU	35627	54313	73918	80474	84323
全社会用电量	万千瓦时	Total Electricity Consumption	10000 kW·h	12577	16029	22736	25710	26648
#工业用电量	万千瓦时	Industrial Electricity Consumption	10000 kW·h	9706	11915	16480	18484	18484
客运量	万人	Passenger Traffic	10000 persons	92. 91	38. 99	20. 53	19. 64	13. 21
货运量	万吨	Freight Traffic	10000 tons	83. 71	115. 30	196. 44	215. 75	219. 45
进出口总额	万美元	Total Imports and Exports	USD10000	22713	27525	38600	50555	52192
#出口	万美元	Exports	USD10000	14238	19570	25258	32321	33901
实际利用外资	万美元	Foreign Capital Actually Used	USD10000	637	1160	674	897	1021
人口变动和婚姻		**Population Changes and Marriages**						
出生	人	Births	person	134	133	119	103	95
死亡	人	Deaths	person	97	104	106	118	116
结婚	对	Marriages	couple	146	117	95	82	109
离婚	对	Divorces	couple	38	43	47	28	30

注:（1）本表价值量指标按当年价格计算。
（2）2018年及以前年份，社会消费品零售总额已根据四经普数据修订，表1-7至1-11同。
（3）2019年起，利用外资采用商务部口径，表1-7同。

Notes:（1）The data in value terms in the table are calculated at current prices.
（2）In 2018 and previous years, the total retail sales of social consumer goods have been adjusted according to the 4th economic census, the same as Tables 1-7 to 1-11 .
（3）From 2019, using foreign capital adopts the standard of Ministry of Commerce， the same as Table 1-7.

表1-7 部分年份国民经济主要指标人均水平
Main Per Capita Indicators of National Economy in Partial Years

单位：元（yuan）

指标	Indicators	2010	2015	2020	2021	2022
经济活动	**Economical Indicators**					
生产总值	Gross Domestic Products (by Registered Population)	71164	97604	134650	153922	163911
农业总产值	Gross Agricultural Output Value	4544	5144	5708	5849	6163
社会消费品零售总额	Total Retail Sales of Consumer Goods	21866	35889	45295	49031	51109
自营进出口额（美元）	Directive Exports and Imports(USD)	11206	11821	15099	19461	19883
#出口（美元）	Export (USD)	7025	8404	9880	12442	12915
实际利用外资（美元）	Foreign Capital Actually Used (USD)	314	498	264	345	389
财政总收入	Financial Revenue	15839	24388	30305	34427	35054
一般公共预算收入	General Public Budget Revenue	7177	11841	16147	18173	17536
一般公共预算支出	General Public Budget Expenditure	8120	14739	18618	20506	22834
人民生活	**People's Livelihood**					
城镇居民人均可支配收入	Annual Disposable Income of Urban Residents	30166	47852	68008	73869	76690
城镇居民人均消费支出	Annual Living Expenditures of Urban Residents	19420	29645	38702	45362	47916
农村居民人均可支配收入	Annual Net Income of Rural Residents	14261	26469	39132	42946	45487
农村居民生活消费支出	Annual Living Expenditure of Rural Residents	9794	17800	23481	27451	29514
人民币住户存款余额	Balance of Saving Deposits of Urban and Rural Households	43154	61790	90468	98358	122636
人均生活用电量（千瓦时）	Residential Electricity Consumption(kW·h)	674	762	1083	1167	1401
社会事业	**Society Indicators**					
人均拥有道路面积(平方米)	Per Capita Area of Roads (sq.m)	19.65	21.56	21.68	20.77	21.76
人均公园绿地面积(平方米)	Per Capita Public Green Area (sq.m)	10.62	11.84	13.86	14.54	14.60

注：本表经济活动部分的数据按常住人口计算。
Note: The data in the economic activity part of this table are calculated according to the resident population.

表1-8 部分年份社会经济发展相对指标
Relative Indicators on Social and Economic Development in Partial Years

指标	Indicators	2010	2015	2020	2021	2022
人口与劳动力	**Population and Labor**					
出生率(‰)	Birth Rate(‰)	8.5	8.3	7.1	6.1	5.6
死亡率(‰)	Death Rate(‰)	6.2	6.5	6.3	7.0	6.8
自然增长率(‰)	Natural Growth Rate(‰)	2.3	1.8	0.8	-0.9	-1.3
人口净迁移率(‰)	Migration Rate(‰)	3.4	3.1	7.8	8.5	5.7
全社会从业人员结构 (%)	**Structure of Total Employment Personnel (%)**					
第一产业比重	Perentage of Primary Industry	6.8	3.7	3.4	3.4	3.3
第二产业比重	Perentage of Secondary Industry	55.9	53.2	50.7	50.9	51.0
第三产业比重	Perentage of Tertiary Industry	37.3	43.1	45.9	45.7	45.7
国民经济	**Domestic Economic**					
第三产业占GDP比重 (%)	Perentage of Tertiary Industry as GDP(%)	40.5	45.9	51.3	49.6	50.4
社会消费品零售额占GDP比重(%)	Perentage of Total Retail Sales of Consumer Goods as GDP(%)	30.7	36.8	33.6	31.9	31.2
财政总收入占GDP比重(%)	Total Fiscal Revenue as Percentage of GDP(%)	22.3	25.0	22.5	22.4	21.4
进出口总额占GDP比重(%)	Total Value of Imports and Exports as Perentage of GDP(%)	106.6	75.4	78.9	81.7	80.7
出口总额占GDP比重(%)	Total Value of Exports as Perentage of GDP(%)	66.8	53.6	51.6	52.2	52.4
研究与实验发展经费占GDP比重 (%)	R&D Expenditure as Percentage of GDP(%)	1.66	2.41	2.86	2.76	2.94
外资项目平均利用合同外资（万美元）	Contractual Foreign Investment on Per Project (USD 10000)	817.4	1723.8	967.0	1532.0	1401.5
金融机构人民币贷款占存款比重 (%)	RMB Loans as Percentage of Deposits in Financial Institutions (%)	96.5	97.2	108.1	108.9	107.2
每公顷播种面积农产品产量（公斤)	Output of Farm Crops Per Hectare of Sowning Area (kg)					

注：2015年及以前年份,在进出口、出口总额占GDP比重中，美元汇率按当年汇率计算。
Note: 2015 and the former years,Total Value of Imports and Exports as Perentage of GDP,Exchange rate of USD are calculated according to the exchange rate of the current year.

表 1－8 续表 Continued

指标	Indicators	2010	2015	2020	2021	2022
粮食	Grain	5765	5897	6059	6009	6228
油料	Oil Plants	2438	2528	2722	2438	2548
蔬菜	Vegetables	31790	31878	31005	30562	31653
城乡居民收入比例	Ratio of Annual Disposable Income of Urban Resident to Rural's	2. 12	1. 81	1. 74	1. 72	1. 69
社会发展	**Social Development**					
日均接待境外旅游者人数（人）	Number of Oversea Tourists Average Daily (person)	2608	4316	153	132	89
日均旅客周转量（万人公里）	Turnover Volume of Passengers Average Daily (10000 persons－km)	3732	1783	688	568	349
日均货物周转量（万吨公里）	Turnover Volume of Freight Traffic Average Daily (10000 tons－km)	43160	59390	113949	120414	129835
每万人拥有在校大学生数（人）	Students Enrollment of Higher Education Per 10000 Persons (person)	245. 3	266. 2	289. 2	298. 9	289. 4
每万人拥有移动电话数	Subscribers of Mobile Telephone Per 10000 Persons (subscriber)	11116	14647	14182	14409	14460
每万人拥有医生数(人)	Number of Doctors Per 10000 Persons (Person)	22. 6	25. 5	33. 9	35. 9	37. 5
每万人拥有病床数（张）	Total Beds of Per 10000 Persons(bed)	45. 5	42. 0	43. 7	47. 3	48. 9
每万人拥有公共图书馆藏书量（册）	Number of Public Libraries Collection Book Per 10000 persons (volume)	12786	11833	18960	18119	20664
每万人拥有公共交通车辆(标台)	Number of Buses Per 10000 Persons (standardstation)	6. 5	14. 7	10. 6	10. 5	10. 3
每十万人拥有律师数（人）	Number of Lawyer Per 100,000 Persons (persons)	16. 1	24. 3	40. 0	45. 2	53. 2
建成区绿化覆盖率 (%)	Coverage Rate of Green Area in Developed Area (%)	37. 52	38. 80	42. 08	43. 29	43. 49
污水处理率 (%)	Percentage of Sewage Disposed (%)	82. 81	91. 38	99. 15	99. 36	99. 60

表1-9 "六五"以来各计划时期社会经济主要指标
Major Social and Economic Indicators of Each Period since "Sixth Five-Year Plan" Period

单位：亿元（100 million yuan）

时期	Period	生产总值 Gross Domestic Product	其中 of Which 第一产业 Primary Industyr	第二产业 Secondary Industyr	第三产业 Tertiary Industry	工业增加值 Value-added of Industry
"六五"时期	"Sixth Five-Year Plan" Period	234.77	61.73	128.15	44.89	118.28
"七五"时期	"Seventh Five-Year Plan" Period	573.47	128.32	322.88	122.27	293.12
"八五"时期	"Eighth Five-Year Plan" Period	1760.35	258.74	1016.18	485.43	893.99
"九五"时期	"Ninth Five-Year Plan" Period	4777.61	450.60	2671.32	1655.69	2412.79
"十五"时期	"Tenth Five-Year Plan" Period	9063.11	564.65	4970.49	3527.95	4421.86
"十一五"时期	"11th Five-Year Plan" Period	19994.20	848.25	11066.49	8079.46	9909.57
"十二五"时期	"12th Five-Year Plan" Period	36706.84	1323.45	19080.15	16303.22	16952.06
"十三五"时期	"13th Five-Year Plan" Period	54946.85	1551.75	26569.39	26825.70	23626.36
"十四五"时期	"14th Five-Year Plan" Period	30299.22	738.16	14410.67	15150.39	12979.23
2021	2021	14594.92	356.16	6997.17	7241.59	6297.53
2022	2022	15704.30	382.00	7413.50	7908.80	6681.70

表1-9 续表1 Continued 1

单位：亿元（100 million yuan）

时期	Period	社会消费品零售总额 Retail Sale of Consumer Goods	自营出口总额（亿美元）Value of Direct Exports(100 million USD)	一般公共预算收入 General Public Budget Revenue	一般公共预算支出 General Public Fiscal Budget Expenditure
"六五"时期	"Sixth Five-Year Plan" Period	87.14	0.04		
"七五"时期	"Seventh Five-Year Plan" Period	223.62	5.88		
"八五"时期	"Eighth Five-Year Plan" Period	657.99	63.86		
"九五"时期	"Ninth Five-Year Plan" Period	1615.27	168.72		
"十五"时期	"Tenth Five-Year Plan" Period	2737.09	654.04	714.48	922.53
"十一五"时期	"11th Five-Year Plan" Period	5991.29	2039.70	1940.58	2209.97
"十二五"时期	"12th Five-Year Plan" Period	12340.63	3325.26	4042.88	4772.55
"十三五"时期	"13th Five-Year Plan" Period	19481.73	4028.47	6718.87	7803.94
"十四五"时期	"14th Five-Year Plan" Period	9545.80	2417.11	3403.24	4132.12
2021	2021	4649.10	1179.71	1723.14	1944.42
2022	2022	4896.70	1237.40	1680.10	2187.70

表1-9 续表2 Continued 2

时期	Period	宁波港域货物吞吐量(万吨) Cargo of Ports Throughpu（10000 tons）	宁波港域集装箱吞吐量（万标箱）Container Throughput (10000 TEU)	全社会用电量（亿千瓦时）Total Electricity Consumption (100 million kWh)	粮食产量（万吨）Yield of Grain (10000 tons)	户籍人口自然增长（人）Population Natural Increase (person)
"六五"时期	"Sixth Five-Year Plan" Period	2840		74.52	913.51	191824
"七五"时期	"Seventh Five-Year Plan" Period	10502	2.2	135.67	936.76	203889
"八五"时期	"Eighth Five-Year Plan" Period	25781	45.3	244.06	907.96	128862
"九五"时期	"Ninth Five-Year Plan" Period	45772	231.5	423.77	850.60	102695
"十五"时期	"Tenth Five-Year Plan" Period	96260	1505.7	955.17	446.52	49734
"十一五"时期	"11th Five-Year Plan" Period	181275	5069.1	1924.91	388.14	60064
"十二五"时期	"12th Five-Year Plan" Period	241884	8548.2	2740.63	335.83	68829
"十三五"时期	"13th Five-Year Plan" Period	280933	12258.6	3771.12	325.52	63325
"十四五"时期	"14th Five-Year Plan" Period	126062	6015.1	1911.07	139.39	-13072
2021	2021	62340	2937.3	938.41	67.79	-5318
2022	2022	63722	3077.8	972.66	71.60	-7754

表1-10 “六五”以来各计划时期社会经济主要指标平均增长率
Growth Rate of Major Social and Economic Indicators of Each Period since "Sixth Five-Year Plan" Period

单位：%

时期	Period	生产总值 Gross Domestic Product	其中 of Which 第一产业 Primary Industyr	第二产业 Secondary Industyr	第三产业 Tertiary Industry	工业增加值 Value-added of Industry
“六五”时期	"Sixth Five-Year Plan" Period	17.2	8.5	21.0	17.7	21.7
“七五”时期	"Seventh Five-Year Plan" Period	8.8	0.9	10.9	9.0	11.0
“八五”时期	"Eighth Five-Year Plan" Period	21.0	7.7	23.4	24.4	24.9
“九五”时期	"Ninth Five-Year Plan" Period	13.0	3.6	13.9	14.2	14.5
“十五”时期	"Tenth Five-Year Plan" Period	13.7	3.9	14.5	14.5	14.1
“十一五”时期	"11th Five-Year Plan" Period	12.1	4.4	11.9	13.4	12.6
“十二五”时期	"12th Five-Year Plan" Period	8.3	1.4	8.3	8.8	8.3
“十三五”时期	"13th Five-Year Plan" Period	6.4	1.8	5.3	8.0	5.9
“十四五”时期	"14th Five-Year Plan" Period	5.8	2.6	5.4	6.4	5.9
2021	2021	8.2	1.1	7.7	9.1	8.5
2022	2022	3.5	4.1	3.2	3.8	3.3

表1-10 续表1 Continued 1

单位：%

时期	Period	固定资产投资 Investment in Fixed Assets	社会消费品零售总额 Retail Sale of Consumer Goods	自营出口总额（亿美元） Value of Direct Exports(100 million USD)	一般公共预算收入 General Public Budget Revenue	一般公共预算支出 General Public Fiscal Budget Expenditure
“六五”时期	"Sixth Five-YearPlan" Period	15.9	17.8		10.1	
“七五”时期	"Seventh Five-YearPlan" Period	19.5	16.8	135.1	11.7	
“八五”时期	"Eighth Five-YearPlan" Period	46.2	32.8	52.0	27.3	
“九五”时期	"Ninth Five-YearPlan" Period	6.5	11.4	17.9	21.9	
“十五”时期	"Tenth Five-YearPlan" Period	30.9	11.8	33.9	26.7	25.8
“十一五”时期	"11th Five-YearPlan" Period	10.4	17.5	18.5	20.2	17.8
“十二五”时期	"12th Five-YearPlan" Period	17.3	14.5	6.6	13.6	15.8
“十三五”时期	"13th Five-YearPlan" Period	6.1	7.1	6.5	8.2	6.8
“十四五”时期	"14th Five-YearPlan" Period	10.7	7.5	17.4	9.5	12.1
2021	2021	11.0	9.7	27.7	14.1	11.6
2022	2022	10.4	5.3	8.0	5.1	12.5

表1-10 续表2 Continued 2

单位：%

时期	Period	宁波港域货物吞吐量 Cargo of Ports Throughpu	宁波港域集装箱吞吐量 Container Throughput	全社会用电量 Total Electricity Consumption	粮食产量 Yield of Grain	户籍人口自然增长率(‰) Natural Increase Rate
“六五”时期	"Sixth Five-Year Plan" Period	26.1		11.7	1.9	8.0
“七五”时期	"Seventh Five-Year Plan" Period	19.7		11.2	0.1	8.2
“八五”时期	"Eighth Five-Year Plan" Period	21.8	48.7	14.5	-1.8	5.1
“九五”时期	"Ninth Five-Year Plan" Period	11.0	41.3	12.9	-5.2	3.9
“十五”时期	"Tenth Five-Year Plan" Period	18.4	42.0	18.8	-9.6	1.8
“十一五”时期	"11th Five-Year Plan" Period	8.9	20.1	11.3	1.7	3.0
“十二五”时期	"12th Five-Year Plan" Period	4.4	8.8	2.6	-1.9	2.4
“十三五”时期	"13th Five-Year Plan" Period	3.3	6.4	7.3	1.8	2.1
“十四五”时期	"14th Five-Year Plan" Period	3.0	6.7	8.2	3.0	-1.1
2021	2021	3.7	8.6	12.8	0.5	-0.9
2022	2022	2.2	4.8	3.7	5.6	-1.3

表1-11 国民经济主要指标比上年增长（1978-2022年）
Growth Rate of Major National Economic Indicators Increase Precding Year(1978-2022)

单位：%

年份 Year	生产总值 Gross Domestic Product	其中 of Which #第二产业 Secondary Industyr	第三产业 Tertiary Industry	工业增加值 Value-added of Industry	固定资产投资 Investment in Fixed Assets	社会消费品零售总额 Retail Sale of Consumer Goods	财政总收入 Financial Revenue
1978	22.5	33.2	6.7		54.9	15.1	22.7
1979	13.4	16.4	18.5	14.1	15.3	24.0	-1.7
1980	17.7	28.4	4.9	38.7	12.3	27.6	15.2
1981	9.3	16.4	12.2	20.3	-1.7	16.4	16.2
1982	13.7	5.5	15.2	4.0	34.1	7.4	9.3
1983	17.7	24.8	16.0	21.3	-10.3	12.2	12.9
1984	18.0	19.5	19.5	25.0	42.4	19.7	15.5
1985	28.1	41.4	26.0	40.7	65.1	34.8	-2.2
1986	9.0	8.0	16.9	7.4	21.7	20.2	12.1
1987	14.1	18.2	11.8	18.6	33.8	16.5	10.8
1988	11.1	16.2	8.0	19.2	21.6	38.3	17.7
1989	4.5	8.8	-3.9	7.2	-8.4	7.7	14.5
1990	5.7	4.0	13.4	3.7	19.8	4.1	4.0
1991	24.9	18.2	55.4	24.0	30.9	15.3	11.9
1992	17.9	26.2	15.3	29.4	48.3	25.3	11.5
1993	20.8	26.4	14.8	26.3	69.5	48.9	42.4
1994	21.1	22.6	25.1	20.5	42.8	38.2	48.8
1995	20.5	24.0	15.5	24.4	43.1	38.8	26.4
1996	17.2	18.5	17.9	18.3	17.3	14.3	24.2
1997	13.7	16.4	15.4	19.4	-3.0	11.3	13.8
1998	11.1	11.5	12.1	12.0	3.1	8.6	16.8
1999	11.0	10.7	12.7	10.6	2.9	10.3	18.7
2000	12.0	12.6	13.2	12.7	13.1	12.6	37.6
2001	12.1	12.9	12.4	12.9	30.4	6.4	32.9
2002	13.2	15.0	12.4	15.0	27.9	11.8	35.8
2003	15.6	16.9	15.9	15.7	39.0	12.7	25.8
2004	15.5	16.6	15.7	16.0	32.1	14.2	-11.3
2005	12.4	11.1	16.3	11.2	21.1	14.0	16.4
2006	13.9	13.0	16.3	14.4	12.5	16.1	20.3
2007	14.7	15.3	15.2	16.6	6.3	17.3	29.0
2008	10.3	9.7	11.8	9.9	8.2	19.6	12.0
2009	8.8	8.2	10.1	8.4	16.0	15.9	19.2
2010	13.1	13.4	13.7	14.0	9.4	19.2	21.3
2011	10.3	9.5	11.9	9.9	17.6	18.4	22.2
2012	7.6	6.4	9.8	6.1	21.6	15.4	7.3
2013	8.2	7.7	9.6	8.0	18.0	13.2	7.5
2014	7.6	8.9	6.3	8.4	16.6	13.5	8.5
2015	8.0	9.3	6.7	9.2	13.0	12.0	11.4
2016	7.2	8.1	6.7	8.6	10.1	10.3	3.4
2017	7.9	6.8	9.7	8.1	3.5	10.4	12.4
2018	7.0	3.4	11.4	3.3	3.6	8.1	9.9
2019	6.8	6.2	7.6	7.0	8.1	7.7	4.9
2020	3.4	3.3	3.5	3.9	5.5	-0.7	1.8
2021	8.2	7.7	9.1	8.5	11.0	9.7	15.1
2022	3.5	3.2	3.8	3.3	10.4	5.3	2.9

表1-11 续表 Continued　　　　单位：%

年份 Year	自营进出口总额 Value of Direct Exports and Imports	#出口 Export	实际利用外资 Foreign Capital Actually Used	宁波港域货物吞吐量 Cargo at Throughput Ports	宁波港域集装箱吞吐量 Container Throughput	城镇居民人均可支配收入 Per Capital Annual Disposable Income of Urban Residents
1978						
1979				10.3		11.1
1980				38.1		26.2
1981				7.1		12.1
1982				6.3		5.8
1983				30.2		4.1
1984				23.6		21.3
1985			1609.5	74.2		38.3
1986	102.0	38.8	39.3	72.8		24.9
1987	-0.9	46.5	-14.2	8.0		7.4
1988	616.4	1348.5	60.6	3.2		27.3
1989	49.2	57.1	155.2	10.3		14.8
1990	35.5	55.3	25.0	15.6		12.7
1991	92.2	70.0	22.0	32.7	63.6	11.2
1992	72.8	64.9	329.0	28.8	47.2	22.5
1993	71.0	41.4	199.7	21.8	49.1	49.0
1994	48.4	57.9	3.9	9.9	58.2	50.8
1995	53.2	29.6	11.4	17.1	28.0	21.1
1996	8.6	2.7	25.7	11.5	26.3	14.8
1997	10.1	25.9	10.5	7.6	27.2	8.6
1998	-8.6	1.0	-9.2	5.9	37.4	1.4
1999	18.9	17.3	3.4	10.9	70.3	3.3
2000	50.5	48.6	19.5	19.5	50.1	15.1
2001	17.9	20.8	40.6	11.3	34.5	9.8
2002	38.0	30.7	42.6	19.8	53.3	8.2
2003	53.3	47.9	38.5	20.4	49.1	10.1
2004	38.8	38.2	21.8	21.8	44.5	11.2
2005	28.5	33.2	9.9	19.0	30.0	9.6
2006	26.0	29.4	5.2	15.2	35.7	13.0
2007	33.8	33.0	3.1	11.5	32.3	13.4
2008	20.1	21.1	1.3	4.8	16.0	13.4
2009	-10.4	-16.6	-13.1	6.1	-3.9	9.2
2010	36.3	34.5	5.3	7.4	24.8	10.2
2011	18.4	17.1	20.9	5.1	11.6	12.9
2012	-1.6	1.0	1.5	4.5	8.0	11.3
2013	3.9	7.0	14.8	9.5	7.0	10.1
2014	4.4	11.3	22.9	6.2	11.5	9.2
2015	-4.0	-2.3	5.2	-3.1	6.0	8.4
2016	-5.0	-7.1	6.6	-2.7	4.4	7.7
2017	21.3	14.3	-10.7	11.1	13.9	7.9
2018	12.9	11.4	7.2	4.5	6.5	8.0
2019	6.9	7.6	19.7	1.3	4.3	7.9
2020	6.7	7.3	4.4	2.9	3.4	4.8
2021	30.3	27.7	32.7	3.7	8.6	8.6
2022	6.3	8.0	13.8	2.2	4.8	3.8

主要统计指标解释

【行政区划】指国家对行政区域的划分。根据宪法规定，我国的行政区域划分如下：⑴全国分为省、自治区、直辖市；⑵省、自治区分为自治州、县、自治县、市；⑶自治州分为县、自治县、市；⑷县、自治县分为乡、民族乡、镇；⑸直辖市和较大的市分为区、县；⑹国家在必要时设立的特别行政区。

【气温】指空气的温度，我国一般以摄氏度（℃）为单位表示。气象观测的温度表是放在离地面约1.5米处通风良好的百叶箱里测量的，因此，通常说的气温指的是离地面1.5米处百叶箱中的温度。其统计计算方法为：

月平均气温是将全月各日的平均气温相加，除以该月的天数而得。

年平均气温是将12个月的月平均气温累加后除以12而得。

【相对湿度】指空气中实际水气压与当时气温下的饱合水气压之比。其统计方法与气温相同。

【降水量】指从天空降落到地面的液态或固态（经融化后）水，未经蒸发、渗透、流失而在地面上积聚的深度。其统计计算方法为：

月降水量是将全月各日的降水量累加而得。

年降水量是将12个月的月降水量累加而得。

【日照时数】指太阳实际照射地面的时间。其统计方法与降水量相同。

【可比价格】指计算各种总量指标所采用的扣除了价格变动因素的价格，可进行不同时期总量指标的对比。按可比价格计算总量指标有两种方法：一种是直接用产品产量乘某一年的不变价格计算；另一种是用价格指数进行缩减。

【不变价格】指以同类产品某年的平均价格作为固定价格，用于计算各年的产品价值。按不变价格计算的产品价值消除了价格变动因素，不同时期对比可以反映生产的发展速度。新中国成立后，随着工农业产品价格水平的变化，国家统计局先后五次制定了全国统一的工业产品不变价格和农业产品不变价格。从1952年到1957年使用1952年工（农）业产品不变价格，从1957年到1970年使用1957年不变价格，从1971年到1980年使用1970年不变价格，从1981年到1990年使用1980年不变价格，从1991年开始使用1990年不变价格。

【平均增长速度】我国计算平均增长速度有两种方法：一种是习惯上经常使用的“水平法”，又称几何平均法，是以间隔期最后一年的水平同基期水平对比来计算平均每年增长（或下降）速度；另一种是“累计法”，又称代数平均法或方程法，是以间隔期内各年水平的总和同基期水平对比来计算平均每年增长（或下降）速度。在一般正常情况下，两种方法计算的平均每年增长速度比较接近；但在经济发展不平衡、出现大起大落时，两种方法计算的结果差别较大。

本年鉴内所列的平均增长速度，除固定资产投资用“累计法”计算外，其余均用“水平法”计算。从某年到某年平均增长速度的年份，均不包括基期年在内。

Explanatory Notes on Main Statistical Indicators

【**Administrative Division**】refers to the division of administrative areas by the state. The Constitution of the People' s Republic of China stipulates that the administrative areas in China are divided as: 1) The whole country is divided into provinces, autonomous regions and municipalities directly under the central government; 2) Provinces and autonomous regions are divided into autonomous prefectures, counties, autonomous counties and cities; 3) Autonomous prefectures are divided into counties, autonomous counties and cities; 4) Counties and autonomous counties are divided into townships, nationality townships and towns; 5) Municipalities and large cities are divided into districts and counties, 6) The state shall, when necessary, establish special administrative regions.

【**Temperature**】refers to the air temperature. China uses centigrade as the unit. The thermometry used for weather observation is put in a breezy shutter, which is 1.5 meters high from the ground. Therefore, the commonly used temperature refers to the temperature in the breezy shutter 1.5 meters away from the ground. The calculation method is as follows:

Monthly average temperature is the summation of average daily temperature of one month divided by the actual days of that particular month.

Annual average temperature is the summation of monthly average of a year divided by 12 months.

【**Relative Humidity**】refers to the ratio of actual water vapor pressure to the saturation water vapor density under the current temperature. The statistical method is the same as that of temperature.

【**Volume of Precipitation**】refers to the deepness of liquid state or solid state (thawed) water falling from the sky to the ground that has not been evaporated, infiltrated or run off. The calculation method is as follows:

Monthly precipitation is the summation of daily precipitation of a month.

Annual precipitation is the summation of 12 months precipitation of a year.

【**Sunshine Hours**】refer to the actual hours of sun irradiating the earth. The calculation method is the same as that of the precipitation.

【**Comparable Prices**】refer to prices that are used to remove the factors of price change in calculating economic aggregates, so as to facilitate comparison of aggregates over time. Two methods are used for calculating economic aggregates at comparable prices: 1. Multiplying the output of products by their constant prices of certain year; 2. Deflation of data at current prices by relevant price index.

【**Constant Price**】refers to the average price of a given product in certain year, which is used for comparison of output value over time. As the output value at constant prices removes the factor of price changes, it reflects the trend of production development over time. Since 1949, with the changes in general price level, National Bureau of Statistics has issued nationally unified constant prices five times: the 1952 constant prices for 1949–1957; the 1957 constant prices for 1957–1971; the 1970 constant prices for 1971–1981; the 1980 constant prices for 1981–1990; and the 1990 constant prices have been used since 1991.

【**Average Annual Growth Rate**】Two methods for calculating average annual growth rate are applied in China, one is often called "level approach", or the method of calculating geometric average, which is derived by comparing the level of the last year of the interval with that of the beginning year; the other is called "accumulative approach" or algebraic average or equation method, which is derived by the summation of the actual figure of each year in the interval divided by the figure in the base year.

Usually the results calculated by the two methods are fairly close, but they differed sharply when uneven economic development occurred with striking fluctuations in growth.

The average annual growth rates listed in this statistical yearbook are calculated by "level approach" except for the growth rate of investment in fixed assets. The base years are not listed when the years are listed for average annual growth rates.

NINGBO 2023 Statistical Yearbook

2 CHAPTER

第二篇

人口和劳动力

POPULATION AND LABOR FORCE

人口和劳动力
Population and Labour Force

主要统计指标
Major Statistics Indicators

2022年末户籍人口数	2022 Year – end Registred Populations	621.07	万人	10000 persons
其中：市区	Urban Districts	314.21	万人	10000 persons
2022年出生人口	Birth Population	34556	人	persons
2022年死亡人口	Death Population	42310	人	persons
2022年人口自然增长率	Natural Growth Rate	-1.25	‰	
2022年人口净迁移率	Migration Rate	5.67	‰	
2022年末人口密度	Density of Population	632.71	人/平方公里	person/sq. km
2022年计划生育率	Rate of Family Planning	98.55	%	
2022年末四上单位从业人员数	Number of Employees in Four Types of Units above Designated Size by the end of 2022	355.57	万人	10000 persons
2022年末四上单位在岗职工数	Number of on – the – job Employees of Four Types of Units above Designated Size by the end of 2022	335.81	万人	10000 persons
2022年四上单位在岗职工平均工资	Average Wage of on – the – job Employees of Four Types of Units above Designated Size in 2022	92484	元	yuan
2022年末城镇登记失业人员数	Number of Registered Urban Unemployment at the Year – end	82735	人	persons
2022年末城镇登记失业率	Registered Urban Unemployed Rate	1.77	%	

表2-1 历年总户数和总人口
Households and Population Over the Years

单位：万人(10000 persons)

年份 Year	总户数（万户） Total Households (10000households)	总人口 Total Population	其中 of Which			
			按性别分 By Sex		按农业和非农业分 By Agriculture & Non - agriculture	
			男性 Male	女性 Female	农业人口 Agriculture	非农业人口 Non-agriculture
1978	123.30	457.70	234.18	223.52	394.28	63.42
1979	124.48	462.07	235.78	226.29	394.31	67.76
1980	128.57	465.99	237.98	228.01	393.13	72.86
1981	136.86	471.76	240.95	230.81	394.39	77.37
1982	140.56	478.33	244.20	234.13	396.40	81.93
1983	143.27	481.46	245.79	235.67	397.68	83.78
1984	147.57	484.18	247.26	236.92	398.64	85.54
1985	153.57	487.74	249.24	238.50	394.50	93.24
1986	158.53	491.89	251.56	240.33	394.69	97.20
1987	164.78	498.15	254.80	243.35	399.48	98.67
1988	170.92	503.06	257.19	245.89	402.81	100.25
1989	175.12	507.64	259.75	247.89	406.08	101.56
1990	176.06	510.76	260.99	249.77	407.78	102.98
1991	179.22	514.16	262.68	251.48	409.61	104.55
1992	180.89	516.72	264.09	252.63	409.90	106.82
1993	182.80	519.98	265.72	254.26	410.17	109.81
1994	184.38	522.85	267.24	255.61	410.17	112.68
1995	186.26	526.20	268.72	257.48	410.94	115.26
1996	186.82	530.08	270.30	259.78	410.57	119.51
1997	188.83	533.31	271.89	261.42	409.81	123.50
1998	190.39	535.27	272.40	262.87	404.79	130.48
1999	192.52	538.41	273.65	264.76	401.29	137.12
2000	193.99	540.94	274.50	266.44	398.91	142.03
2001	196.10	543.34	275.50	267.84	392.48	150.86
2002	198.94	546.19	276.60	269.60	383.76	162.43
2003	203.47	549.07	277.64	271.44	380.26	168.81
2004	207.01	552.69	278.84	273.85	376.50	176.19
2005	211.17	556.70	280.35	276.35	374.09	182.61
2006	215.03	560.45	281.71	278.74	371.47	188.98
2007	218.77	564.56	283.42	281.14	370.35	194.21
2008	221.48	568.09	284.84	283.25	369.60	198.49
2009	222.46	571.02	285.96	285.05	368.98	202.04
2010	222.98	574.08	287.15	286.93	368.86	205.23
2011	223.79	576.40	287.90	288.50	368.23	208.18
2012	223.46	577.71	288.30	289.41	366.26	211.45
2013	223.56	580.15	289.15	290.99	365.80	214.35
2014	224.07	583.78	290.52	293.26	366.05	217.73
2015	224.60	586.57	291.55	295.03		
2016	225.81	590.96	293.39	297.57		
2017	227.49	596.93	295.98	300.95		
2018	232.13	602.96	298.51	304.45		
2019	236.63	608.47	300.81	307.66		
2020	240.04	613.66	302.86	310.79		
2021	243.30	618.33	304.45	313.89		
2022	245.20	621.07	305.24	315.83		

注：自2015年起，宁波市公安局取消“农业人口”和“非农业人口”指标。
Note：Since 2015, the Ningbo Municipal Public Security Bureau to cancel the agricultural population and non-agricultural population index

表2-2 历年人口自然变动情况
Natural Changes of Population Over the Years

单位：‰

年份 Year	出生 Birth		死亡 Death		自然增长 Natural Growth	
	人数（人） Population (person)	出生率 Birth Rate	人数（人） Population (person)	死亡率 Death Rate	人数（人） Population (person)	自然增长率 Natural Growth Rate
1978	75180	15.06	26150	5.74	49030	9.32
1979	71642	15.58	27393	5.96	44249	9.62
1980	57417	12.37	27989	6.03	29428	6.34
1981	78132	16.66	28557	6.09	49575	10.57
1982	84905	17.87	28258	5.95	56647	11.92
1983	69668	14.52	30875	6.43	38793	8.09
1984	51040	10.57	28114	5.82	22926	4.75
1985	53366	10.98	29483	6.07	23883	4.91
1986	62535	12.77	28738	5.87	33797	6.90
1987	83541	16.88	30239	6.11	53302	10.77
1988	69248	13.83	30171	6.03	39077	7.80
1989	71283	14.11	30364	6.01	40919	8.10
1990	67464	13.25	30670	6.02	36794	7.23
1991	60140	11.74	29329	5.75	30811	6.01
1992	50700	10.22	30573	5.93	20127	4.29
1993	55242	10.66	29169	5.63	26073	5.03
1994	54990	10.55	30050	5.76	24940	4.78
1995	59600	11.36	32689	6.23	26911	5.13
1996	58282	11.04	30652	5.80	27630	5.24
1997	55231	10.39	31417	5.91	23814	4.48
1998	47116	8.82	32902	6.16	14214	2.66
1999	51544	9.57	31237	5.80	20307	3.77
2000	50168	9.30	33438	6.20	16730	3.10
2001	39867	7.35	30632	5.65	9235	1.70
2002	41404	7.60	32361	5.94	9043	1.66
2003	42445	7.80	35173	6.40	7272	1.30
2004	49192	8.93	36558	6.64	12634	2.29
2005	45185	8.15	33635	6.06	11550	2.08
2006	41749	7.47	31380	5.62	10369	1.86
2007	46830	8.33	33737	6.00	13093	2.33
2008	46155	8.15	33804	5.97	12351	2.18
2009	45114	7.92	34277	6.02	10837	1.90
2010	48837	8.53	35423	6.19	13414	2.34
2011	46103	8.01	34816	6.05	11287	1.96
2012	49998	8.66	37907	6.57	12091	2.10
2013	49321	8.53	35514	6.15	13807	2.38
2014	56398	9.69	35528	6.10	20870	3.59
2015	48612	8.31	37838	6.47	10774	1.84
2016	51100	8.68	34349	5.83	16751	2.85
2017	61258	10.31	43190	7.27	18068	3.04
2018	51061	8.51	40089	6.68	10972	1.83
2019	49464	8.17	36526	6.03	12938	2.14
2020	43521	7.09	38925	6.34	4596	0.75
2021	37599	6.10	42917	6.97	-5318	-0.86
2022	34556	5.58	42310	6.83	-7754	-1.25

表2-3 历年人口迁移情况
Bacis Statistics on Migration Over the Years

单位：人(person)

年份 Year	迁入 Inflows	其中 of Which		迁出 Outflows	其中 of Which		净迁移率(‰) Migration Rate(‰)
		省内迁入 From Zhejiang	省外迁入 Form Other Province		迁往省内 Outflow to Zhejiang	迁往省外 Outflow to Other Province	
1990	43055	34763	8292	43996	35646	8350	-0. 18
1991	35526	27628	7898	32260	25142	7118	0. 64
1992	54895	46773	8122	49969	43721	6248	0. 96
1993	51257	41921	9336	43716	36697	7019	1. 45
1994	55877	46390	9487	49826	42731	7095	1. 16
1995	61832	50483	11349	52873	45598	7275	1. 71
1996	66392	53141	13251	55103	47097	8006	2. 14
1997	64083	51097	12986	53669	45306	8363	1. 96
1998	73735	59605	14130	67191	58068	9123	1. 22
1999	99809	82531	17278	89491	79170	10321	1. 92
2000	85277	66946	18331	73024	60774	12250	2. 27
2001	112559	91837	20722	95907	82261	13646	3. 07
2002	105609	77127	28482	85498	71518	13980	3. 69
2003	105057	76140	28917	80102	65019	15083	4. 56
2004	104523	72455	32068	74307	59665	14642	5. 49
2005	93433	64157	29276	62900	48874	14026	5. 50
2006	90684	60320	30364	59694	46742	12952	5. 55
2007	85199	55378	29821	54649	44955	9694	5. 43
2008	77022	46195	30827	52036	40749	11287	4. 41
2009	69949	40163	29786	48037	37595	10442	3. 85
2010	67588	40093	27495	47814	37584	10230	3. 45
2011	56088	31626	24462	42543	31859	10684	2. 35
2012	47704	25619	22085	39715	28056	11659	1. 38
2013	46493	24467	22026	34645	22518	12127	2. 05
2014	67125	41165	25960	48879	36593	12286	3. 14
2015	40775	15254	25521	22674	11705	10969	3. 09
2016	46617	16728	29889	19171	10685	8486	4. 66
2017	66083	20874	45209	24261	15011	9250	7. 04
2018	75202	26287	48915	25440	15715	9725	8. 29
2019	65642	21696	43946	23145	13940	9205	7. 02
2020	71682	22834	48848	24115	14970	9145	7. 75
2021	76844	21736	55108	24645	14877	9768	8. 47
2022	53936	15757	38179	18779	11308	7471	5. 67

表2-4 各区（县、市）人口密度（2022年）
Density of Population by Region（2022）

单位：人/ 平方公里(person/sq.km)

年份 Year	全市 Total	市区 Urban District	海曙 Haishu	江北 Jiangbei	镇海 Zhenhai	北仑 Beilun	鄞州 Yinzhou	奉化 Fenghua	余姚 Yuyao	慈溪 Cixi	宁海 Ninghai	象山 Xiangshan
2022	632. 71	842. 62	1081. 16	1361. 90	1226. 55	750. 47	1213. 42	375. 84	553. 54	785. 53	341. 71	389. 90

表2-5 各区（县、市）人口、户口情况（2022年底）
Basic Statistics on Population and Households by Region(End of 2022)

指标	单位	Indicators	Unit	全市 Total	市区 Urban District
总户数	**户**	**Total Households**	**household**	**2451951**	**1266008**
总人口	**人**	**Total Population**	**person**	**6210691**	**3142120**
男性	人	Male	person	3052406	1527290
女性	人	Female	person	3158285	1614830
城镇人口	人	Urban population Population	person	4257387	2351926
平均人口	**人**	**Average Population**	**person**	**6197008**	**3127283**
出生人数	**人**	**Birth Population**	**person**	**34556**	**19742**
男性	人	Male	person	18062	10260
女性	人	Female	person	16494	9482
出生率	‰	Birth Rate	‰	5. 58	6. 31
死亡人数	**人**	**Death Population**	**person**	**42310**	**18841**
男性	人	Male	person	23785	10707
女性	人	Female	person	18525	8134
死亡率	‰	Death Rate	‰	6. 83	6. 02
本年自然增加人数	**人**	**Natural Growth Population**	**person**	**-7754**	**901**
人口自然增长率	‰	Natural Growth Rate	‰	-1. 25	0. 29
迁入人数	**人**	**Number of the Persons Moved in**	**person**	**53936**	**37886**
省内迁入	人	From Zhejiang Province	person	15757	11933
省外迁入	人	From Other Province	person	38179	25953
迁出人数	**人**	**Number of the Persons Moved Out**	**person**	**18779**	**9086**
迁往省内	人	To Zhejiang Province	person	11308	4256
迁往省外	人	To Other Province	person	7471	4830

注：本表数据来自宁波市公安局。
Note: Data in this table are obtained from Bureau of Public Security of Ningbo Municipality.

各区 by Districts						余姚市 Yuyao	慈溪市 Cixi	宁海县 Ninghai	象山县 Xiangshan
海曙区 Haishu	江北区 Jiangbei	镇海区 Zhenhai	北仑区 Beilun	鄞州区 Yinzhou	奉化区 Fenghua				
261279	**119418**	**123431**	**182024**	**395412**	**184444**	**331187**	**426116**	**244970**	**183670**
643291	**283276**	**301731**	**449532**	**987720**	**476570**	**830862**	**1069100**	**629770**	**538839**
311589	136721	146342	215984	478665	237989	407427	521783	324047	271859
331702	146555	155389	233548	509055	238581	423435	547317	305723	266980
516724	232661	260809	313116	805711	222905	643408	791994	257080	212979
642535	**280685**	**298201**	**446938**	**981709**	**477216**	**831923**	**1067031**	**630611**	**540160**
3701	**1950**	**2267**	**2887**	**6815**	**2122**	**3886**	**5558**	**3200**	**2170**
1881	1007	1157	1544	3561	1110	1990	2954	1698	1160
1820	943	1110	1343	3254	1012	1896	2604	1502	1010
5.76	6.95	7.60	6.46	6.94	4.45	4.67	5.21	5.07	4.02
4498	**1601**	**1615**	**2714**	**4615**	**3798**	**7108**	**8170**	**4249**	**3942**
2530	924	960	1526	2609	2158	3920	4432	2463	2263
1968	677	655	1188	2006	1640	3188	3738	1786	1679
7.00	5.70	5.42	6.07	4.70	7.96	8.54	7.66	6.74	7.30
–797	**349**	**652**	**173**	**2200**	**–1676**	**–3222**	**–2612**	**–1049**	**–1772**
-1.24	1.24	2.19	0.39	2.24	-3.51	-3.87	-2.45	-1.66	-3.28
6701	**4576**	**5956**	**7575**	**11377**	**1701**	**3983**	**9427**	**1334**	**1306**
2464	1615	1730	1021	4729	374	964	2064	425	371
4237	2961	4226	6554	6648	1327	3019	7363	909	935
1582	**1246**	**1073**	**1176**	**3400**	**609**	**2881**	**2681**	**1954**	**2177**
807	508	529	463	1635	314	2252	1706	1478	1616
775	738	544	713	1765	295	629	975	476	561

表2-6 部分年份各区（县、市）总户数与总人口
Total Households and Population by Region in Partial Years

单位：人（person)

指标	Indicators	2018	2019	2020	2021	2022
总户数(户)	**Total Households (Household)**	**2321348**	**2366343**	**2400404**	**2432993**	**2451951**
海曙区	Haishu	249854	253617	257050	259966	261279
江北区	Jiangbei	107784	109990	113718	117079	119418
镇海区	Zhenhai	104841	109757	115443	120147	123431
北仑区	Beilun	169153	172624	175490	179759	182024
鄞州区	Yinzhou	356224	369461	380827	389996	395412
奉化区	Fenghua	182202	183066	183611	184201	184444
余姚市	Yuyao	319681	327148	328730	330445	331187
慈溪市	Cixi	416692	417394	420233	423656	426116
宁海县	Ninghai	233037	241163	242772	244445	244970
象山县	Xiangshan	181880	182123	182530	183299	183670
总人口	**Total Population**	**6029568**	**6084707**	**6136558**	**6183324**	**6210691**
海曙区	Haishu	629970	633478	637638	641778	643291
江北区	Jiangbei	257730	262756	271024	278093	283276
镇海区	Zhenhai	260828	271619	284262	294671	301731
北仑区	Beilun	423717	429661	435425	444343	449532
鄞州区	Yinzhou	902151	930518	955307	975698	987720
奉化区	Fenghua	481308	480597	479397	477862	476570
余姚市	Yuyao	836306	835927	834345	832984	830862
慈溪市	Cixi	1055702	1059605	1061711	1064962	1069100
宁海县	Ninghai	633256	633918	633255	631452	629770
象山县	Xiangshan	548600	546628	544194	541481	538839

表 2－6 续表 Continued　　　　单位：人（person）

指标	Indicators	2018	2019	2020	2021	2022
男性人数	**Number of Male**	**2985080**	**3008088**	**3028613**	**3044474**	**3052406**
海曙区	Haishu	308051	309163	310682	311662	311589
江北区	Jiangbei	125690	127936	131573	134590	136721
镇海区	Zhenhai	128736	133577	139189	143438	146342
北仑区	Beilun	206275	208689	210894	214190	215984
鄞州区	Yinzhou	440932	453951	465068	473676	478665
奉化区	Fenghua	241378	240875	240030	238903	237989
余姚市	Yuyao	412214	411639	410357	408969	407427
慈溪市	Cixi	517962	519395	519774	520548	521783
宁海县	Ninghai	326403	326564	326102	325091	324047
象山县	Xiangshan	277439	276299	274944	273407	271859
女性人数	**Number of Female**	**3044488**	**3076619**	**3107945**	**3138850**	**3158285**
海曙区	Haishu	321919	324315	326956	330116	331702
江北区	Jiangbei	132040	134820	139451	143503	146555
镇海区	Zhenhai	132092	138042	145073	151233	155389
北仑区	Beilun	217442	220972	224531	230153	233548
鄞州区	Yinzhou	461219	476567	490239	502022	509055
奉化区	Fenghua	239930	239722	239367	238959	238581
余姚市	Yuyao	424092	424288	423988	424015	423435
慈溪市	Cixi	537740	540210	541937	544414	547317
宁海县	Ninghai	306853	307354	307153	306361	305723
象山县	Xiangshan	271161	270329	269250	268074	266980

表2-7　部分年份各区（县、市）人口自然变动情况
Natural Changes of Population by Region in Partial Years

单位：人（person）

指标	Indicators	2018	2019	2020	2021	2022
出生人口	**Birth**	**51061**	**49464**	**43521**	**37599**	**34556**
海曙区	Haishu	5348	5121	4528	3974	3701
江北区	Jiangbei	2378	2412	2368	2035	1950
镇海区	Zhenhai	2605	2767	2644	2451	2267
北仑区	Beilun	4072	3922	3450	2978	2887
鄞州区	Yinzhou	9608	9567	8387	7425	6815
奉化区	Fenghua	3212	2891	2522	2190	2122
余姚市	Yuyao	5805	5670	4881	4271	3886
慈溪市	Cixi	7318	7382	6476	5871	5558
宁海县	Ninghai	6482	5889	5003	3848	3200
象山县	Xiangshan	4233	3843	3262	2556	2170
死亡人口	**Death**	**40089**	**36526**	**38925**	**42917**	**42310**
海曙区	Haishu	4209	3594	3679	4385	4498
江北区	Jiangbei	1594	1388	1492	1732	1601
镇海区	Zhenhai	1653	1418	1400	1602	1615
北仑区	Beilun	2506	2426	2548	2541	2714
鄞州区	Yinzhou	5117	3991	4574	5599	4615
奉化区	Fenghua	3681	2849	3177	4085	3798
余姚市	Yuyao	6523	6209	6611	7141	7108
慈溪市	Cixi	7427	7281	7929	7980	8170
宁海县	Ninghai	3708	3688	3928	4048	4249
象山县	Xiangshan	3671	3682	3587	3804	3942

表 2 – 7 续表 Continued　　　　单位：人（person)

指标	Indicators	2018	2019	2020	2021	2022
自然增长	**Natural Growth**	**10972**	**12938**	**4596**	**–5318**	**–7754**
海曙区	Haishu	1139	1527	849	-411	-797
江北区	Jiangbei	784	1024	876	303	349
镇海区	Zhenhai	952	1349	1244	849	652
北仑区	Beilun	1566	1496	902	437	173
鄞州区	Yinzhou	4491	5576	3813	1826	2200
奉化区	Fenghua	-469	42	-655	-1895	-1676
余姚市	Yuyao	-718	-539	-1730	-2870	-3222
慈溪市	Cixi	-109	101	-1453	-2109	-2612
宁海县	Ninghai	2774	2201	1075	-200	-1049
象山县	Xiangshan	562	161	-325	-1248	-1772
自然增长率(‰)	**Natural Growth Rate(‰)**	**1.83**	**2.14**	**0.75**	**–0.86**	**–1.25**
海曙区	Haishu	1.81	2.42	1.34	-0.64	-1.24
江北区	Jiangbei	3.08	3.93	3.28	1.10	1.24
镇海区	Zhenhai	3.73	5.07	4.48	2.93	2.19
北仑区	Beilun	3.74	3.51	2.09	0.99	0.39
鄞州区	Yinzhou	5.06	6.09	4.04	1.89	2.24
奉化区	Fenghua	-0.97	0.09	-1.36	-3.96	-3.51
余姚市	Yuyao	-0.86	-0.64	-2.07	-3.44	-3.87
慈溪市	Cixi	-0.10	0.10	-1.37	-1.98	2.45
宁海县	Ninghai	4.38	3.47	1.70	-0.32	-1.66
象山县	Xiangshan	1.02	0.29	-0.60	-2.30	-3.28

表2-8 部分年份各区（县、市）人口迁移情况
Migration of Population by Region in Partial Years

单位：人（person）

指标	Indicators	2018	2019	2020	2021	2022
迁入人口	**Population Inflows**	**75202**	**65642**	**71682**	**76844**	**53936**
海曙区	Haishu	11315	9483	11605	10513	6701
江北区	Jiangbei	6406	5233	6852	6688	4576
镇海区	Zhenhai	9212	8734	9405	9077	5956
北仑区	Beilun	11587	8179	9192	12305	7575
鄞州区	Yinzhou	21443	18403	18810	18574	11377
奉化区	Fenghua	1950	1687	1691	2182	1701
余姚市	Yuyao	3651	3787	3884	5115	3983
慈溪市	Cixi	7016	7247	7584	9396	9427
宁海县	Ninghai	1320	1621	1344	1378	1334
象山县	Xiangshan	1302	1268	1315	1616	1306
其中：省内迁入	**of Which: From Zhejiang**	**26287**	**21696**	**22834**	**21736**	**15757**
海曙区	Haishu	5218	4106	4398	3750	2464
江北区	Jiangbei	2507	1936	2407	2251	1615
镇海区	Zhenhai	3035	2567	2509	2438	1730
北仑区	Beilun	2068	1466	1519	1535	1021
鄞州区	Yinzhou	9996	8323	8275	7463	4729
奉化区	Fenghua	437	321	395	461	374
余姚市	Yuyao	1012	925	990	1151	964
慈溪市	Cixi	1213	1217	1477	1797	2064
宁海县	Ninghai	405	487	427	393	425
象山县	Xiangshan	396	348	437	497	371

表 2－8 续表 Continued　　　　单位：人（person)

指标	Indicators	2018	2019	2020	2021	2022
迁出人口	**Population Outflows**	**25440**	**23145**	**24115**	**24645**	**18779**
海曙区	Haishu	1941	1766	1830	1913	1582
江北区	Jiangbei	1269	1207	1142	1372	1246
镇海区	Zhenhai	944	970	1025	1120	1073
北仑区	Beilun	1652	1490	1467	1717	1176
鄞州区	Yinzhou	3608	3429	3596	4044	3400
奉化区	Fenghua	1371	857	820	827	609
余姚市	Yuyao	3907	3576	3737	3613	2881
慈溪市	Cixi	3893	3425	4032	4016	2681
宁海县	Ninghai	3208	3057	3066	2943	1954
象山县	Xiangshan	3647	3368	3400	3080	2177
其中：迁往省内	**Of Which: To Zhejiang**	**15715**	**13940**	**14970**	**14877**	**11308**
海曙区	Haishu	938	814	923	951	807
江北区	Jiangbei	530	489	492	584	508
镇海区	Zhenhai	398	419	506	494	529
北仑区	Beilun	584	517	542	655	463
鄞州区	Yinzhou	1550	1477	1690	1909	1635
奉化区	Fenghua	812	406	369	428	314
余姚市	Yuyao	2873	2601	2807	2705	2252
慈溪市	Cixi	2519	2193	2640	2639	1706
宁海县	Ninghai	2514	2337	2322	2152	1478
象山县	Xiangshan	2997	2687	2679	2360	1616

表2-9　各区（县、市）计划生育情况(2022年)
Basic Statistics on Family Planning by Region（2022）

指标	单位	Indicators	Unit	全市 Total	市区 Urban District
计划生育率	%	Rate of Family Planning	%	98. 55	98. 72
年内出生人数	人	Number of Birth in This Year	person	28186	14504
#女	人	Female	person	13438	6974
1. 一孩人数	人	One－Child	person	18615	9586
#计划内	人	Under Control	person	18408	9500
2. 两孩人数	人	Two－Child	person	8790	4539
#计划内	人	Under Control	person	8632	4459
3. 三孩人数	人	Three－Child	person	741	364
#政策性	人	Policy	person	711	351
4. 多孩人数	人	Over Two Child	person	40	15
#政策性	人	Policy	person	26	9
计划内出生人数	人	Number of Birth Under Control	person	27777	14319
计划外出生人数	人	Number of Birth Out of Control	person	409	185
1. 一孩人数	人	One－Child	person	207	86
2. 两孩人数	人	Two－Child	person	158	80
3. 三孩人数	人	Three－Child	person	30	13
4. 多孩人数	人	Over Two Child	person	14	6
育龄妇女人数	万人	Number of Women at Child－Bearing Age	10000 persons	136. 84	70. 10
已婚育龄妇女人数	万人	Number of Married Women at Child－Bearing Age	10000 persons	95. 53	49. 51
#已有一孩	万人	1st Birth	10000 persons	57. 68	30. 81
#已领独生证	万人	With One－Child Certificate	10000 persons	20. 61	11. 75
#已婚育龄妇女一孩率	%	Rate of 1st Birth of Married Women at Child－Bearing Age	%	60. 38	62. 23
#已婚育龄妇女领独生证率	%	Rate of One－Child Certificate	%	21. 58	23. 73
初婚妇女人数	人	Number of First Married Women	person	17072	7141
已婚育龄妇女节育率	%	Rate of Controlling－Birth for Married Women at Child－Bearing Age	%	80. 73	83. 00
采取节育措施人数	万人	Number of Controlling－Birth Method	10000 persons	77. 12	41. 09
年内节育手术例数	例	Number of Controlling－Birth Surgery in This Year	case	3069	262
年内取环例数	例	Number of Remove Contraceptive	case	811	19
出生率	‰	Brith Rate	‰	4. 55	4. 64
死亡率	‰	Death Rate	‰	6. 83	6. 02

各区 by Districts						余姚市 Yuyao	慈溪市 Cixi	宁海县 Ninghai	象山县 Xiangshan
海曙区 Haishu	江北区 Jiangbei	镇海区 Zhenhai	北仑区 Beilun	鄞州区 Yinzhou	奉化区 Fenghua				
98.69	97.03	98.46	99.12	98.96	99.22	98.90	98.60	97.87	97.72
2816	1415	1492	2043	4810	1928	3551	4655	3243	2233
1401	673	754	948	2294	904	1708	2195	1529	1032
1944	926	936	1345	3092	1343	2502	3287	1858	1382
1924	908	926	1333	3078	1331	2480	3250	1825	1353
812	457	512	628	1583	547	987	1266	1205	793
798	437	502	622	1556	544	975	1248	1176	774
59	31	41	69	128	36	58	96	170	53
57	28	39	69	122	36	56	88	166	50
1	1	3	1	7	2	4	6	10	5
		2	1	4	2	1	4	7	5
2779	1373	1469	2025	4760	1913	3512	4590	3174	2182
37	42	23	18	50	15	39	65	69	51
20	18	10	12	14	12	22	37	33	29
14	20	10	6	27	3	12	18	29	19
2	3	2		6		2	8	4	3
1	1	1		3		3	2	3	
13.73	6.35	6.44	9.93	22.96	10.68	17.63	22.28	14.55	12.29
9.68	4.48	4.85	7.28	16.33	6.88	12.38	15.34	10.10	8.20
6.09	2.85	2.99	4.51	10.26	4.11	7.78	9.65	4.81	4.63
2.13	1.05	1.22	1.78	3.65	1.92	2.57	3.18	1.59	1.53
62.89	63.67	61.66	61.94	62.82	59.71	62.82	62.90	47.64	56.49
22.00	23.46	25.16	24.45	22.35	27.89	20.75	20.73	15.70	18.61
1640	521	891	1131	1737	1221	3220	3624	1596	1491
81.78	76.33	80.86	86.62	83.71	85.03	80.68	81.94	72.04	75.59
7.92	3.42	3.92	6.31	13.67	5.85	9.99	12.57	7.27	6.20
41	30	34	29	109	19	94	222	2170	321
5	2		3	9		18	82	556	136
4.38	5.04	5.00	4.57	4.90	4.04	4.27	4.36	5.14	4.13
7.00	5.70	5.42	6.07	4.70	7.96	8.54	7.66	6.74	7.30

表2-10 各区（县、市）婚姻状况（2022年）
Basic Statistics on Marital by Region（2022）

指标	单位	Indicators	Unit	全市 Total	市区 Urban District
准予登记结婚数	对	**Registering Marrige Permitted**	**couple**	**39767**	**21264**
#涉外婚姻	人	Chinese－Foreign Marrige	person	152	
(1) 国内公民	人	Demestic Citizen	person	76	
#女性	人	Female	person		
(2) 港澳台同胞	人	Chinese of Hong Kong, Macao and Taiwan	person	32	
(3) 华侨	人	Overseas Chinese	person	2	
(4) 外国人	人	Foreigner	person	42	
1. 初婚人数	人	First Marriage	person	62744	33713
2. 再婚人数	人	Remarriage	person	11234	5605
#再婚中恢复结婚	对	Resume Marriage	couple	2778	1605
准予离婚数	对	**Divorce Approved**	**couple**	**10982**	**6407**

注：本表数据由市民政局提供。
Note: Data in this table are obtained from Ningbo Municipal Bureau of Civil Affairs.

表2-11 主要年份婚姻状况
Marriage Statistics in Main Years

年份 Year	准予登记结婚（对） Marriage Registration Permitted (Couple)	初婚（人） First Marriage (person)	再婚（人） Remarriage (person)	再婚中恢复结婚（对） Resume Marriage (Couple)	准予离婚数（对） Divorce Approved (Couple)
2000	40505	74415	6125	242	3781
2001	38813	70658	6326	288	4206
2002	46931	85892	7572	371	4444
2003	42075	75735	8097	394	5538
2004	48214	86584	9518	743	7570
2005	39445	68699	9835	525	8570
2006	51725	90762	12688	736	9687
2007	41954	73877	10031	840	10232
2008	51956	90228	13684	509	11376
2009	46181	77918	14444	961	12698
2010	52508	87780	17236	1333	13754
2011	49710	83624	15796	2291	13911
2012	53721	92191	15251	2787	14893
2013	53742	71166	14968	6998	16414
2014	57597	91632	23562	4306	15045
2015	42628	64369	20887	7616	15823
2016	45861	69776	13456	4098	17456
2017	36133	56228	16038	4022	17819
2018	40855	60483	20955	4000	17604
2019	32604	45405	12182	7383	17766
2020	34772	51325	18219	3492	17078
2021	29997	43216	16778	2910	10243
2022	39767	62744	11234	2778	10982

各区 by Districts						余姚市 Yuyao	慈溪市 Cixi	宁海县 Ninghai	象山县 Xiangshan
海曙区 Haishu	江北区 Jiangbei	镇海区 Zhenhai	北仑区 Beilun	鄞州区 Yinzhou	奉化区 Fenghua				
4943	**2833**	**3009**	**2482**	**5444**	**2477**	**5288**	**6440**	**4395**	**2380**

海曙区 Haishu	江北区 Jiangbei	镇海区 Zhenhai	北仑区 Beilun	鄞州区 Yinzhou	奉化区 Fenghua	余姚市 Yuyao	慈溪市 Cixi	宁海县 Ninghai	象山县 Xiangshan
8239	4709	4985	3415	8526	3724	8451	9956	7220	3404
1031	639	695	917	1460	826	1417	2108	1206	898
308	159	169	316	451	202	354	408	182	229
1138	**701**	**698**	**1128**	**1956**	**773**	**1099**	**1436**	**1073**	**967**

涉外婚姻（人）Chinese－Foreign Marriage (person)	其中：of Which				
	国内公民（人）Chinese Citizens (person)	#女性 Female	港澳台同胞（人）Cninese of HongKong, Macao,Taiwan (person)	华侨（人）Overseas Chinese (person)	外国人（人）Foreigner (person)
235	235	229	177	7	51
321	321	313	249	10	62
199	199	189	137	10	52
159	159	152	106	8	45
163	163	154	88	14	61
178	178	166	96	9	73
181	178	162	100	13	71
170	170	154	78	10	82
172	168	148	60	17	99
162	160	133	63	7	94
138	136	114	44	8	88
306	153	127	69	4	80
284	142	113	45	9	88
326	160	113	58	5	103
232	114	103	30	6	82
232	111	103	41	7	73
294	146	135	53	4	91
224	108	79	36	2	78
272	130	92	37	3	112
238	119	85	26	5	88
120	60	42	11		49
67	66	47	25	1	42
152	76		32	2	42

表2-12 部分年份年末各区（县、市）常住人口
Resident Population at the End of Some Years

年份 Year	全市 Total	海曙区 Haishu	江北区 Jiangbei	镇海区 Zhenhai	北仑区 Beilun
2011	785. 1	90. 9	37. 7	40. 8	63. 1
2012	804. 1	92. 9	38. 9	41. 9	64. 5
2013	821. 6	94. 6	40. 0	43. 0	65. 7
2014	841. 6	96. 9	41. 4	44. 3	67. 1
2015	858. 2	97. 8	42. 2	46. 4	69. 0
2016	872. 8	99. 5	43. 2	47. 4	70. 2
2017	890. 3	100. 1	44. 3	47. 9	73. 3
2018	911. 5	102. 1	45. 8	49. 0	78. 1
2019	929. 4	103. 9	47. 8	50. 2	80. 1
2020	942. 0	104. 3	49. 0	51. 1	83. 1
2021	954. 4	105. 3	49. 5	51. 2	85. 0
2022	961. 8	105. 8	50. 3	51. 6	87. 9

注：（1）本表和2-13表2020年前的数据已根据七普数据修订。
（2）各区（县、市）2020年前的数据均按2021年的行政区划同口径调整：其中鄞州区数据包含高新区全部；镇海区数据不包括高新区的贵驷街道，表2-13同。

Notes: (1)The data in this table and Table 2-13 has been revised according to the data of the seventh population census.
(2)The data of all districts and counties (cities) are adjusted according to the same caliber of administrative divisions in 2021: the data of Yinzhou District includes all of the high tech Zone; The data of Zhenhai District does not include Guisi street of high tech Zone,the same as Table 2-13.

单位：万人（10000 persons）

鄞州区 Yinzhou	奉化区 Fenghua	余姚市 Yuyao	慈溪市 Cixi	宁海县 Ninghai	象山县 Xiangshan
128.0	51.0	103.5	151.6	66.2	52.2
131.0	52.4	105.5	156.2	67.4	53.5
133.8	53.8	107.2	160.5	68.4	54.6
137.3	54.8	109.5	165.6	69.0	55.7
140.1	55.7	111.5	170.3	69.0	56.3
142.8	56.6	113.5	173.7	69.3	56.5
147.5	57.0	118.5	175.5	69.5	56.6
152.6	57.3	123.0	177.3	69.6	56.7
157.6	57.8	123.4	182.1	69.7	56.8
161.2	57.8	125.6	183.3	69.7	56.9
164.8	58.4	126.1	185.9	70.8	57.4
166.2	58.6	126.4	186.5	70.9	57.6

表2-13 部分年份年末各区（县、市）城镇常住人口比重
Proportion of Urban Resident Population at the End of Some Years

年份 Year	全市 Total	海曙区 Haishu	江北区 Jiangbei	镇海区 Zhenhai	北仑区 Beilun
2011	68.7	80.5	73.9	60.9	71.5
2012	69.1	81.1	74.6	63.2	72.0
2013	70.2	81.4	75.0	66.5	72.2
2014	71.0	81.8	75.5	69.3	72.6
2015	72.5	82.8	77.1	72.7	74.4
2016	73.7	83.3	79.2	76.1	75.0
2017	74.7	84.1	80.0	79.8	75.3
2018	75.7	85.0	80.9	82.7	75.6
2019	77.5	86.5	82.6	87.4	76.4
2020	78.0	87.0	83.0	89.9	76.7
2021	78.4	87.6	83.6	90.4	77.1
2022	78.9	88.1	84.7	91.1	77.8

单位：%

鄞州区 Yinzhou	奉化区 Fenghua	余姚市 Yuyao	慈溪市 Cixi	宁海县 Ninghai	象山县 Xiangshan
76.8	48.9	66.7	72.6	56.3	54.9
77.0	49.0	67.2	72.7	56.4	55.0
77.7	50.2	69.1	74.0	57.2	56.2
78.3	50.6	70.5	74.6	58.1	56.5
79.3	52.5	72.3	75.8	59.4	57.7
79.9	55.5	73.4	76.5	60.6	59.5
80.5	56.2	74.9	77.4	61.1	60.2
81.0	57.2	76.8	78.0	61.9	60.8
82.0	59.6	80.4	79.4	62.8	61.1
82.2	60.0	80.8	79.7	62.9	61.4
82.7	60.5	81.0	79.9	63.4	61.6
83.0	61.2	81.4	80.1	63.7	62.5

表2-14 全市四上单位从业人员和劳动报酬情况(2022年) Employees and Payment of Four Types of Units above Designated Size（2022）

指标	Indicators
总计	**Total**
按国民经济行业分组	**Grouped by Sector**
农、林、牧、渔业	Framing, Forestry, Animal Husbandry and Fishery
采矿业	Mining and Quarrying
制造业	Manufacturing
电力、燃气及水的生产和供应业	Electric Power, Gas and Water Production and Supply
建筑业	Construction
交通运输、仓储和邮政业	Transport, Storage and Post
信息传输、计算机服务和软件业	Information Transmission, Computer Service and Software
批发与零售业	Wholesale and Retail Trade
住宿与餐饮业	Hotels and Catering Trade
金融业	Financial Industries
房地产业	Real Estate Trade
租赁与商务服务业	Leasing and Business Services
科学研究、技术服务与地质勘查业	Scientific Research, Technical Service and Geologic Prospect
水利环境和公共设施管理业	Water Conservancy, Environment and Public Facility Manageme
居民服务和其他服务业	Resident Service and Other Service Industries
教育	Education
卫生、社会保障和社会福利业	Health Care, Sports and Social Welfare
文化、体育和娱乐业	Culture, Sports and Entertainment
公共管理与社会组织	Public Management and Social Organizations

单位从业人员年末人数（人）Number of Employees at the Year – end (person)	其中 of Which		在岗职工平均工资（含劳务派遣）（元）Average Wage of Staff and Workers (yuan)
	女性 Female	在岗职工合计 Working Staff and Workers	
3555697	**1246092**	**3358068**	**92484**
654	134	649	114911
1591306	685305	1576282	92056
14338	3107	13868	178789
538523	65503	491657	77495
216469	113811	211554	125281
96809	27692	95043	129588
47219	24343	44512	64077
58010	17910	56983	119726
100163	47101	90308	83757
777595	218351	666980	80501
55274	16443	54394	179994
10382	4167	9159	67326
28354	9253	27202	66303
1634	984	1560	141001
13107	9225	12466	130563
5860	2763	5451	109102

表2-15 部分年份按国民经济行业分组的从业人员数（四上单位）
Employees Grouped by Sectors in Partial Years（Four Types of Units Above Designated Size）

单位：万人（10000 persons）

指标	Indicators	2020	2021	2022
从业人员数	**Number of Employed Person**	**323.92**	**338.12**	**355.57**
按国民经济行业分组	**Group by Sector**			
农、林、牧、渔业	Framing, Forestry, Animal Husbandry and Fishery			
采矿业	Mining and Quarrying	0.09	0.06	0.07
制造业	Manufacturing	151.75	163.01	159.13
电力、燃气及水的生产和供应业	Electric Power, Gas and Water Production and Supply	1.46	1.39	1.43
建筑业	Construction	61.83	59.58	53.85
交通运输、仓储和邮政业	Transportation, Storage and Post	18.61	10.10	21.65
信息传输、计算机服务和软件业	Information Transmission, Computer Service and Software	2.39	2.57	9.68
批发和零售业	Wholesale and Retail Trade	18.80	21.36	4.72
住宿和餐饮业	Hotel and Catering Services	4.25	4.53	5.80
金融业	Financial Industries			
房地产业	Real Estate Industries	9.30	10.17	10.02
租赁和商务服务业	Leasing and Business Service Industries	46.02	54.68	77.76
科学研究、技术服务和地质勘查业	Scientific Research, Technical Service and Geologic Prospecting	4.28	5.05	5.53
水利、环境和公共设施管理业	Water Conservancy, Environment and Public Facility Management	0.82	1.13	1.04
居民服务和其他服务业	Resident Service and Other Service Industries	2.15	2.35	2.84
教育	Education	0.34	0.23	0.16
卫生、社会保障和社会福利业	Health Care, Social Security and Social Welfare	1.19	1.28	1.31
文化、体育和娱乐业	Culture, Sports and Entertainment	0.67	0.62	0.59
公共管理和社会组织	Public Management and Social Organizations			
国际组织	International Organizations			

表2-16 部分年份按行业分组的从业人员平均工资（四上单位）
Average Wage of Employees Grouped by Sectors in Partial Years （Four Types of Units Above Designated Size）

单位：元（yuan）

指标	Indicators	2020	2021	2022
总计	**Total**	**77758**	**89495**	**90765**
按国民经济行业分组	**Grouped by Sector**			
农、林、牧、渔业	Framing, Forestry, Animal Husbandry and Fishery			
采矿业	Mining and Quarrying	84721	96794	114194
制造业	Manufacturing	78370	89160	91926
电力、燃气及水的生产和供应业	Electric Power, Gas and Water Production and Supply	158234	163915	175798
建筑业	Construction	71809	76955	76699
交通运输、仓储和邮政业	Transport, Storage and Post	64802	105338	123389
信息传输、计算机服务和软件业	Information Transmission, Computer Service and Software	128456	148877	128740
批发与零售业	Wholesale and Retail Trade	95294	110744	62619
住宿与餐饮业	Hotel and Catering Services	56452	62888	119427
金融业	Financial Industries			
房地产业	Real Estate Industries	82138	86151	80285
租赁与商务服务业	Leasing and Business Service	66833	82284	77322
科学研究、技术服务与地质勘查业	Scientific Research, Technical Service and Geologic Prospecting	161687	168920	178393
水利环境和公共设施管理业	Water Conservancy, Environment and Public Facility Management	62069	61589	63291
居民服务和其他服务业	Resident Service and Other Service	58249	66687	65458
教育	Education	125265	128250	138386
卫生、社会保障和社会福利业	Health Care, Social Security and Social Welfare	117899	124026	127905
文化、体育和娱乐业	Culture, Sports and Entertainment	90848	100557	106379
公共管理与社会组织	Public Management and Social Organizations			

表2-17 各区（县、市）就业人员数（2007-2022年）
Number of Employed Persons by Region (2007-2022)

单位：万人（10000 persons）

年份 Year	全市 Total	海曙区 Haishu	江北区 Jiangbei	镇海区 Zhenhai	北仑区 Beilun	鄞州区 Yinzhou	奉化区 Fenghua	余姚市 Yuyao	慈溪市 Cixi	宁海县 Ninghai	象山县 Xiangshan
2007	435.23	45.43	25.06	24.90	45.03	78.09	24.74	52.44	83.55	28.43	27.56
2008	440.02	45.93	25.34	25.17	45.52	78.95	25.01	53.02	84.47	28.74	27.86
2009	447.65	46.73	25.78	25.61	46.31	80.32	25.44	53.94	85.94	29.24	28.35
2010	452.31	47.21	26.04	25.88	46.79	81.16	25.71	54.50	86.83	29.54	28.64
2011	463.83	48.41	26.71	26.53	47.98	83.22	26.36	55.89	89.04	30.30	29.37
2012	467.75	48.82	26.93	26.76	48.39	83.93	26.58	56.36	89.80	30.55	29.62
2013	473.60	49.43	27.27	27.09	49.00	84.98	26.92	57.07	90.92	30.94	29.99
2014	484.26	50.55	27.88	27.70	50.10	86.89	27.52	58.35	92.97	31.63	30.67
2015	495.35	51.70	28.52	28.34	51.25	88.88	28.15	59.69	95.09	32.36	31.37
2016	513.27	53.57	29.55	29.36	53.10	92.09	29.17	61.85	98.54	33.53	32.50
2017	529.21	55.24	30.47	30.27	54.75	94.96	30.08	63.77	101.60	34.57	33.51
2018	555.39	57.97	31.98	31.77	57.46	99.65	31.57	66.92	105.16	37.14	35.77
2019	569.45	59.44	32.79	32.58	58.91	102.18	32.36	68.62	109.32	37.20	36.06
2020	589.43	62.32	33.48	33.27	59.77	107.29	33.79	72.20	110.59	39.39	37.32
2021	600.10	63.41	34.07	33.88	60.87	109.16	34.39	73.54	112.68	40.10	37.99
2022	599.02	63.30	34.02	33.83	60.78	108.97	34.31	73.41	112.51	40.00	37.90

表2-18 各区（县、市）分三次产业就业人员数（2021-2022年）
Number of Employed Persons by Type of Industry and Region (2021–2022)

单位：万人(10000 persons)

区域	District	就业人员总数 Number of Employed Persons		第一产业 Primary Industry		第二产业 Secondary Industry		第三产业 Tertiary Industry	
		2021	2022	2021	2022	2021	2022	2021	2022
全市	Total	600.10	599.02	20.02	19.70	305.66	305.56	274.42	273.76
海曙	Haishu	63.41	63.30	0.79	0.78	25.05	25.04	37.58	37.49
江北	Jiangbei	34.07	34.02	0.33	0.32	14.11	14.10	19.64	19.59
镇海	Zhenhai	33.88	33.83	0.37	0.36	17.38	17.38	16.13	16.09
北仑	Beilun	60.87	60.78	0.72	0.71	32.68	32.67	27.47	27.40
鄞州	Yinzhou	109.16	108.97	1.07	1.06	40.84	40.83	67.24	67.08
奉化	Fenghua	34.39	34.31	2.45	2.41	17.19	17.18	14.75	14.72
余姚	Yuyao	73.54	73.41	3.64	3.58	45.08	45.06	24.83	24.77
慈溪	Cixi	112.68	112.51	3.81	3.75	71.17	71.15	37.70	37.61
宁海	Ninghai	40.10	40.00	3.26	3.21	20.80	20.79	16.03	15.99
象山	Xiangshan	37.99	37.90	3.58	3.52	21.36	21.35	13.06	13.02

表2-19 部分年份城镇登记失业人数和城镇登记失业率
Number of Registered Urban Unemployed and Registered Urban Unemployed Rate in Partial Years

单位：人（person）

指标	Indicators	2018	2019	2020	2021	2022
新增失业人员	Newly Added Unemployment	62310	86267	131821	120085	101533
#女性	Female	33257	45777	59065	55732	51473
失业人员转就业人数	Unemployed to Reemployed	61604	75116	70850	84830	95020
#女性	Female	33207	39112	31313	34270	48651
城镇登记失业人员数	Registered Urban Unemployment	61357	57080	93669	97468	82735
#女性	Female	29609	30042	46103	52761	46812
#长期失业者	Long-term Unemployed	42802	30198	27440	54267	42214
城镇登记失业率(%)	Registered Urban Unemployed Rate(%)	1.79	1.61	2.22	2.31	1.77

表2-20 部分年份社会保险基本情况
Basic Statistics on Social Insurance in Partial Years

单位：万人（10000 persons）

指标	Indicators	2018	2019	2020	2021	2022
企业养老保险参保人数	Number of Staff and Worker Participated in Basic Pension Insurance at the year-end	453.03	468.25	487.38	511.21	526.71
企业养老保险实际缴费人数	Number of Factial Pay Participated in Basic Pension Insurance at the year-end	338.19	332.86	346.85	365.66	373.51
基本医疗保险参保人数	Population Participated Medical Insurance at the year-end	405.00	426.60	451.30	477.12	501.63
失业保险参保人数	Population Participated Unemployment Insurance at the year-end	281.82	297.21	318.40	333.54	341.59
工伤保险参保人数	Population Participated Work Injury Insurance at the year-end	369.92	375.47	415.64	443.23	451.47
生育保险参保人数	Population Participated Maternity Insurance at the year-end	278.18	276.06	422.06	313.92	376.96
被征地人员养老保障参保人数	Number of Taken Over Land Farmers Participated in Rural Social Old-aged Security	33.92	32.98	32.98	30.35	28.57

表2-21 各区（县、市）城镇就业和失业人员变化情况（2022年底）
Number of Urban Employed and Unemployed by Region (End of 2022)

单位：人(person)

指标	Indicators	全市 Total	市区 Urban District	海曙区 Haishu	江北区 Jiangbei	镇海区 Zhenhai	北仑区 Beilun
上期末结转的失业人数	**From the Previous Year**	**97468**	**58334**	**11938**	**5697**	**11449**	**6040**
本期增加的失业人员	**Newly Added in this Year**	**101533**	**61112**	**16051**	**5302**	**9715**	**5690**
#女性	Female	51473	32790	9699	2802	4733	3142
由就业转失业	Reemployed to Unemployed	84041	54720	12609	4993	9188	5229
本期失业人员就业人数	**Unemployed to Reemployed at This Year**	**95020**	**52689**	**9814**	**5459**	**9798**	**5730**
#女性	Female	48651	28009	5824	2723	4876	3235
期末实有登记失业人数	**Registered Unemployment at the Year－end**	**82735**	**51670**	**12307**	**4912**	**8788**	**4962**
#女性	Female	46812	31412	7594	2500	6046	2799
长期失业者	Long－term Unemployment	42214	26085	7206	2535	3958	2555
城镇登记失业率(%)	**Registered Urban Unemployed Rate (%)**	**1.77**	**1.86**	**2.22**	**1.74**	**1.88**	**1.63**

指标	Indicators	鄞州区 Yinzhou	奉化区 Fenghua	余姚市 Yuyao	慈溪市 Cixi	宁海县 Ninghai	象山县 Xiangshan
上期末结转的失业人数	**From the Previous Year**	**16836**	**6374**	**13702**	**16210**	**5077**	**4145**
本期增加的失业人员	**Newly Added in this Year**	**17260**	**7094**	**15162**	**15154**	**6082**	**4023**
#女性	Female	9096	3318	7052	5860	3347	2424
由就业转失业	Reemployed to Unemployed	15710	6991	12217	9416	3670	4018
本期失业人员就业人数	**Unemployed to Reemployed at This Year**	**14714**	**7174**	**12452**	**19927**	**5061**	**4891**
#女性	Female	7219	4132	6408	8404	2637	3193
期末实有登记失业人数	**Registered Unemployment at the Year－end**	**15731**	**4940**	**13449**	**10456**	**3883**	**3277**
#女性	Female	8506	3967	6522	4743	2259	1876
长期失业者	Long－term Unemployment	7525	2306	6960	5673	1987	1509
城镇登记失业率(%)	**Registered Urban Unemployed Rate (%)**	**1.75**	**1.84**	**2.25**	**1.17**	**1.67**	**1.31**

主要统计指标解释

【出生率（又称粗出生率）】指在一定时期内（通常为一年）平均每千人所出生的人数的比率，一般用千分率表示。计算公式为：

出生率＝年出生人数／年平均人数×1000‰

式中：出生人数指活产婴儿，即胎儿脱离母体时（不管怀孕月数），有过呼吸或其他生命现象。年平均人数指年初、年底人口数的平均数，也可用年中人口数代替。

【死亡率（又称粗死亡率）】指在一定时期内（通常为一年）一定地区的死亡人数与同期平均人数（或期中人数）之比，一般用千分率表示。计算公式为：

死亡率＝年死亡人数／年平均人数×1000‰

【人口自然增长率】指在一定时期内（通常为一年）人口自然增加数（出生人数减死亡人数）与该时期内平均人数（或期中人数）之比，一般用千分率表示。计算公式为：

人口自然增长率＝（本年出生人数－本年死亡人数）／年平均人数×1000‰＝人口出生率－人口死亡率

【经济活动人口】指在16岁以上，有劳动能力，参加或要求参加社会经济活动的人口；包括从业人员和失业人员。

【单位从业人员】各单位的从业人员是指在各级国家机关、政党机关、社会团体及企业、事业单位中工作，并取得劳动报酬的全部人员。包括：在岗职工、再就业的离退休人员、民办教师以及在各单位中工作的外方人员和港澳台方人员、兼职人员、聘用的外单位下岗人员、借用的外单位人员和第二职业者。不包括离开本单位仍保留劳动关系的职工。

【在岗职工】指在本单位工作并由单位支付劳动报酬的职工。包括由单位派出学习、劳务及病伤产假且仍由单位支付劳动报酬的人员。

【职工平均工资】指企业、事业、机关单位的职工在一定时期内平均每人所得的货币工资额。它表明一定时期职工工资收入的高低程度，是反映职工工资水平的主要指标。计算公式为：

职工平均工资＝报告期实际支付的全部职工工资总额／报告期全部职工平均人数

【专业技术人员】指从事专业技术和从事专业技术管理工作的人员。统计对象为事业、企业单位中已经聘任专业技术职务从事专业技术工作的人员，以及未聘任专业技术职务，现在专业技术岗位上工作的具有中专以上学历的人员。

【城镇登记失业人员】指有非农业户口，在一定的劳动年龄内，有劳动能力，无业而要求就业，并在当地就业服务机构进行求职登记的人员。

【城镇登记失业率】指城镇登记失业人数同城镇从业人数与城镇登记失业人数之和的比。计算公式为：

城镇登记失业率=城镇登记失业人数／（城镇从业人数+城镇登记失业人数）×100%

【四上单位】指规模以上工业、限额以上批发零售业和限额以上住宿餐饮业、有资质的建筑业和房地产开发经营业、规模以上服务业单位。

Explanatory Notes on Main Statistical Indicators

【Birth Rate or (Crude Birth Rate)】 refers to the ratio of the number of births to the average population (or mid–period population) during a certain period of time (usually a year) which is often expressed in ‰. Birth rate in the chapter refers to annual birth rate. The following formula is used:

Birth Rate = Number of Births/Average Number of Population × 1000‰

Number of births refers to live births i.e. the births when babies had showed any vital phenomena regardless of the length of pregnancy.Annual Average Number of Population is the average of the number of population at the beginning of the year and that at the end of the year. Sometimes it is substituted for with the mid year population.

【Death Rate (or Crude Death Rate)】 refers to the ratio of the number of deaths to the average population (or mid–period population) during a certain period of time (usually a year) which is often expressed in ‰. Death rate in the chapter refers to annual death rate. The following formula is used:

Death Rate= Number of Deaths/Annual Average Number of Population × 1000‰

【Natural Growth Rate of Population】 refers to the ratio of natural increase in population (number of births minus number of deaths) in a certain period of time (usually a year) to the average population (or mid–period population) of the same period which is often expressed in ‰. The following formulas are applied:

Natural Growth of Population = (Number of Births–Number of Deaths)/Average Number of Population × 1000‰

Natural Growth Rate of Population = Birth Rate–Death Rate

【Economically Active Population】 refers to the population aged 16 and over who are capable to work, are participating in or willing to participate in economic activities, including employed persons and unemployed persons.

【Employees of the Unit】 refers to the personnel who work in the government offices, political parties, social communities, enterprises and public undertakings and get paid. Including: on–the–job employees, reemployed retirees, teachers in schools run by the local people, personnel from abroad or HK, Macao, TW who work in the unit, persons on part time, laid–off personnel from other units, hands borrow ed from other units and concurrent employees. Employees who had left their units but still retain labor contracts with them are excluded.

【Full Employed Staff and Workers】 refers to the employees who work for the unit and get paid by it, including those who are leave because of illness, injuries and pregnancies.

【Average Wage of Staff and Workers】 refers to the average wage in money terms per person during a certain period of time for staff and workers in enterprises, institutions, and government agencies, which reflects the general level of wage income during a certain period of time and is calculated as follows:

Average Wage of Staff and Workers = Total Wages of Staff and Workers in Reference Period/Average Number of Staff and Workers in Reference Period.

【Specialized Technical Personnel】 refer to the professional technology and administrative personnel. Its statistical targets include personnel who had been employed and given professional posts by the enterprises and pubic under takings, and the personnel who work in the unit have degrees higher than polytechnic school, but not given professional posts.

【Registered Urban Unemployed Persons】 The registered unemployed persons in urban areas refer to the persons who are registered as permanent residents in the urban areas engaged in non–agricultural activities, aged within the range of working age, capable to labor, unemployed but desirous to be employed and have been registered at the local employment service agencies to apply for a job.

【Registered Urban Unemployment Rate】 Registered unemployment rate in urban areas refers to the ratio of the number of the registered unemployed persons to the sum of the number of employed persons and the registered unemployed persons . The formula is as follows:

Registered urban unemployment rate = number of registered urban unemployed persons ÷ (number of urban employed persons + number of registered urban unemployed persons) × 100%.

【Four Types of Units above Designated Size】 Refers to industries above Designated Size, wholesale and retail industries above Designated Size, accommodation and catering industries above Designated Size, qualified construction industry and real estate development business units, and service enterprises above designated size.

NINGBO 2023 Statistical Yearbook

3

CHAPTER

第三篇

国民经济核算

INVESTMENT IN FIXED ASSETS AND CONSTRUCTION

国民经济核算
National Economic Accounting

主要统计指标
Major Statistics Indicators

		2021年	2022年
地区生产总值（亿元）	Gross Domestic Product（100 million yuan）	14703.2	15704.3
第一产业	Primary Industry	359.3	382.0
第二产业	Secondary Industry	6867.3	7413.5
第三产业	Tertiary Industry	7476. 6	7908.8
地区生产总值构成（%）	Composition of Gross Domestic Product	100. 0	100.0
第一产业	Primary Industry	2.4	2.4
第二产业	Secondary Industry	46.7	47.2
第三产业	Tertiary Industry	50.9	50.4
地区生产总值增长速度（%）	Growth Rate of Gross Domestic Product	8.2	3.5
第一产业	Primary Industry	1.1	4.1
第二产业	Secondary Industry	7.7	3.2
第三产业	Tertiary Industry	9.1	3.8
人均地区生产总值（元）	Per capita Gross Domestic Product(yuan)	155064	163911
人均地区生产总值增长速度（%）	Growth Rate of Per Capita Gross Domestic Product	6.8	2.5

表3-1 历年生产总值
Gross Domestic Product Over the Years

单位：亿元（100 million yuan）

年份 Year	生产总值 Gross Domestic Product	其中 of Which				人均生产总值（元） Per Capita GDP (yuan)
		第一产业 Primary Industry	第二产业 Secondary Industry	第三产业 Tertiary Industry	工业 Industry	
1978	20. 17	6. 52	9. 69	3. 96	8. 62	437
1979	24. 15	7. 99	11. 43	4. 73	10. 11	522
1980	29. 53	8. 68	15. 54	5. 31	14. 21	634
1981	31. 99	7. 85	18. 11	6. 03	16. 82	680
1982	36. 88	11. 20	18. 79	6. 89	17. 26	776
1983	41. 68	10. 91	22. 63	8. 14	21. 22	864
1984	53. 17	14. 93	28. 23	10. 01	26. 02	1096
1985	71. 05	16. 84	40. 40	13. 81	36. 96	1462
1986	80. 22	18. 61	44. 47	17. 14	40. 59	1638
1987	95. 99	22. 11	53. 99	19. 89	48. 76	1939
1988	118. 62	27. 11	66. 42	25. 09	60. 28	2370
1989	137. 25	31. 14	77. 69	28. 42	71. 02	2716
1990	141. 40	29. 35	80. 31	31. 74	72. 46	2777
1991	169. 87	32. 75	98. 39	38. 73	88. 69	3315
1992	213. 05	35. 32	128. 70	49. 03	116. 20	4133
1993	315. 11	46. 09	189. 12	79. 90	165. 61	6079
1994	459. 66	63. 47	260. 98	135. 21	227. 59	8816
1995	602. 65	81. 11	338. 99	182. 55	295. 90	11489
1996	784. 07	92. 21	442. 64	249. 22	390. 74	14846
1997	879. 10	84. 53	500. 05	294. 52	452. 24	16534
1998	952. 79	87. 77	528. 73	336. 29	478. 67	17833
1999	1017. 08	91. 85	564. 07	361. 16	512. 84	18946
2000	1144. 57	94. 24	635. 83	414. 50	578. 30	21208
2001	1278. 75	98. 52	690. 81	489. 42	624. 92	23587
2002	1453. 34	103. 60	793. 01	556. 73	715. 24	23302
2003	1749. 27	109. 75	954. 04	685. 48	847. 79	27493
2004	2119. 65	120. 54	1176. 97	822. 14	1036. 42	32562
2005	2462. 09	132. 25	1355. 66	974. 18	1197. 50	37046
2006	2891. 84	132. 73	1602. 88	1156. 23	1434. 14	42555
2007	3449. 62	150. 87	1923. 42	1375. 33	1731. 59	49588
2008	3982. 92	165. 95	2224. 41	1592. 56	1989. 04	56129
2009	4405. 12	182. 04	2400. 69	1822. 39	2141. 05	61051
2010	5264. 70	216. 66	2915. 09	2132. 95	2613. 74	70734
2011	6212. 56	251. 58	3394. 02	2566. 96	3031. 87	80359
2012	6862. 02	263. 99	3572. 82	3025. 21	3184. 04	86358
2013	7432. 09	265. 15	3794. 14	3372. 80	3381. 56	91432
2014	7904. 81	267. 60	4108. 26	3528. 95	3636. 71	95055
2015	8295. 35	275. 13	4210. 91	3809. 31	3717. 89	97604
2016	8972. 83	290. 72	4463. 78	4218. 33	3953. 81	103672
2017	10146. 55	297. 05	5119. 01	4730. 49	4579. 74	115099
2018	11193. 14	302. 33	5507. 15	5383. 66	4898. 77	124244
2019	12035. 11	323. 14	5686. 34	6025. 63	5047. 01	130752
2020	12599. 22	338. 52	5793. 11	6467. 59	5147. 04	134650
2021	14703. 20	359. 28	6867. 26	7476. 66	6163. 12	155064
2022	15704. 30	381. 99	7413. 47	7908. 84	6681. 72	163911

注：（1）本章数据经全国第四次经济普查和第七次人口普查数据修订，2022年为快报数据。
（2）人均生产总值1978–2001年按户籍人口计算，2001年以后按常住人口计算。

Notes:（1）The data in this chapter are revised by the data of the 4th economic census and the 7th population census, and the data in 2022 are fast report data.
（2）The per capita GDP of 1978–2001 is calculated by registered residence population. After 2001, the per capita GDP is calculated according to the permanent population.

表3-2 历年生产总值指数（以1978年为100）
Index of Gross Domestic Product Over the Years(Take the Data of 1978 as 100)

年份 Year	生产总值 Gross Domestic Product	其中 of Which				人均生产总值 Per Capita GDP
		第一产业 Primary Industry	第二产业 Secondary Industry	第三产业 Tertiary Industry	工业 Industry	
1978	100. 0	100. 0	100. 0	100. 0	100. 0	100. 0
1979	113. 4	106. 4	116. 4	118. 5	114. 1	113. 1
1980	133. 5	108. 8	149. 5	124. 3	158. 3	132. 3
1981	145. 9	103. 2	174. 0	139. 5	190. 5	143. 1
1982	165. 9	134. 8	183. 6	160. 8	198. 2	161. 1
1983	195. 2	143. 1	229. 1	186. 5	240. 4	186. 8
1984	230. 4	162. 9	273. 8	222. 9	300. 5	219. 2
1985	295. 1	163. 7	387. 1	281. 0	422. 8	278. 9
1986	321. 7	171. 5	418. 1	328. 5	454. 0	301. 6
1987	367. 0	177. 4	494. 2	367. 4	538. 5	340. 6
1988	407. 8	170. 3	574. 2	396. 9	641. 9	374. 1
1989	426. 1	163. 6	624. 8	381. 4	688. 1	387. 3
1990	450. 4	171. 2	649. 8	432. 4	713. 5	406. 3
1991	562. 5	188. 8	768. 0	671. 7	884. 8	504. 2
1992	663. 2	184. 1	969. 2	774. 6	1144. 9	591. 0
1993	801. 2	203. 0	1225. 1	889. 4	1446. 5	710. 0
1994	970. 2	217. 2	1502. 0	1113. 0	1743. 0	854. 7
1995	1169. 1	247. 7	1862. 5	1285. 7	2168. 0	1023. 8
1996	1370. 2	269. 2	2207. 1	1515. 2	2565. 5	1191. 7
1997	1558. 0	252. 2	2569. 0	1748. 3	3062. 9	1345. 9
1998	1730. 9	265. 1	2864. 4	1960. 4	3429. 1	1488. 0
1999	1921. 3	286. 6	3170. 9	2208. 4	3791. 0	1643. 9
2000	2151. 9	296. 0	3570. 5	2499. 7	4273. 8	1831. 5
2001	2412. 2	310. 8	4032. 7	2810. 1	4825. 1	2043. 7
2002	2730. 6	322. 7	4637. 6	3159. 1	5548. 9	2276. 6
2003	3156. 6	334. 3	5421. 7	3661. 1	6420. 0	2579. 8
2004	3645. 9	351. 0	6319. 6	4234. 2	7447. 2	2872. 7
2005	4096. 3	357. 7	7019. 6	4925. 9	8278. 9	3161. 3
2006	4664. 1	375. 0	7932. 6	5727. 6	9469. 9	3520. 2
2007	5351. 6	395. 3	9144. 7	6595. 3	11038. 3	3945. 6
2008	5903. 4	411. 6	10032. 5	7375. 1	12130. 1	4267. 0
2009	6421. 9	427. 4	10853. 7	8119. 5	13147. 7	4564. 9
2010	7264. 2	443. 7	12307. 2	9229. 3	14989. 5	5005. 7
2011	8010. 2	461. 5	13478. 2	10331. 0	16476. 6	5314. 2
2012	8615. 6	466. 6	14334. 7	11341. 1	17477. 9	5561. 2
2013	9318. 6	459. 4	15440. 7	12424. 6	18875. 0	5879. 8
2014	10023. 0	468. 1	16811. 4	13210. 4	20455. 7	6181. 8
2015	10822. 4	476. 3	18375. 9	14096. 2	22340. 3	6531. 0
2016	11606. 3	484. 3	19867. 4	15037. 7	24265. 1	6877. 8
2017	12528. 9	494. 9	21211. 7	16492. 0	26223. 3	7289. 4
2018	13403. 9	496. 4	21926. 9	18364. 1	27099. 8	7631. 0
2019	14309. 6	507. 4	23025. 1	19978. 3	28600. 8	7973. 6
2020	14789. 3	520. 0	23780. 6	20671. 3	29706. 9	8106. 6
2021	16008. 0	525. 5	25607. 3	22556. 0	32243. 1	8658. 9
2022	16573. 2	547. 2	26439. 5	23401. 8	33291. 1	8872. 7

表3-3 历年生产总值比上年增长
Growth Rate of Gross Domestic Product Raised Preceding Year Over the Years

单位：%

年份 Year	生产总值 Gross Domestic Product	其中 of Which				人均生产总值 Per Capita GDP
		第一产业 Primary Industry	第二产业 Secondary Industry	第三产业 Tertiary Industry	工业 Industry	
1978	22.5	19.8	33.2	6.7		21.4
1979	13.4	6.4	16.4	18.5	14.1	13.1
1980	17.7	2.3	28.4	4.9	38.7	16.9
1981	9.3	-5.2	16.4	12.2	20.3	8.2
1982	13.7	30.6	5.5	15.2	4.0	12.6
1983	17.7	6.2	24.8	16.0	21.3	15.9
1984	18.0	13.8	19.5	19.5	25.0	17.4
1985	28.1	0.5	41.4	26.0	40.7	27.2
1986	9.0	4.8	8.0	16.9	7.4	8.1
1987	14.1	3.4	18.2	11.8	18.6	12.9
1988	11.1	-4.0	16.2	8.0	19.2	9.9
1989	4.5	-3.9	8.8	-3.9	7.2	3.5
1990	5.7	4.6	4.0	13.4	3.7	4.9
1991	24.9	10.3	18.2	55.4	24.0	24.1
1992	17.9	-2.5	26.2	15.3	29.4	17.2
1993	20.8	10.3	26.4	14.8	26.3	20.1
1994	21.1	7.0	22.6	25.1	20.5	20.4
1995	20.5	14.0	24.0	15.5	24.4	19.8
1996	17.2	8.7	18.5	17.9	18.3	16.4
1997	13.7	-6.3	16.4	15.4	19.4	12.9
1998	11.1	5.1	11.5	12.1	12.0	10.6
1999	11.0	8.1	10.7	12.7	10.6	10.5
2000	12.0	3.3	12.6	13.2	12.7	11.4
2001	12.1	5.0	12.9	12.4	12.9	11.6
2002	13.2	3.8	15.0	12.4	15.0	11.4
2003	15.6	3.6	16.9	15.9	15.7	13.3
2004	15.5	5.0	16.6	15.7	16.0	11.4
2005	12.4	1.9	11.1	16.3	11.2	10.0
2006	13.9	4.8	13.0	16.3	14.4	11.4
2007	14.7	5.4	15.3	15.2	16.6	12.1
2008	10.3	4.1	9.7	11.8	9.9	8.1
2009	8.8	3.8	8.2	10.1	8.4	7.0
2010	13.1	3.8	13.4	13.7	14.0	9.7
2011	10.3	4.0	9.5	11.9	9.9	6.2
2012	7.6	1.1	6.4	9.8	6.1	4.6
2013	8.2	-1.5	7.7	9.6	8.0	5.7
2014	7.6	1.9	8.9	6.3	8.4	5.1
2015	8.0	1.8	9.3	6.7	9.2	5.7
2016	7.2	1.7	8.1	6.7	8.6	5.3
2017	7.9	2.2	6.8	9.7	8.1	6.0
2018	7.0	0.3	3.4	11.4	3.3	4.7
2019	6.8	2.2	5.0	8.8	5.5	4.5
2020	3.4	2.5	3.3	3.5	3.9	1.7
2021	8.2	1.1	7.7	9.1	8.5	6.8
2022	3.5	4.1	3.2	3.8	3.3	2.5

表3-4 历年生产总值构成
Structure of Gross Domestic Product Over the Years

单位：%

年份 Year	生产总值 Gross Domestic Product	其中 of Which			
		第一产业 Primary Industry	第二产业 Secondary Industry	第三产业 Tertiary Industry	工业 Industry
1978	100.00	32.34	48.06	19.60	42.75
1979	100.00	33.08	47.33	19.59	41.87
1980	100.00	29.41	52.61	17.98	48.11
1981	100.00	24.54	56.61	18.85	52.58
1982	100.00	30.37	50.94	18.69	46.80
1983	100.00	26.18	54.29	19.53	50.91
1984	100.00	28.08	53.09	18.83	48.94
1985	100.00	23.71	56.85	19.44	52.02
1986	100.00	23.20	55.43	21.37	50.60
1987	100.00	23.04	56.24	20.72	50.80
1988	100.00	22.85	56.00	21.15	50.82
1989	100.00	22.69	56.61	20.70	51.75
1990	100.00	20.76	56.80	22.44	51.25
1991	100.00	19.28	57.92	22.80	52.21
1992	100.00	16.58	60.41	23.01	54.54
1993	100.00	14.63	60.02	25.35	52.56
1994	100.00	13.81	56.77	29.42	49.51
1995	100.00	13.46	56.25	30.29	49.10
1996	100.00	11.76	56.45	31.79	49.83
1997	100.00	9.62	56.88	33.50	51.44
1998	100.00	9.21	55.49	35.30	50.24
1999	100.00	9.03	55.46	35.51	50.42
2000	100.00	8.23	55.55	36.22	50.53
2001	100.00	7.71	54.02	38.27	48.87
2002	100.00	7.13	54.56	38.31	49.21
2003	100.00	6.27	54.54	39.19	48.46
2004	100.00	5.68	55.53	38.79	48.90
2005	100.00	5.37	55.06	39.57	48.64
2006	100.00	4.59	55.43	39.98	49.59
2007	100.00	4.37	55.76	39.87	50.20
2008	100.00	4.17	55.85	39.98	49.94
2009	100.00	4.13	54.50	41.37	48.60
2010	100.00	4.12	55.37	40.51	49.65
2011	100.00	4.05	54.63	41.32	48.80
2012	100.00	3.85	52.07	44.08	46.40
2013	100.00	3.57	51.05	45.38	45.50
2014	100.00	3.39	51.97	44.64	46.01
2015	100.00	3.32	50.76	45.92	44.82
2016	100.00	3.24	49.75	47.01	44.06
2017	100.00	2.93	50.45	46.62	45.14
2018	100.00	2.70	49.20	48.10	43.77
2019	100.00	2.68	47.25	50.07	41.94
2020	100.00	2.69	45.98	51.33	40.85
2021	100.00	2.44	46.71	50.85	41.92
2022	100.00	2.43	47.21	50.36	42.55

表3-5 按产业划分的生产总值(2021-2022年)
Gross Domestic Product Classified by Industries（2021–2022）

单位：万元 (10000 yuan)

指标	Indicators	2021	2022	发展速度(%) Growth Rate over 2021(%)
宁波市生产总值	**Gross Domestic Product**	**147032016**	**157042963**	**103. 5**
第一产业	Primary Industry	3592773	3819926	104. 1
第二产业	Secondary Industry	68672666	74134665	103. 2
第三产业	Tertiary Industry	74766577	79088372	103. 8
按国民经济行业（2017）分类	**Group by Sector（2017）**			
农林牧渔业	Agriculture, Forestry, Animal Husbandry and Fishery	3759938	4003568	104. 2
工业	Industry	61631186	66817224	103. 3
建筑业	Constructions	7144661	7427378	103. 3
批发和零售业	Retail and Wholesale Industries	17569417	18705990	103. 3
交通运输、仓储和邮政业	Transportation, Storage and Post	6181446	6560725	100. 4
住宿和餐饮业	Hoteling and Catering	1682472	1770828	103. 5
信息传输、软件和信息技术服务业	Information Transmission, Software and Information Technology Service	2004904	2295204	112. 2
金融业	Financial Industry	11583276	12668164	106. 8
房地产业	Real Estate Industry	10726724	10358438	95. 2
租赁和商务服务业	Leasehold and Business Service	8894631		
科学研究和技术服务业	Scientific Research and Technology Service	2840292		
水利、环境和公共设施管理业	Water Conservancy, Environment and Public Facility Management	316965		
居民服务、修理和其他服务业	Residential Service, Repairing & Maintenance and Other Service	1549110		
教育	Education	3568747		
卫生和社会工作	Health Care and Social Work	2742071		
文化、体育和娱乐业	Culture, Sports and Entertainment	1088044		
公共管理、社会保障和社会组织	Public Management, Social Security and Social Organizations	3748132		

表3-6 生产总值项目构成（1993-2022年）
Structure of Gross Domestic Product（1993–2022）

单位：万元 (10000 yuan)

年份 Year	总计 Gross Domestic Product				
	增加值 Value-Added	其中 of Which			
		劳动者报酬 Compensation of Employees	生产税净额 Net Taxes on Production	固定资产折旧 Depreciation of Fixed Assets	营业盈余 Operating Surplus
1993	3151137	1506857	499355	311430	833495
1994	4596645	2480140	699264	432964	984277
1995	6026524	3092917	953362	589020	1391225
1996	7840727	4197455	1297978	761269	1584025
1997	8791042	4760824	1466876	1000186	1563156
1998	9527859	4405743	1756795	1329018	2036303
1999	10170826	4858140	1765615	1485977	2061094
2000	11445653	5197257	1898185	1503767	2846444
2001	12787531	6129433	1872390	1619514	3166194
2002	14533421	6574217	2288833	1702915	3967456
2003	17492728	7522559	2888138	1983778	5098253
2004	21196516	8262149	3418924	2625370	6890073
2005	24620902	9538821	3773844	3181265	8126972
2006	28918352	11269709	4850964	3792688	9004991
2007	34496205	12842875	5480436	4719343	11453551
2008	39829199	16637991	6573061	5764661	10853486
2009	44051239	15978906	8653924	5399880	14018529
2010	52646956	19765807	10039359	5826324	17015466
2011	62125617	24885134	12311073	7263773	17665637
2012	68620203	29175512	13587404	8765865	17091422
2013	74320916	33540613	13716206	8962255	18101842
2014	79048111	36239815	14953627	9485037	18369632
2015	82953506	41180382	15554505	11379178	14839441
2016	89728271	42257341	16536001	10885607	20049322
2017	101465516	46487373	18645727	11932131	24400285
2018	111931398	52932036	18011298	15167592	25820472
2019	120351140	59156181	17623655	16223958	27347346
2020	125992175	60066403	18351852	18456144	29117776
2021	147032016	72160762	18596921	19220409	37053924
2022	157042963				

表 3－6 续表 1 Continued 1　　　　单位：万元 (10000 yuan)

年份 Year	第一产业 Primary Industry				
	增加值 Value-Added	其中 of Which			
		劳动者报酬 Compensation of Employees	生产税净额 Net Taxes on Production	固定资产折旧 Depreciation of Fixed Assets	营业盈余 Operating Surplus
1993	460932	362995	6022	12583	79332
1994	634751	497816	11730	16599	108606
1995	811080	642492	17182	24416	126990
1996	922101	715773	17978	29039	159311
1997	845307	665351	21563	32441	125952
1998	877645	691633	15435	34769	135808
1999	918527	722231	15389	38032	142875
2000	942353	737186	14797	39345	151025
2001	985257	770231	15638	41004	158384
2002	1035968	812679	16182	43465	163642
2003	1097567	861928	10418	46163	179058
2004	1205371	1165332	1293	38746	
2005	1322475	1250992	14514	56969	
2006	1327333	1275691	-9016	60658	
2007	1508691	1473039	-33634	69286	
2008	1659473	1642880	-60710	77303	
2009	1820386	1770865	-42211	91732	
2010	2166591	2118691	-59238	107138	
2011	2515768	2462074	-69505	123199	
2012	2639891	2582298	-73809	131402	
2013	2651482	2596009	-79166	134639	
2014	2675972	2620494	-79625	135103	
2015	2751342	2692108	-81829	141063	
2016	2907179	2841598	-84286	149867	
2017	2970472	2909382	-92153	153243	
2018	3023255	2966835	-98777	155197	
2019	3231376	3171826	-104007	163557	
2020	3385226	3320311	-108254	173169	
2021	3592773	3524971	-116165	128777	55190
2022	3819926				

表 3－6 续表 2 Continued 2　　　　单位：万元 (10000 yuan)

年份 Year	第二产业 Secondary Industry				
	增加值 Value-Added	其中 of Which			
		劳动者报酬 Compensation of Employees	生产税净额 Net Taxes on Production	固定资产折旧 Depreciation of Fixed Assets	营业盈余 Operating Surplus
1993	1891201	822727	360007	189250	519217
1994	2609752	1307376	541991	254130	506255
1995	3389919	1499859	728377	342581	819102
1996	4426403	2279485	966565	422195	758158
1997	5000559	2709675	1035314	520105	735465
1998	5287306	2080907	1265643	708150	1232606
1999	5640654	2355823	1271128	809524	1204179
2000	6358306	2462503	1378338	794615	1722850
2001	6908111	2768675	1404624	806206	1928606
2002	7930119	3381081	1752335	730237	2066466
2003	9540385	4030508	1808864	912346	2788667
2004	11769706	4360196	2305394	1305425	3798691
2005	13556610	4952204	2504702	1658563	4441141
2006	16028733	6113649	3285801	2219595	4409688
2007	19234183	7005672	3824969	2568729	5834813
2008	22244101	9744814	3606886	3587172	5305229
2009	24006883	8140710	5177253	3061500	7627420
2010	29150892	10161373	5733699	3133720	10122100
2011	33940182	12917553	7063591	4091788	9867250
2012	35728227	14777150	7496727	4658662	8795688
2013	37941374	14799250	8169467	4719752	10252905
2014	41082657	16879724	8051414	4832571	11318948
2015	42109110	18169898	9001508	5563188	9374516
2016	44637812	18616512	9002861	5572488	11445951
2017	51190091	20422135	10616302	5918185	14233469
2018	55071519	23551858	10603932	7323422	13592307
2019	56863417	24476964	9948536	7734947	14702970
2020	57931094	24957574	10164477	8199575	14609468
2021	68672666	30446445	10170090	8019594	20036537
2022	74134665				

表 3 – 6 续表 3 Continued 3

单位：万元 (10000 yuan)

年份 Year	第三产业 Tertiary Industry				
	增加值 Value-Added	其中 of Which			
		劳动者报酬 Compensation of Employees	生产税净额 Net Taxes on Production	固定资产折旧 Depreciation of Fixed Assets	营业盈余 Operating Surplus
1993	799004	321135	133326	109597	234946
1994	1352142	674948	145543	162235	369416
1995	1825525	950566	207803	222023	445133
1996	2492223	1202197	313435	310035	666556
1997	2945176	1385798	409999	447640	701739
1998	3362908	1633203	475717	586099	667889
1999	3611645	1780086	479098	638421	714040
2000	4144994	1997568	505050	669807	972569
2001	4894163	2590527	452128	772304	1079204
2002	5567334	2380457	520316	929213	1737348
2003	6854776	2630123	1068856	1025269	2130528
2004	8221439	2736621	1112237	1281199	3091382
2005	9741817	3335625	1254628	1465733	3685831
2006	11562286	3880369	1574179	1512435	4595303
2007	13753331	4364164	1689101	2081328	5618738
2008	15925625	5250297	3026885	2100186	5548257
2009	18223970	6067331	3518882	2246648	6391109
2010	21329473	7485743	4364898	2585466	6893366
2011	25669667	9505507	5316987	3048786	7798387
2012	30252085	11816064	6164486	3975801	8295734
2013	33728060	16145354	5625905	4107864	7848937
2014	35289482	16739597	6981838	4517363	7050684
2015	38093054	20318376	6634826	5674927	5464925
2016	42183280	20799231	7617426	5163252	8603371
2017	47304953	23155856	8121578	5860703	10166816
2018	53836624	26413343	7506143	7688973	12228165
2019	60256347	31507391	7779126	8325454	12644376
2020	64675855	31788518	8295629	10083400	14508308
2021	74766577	38189346	8542996	11072038	16962197
2022	79088372				

表3-7 各区（县、市）按产业划分的生产总值（2021年）
Gross Domestic Product Classified by Industries and by Region（2021）

指标	Indicators	全市 Total	海曙区 Haishu	江北区 Jiangbei
地区生产总值	**Gross Domestic Product**	**147032016**	**14256160**	**7991009**
第一产业	Primary Industry	3592773	166177	85318
第二产业	Secondary Industry	68672666	4002833	2542661
第三产业	Tertiary Industry	74766577	10087150	5363030
农林牧渔业	Agriculture, Forestry, Animal Husbandry and Fishery	3759938	174309	90392
工业	Industry	61631186	3180391	2104833
建筑业	Constructions	7144661	824173	441017
批发和零售业	Retail and Wholesale Industries	17569417	1752799	975804
交通运输、仓储和邮政业	Transportation, Storage and Post	6181446	1041647	599720
住宿和餐饮业	Hoteling and Catering	1682472	236366	78536
信息传输、软件和信息技术服务业	Information Transmission, Software and Information Technology Service	2004904	258171	119991
金融业	Financial Industry	11583276	1530446	629960
房地产业	Real Estate Industry	10726724	1238096	838297
租赁和商务服务业	Leasehold and Business Service	8894631	1976771	1101906
科学研究和技术服务业	Scientific Research and Technology Service	2840292	327883	169606
水利、环境和公共设施管理业	Water Conservancy, Environment and Public Facility Management	316965	69319	21823
居民服务、修理和其他服务业	Residential Service, Repairing & Maintenance and Other Service	1549110	131418	102334
教育	**Education**	3568747	514402	369561
卫生和社会工作	Health Care and Social Work	2742071	532430	142845
文化、体育和娱乐业	Culture, Sports and Entertainment	1088044	87050	42491
公共管理、社会保障和社会组织	Public Management, Social Security and Social Organizations	3748132	380489	161893

单位：万元 (10000 yuan)

镇海区 Zhenhai	北仑区 Beilun	鄞州区 Yinzhou	奉化区 Fenghua	余姚市 Yuyao	慈溪市 Cixi	宁海县 Ninghai	象山县 Xiangshan
12522106	**24415155**	**25759988**	**8514695**	**14433040**	**23785493**	**8378775**	**6699118**
70593	88850	289854	337953	506638	617086	511604	907131
8350238	11894569	7005598	5112572	8622109	14120323	4042561	2612038
4101275	12431736	18464536	3064170	5304293	9048084	3824610	3179949
73855	93624	312783	351345	533364	640394	532209	945709
7810365	11253294	5591789	4605369	8130458	13142364	3568185	1867006
547090	670353	1417166	508072	492566	978812	491316	774603
685081	5784321	3175072	537696	1115711	1976760	798315	521768
499360	1783599	796390	267725	210485	714768	273769	241812
84738	145753	365202	97037	172809	264001	133791	109713
115302	351450	685854	80298	118827	169360	93743	65841
473393	842763	4600765	477486	865916	1425615	445755	393635
737756	847922	2414557	591863	1131106	1647819	809961	463706
549520	1157889	2615542	189131	205341	350517	320856	325736
208919	220697	984896	48974	90350	744767	75017	46167
27070	38103	79967	12682	23024	4232	24851	5993
73786	289673	248761	99528	160848	227931	103088	107792
263023	250214	841575	122942	314849	481647	194060	185562
149173	216650	752430	133572	222093	324591	108643	165365
49581	102577	221676	73251	120445	130509	76436	198244
174094	366273	655563	317724	524848	561406	328780	280466

表3-8 各区（县、市）按产业划分的生产总值（2022年）
Gross Domestic Product Classified by Industries and by Region（2022）

指标	Indicators	全市 Total	海曙区 Haishu	江北区 Jiangbei
地区生产总值	**Gross Domestic Product**	**157042963**	**15012748**	**8603155**
第一产业	Primary Industry	3819926	171793	89439
第二产业	Secondary Industry	74134665	4258353	2710647
第三产业	Tertiary Industry	79088372	10582602	5803069
农林牧渔业	Agriculture, Forestry, Animal Husbandry and Fishery	4003568	180836	94919
工业	Industry	66817224	3378825	2254734
建筑业	Constructions	7427378	881315	459329
批发和零售业	Retail and Wholesale Industries	18705990	1854394	1024611
交通运输、仓储和邮政业	Transportation, Storage and Post	6560725	911848	597515
住宿和餐饮业	Hoteling and Catering	1770828	248614	84236
信息传输、软件和信息技术服务业	Information Transmission, Software and Information Technology Service	2295204	322405	126416
金融业	Financial Industry	12668164	1549621	710946
房地产业	Real Estate Industry	10358438	1314887	775426
租赁和商务服务业	Leasehold and Business Service			
科学研究和技术服务业	Scientific Research and Technology Service			
水利、环境和公共设施管理业	Water Conservancy, Environment and Public Facility Management			
居民服务、修理和其他服务业	Residential Service, Repairing & Maintenance and Other Service			
教育	**Education**			
卫生和社会工作	Health Care and Social Work			
文化、体育和娱乐业	Culture, Sports and Entertainment			
公共管理、社会保障和社会组织	Public Management, Social Security and Social Organizations			

单位：万元 (10000 yuan)

镇海区 Zhenhai	北仑区 Beilun	鄞州区 Yinzhou	奉化区 Fenghua	余姚市 Yuyao	慈溪市 Cixi	宁海县 Ninghai	象山县 Xiangshan
13742923	**26308414**	**27347839**	**9072828**	**15135928**	**25215814**	**9007216**	**7200357**
73187	89240	307279	359780	537583	660105	545151	984458
9549213	13001273	7511622	5473704	8982721	15313453	4364870	2737481
4120523	13217901	19528938	3239344	5615624	9242256	4097195	3478418
76808	94671	332700	374355	566653	685517	567641	1026583
9001851	12335518	6063404	4928526	8442891	14244732	3865601	2057083
555554	697675	1451964	546230	540778	1069614	517652	712301
713488	6094938	3355725	615223	1270991	2135893	884293	586766
506166	1945267	840757	263391	217765	604606	307931	285677
86287	146936	371436	106326	187030	279724	141257	114443
104383	403971	707651	92187	104825	255266	119475	67367
530050	916341	4994059	482881	911735	1577511	505093	424837
660866	815385	2410831	586949	1150178	1477094	794829	462930

表3-9 各区（县、市）历年生产总值（1993-2022年）
Gross Domestic Product by Region（1993-2022）

年份 Year	地区生产总值（GDP） 海曙区 Haishu	江北区 Jiangbei	镇海区 Zhenhai	北仑区 Beilun
1993	48686	80429	242674	339277
1994	71513	113427	331474	463267
1995	91295	145894	431052	641800
1996	110651	170417	526367	760077
1997	129666	191695	599886	876112
1998	145738	202629	646998	995001
1999	158424	222260	738254	1116166
2000	180641	249215	823575	1216294
2001	208072	284411	907231	1401741
2002	236375	328030	1109097	1603120
2003	298420	426195	1285856	1917693
2004	358183	821151	1843957	2340944
2005	2180997	1019034	1914261	2712745
2006	2470987	1213686	1923438	3120567
2007	2870293	1393385	2386386	3774400
2008	3321879	1566272	1528519	4229728
2009	3384788	1601461	3411217	4581760
2010	3841392	1974118	4520688	6279402
2011	4424468	2344211	5700880	6807479
2012	4675192	2664595	5853456	7104425
2013	5064498	2956865	6343101	7788624
2014	5298545	3229047	6405982	12528890
2015	5501335	3954210	7217527	12985568
2016	9407264	4539545	7947386	14087215
2017	10256115	5142969	8991099	16885951
2018	11122090	5877391	9612146	18407425
2019	11758030	6511333	10123173	19803745
2020	12113540	7104945	10301846	20346172
2021	14256160	7991009	12522106	24415155
2022	15012748	8603155	13742923	26308414

注：(1) 海曙区2004年以前为区属口径，2005-2015年为原海曙区口径，2016年以后为新海曙区口径。
(2) 江北区2004年以前为区属口径。
(3) 鄞州区2016年起为新鄞州区口径。
(4) 2016年中烟搬迁至奉化。

Notes:(1) Haishu District was under the jurisdiction of the district before 2004, the former from 2005 to 2015, and the new one after 2016.
(2) Jiangbei District was under the jurisdiction of the district before 2004.
(3) Yinzhou District has adopted the new caliber since 2016.
(4) In 2016,Ningbo cigarette factory of China tobacco company moved to Fenghua.

单位：万元 (10000 yuan)

Gross Domestic Product

鄞州区 Yinzhou	奉化区 Fenghua	余姚市 Yuyao	慈溪市 Cixi	宁海县 Ninghai	象山县 Xiangshan
547059	181515	435727	480074	171622	224600
736368	254753	626039	706881	274011	339300
923776	335178	829673	953238	361600	421500
1078781	395357	1016980	1109172	452943	518000
1171975	431102	1126097	1225145	450106	545800
1243672	462295	1211576	1323248	495598	599900
1346390	506220	1334234	1475464	549806	662700
1548726	590290	1466656	1703490	627532	707500
1737826	656109	1621011	1920934	673962	780600
2007902	775788	1834749	2171658	791109	872600
2427317	935589	2129229	2593673	950834	1008900
2884370	1096366	2531410	3147150	1116576	1163300
3531389	1248225	2996709	3754080	1312445	1346157
4301423	1451339	3587029	4501355	1606102	1575724
5304586	1679726	4237376	5314195	1943372	1927501
6507677	1877501	4884997	6012271	2177708	2204784
7000712	1936409	4921159	6221232	2359377	2354941
8146266	2248707	5706688	7506124	2782974	2708271
9438541	2596451	6667192	8699231	3227011	3206918
10937592	2738975	7170001	9532024	3517758	3424964
12070432	2949567	7582552	10498501	3856213	3693463
12966399	3134865	7948808	11555469	4309934	3886401
13008589	3339493	8023365	12075056	4800626	3916508
16366805	5012040	8869769	13160172	5317914	4376693
18313639	5536458	9891091	15791540	5883419	4646164
20317150	6141113	10809063	17935978	6559795	5149199
22088412	6633075	11616171	19306773	7009576	5501025
22704254	7420090	12290585	20286375	7203179	5895054
25759988	8514695	14433040	23785493	8378775	6699118
27347839	9072828	15135928	25215814	9007216	7200357

表3-10 各区（县、市）历年生产总值指数（1993-2022年）
Indices of Gross Domestic Product by Region（1993–2022）

以上年为100

年份 Year	海曙区 Haishu	江北区 Jiangbei	镇海区 Zhenhai	北仑区 Beilun
1993	121.8	109.8	110.3	112.0
1994	105.4	112.1	119.4	112.9
1995	120.5	109.9	112.4	112.9
1996	117.9	116.3	118.9	119.7
1997	115.0	110.5	113.3	117.5
1998	114.6	109.9	110.3	115.2
1999	111.9	114.8	113.7	112.5
2000	112.9	110.8	106.7	112.6
2001	116.7	112.2	111.3	114.3
2002	116.5	113.5	124.3	115.7
2003	118.1	116.5	112.2	117.7
2004	118.7	156.3	133.0	118.1
2005	112.0	114.1	98.1	112.1
2006	112.5	114.2	96.5	113.8
2007	112.3	108.8	120.0	114.0
2008	110.9	109.1	59.4	110.6
2009	105.7	105.2	111.4	110.6
2010	110.0	115.3	112.4	114.2
2011	108.6	109.8	112.8	111.7
2012	106.9	105.7	104.2	107.7
2013	106.6	109.0	109.6	109.5
2014	105.7	108.1	106.4	109.3
2015	107.6	109.2	108.5	105.1
2016	105.5	113.0	108.1	109.5
2017	106.3	109.9	104.5	112.3
2018	107.0	109.9	103.3	107.3
2019	106.1	108.1	107.1	106.5
2020	102.0	103.7	102.9	103.6
2021	109.3	109.7	107.0	108.1
2022	102.7	104.9	105.9	104.2

注：2016年中烟搬迁至奉化。
Note: In 2016,Ningbo cigarette factory of China tobacco company moved to Fenghua.

Take the data of the Previous Year as 100

鄞州区 Yinzhou	奉化区 Fenghua	余姚市 Yuyao	慈溪市 Cixi	宁海县 Ninghai	象山县 Xiangshan
125. 5	118. 3	127. 6	120. 1	124. 7	135. 4
115. 6	118. 4	119. 3	126. 0	119. 3	123. 9
107. 2	116. 3	114. 0	118. 3	117. 7	111. 2
115. 7	114. 2	120. 2	115. 1	116. 8	119. 3
110. 7	109. 4	113. 7	111. 6	108. 4	107. 8
111. 9	110. 6	112. 2	110. 5	112. 8	114. 2
110. 0	110. 9	110. 9	111. 1	111. 3	112. 4
113. 0	111. 8	110. 5	112. 2	111. 4	110. 3
112. 7	112. 6	110. 0	112. 4	111. 4	111. 9
114. 7	116. 8	112. 3	113. 7	113. 2	112. 7
115. 9	118. 0	114. 8	115. 6	117. 6	114. 8
115. 6	115. 1	116. 3	115. 3	115. 5	111. 1
114. 4	113. 6	114. 2	115. 0	113. 3	113. 1
113. 4	115. 5	114. 7	115. 6	119. 8	114. 5
116. 7	112. 8	114. 4	114. 8	116. 1	116. 8
114. 0	108. 1	109. 0	108. 8	108. 0	110. 3
110. 0	105. 8	108. 2	107. 9	108. 5	107. 6
112. 4	111. 7	112. 7	115. 1	113. 8	110. 2
109. 9	109. 3	110. 9	110. 7	111. 1	109. 5
109. 4	105. 6	108. 8	109. 7	108. 4	106. 1
109. 5	106. 9	107. 0	111. 2	109. 3	108. 3
108. 5	106. 3	108. 4	108. 7	106. 7	108. 3
107. 9	106. 5	107. 4	107. 6	108. 6	107. 2
107. 0	151. 8	107. 0	109. 6	107. 1	105. 0
106. 9	105. 5	107. 4	113. 4	107. 9	106. 1
105. 2	105. 8	107. 8	110. 0	107. 9	106. 8
107. 0	105. 5	107. 9	106. 4	106. 1	105. 6
102. 5	104. 1	105. 1	105. 1	103. 4	101. 9
107. 1	105. 7	109. 1	108. 2	108. 8	108. 3
103. 0	102. 4	101. 9	102. 3	104. 3	105. 2

表3-11 部分年份按支出法计算的生产总值
Gross Domestic Product Calculated with Expenditure Approach in Partial Years

单位：亿元 (100 million yuan)

指标	Indicators	2020	2021	2022
支出法生产总值	**Gross Domestic Product**	**12599. 22**	**14703. 20**	
最终消费	Final Consumption	5462. 74	6161. 32	
居民消费	Resident Consumption	4300. 48	4955. 45	
城镇居民	Urban Resident	3503. 00	4141. 12	
农村居民	Rural Resident	797. 48	814. 33	
政府消费	Government Consumption	1162. 26	1205. 87	
资本形成总额	Total Capital Formation	6302. 80	6706. 33	
固定资本形成总额	Fixed Capital Formation	5568. 62	5719. 21	
存货变动	Stock Change	734. 18	987. 12	
货物和服务净流出	Net Outflows of Goods and Services	833. 68	1835. 55	

注：暂未开展2022年支出法GDP的核算，表3-12同。
Note： GDP accounting of expenditure method in 2022 has not been carried out yet, the same as table 3-12.

表3-12 部分年份按支出法计算的生产总值指数（以上年为100）
Index of Gross Domestic Product Calculated with Expenditure Approach in Partial Years(Preceding Year=100)

指标	Indicators	2020	2021	2022
支出法生产总值	**Gross Domestic Product**	**103. 4**	**108. 2**	
最终消费	Final Consumption	105. 2	107. 0	
居民消费	Resident Consumption	104. 2	108. 5	
城镇居民	Urban Resident	98. 5	111. 0	
农村居民	Rural Resident	138. 6	97. 6	
政府消费	Government Consumption	109. 2	101. 7	
资本形成总额	Total Capital Formation	162. 9	103. 7	
固定资本形成总额	Fixed Capital Formation	143. 4	100. 8	
存货变动	Stock Change	1508. 7	126. 1	
货物和服务净流出	Net Outflows of Goods and Services	34. 9	150. 1	

主要统计指标解释

【国内生产总值（GDP）】指一个国家（或地区）所有常住单位在一定时期内生产活动的最终成果。国内生产总值有三种表现形态，即价值形态、收入形态和产品形态。从价值形态看，它是所有常住单位在一定时期内生产的全部货物和服务价值超过同期中间投入的全部非固定资产货物和服务价值的差额，即所有常住单位的增加值之和；从收入形态看，它是所有常住单位在一定时期内创造并分配给常住单位和非常住单位的初次收入分配之和；从产品形态看，它是所有常住单位在一定时期内最终使用的货物和服务价值与货物和服务净出口价值之和。在实际核算中，国内生产总值有三种计算方法，即生产法、收入法和支出法。三种方法分别从不同的方面反映国内生产总值及其构成。

【三次产业】根据社会生产活动历史发展的顺序对产业结构的划分，产品直接取自自然界的部门为第一产业；对初级产品进行再加工的部门称为第二产业；为生产和消费提供服务的部门称为第三产业。它是世界上通用的产业结构分类，但各国的划分不尽一致。我国的三次产业划分为：

第一产业是指农、林、牧、渔业（不含农、林、牧、渔服务业）。

第二产业是指采矿业（不含开采辅助活动），制造业（不含金属制品、机械和设备修理业），电力、热力、燃气及水生产和供应业，建筑业。

第三产业即服务业，是指除第一产业、第二产业以外的其他行业。

【劳动者报酬】指劳动者因从事生产活动所获得的全部报酬。包括劳动者获得的各种形式的工资、奖金和津贴，既包括货币形式的，也包括实物形式的；还包括劳动者所享受的公费医疗和医药卫生费、上下班交通补贴和单位支付的社会保险费等。

【生产税净额】指生产税减生产补贴后的余额。生产税指政府对生产单位生产、销售和从事经营活动以及因从事生产活动使用某些生产要素（如固定资产、土地、劳动力）所征收的各种税、附加费和规费。生产补贴与生产税相反，指政府对生产单位的单方面收入转移，因此视为负生产税，包括政策亏损补贴、粮食系统价格补贴、外贸企业出口退税收入等。

【固定资产折旧】指一定时期内为弥补固定资产损耗按照核定的固定资产折旧率提取的固定资产折旧，或按国民经济核算统一规定的折旧率虚拟计算的固定资产折旧。它反映了固定资产在当期生产中的转移价值。各类企业和企业化管理的事业单位的固定资产折旧是指实际计提并计入成本费中的折旧费；不计提折旧的政府机关、非企业化管理的事业单位和居民住房的固定资产折旧是按照统一规定的折旧率和固定资产原值计算的虚拟折旧。原则上，固定资产折旧应按固定资产的重置价值计算，但是目前我国尚不具备对全社会固定资产进行重估价的基础，所以暂时只能采用上述办法。

【营业盈余】指常住单位创造的增加值扣除劳动者报酬、生产税净额和固定资产折旧后的余额。它相当于企业的营业利润加上生产补贴，但要扣除从利润中开支的工资和福利等。

【支出法国内生产总值】指一个国家(或地区)所有常住单位在一定时期内用于最终消费、资本形成总额，以及货物和服务的净出口总额，它反映本期生产的国内生产总值的使用及构成。

【最终消费】指常住单位在一定时期内对于货物和服务的全部最终消费支出，也就是常住单位为满足物质、文化和精神生活的需要，从本国经济领土和国外购买的货物和服务的支出；不包括非常住单位在本国经济领土内的消费支出。最终消费分为居民消费和政府消费。

【资本形成总额】指常住单位在一定时期内获得的减去处置的固定资产加存货的变动，包括固定资本形成总额和存货增加。

Explanatory Notes on Main Statistical Indicators

【Gross Domestic Product (GDP)】 refers to the final products of all resident units in a country (or a region) during a certain period of time. Gross domestic product is expressed in three different forms, i.e. value, income, and products respectively. The form of value refers to the total value of all products and services produced by all resident units during a certain period of time ,minus total value of intimidate input of materials and services of the nature of non–fixed assets or the summation of the value–added of all resident units; the form of income includes all the income created by all resident units and distributed primarily to all resident and non–resident units; the form of products refers to the value of all final goods and services for final use by all resident units plus the value of net exports of goods and services during a given period of time. In the practice of national accounting, gross domestic product is calculated with three approaches, i.e. production approach, income approach, and expenditure approach, which reflect gross domestic product and its composition from different aspects.

【Three Industries Industry】 structure has been classified according to the historical sequence of development. Primary industry refers to extraction of natural resources; secondary industry involves processing of primary products; and tertiary industry provides services of various kinds for production and consumption. The above classification is universal although it various to some extent from country to country. Industry in China comprises;

The primary industry refers to agriculture, forestry, animal husbandry and fishery (excluding agriculture, forestry, animal husbandry and Fishery Services).

The secondary industry refers to mining (excluding mining auxiliary activities), manufacturing (excluding metal products, machinery and equipment repair), power, heat, gas and water production and supply, and construction.

The tertiary industry, namely the service industry, refers to other industries except the primary industry and the secondary industry.

【Laborers' Remuneration】 refers to the whole payment of various forms earned by the laborers from the productive activities they are engaged in. It includes wages, bonuses and allowances the laborers earned in monetary form and in kind. It also includes the free medical services provided to the laborers and the medicine expenses, traffic subsidies and social insurance fee paid by the laborers' working units for them.

【Net Taxes on Production】 refers to the residual of the taxes on production minus the subsidies on production. The taxes on production refers to the various taxes, extra charges and fees levied on the production units on their production, sale and business activities as well as on some factors of production, such as fixed assets, land and labor force, used in the production activities they are engaged in. In contrast to the taxes on production, the subsidies on production refer to the unilateral transfer of part of the government' s revenue to the production units and is therefore regarded as negative taxes on production. They include subsidies on the loss due to implementation of government policies, price subsidies to the grain institutions, foreign trade corporations receipts from drawback, etc.

【Depreciation of Fixed Assets】 refers to the depreciation of fixed assets of a given period, drawn in accordance with the stipulated depreciation rate for the purpose of compensating the wear loss of the fixed assets or the depreciation of fixed assets calculated in a fictitious way in accordance with the stipulated unified depreciation rate in the national economic accounting system. It reflects the value of transfer of the fixed assets in the production of the current period. The depreciation of fixed assets in various enterprises and institutions managed as enterprises refers to the depreciation expenses actually drawn and calculated as part of the cost. In government agencies and institutions not managed as enterprises which do not draw the depreciation expenses, as well as for the houses of residents, the depreciation of fixed assets is the imputed depreciation, which is calculated in accordance with the stipulated unified depreciation rate. In principle, the depreciation of fixed assets should be calculated on the basis of the re–purchased value of the fixed assets. However, there is no actual condition to re–evaluate all the fixed assets in China. Therefore, the above–mentioned methods are temporarily adopted at present.

【Operating Surplus】 refers to the balance of the value added created by the resident units deducting the laborers' remuneration, net taxes on production and the depreciation of fixed assets. It is equivalent to the business profit of the enterprises plus subsidies on production, but the wages and welfare expenses paid from the profits should be deducted.

【GDP Calculated with Expenditure Approach】 refers to total expenditure on final consumption, total capital formation and net export of goods and services by resident units of a country in a certain period of time. It reflects the composition of GDP by its use.

【Final Consumption】 refers to the total expenditure of resident units on final consumption of goods and services in a certain period, namely the expenditure of the resident units for purchases of goods and services from domestic economic territory and abroad to meet the requirements of material, cultural and spiritual life. It excludes the expenditure of non–resident units on consumption in the economic territory of the country. The final consumption is classified into household consumption and government consumption.

【Total Capital Formation】refers to the fixed assets acquired minus those disposed and the change in inventory, including the total fixed assets formation and the increase in inventory.

NINGBO
2023
Statistical Yearbook

4
CHAPTER

第四篇

财政、金融、保险、证券

FINANCE,BANKING, INSURANCE AND SECURITIES

财政、金融、保险、证券
Price Index and People's Livelihood

主要统计指标
Major Statistics Indicators

2022年全市财政总收入	Total Financial Revenue	3358.63	亿元	100 million yuan
比上年增长	Increase Over Last Year	2.9	%	
2022年一般公共预算收入	General Public Budget Revenue	1680. 23	亿元	100 million yuan
比上年增长	Increase Over Last Year	-2. 5	%	
2022年一般公共预算支出	General Public Financial Budget Expenditure	2187. 81	亿元	100 million yuan
比上年增长	Increase Over Last Year	12. 5	%	
2022年金融机构本外币存款余额	Total Deposits in RMB and Foreign Currency	31302. 66	亿元	100 million yuan
比上年增长	Increase Over Last Year	15. 0	%	
2022年本外币住户存款余额	Household Savings Deposits in RMB and Foreign Cu	11841. 58	亿元	100 million yuan
比上年增长	Increase Over Last Year	25. 0	%	
2022年金融机构本外币贷款余额	Total Loans in RMB and Foreign Currency	32986. 07	亿元	100 million yuan
比上年增长	Increase Over Last Year	13. 57	%	
2022年保费收入	Premiums	416. 09	亿元	100 million yuan
比上年增长	Increase Over Last Year	10. 9	%	
2022年赔付支出	Claim and Payment	163. 42	亿元	100 million yuan
比上年增长	Increase Over Last Year	2. 3	%	
2022年证券成交总额	Total Negotiable Securities Turnover	120020. 28	亿元	100 million yuan
比上年增长	Increase Over Last Year	-2. 7	%	

表4-1 历年公共财政预算收入及支出情况
The Public Fiscal Budget Revenue and Expenditure Over Years

单位：万元（10000 yuan）

年份 Year	财政总收入 Financial Revenue	一般公共预算收入 General Public Budget Revenue	一般公共预算支出 General Public Fiscal Budget Expenditure
1978	49697		
1979	48860		
1980	56290		
1981	65432		
1982	71546		
1983	80801		
1984	93318		
1985	91237		
1986	102264		
1987	113351		
1988	133395		
1989	152751		
1990	158910		
1991	177875		
1992	198354		
1993	282429		
1994	420202		
1995	531135		
1996	659529		
1997	750412		
1998	876351		
1999	1039976		
2000	1431511	643518	839068
2001	1903064	991088	1162797
2002	2583984	1118368	1452639
2003	3250078	1394092	1802609
2004	4009592	1517489	2159498
2005	4664968	2123797	2647749
2006	5611702	2573799	2926969
2007	7239222	3291218	3710400
2008	8109020	3903874	4394083
2009	9662496	4327676	5060788
2010	11717470	5309278	6007447
2011	14317563	6575531	7507223
2012	15365101	7255003	8284437
2013	16511797	7928080	9398939
2014	17908862	8606120	10008563
2015	20727267	10064065	12526362
2016	21457622	11145409	12892601
2017	24158286	12452880	14106049
2018	26553064	13796865	15941000
2019	27849497	14685072	17678895
2020	28355977	15108432	17420878
2021	32643853	17231388	19444158
2022	33586340	16802309	21878133

注：本表至4-2表数据来自宁波市财政局。根据新修改的《预算法》，对财政收入的指标表述进行了规范，原“地方财政收入”改名为“一般公共预算收入”，具体统计口径保持不变。

Note:Data from Tables 4-1 to 4-2 are obtained from Finance Bureau of Ningbo."According to newly modified Budget Law, the expression of fiscal revenue was regulated as the original “local financial revenue” was changed to “general public budget revenue”, with the specific statistical caliber unchanged.

表4-2 各区（县、市）财政收入及支出情况(2022年)
Basic Statistics on Financial Revenue by Region(2022)

指标	Indicators	全市 Total	市区 Urban District	海曙区 Haishu
一、财政总收入	**Total Financial Revenue**	**33586340**	**25916696**	**2076301**
一般公共预算收入	General Public Budget Revenue	16802309	12314741	1170566
1. 税收收入小计	Total Tax Revenue	13825149	10357241	1078622
2. 非税收收入小计	Total non – Tax Revenue	2977160	1957500	91944
二、一般公共预算支出	**General Public Fiscal Budget Expenditure**	**21878133**	**15838402**	**1383524**
一般公共服务	General Public Service	1791137	1239275	227611
住房保障	Housing security	682642	509962	85341
教育	Education	2987893	1926968	231406
科学技术	Science and Technology	1509955	952886	62806
社会保障和就业	Social Security and Reemployment	2375970	1516464	150312
卫生健康	Health Care	1925322	1296168	129845
节能环保	Energy Saving and Environmental Protection	312371	270743	6678
城乡社区服务	Community Service in Urban and Rural Areas	3032076	2612004	177375

单位：万元(10000 yuan)

江北区 Jiangbei	镇海区 Zhenhai	北仑区 Beilun	鄞州区 Yinzhou	奉化区 Fenghua	余姚市 Yuyao	慈溪市 Cixi	宁海县 Ninghai	象山县 Xiangshan
1775273	**1292601**	**9053502**	**4678678**	**1071463**	**2057850**	**3640792**	**970993**	**1000009**
1019419	744025	4241297	2795978	692970	1207431	2047306	624665	608166
926614	592138	3863774	2500937	545152	943435	1639164	451722	433587
92805	151887	377523	295041	147818	263996	408142	172943	174579
945557	**1075739**	**3718022**	**2697215**	**1073185**	**1489567**	**2508550**	**1024918**	**1016696**
93076	93732	182200	224881	156137	123870	204527	94840	128625
56406	40833	49129	114948	32406	25562	82192	34912	30014
130532	162807	233990	379663	162851	272115	450000	181312	157498
49545	49180	362004	212085	57281	83886	385492	31178	56513
104806	139781	250804	347980	189253	246801	245596	175852	191257
71021	99884	178642	301351	74648	176401	229893	129226	93634
6920	6964	172777	21454	4912	20465	11716	4196	5251
123064	241664	415265	435012	76830	77789	234581	65537	42165

表4-3 历年金融机构人民币存贷款与现金收支情况

Savings Deposits and Loans Balances of Financial Institutions and Cash Revenue and Expenditures Over the Years(RMB)

单位：万元 (10000 yuan)

年份 Year	存款余额 Deposits Balance	#住户存款 household Savings	贷款余额 Loans Balance	现金收入 Cash Income	现金支出 Cash Expenditure	货币投放（+）回笼（-） Currency Issues (+) or Cash Withdrawal(-)
1978	50194	14997	68843	92387	101326	8939
1979	64379	20612	78939	119923	130544	10621
1980	90536	28781	107339	159955	174339	14384
1981	107253	34418	114394	187306	198061	10755
1982	130697	46298	130617	216530	227547	11017
1983	154150	60536	146636	277321	288711	11390
1984	207363	81558	242546	356422	392814	36392
1985	266510	109853	304823	522442	562304	39862
1986	354390	149451	414921	640814	679516	38702
1987	445081	199524	522160	860563	926247	65684
1988	522116	215357	643234	1212594	1328827	116233
1989	639228	317572	765704	1344442	1415310	70868
1990	899295	461220	973946	1044032	1102545	58513
1991	1180588	605796	1227009	1321446	1401416	79970
1992	1605229	792466	1603689	1957225	2099612	142387
1993	2012813	979740	2116122	3295921	3441608	145687
1994	2972601	1468634	2671174	4949086	5199010	249924
1995	4546806	2094162	3892271	7121855	7452530	330675
1996	5981440	2846051	5240845	9312625	9789622	476997
1997	7172242	3644769	5747533	12202712	12646470	443758
1998	8552754	4596343	6700817	19733593	20136905	403312
1999	10080232	5296350	7734820	24090235	24591240	501005
2000	11729400	5860592	8831213	30467325	31088353	621028
2001	14445304	6994639	10515601	36286694	37062049	775355
2002	19062375	8623909	14794722	49240318	50379541	1139223
2003	26290346	10596339	21027772	68390220	69703625	1313405
2004	30917954	12089813	24836090	90446530	91895140	1448610
2005	37919362	14588012	29597759	100679426	102368573	1689147
2006	45734811	17520388	37274957	121414154	123296128	1881974
2007	51772379	18274856	47359146	153033733	155234259	2200526
2008	62164580	23670651	56727416	155387621	157911068	2523447
2009	80839363	28695587	74248698	143230611	145798647	2568037
2010	95520308	32822564	90006170	158421425	161613115	3191690
2011	104359176	36662324	102099855			
2012	116023188	41759634	113003187			
2013	127405215	45623634	124932759			
2014	133074057	47803126	136106069			
2015	154002364	53028406	149669245			
2016	161960114	56894416	158067586			
2017	173925325	59026776	171252864			
2018	185325127	65612648	193411109			
2019	202908596	74754684	217742284			
2020	231666786	85220707	250519770			
2021	261876551	93873063	285131589			
2022	302037454	117497481	323772756			

注：（1）本表至4-7表数据来自中国人民银行宁波中心支行，2011年现金收支统计制度取消。
（2）根据人民银行总行调整，2015年起城乡居民储蓄变更为住户存款。

Notes: (1) Data from Tables 4-3 to 4-7 are obtained from Central Subbranch of Ningbo of The People's Bank of China. Cancel the cash income and expenditure statistics system in 2011.
(2) According to the people's Bank of the head office to adjust, 2015 from urban and rural residents to change the household savings.

表4-4 金融机构人民币信贷资金来源主要指标(2022年)
Main Indicators of Credit Funds of Financial Institutions-sources of Funds (RMB)(2022)

(年末余额）单位：万元（year-end)(10000 yuan)

指标	Indicators	2022
资金来源总计	**Total capital source**	**454570085**
一、各项存款	Total deposits	302037454
（一）境内存款	Domestic deposits	301121849
1. 住户存款	Household deposits	117497481
（1）活期存款	Current deposit	38499397
（2）定期及其他存款	Fixed deposit and other deposits	78998084
其中：结构性存款	Among: Structural deposits	1979030
保证金存款	Margin deposit for security	300513
2. 非金融企业存款	Non-financial business deposit	109354501
（1）活期存款	Current deposit	31124507
（2）定期及其他存款	Fixed deposit and other deposits	78229995
其中：结构性存款	Among:Structural deposits	4904352
保证金存款	Margin deposit for security	13987420
3. 机关团体存款	Institution and group deposits	35726543
4. 财政性存款	Fiscal deposit	10946052
5. 非银行业金融机构存款	Non-banking financial institutions deposits	27597272
（二）境外存款	Overseas deposits	915605
二、金融债券	Financial bond	12684182
其中：境外发行	Among: overseas issuance	
三、卖出回购资产	Repurchased assets sales	498092
四、借款及非银行业金融机构拆入	Loan and money borrowed from financial institutions	563895
五、联行往来（净）	Inter - branches accounts (net)	86869152
六、应付及暂收款	Payables and suspense credits	8164469
七、各项准备	Reserve	8767651
八、所有者权益	Owner's equity	25968215
其中：实收资本	Among: Paid-up capital	5725364
九、其他	Others	9016977

注：本表根据人民银行信贷收支年报格式进行相应调整。
Note: this sheet shall be adjusted according to the annual format of bank credit receipts and payments by People's Bank of China

表4-5 金融机构人民币信贷资金运用主要指标(2022年)
Main Indicators of Credit Funds of Financial Institutions-use of Funds (RMB)(2022)

(年末余额）单位：万元（year-end)(10000 yuan)

指标	Indicators	2022
资金运用总计	**Total application of funds**	**454570085**
一、各项贷款	All loans	323772756
（一）境内贷款	Domestic loan	323712143
1. 住户贷款	Household loans	115373548
（1）短期贷款	Short-term loan	33597839
消费贷款	Consumption loan	16068928
经营贷款	Business loan	17528912
（2）中长期贷款	Medium and long term loan	81775709
消费贷款	Consumption loan	70268133
经营贷款	Business loan	11507576
2. 企（事）业单位贷款	Non-financial business and institution and group loans	208290595
（1）短期贷款	Short-term loan	77205061
（2）中长期贷款	Medium and long term loan	100448964
（3）票据融资	Bill financing	20678276
（4）融资租赁	Finance lease	9493921
（5）各项垫款	Monies advanced	464373
3. 非银行业金融机构贷款	Non-banking financial institutions loans	48000
（二）境外贷款	Overseas loan	60613
二、债券投资	Bond investment	76682591
其中：境外债券	Among: overseas bond	94908
三、股权及其他投资	Stock rights and other investments	47353098
四、买入返售资产	Purchase of resold assets	1424047
五、存放非银行业金融机构款项	Deposits in non-banking financial institution	579975
六、联行往来（净）	Inter-branches accounts (net)	
其中：境内存放二级准备金	Among: secondary reserve deposited domestically	1108033
七、金银占款	Funds outstanding for gold and silver	
八、中央银行外汇占款	Foreign exchange trading	
九、应收及预付款	Receivables and advance payment	2676574
十、投资性房地产	Investment real estate	3451
十一、固定资产	Fixed assets	2077594

表4-6 各县（市）金融机构人民币存贷款情况（2022年）
Savings Deposits and Loans Balances of Financial Institutions by Region(RMB)(2022)

单位：万元（10000 yuan）

地区	Region	存款余额 Deposits	其中 of Which：非金融企业存款 Non-financial business deposits	其中 of Which：住户存款 Household deposits	其中：活期存款 Among: current deposits	贷款余额 Loans	其中 of Which：企(事)业单位贷款 Loans from enterprises (Institutions)	其中 of Which：住户贷款 Residents loans
全市	**Total**	**302037454**	**109354501**	**117497481**	**38499397**	**323772756**	**208290595**	**115373548**
市区	Urban Districts	216282163	82866462	69519577	22393629	236370910	149400436	86876131
余姚市	Yuyao	26182098	8067503	15250007	4586972	22185111	15589847	6594367
慈溪市	Cixi	39506954	11312510	22344662	6791235	36412497	24475581	11933656
宁海县	Ninghai	10651522	4021443	5220180	2340448	15584235	10556350	5027773
象山县	Xiangshan	9414715	3086583	5163054	2387113	13220003	8268381	4941621

注：（1）市区包括海曙区、江北区、镇海区、北仑区、鄞州区和奉化区。
（2）2015年人民银行对存贷款统计口径进行调整，本表根据人民银行信贷收支年报格式做了相应调整。
Notes：（1）Urban districts include Haishu, Jiangbei, Zhenhai, Beilun, Yinzhou and Fenghua.
（2）In 2015, The People's bank of China adjusted the statistical specification of loans and deposits, this sheet shall be adjusted according to the annual format of bank credit receipts and payments by People's Bank of China.

表4-7 部分年份金融机构本外币存贷款情况
Savings Deposits and Loans Balances of Financial Institutions in Partial Years (in RMB and Foreign Currency)

单位：万元（10000 yuan）

指标	Indicators	2019	2020	2021	2022
本外币存款余额	**Total Deposits in RMB and Foreign Currency**	**208578114**	**239881825**	**272288682**	**313026567**
#人民币	RMB	202908596	231666786	261876551	302037454
外币	Foreign Currency	812694	1259029	1633096	1577853
#住户存款	Household Deposits in RMB and Foreign Currency	75669406	86110746	94703909	118415844
本外币贷款余额	**Total Loans in RMB and Foreign Currency**	**221872366**	**254516344**	**290454746**	**329860745**
#人民币	RMB	217742284	250519770	285131589	323772756
外币	Foreign Currency	592025	612511	834913	874133

表4-8 保险公司业务经济技术指标（2022年）
Economic and Technical Indicators of Insurance Companies(2022)

单位：万元（10000 yuan）

指标	Indicators	保费收入 Premiums 绝对量 Total	保费收入 Premiums 同比增长(%) Growth Rate(%)	赔付支出 Claim and Payment 绝对量 Total	赔付支出 Claim and Payment 同比增长(%) Growth Rate(%)
合计	**Total**	**4160922**	**10. 93**	**1634170**	**2. 29**
财产险	Property Insurance	1906465	8. 52	1177249	-2. 23
#机动车辆保险	Motor Vehicle Insurance	1246097	8. 29	848643	3. 30
人身险	Life Insurance	2254457	13. 05	456921	16. 12
寿险	Life insurance	1707250	18. 08	274861	22. 70
健康险	Health insurance	438851	1. 01	146042	5. 40
人身意外伤害险	Personal Accident Insurance	108357	-4. 86	36018	16. 49
按公司类别分	**Of Which**				
财产保险公司	**PropertyInsuranceCompanies**	**2062536**	**7. 86**	**1248854**	**-1. 27**
财产险	Property Insurance	1906465	8. 52	1177249	-2. 23
#机动车辆保险	Motor Vehicle Insurance	1246097	8. 29	848643	3. 30
人身险	Life Insurance	156071	0. 37	71606	17. 75
健康险	Health insurance	88181	3. 09	50020	16. 14
人身意外伤害险	Personal Accident Insurance	67890	-2. 95	21585	21. 66
人寿保险公司	**Property Insurance Companies**	**2098386**	**14. 12**	**385315**	**15. 83**
人身险	Life Insurance	2098386	14. 12	385315	15. 83
寿险	Life insurance	1707250	18. 08	274861	22. 70
健康险	Health insurance	350670	0. 50	96022	0. 56
人身意外伤害险	Personal Accident Insurance	40467	-7. 91	14432	9. 53

注：（1）本表数据来自于中国银行保险监督管理委员会宁波监管局。
（2）因部分机构正在进行风险处置，行业汇总数据口径暂不包括这部分机构。

Notes:(1)Data in this table are obtained from China Insurance Regulatory Commission Ningbo Bureau.
(2)As some institutions are in the process of risk disposal, the industry summary data does not include these institutions for the time being.

表4-9 部分年份保险业务情况
Conditions of Insurance Business in Partial Years

单位：亿元（100 million yuan）

指标	Indicators	2016	2017	2018	2019	2020	2021	2022
保费收入	**Premiums**	**257.56**	**302.95**	**320.59**	**375.83**	**390.72**	**375.10**	**416.09**
财产险	Property Insurance	127.22	138.93	152.84	165.55	174.12	175.68	190.65
人身险	Life Insurance	130.34	164.02	167.75	210.28	216.59	199.42	225.45
赔付支出	**Claim and Payment**	**115.35**	**113.32**	**130.08**	**147.70**	**148.70**	**159.75**	**163.42**
财产险	Property Insurance	78.97	80.70	96.25	108.60	109.36	120.41	117.72
人身险	Life Insurance	36.38	32.62	33.83	39.11	39.34	39.35	45.69

注：2011年起，保险业采用新会计准则二号解释的新口径。
Note：From 2011,the insurance industry in accordance with the new accouting standards new diameter calculation.

表4-10 证券市场基本情况（2022年）
Basic Statistics on Securities Markets(2022)

指标	单位	Indicators	Unit	绝对量 Total	比上年增长(%) Growth Rate(%)
上市公司总家数	家	Total Listed Companies (A Share and H Share)	Unit	114	6.54
#A股上市公司	家	A Share Companies	Unit	114	6.54
A股上市公司总股本	亿股	Total Issued Capital of Listed Companies (A Share)	100 million shares	928.40	10.70
A股上市公司总市值	亿元	Total Market Capitalization of Listed Companies (A Share)	100 million yuan	13798.18	-7.02
境内证券市场融资额	亿元	Total Financing on Securities Markets in Mainland	100 million yuan	972.72	-2.52
证券成交总额	亿元	Total Negotiable Securities Turnover	100 million yuan	120020.28	-2.71
#股票和基金	亿元	Stock and Fund	100 million yuan	65157.91	-14.80
证券客户交易结算资金余额	亿元	Total Exchange and Settlement Capital of Securities Customer	100 million yuan	252.79	3.20
指定与托管证券市值	亿元	Securities Market Capitalization of Appointment and Trusteeship	100 million yuan	12652.39	7.16
证券投资者股票账户数	万户	Total Stock Investors	10000 accounts	285.99	10.15
证券公司分支机构利润总额	亿元	Total Profits of Branch of Securities Company	100 million yuan	4.42	-41.21
期货代理交易量	万手	Futures Trading Volume	10000 pieces	11153.99	-1.31
期货代理交易额	亿元	Futres Agency Turnover	100 million yuan	72733.53	-2.17
期货保证金余额	亿元	Futures Margin Amount	100 million yuan	138.91	31.78
期货投资者开户数	万户	Total Future Investors	10000 accounts	5.96	9.36

注：本表数据来自于中国证券监督管理委员会宁波监管局。
Note:Data in this table are obtained from China Securities Regulatory Commission Ningbo Bureau.

表4-11 银行业分支机构及人员数（2022年）
Branches and Personnel of the Banking Sector(2022)

单位：家（Unit）

行列名称	Rank name	法人 Corporation	分行（分公司）Branch	支行 Subbranch	分理处（储蓄所）Saving Branch	机构小计 Total	人员数（人）Employee (Person)
政策性银行合计	**Policy Bank**		**3**	**8**		**11**	**411**
国家开发银行	China Development Bank		1			1	157
进出口银行	Export－Import Bank		1			1	73
农业发展银行	Agricultural Development Bank of China		1	8		9	181
大型银行合计	**State－owned Commercial Bank**		**22**	**640**	**260**	**922**	**17990**
工商银行	Industrial and Commercial Bank of China		5	156	1	162	4027
农业银行	Agricultural Bank of China		6	154	11	171	3942
中国银行	Bank of China		6	113		119	3093
建设银行	China Constuction Bank		3	123	2	128	3272
交通银行	Bank of Communications		1	40		41	987
邮储银行	Postal Savings Bank of China		1	54	246	301	2669
股份制商业银行合计	**Joint－stock Commercial Bank**		**12**	**254**		**266**	**7562**
中信银行	China CITIC Bank		1	28		29	867
光大银行	China Everbright Bank Co.,Ltd.		1	33		34	726
华夏银行	Huaxia Bank		1	10		11	313
广发银行	China Guangfa Bank		1	17		18	498
平安银行	Ping An Bank Co.,Ltd		1	16		17	546
招商银行	China Merchants Bank		1	26		27	1075
浦发银行	Shanghai Pudong Development Bank		1	29		30	1005
兴业银行	Industrial Bank Co., Ltd.		1	28		29	688
民生银行	China Minsheng Bank Co., Ltd.		1	43		44	788
浙商银行	China Zheshang Bank Co., Ltd.		1	17		18	701
恒丰银行	EverGrowing Bank Co.,Ltd		1	6		7	257
渤海银行	China Bohai Bank		1	1		2	98
城市商业银行合计	**City Commercial Bank**	**3**	**10**	**383**		**396**	**14639**
宁波银行	Bank of Ningbo	1		245		246	9270
宁波通商银行	Ningbo Commerce Bank Company Limited	1		8		9	795

表4-11 续表 Continued　　单位：家（Unit）

行列名称	Rank name	法人 Corporation	分行（分公司）Branch	支行 Subbranch	分理处（储蓄所）Saving Branch	机构小计 Total	人员数（人）Employee (Person)
宁波东海银行	Ningbo Donghai Bank		1	11		12	445
上海银行	Shanghai Bank		1	10		11	426
徽商银行	Huishang Bank		1	15		16	254
温州银行	Wenzhou Bank		1	7		8	233
泰隆银行	Zhejiang Tailong Commercial Bank		1	32		33	951
临商银行	Linshang Bank		1	6		7	293
杭州银行	Bank of Hangzhou		1	10		11	540
民泰银行	Zhejiang Mintai Commercial Bank		1	10		11	362
稠州银行	Zhejiang Chouzhou Commercial Bank		1	8		9	298
台州银行	Taizhou Bank		1	19		20	518
北京银行	Bank of Beijing		1	2		3	254
农村中小金融机构合计	**Rural Small and Medium Financial Institutions**	**21**		**210**	**467**	**698**	**8145**
农村合作金融机构合计	Rural Cooperative Financial Institutions	9		189	460	658	7486
村镇银行合计	Village Banks combined	12		21	7	40	659
非银行金融机构合计	**Non-bank Financial Institutions**	**3**	**1**			**4**	**545**
信托投资公司	Trust and Investment Corporation	1				1	72
财务公司	Finance Company	1				1	48
租赁公司	Leasing Company	1	1			2	425
外资银行合计	**Foreign Bank**		**7**	**2**		**9**	**159**
恒生银行（中国）	Hang Seng Bank(China)		1			1	13
汇丰银行（中国）	HSBCBank (China)		1	1		2	44
渣打银行（中国）	Standard Chartered Bank (China)		1	1		2	32
东亚银行（中国）	The Bank of East Asia Limited		1			1	8
兆丰银行	Mega Bank		1			1	26
富邦华一银行	Fubon Bank		1			1	17
首都银行	Metrobank		1			1	19
宁波市辖合计	**Ningbo governs combined**	**27**	**55**	**1497**	**727**	**2306**	**49451**

注：（1）本表数据来自国家金融监督管理总局宁波监管局。
（2）本表数据未包含宁银理财。

Notes:（1）Data in this table are obtained from China Banking Regulatory Commission Ningbo Regulatory Bureau.
（2）The data in this table does not include Ningyin Wealth Management.

主要统计指标解释

【财政收入】国家财政参与社会产品分配所取得收入，是实现国家职能的财力保证。财政收入包括的内容几经变化，目前主要包括：

(1)各项税收 包括增值税、营业税、消费税、土地增值税、城市维护建设税、资源税、城市土地使用税、印花税、固定资产投资方向调节税、个人所得税、企业所得税、关税、农牧业税和耕地占用税等。

(2)专项收入 包括征收排污费、征收城市水资源费收入，教育费附加收入等。

(3)其他收入 包括基本建设贷款归还收入、国家能源交通重点建设基金收入、国家预算调节基金等。

(4)国有企业计划亏损补贴 这项为负收入，冲减财政收入。

【财政支出】国家财政将筹集起来的资金进行分配使用，以满足经济建设和各项事业的需要，主要包括（2007年支出项目作过调整）：

(1)基本建设支出

(2)企业挖潜改造资金

(3)地质勘探费用

(4)科技三项费用

(5)支援农村生产支出

(6)农林水利气象等部门的事业费用

(7)工业交通商业等部门的事业费

(8)文教科学卫生事业费

(9)抚恤和社会福利救济费

(10)国防支出

(11)行政管理费

(12)价格补贴支出

【存款】企业、机关、团体或居民根据可以收回的原则，把货币资金存入银行或其他信用机构保管并取得一定利息的一种信用活动形式。根据存款对象的不同可划分为企业存款、财政存款、机关团体存款、基本建设存款、城镇储蓄存款、农村存款等科目。它是银行信贷资金的主要来源。

【贷款】银行或其他信用机构根据必须归还的原则，按一定利率，为企业、个人等提供资金的一种信用活动形式。我国银行贷款分为流动资金贷款、固定资产贷款、城乡个体工商户贷款以农业贷款等科目。

【承保额】又叫保险金额。它是保险人员对被保险人负提损失补偿或约定给付的金额。它是保险合同上的最高责任额，也是计算保费的依据。

【保费】又叫保险费。是保险人根据保险合同的有关规定，为被保险人取得因约定危险事故发生所造成的经济损失补偿(或给付)权利，付给保险人的代价。包括财产险和人身险储金收入。

【赔款】保险事故发生后，经查证确属保险责任范围以内的保险标的损失，保险人根据保险合同的规定履行赔偿义务，给与被保险人的款项叫做赔款。赔款可以分为已决赔款和未决赔款两种。

Explanatory Notes on Main Statistical Indicators

【Government Revenue】 refers to the revenue of government finance by means of participating the distribution of the social products, which is the financial resources for ensuring the government to function. The contents of government revenue have been changed several times. Now it includes the following main items:

(1) Various tax revenue, including value added tax, business tax, consumption tax, land value added tax, tax on city maintenance and construction, resources tax, tax on the urban land, stamp tax, tax on the adjustment of orientation of investment in the fixed assets, personal income tax, tariff, tax on agriculture and animal husbandry and tax on occupation of cultivated land, etc.

(2) Special revenues, including revenue collected from imposing fee on sewage treatment, revenue collected from imposing fee on urban water resources, and extra–charges for educations, etc.

(3) Other revenues, including revenue from the re–payment of capital construction loan, the funds for the state key construction projects in energy industry and transportation, and the funds for state budget adjustment, etc.

(4) Planned subsidies for the losses of the state–=owned enterprises. This is an item of negative revenue, used to eat up part of the government revenue.

【Government Expenditure】 refers to the distribution and use of the funds the government finance has raised, so as to meet the needs of economic construction and various causes. It included the following main items (The items have changed from the year of 2007):

(1) Expenditure for capital construction

(2) Innovation funds of the enterprises

(3) Geological prospecting expenses

(4) Expenditures for science and technology promotion

(5) Expenditure for supporting rural production

(6) Operating expenses of departments of farming, forestry, water conservancy and meteorology etc.

(7) Operating expenses of departments of industry, transport and commerce

(8) Operating expenses of departments of culture, education, science and public health

(9) Pension for the disabled or the families of the bereaved and relief funds for social welfare

(10) Expenditures for national defense

(11) Administrative expenses

(12) Expenditure for price subsidies

【Deposit】 is a form a of credit by which enterprises, institutions, organizations or residents can put money into banks and other credit institutions for safekeeping and interest earning under the principle of free withdrawal. According to different depositors, deposits are divided into enterprise deposits, deposits of government agencies and institutions, capital construction deposits, urban savings deposits, rural deposits and other deposits. Deposits are major sources of the credit funds of banks.

【Loan】 is a form a of credit by which banks and other institutions provide funds at a certain interest rate to enterprise sand individuals in light of the principle of unconditional re–payment. Loans from Chinese banks include circulating capital loans, fixed assets loans, loans to urban and rural individuals engaged in industrial and commercial business and agricultural loans.

【Amount Insured】 refers to the amount of compensation for loss or agreed sum of money to be paid by the insurer to the insurant. It is the maximum amount of liabilities written in the insurance contract and is also used as a basis to calculate the premium.

【Premium】 is the fee paid by the insurant based on a proportion of the benefit he or she may get from the insurance plus the insurance value. It includes the income from the deposit of property insurance and personal insurance.

【Settled Claim】 is the compensation paid by the insurer to the insurant in accordance with the insurance contract for the loss which has been checked and found to be in the range of liability of insurance after an accident has happened to the insured property or to a person who has insured for his life. It is further divided into settled and unsettled claim.

NINGBO 2023 Statistical Yearbook

5 CHAPTER

第五篇

物价指数和人民生活

PRICES INDEX AND PEOPLE'S LIVELIHOOD

物价指数和人民生活
Prices Index and People's Livelihood

主要统计指标
Major Statistics Indicators

以上年价格为 100	The Price of Preceding Year is Taken as 100			
2022年市区居民消费价格指数	Consumer Price Index in Urban Area	102. 3		
2022年市区商品零售价格指数	Retail Price Index in Urban Area	104. 1		
2022年工业生产者出厂价格指数	Industrial Producer Ex – factory Price Index	105. 3		
2022年工业生产者购进价格指数	Industrial Producer Purchase Price Index	110. 8		
2022年城镇居民人均可支配收入	Per Capital Disposable Income of Urban Resident	76690	元	yuan
2022年城镇居民人均消费支出	Per Capita Living Expenditure of Urban Resident	47916	元	yuan
2022年农村居民人均可支配收入	Per Capital Net Income of Rural Resident	45487	元	yuan
2022年农村居民人均消费支出	Per Capita Living Expenditures of Rural Resident	29514	元	yuan

表5-1 市区居民消费价格指数及商品零售价格指数(以上年价格为100)
Consumer Price Indices and Retail Price Indices in Urban Area(Preceding Year=100)

年份 Year	各年以上年价格为100（The Price of Preceding Year is Taken as 100）		
	居民消费价格指数 General Consumer Price Index	#服务 Service	商品零售价格指数 Retail Price Index
1978	100.0	104.4	99.3
1985	116.6	113.6	116.9
1986	106.4	106.0	106.4
1987	110.6	105.2	111.1
1988	124.2	123.9	124.2
1989	116.7	111.6	117.1
1990	104.0	113.7	103.2
1991	106.8	111.5	106.4
1992	112.2	119.5	111.4
1993	126.0	149.5	122.8
1994	123.5	129.8	118.0
1995	119.1	129.8	112.6
1996	110.4	122.0	106.3
1997	103.9	119.5	100.8
1998	99.8	108.4	97.6
1999	100.1	117.8	97.3
2000	100.3	114.0	98.3
2001	99.3	105.4	94.8
2002	99.2	100.6	98.6
2003	101.2	101.3	101.6
2004	102.7	101.9	102.0
2005	102.0	101.7	101.1
2006	101.9	101.2	101.8
2007	103.9	100.6	103.3
2008	105.0	98.2	107.1
2009	99.4	97.7	98.8
2010	103.7	102.0	103.9
2011	105.3	101.8	105.7
2012	101.7	99.5	101.8
2013	102.2	103.8	101.0
2014	101.9	103.6	100.3
2015	101.8	102.4	100.4
2016	102.1	101.7	101.8
2017	101.8	103.4	101.1
2018	102.2	102.2	102.1
2019	103.0	102.6	102.3
2020	101.9	101.7	100.2
2021	102.1	101.4	103.3
2022	102.3	100.6	104.1

表5-2 市区居民消费价格指数及商品零售价格指数(以1952年为100)
Consumer Price Indices and Retail Price Indices in Urban Area (Take Data in 1952 as 100)

年份 Year	以1952年为100 (Take data in 1952 as 100) 居民消费价格指数 Consumer Price Index	#服务 Service	商品零售价格指数 Retail Price Index
1953	106.8	100.0	106.1
1957	110.7	113.6	108.8
1965	117.2	114.2	116.4
1975	116.5	105.2	116.5
1978	116.3	109.8	115.4
1980	135.4	109.8	124.6
1985	171.6	137.4	158.2
1989	292.7	211.8	272.1
1990	304.4	240.9	280.8
1991	325.1	268.5	298.7
1992	364.7	320.9	332.8
1993	459.6	479.8	408.7
1994	567.6	622.7	482.2
1995	676.0	808.3	543.0
1996	746.3	986.1	577.2
1997	775.4	1178.4	581.8
1998	773.8	1277.4	567.8
1999	774.6	1504.8	552.5
2000	776.9	1715.5	543.1
2001	771.5	1808.1	514.9
2002	765.3	1819.0	507.7
2003	774.5	1842.6	515.8
2004	795.4	1877.6	526.1
2005	811.3	1909.6	531.9
2006	826.8	1932.5	541.5
2007	859.0	1944.1	559.3
2008	901.9	1909.1	599.1
2009	896.5	1865.2	591.9
2010	929.7	1902.5	614.9
2011	979.0	1936.7	650.0
2012	995.6	1927.0	661.7
2013	1017.5	2000.3	668.3
2014	1036.8	2072.3	670.3
2015	1055.5	2122.0	673.0
2016	1077.7	2158.1	685.1
2017	1097.1	2231.5	692.6
2018	1121.3	2281.5	707.1
2019	1154.5	2341.5	723.6
2020	1176.1	2381.2	725.4
2021	1200.8	2414.6	749.4
2022	1228.4	2429.1	780.1

表5-3 市区居民消费价格分类指数
Consumer Price Indices by Category in Urban Area

(以上年价格为100 The Price of Preceding Year is Taken as 100)

指标	Indicators	2019	2020	2021	2022
居民消费价格指数	**Consumer Price Index**	**103. 0**	**101. 9**	**102. 1**	**102. 3**
服务价格指数	**Price Index for Service**	**102. 6**	**101. 7**	**101. 4**	**100. 6**
一、食品烟酒	Food, Tobacco and Liquor	105. 2	106. 2	102. 1	103. 1
1. 食品	Food	106. 1	107. 8	101. 5	103. 7
#粮食	Grain	100. 5	101. 7	102. 3	102. 9
食用油	Edible Oil and Fats	99. 1	106. 1	119. 5	110. 6
菜及食用菌	Vegetables and Edible Fungi	105. 0	103. 3	110. 1	101. 3
畜肉类	Meat of Livestock	125. 3	137. 6	83. 2	95. 2
禽肉类	Meat of Poultry	107. 6	102. 1	94. 2	105. 7
水产品	Aquatic Products	98. 6	100. 3	107. 3	104. 1
蛋类	Eggs	103. 7	97. 4	104. 7	103. 2
干鲜瓜果类	Dried and Fresh Melons and Fruits	106. 5	92. 5	104. 4	113. 2
2. 茶及饮料	Tea and Beverages	103. 2	98. 6	103. 7	104. 3
3. 烟酒	Tobacco and Liquor	101. 0	100. 3	101. 8	101. 9
4. 在外就餐	Dining Out	104. 6	104. 8	103. 9	102. 0
二、衣着	Clothing	102. 8	99. 9	99. 6	99. 7
1. 服装	Garments	103. 2	100. 5	99. 6	99. 9
2. 鞋类	Footwear	101. 6	97. 2	99. 6	98. 5
三、居住	Residence	101. 1	100. 9	100. 8	100. 4
四、生活用品及服务	Articles for Daily Use and Services	103. 0	101. 5	102. 3	101. 0
#家具及室内装饰品	Furniture and Interior Decorations	104. 0	100. 7	102. 3	100. 2
家用器具	Home Appliances	99. 0	97. 2	101. 7	101. 6
家用纺织品	Home Textiles	108. 7	100. 0	100. 8	101. 9
五、交通通信	Transport and Communications	98. 8	94. 6	105. 3	105. 8
1. 交通	Transport	98. 0	93. 2	105. 5	107. 8
2. 通信	Communications	100. 7	97. 8	104. 6	99. 4
六、教育文化娱乐	Education, Culture and Recreation	104. 5	103. 1	104. 4	102. 2
1. 教育	Education	106. 3	106. 0	105. 1	102. 8
2. 文化娱乐	Culture and Recreation	102. 1	99. 2	103. 2	101. 3
七、医疗保健	Health Care	104. 3	98. 9	100. 4	101. 8
1. 药品及医疗器具	Medicine and Medical Instrument	107. 1	95. 9	98. 7	106. 1
2. 医疗服务	Medical Services	102. 1	101. 4	101. 1	100. 0
八、其他用品及服务	Other Articles and Services	105. 0	105. 3	97. 3	101. 5

表5-4 市区商品零售价格分类指数
Retail Price Index by Category of Commodities in Urban Area

(以上年价格为100 The Price of Preceding Year is Taken as 100)

指标	Indicators	2019	2020	2021	2022
商品零售价格总指数	**Retail Price Index**	**102.3**	**100.2**	**103.3**	**104.1**
一、食品	Food	105.8	107.2	102.1	103.2
#粮食	Grain	100.5	101.7	102.3	102.9
食用油	Edible Oil and Fats	98.3	104.8	119.5	110.6
菜及食用菌	Vegetables and Edible Fungi	105.0	103.3	110.1	101.3
畜肉类	Meat of Livestock	125.3	137.6	83.2	95.2
禽肉类	Meat of Poultry	107.6	102.1	94.2	105.7
水产品	Aquatic Products	98.8	100.0	107.2	104.1
蛋类	Eggs	103.7	97.4	104.7	103.2
干鲜瓜果类	Dried and Fresh Melons and Fruits	106.5	92.5	104.4	113.2
餐饮业零售	Catering Retail	104.6	104.8	103.9	102.0
二、饮料、烟酒	Beverages, Tobacco and Liquor	101.7	99.9	102.1	102.2
三、服装、鞋帽	Garments, Shoes and Hats	102.9	99.8	99.5	99.5
四、纺织品	Textiles	108.8	100.1	100.3	101.1
五、家用电器及音像器材	Household Appliances, Music and Video Equipment	97.7	98.0	102.6	100.1
六、文化办公用品	Cultural and Office Appliances	98.6	100.6	103.9	100.9
七、日用品	Articles for Daily Use	103.5	102.1	101.0	100.8
八、体育娱乐用品	Sports and Recreation Articles	102.3	102.6	101.6	101.6
九、交通、通信用品	Transportation and Communication Appliances	99.8	97.1	102.9	101.2
十、家具	Furniture	104.4	101.2	102.5	100.2
十一、化妆品	Cosmetics	102.9	102.2	99.5	99.7
十二、金银饰品	Gold and Silver Ornaments	108.8	121.0	96.1	101.6
十三、中西药品及医疗保健用品	Traditional Chinese and Western Medicines and Health Care Articles	107.3	95.5	98.8	106.0
十四、书报杂志及电子出版物	Books, Newspapers, Magazines and Electronic Publications	104.5	100.5	100.3	101.5
十五、燃料	Fuels	94.7	89.1	118.4	122.3
十六、建筑材料及五金电料	Building Materials and Hardware	100.8	100.4	104.6	101.8

表5-5 部分年份工业生产者出厂价格指数
Industrial Producer Ex-factory Price Index in Partial Years

指标	Indicators	各年以上年价格为100 (The Price of Preceeding Years is Taken as 100)				
		2018	2019	2020	2021	2022
总指数	**Combined Index**	**104.2**	**97.9**	**95.7**	**108.5**	**105.3**
轻工业	Light Industry	101.4	100.1	98.1	102.7	103.0
以农产品为原料	Using Farm Products as Raw Materials	101.3	100.0	99.4	103.4	102.3
以非农产品为原料	Using Non Farm Products as Raw Materials	101.5	100.1	97.1	102.4	103.4
重工业	Heavy Industry	105.3	97.1	94.8	110.5	106.0
采掘	Mining and Quarrying Industry	111.0	109.1	111.6	100.1	97.1
原材料	Raw Material Industry	110.7	94.0	86.5	119.4	114.3
加工	Manufacturing Industry	102.1	99.0	99.5	105.7	101.5
生产资料	Production Goods	105.3	97.0	94.5	110.7	105.8
采掘	Mining and Quarrying Industry	111.0	109.1	111.6	100.1	97.1
原材料	Raw Material Industry	110.8	93.9	86.1	119.2	114.1
加工	Manufacturing Industry	102.2	98.8	99.1	106.4	101.6
生活资料	Means of Subsistence	100.5	101.0	99.5	99.9	102.8
食品	Food	100.6	101.8	98.1	97.7	106.3
衣着	Garments	99.6	100.9	99.8	99.4	102.7
一般日用品	Articles for Daily Use	100.4	100.9	99.7	99.7	104.1
耐用消费品	Durable Consumer Goods	101.1	100.9	99.8	100.6	101.5

表5-6 部分年份工业生产者购进价格指数
Purchase Price Index of Industrial Producers in Partial Years

指标	Indicators	各年以上年价格为100 (The Price of Preceeding Years is Taken as 100)				
		2018	2019	2020	2021	2022
总指数	**Combined Index**	**107.5**	**96.2**	**92.3**	**121.2**	**110.8**
燃料动力类	Fuels and Energy	117.9	96.1	85.9	132.8	134.6
黑色金属材料类	Ferrous Metals	103.9	96.1	97.7	124.7	97.1
有色金属材料及电线类	Nonferrous Metal and Electric Wire	104.9	94.5	100.9	134.1	102.4
化工原料类	Chemical Raw Materials	110.0	90.3	82.3	128.0	110.0
木材及纸浆类	Wood and Paper Pulps	103.7	93.1	93.4	109.0	103.6
建筑材料及非金属类	Building Materials and Nonmetal Minerals	130.2	103.5	90.0	106.3	94.8
其他工业原材料及半成品类	Other Industrial Raw and Processed Materials	99.5	97.9	97.7	107.7	103.3
农副产品类	Farm and Sideline Products	98.9	98.6	95.7	101.8	103.5
纺织原料类	Textile Raw Materials	101.6	98.8	99.2	103.3	106.2

表5-7 住宅销售价格指数(2022年)
Residential Building Sales Price Index（2022）

(以上年同期价格为100 The Price of Preceding Years is Taken as 100)

月份	Month	新建商品住房 New Commodity Housing	按套型分 By House Size			二手住宅 Second-hand Residential Buildings	按套型分 By House Size		
			90m²及以下 90 Sq.m and Below	90-144m² 90-144 Sq.m	144m²以上 More than 144 Sq.m		90m²及以下 90 Sq.m and Below	90-144m² 90-144 Sq.m	144m²以上 More than 144 Sq.m
一月份	January	103.3	103.1	103.3	103.3	101.8	100.9	102.5	102.1
二月份	February	103.5	103.3	103.6	103.3	101.5	100.6	102.3	101.8
三月份	March	102.8	103.0	102.9	102.4	100.9	100.0	101.6	101.5
四月份	April	102.0	101.7	102.0	101.9	100.1	99.6	100.5	100.7
五月份	May	101.3	101.0	101.4	101.3	99.4	99.1	99.6	99.5
六月份	June	100.8	101.1	100.7	101.0	99.2	99.2	99.3	99.3
七月份	July	100.3	100.6	100.3	100.3	99.1	99.3	98.9	98.9
八月份	August	100.3	100.6	100.2	100.3	98.6	98.7	98.4	98.7
九月份	September	100.4	100.8	100.3	100.5	98.5	98.8	98.2	98.6
十月份	October	100.9	101.7	100.7	100.8	98.3	98.3	98.4	98.4
十一月份	November	101.2	102.4	101.0	101.0	98.2	98.4	97.9	98.4
十二月份	December	101.8	102.7	101.7	101.4	98.4	98.7	98.1	98.6

表5-8 历年城乡居民人均收支及住房情况
Per Capita Annual Income and Living Expenditures and Housing Conditions of Urban and Rural Residents Over the Years

单位：平方米(sq.m)

年份 Year	居民人均可支配收入（元） Per Capita Disposable Income of Residents(Yuan)			居民人均消费支出（元） Per Capita Living Expenditure of Residents(Yuan)			居民人均自有现住房面积 Per Capita Private Housing Area of Residents		
	全体 Total	城镇 Urban	农村 Rural	全体 Total	城镇 Urban	农村 Rural	全体 Total	城镇 Urban	农村 Rural
1978		306			299				
1979		340			332				
1980		429	222		419	183			
1981		481	217		490	274			
1982		509	353		492	338			
1983		530	340		502	375		12.62	
1984		643	483		561	428		12.84	
1985		889	627		862	564		12.94	21.30
1986		1110	735		1057	673		12.92	22.80
1987		1192	871		1076	762		13.44	24.50
1988		1518	1066		1469	964		14.49	26.00
1989		1742	1199		1543	1051		15.32	27.30
1990		1963	1254		1628	1166		15.56	27.70
1991		2182	1441		1854	1221		15.93	29.90
1992		2674	1624		2204	1368		16.00	31.00
1993		3983	2060		3139	1599		16.08	30.20
1994		6008	2685		4442	2215		17.25	33.60
1995		7275	3484		5566	2432		17.41	31.30
1996		8354	4267		6545	3283		17.09	30.75
1997		9069	4568		7189	3483		17.42	39.95
1998		9193	4697		7912	3589		18.21	37.58
1999		9492	4798		7493	3591		19.40	39.78
2000		10921	5069		7997	3929		20.34	41.57
2001		11991	5362		9463	4383		21.53	43.14
2002		12970	5764		9396	4508		21.86	45.74
2003		14277	6221		10463	4194		23.22	46.86
2004		15882	7018		11283	6102		23.85	49.90
2005		17408	7810		11758	6623		24.92	50.44
2006		19674	8847		12666	7378		24.91	51.88
2007		22307	10051		13921	8062		26.09	53.24
2008		25304	11450		16379	9174		28.85	55.86
2009		27368	12641		18203	9789		29.72	55.88
2010		30166	14261		19420	9794		30.22	56.00
2011		34058	16518		21779	11253		32.88	57.22
2012		37902	18475		23288	12699		32.55	58.29
2013	34657	41729	20534	21728	24685	13915	40.19	33.58	58.87
2014	38074	44155	24283	24324	27893	16228	42.29	39.70	47.76
2015	41373	47852	26469	26056	29645	17800	43.28	40.33	49.28
2016	44641	51560	28572	27891	31584	19313	44.47	41.82	49.83
2017	48233	55656	30871	29316	33197	20239	45.57	43.26	50.20
2018	52402	60134	33633	32200	36712	21248	48.98	46.36	56.40
2019	56982	64886	36632	33944	38274	22797	49.64	46.80	57.80
2020	59952	68008	39132	34455	38702	23481	49.98	47.11	58.24
2021	65436	73869	42946	40478	45362	27451	49.63	46.69	58.30
2022	68348	76690	45487	42997	47916	29514	49.44	46.42	58.51

注：2014年（含）之后为城乡住户一体化新口径，2013年（含）之前城镇均为市区口径，2013年（含）之前农村居民可支配收入指人均纯收入口径。

Note: After 2014(inclusive), it is a new criterion for the integration of urban and rural households.Before 2013(inclusive) the per capita disposable income of urban residents is the urban criterion, and before 2013(inclusive) the disposable income of rural residents refers to the per capita net income criterion.

表5-9 分城乡居民收入与支出(2022年)
Urban and Rural Residents Income and Expenditure（2022）

指标	Indicators	单位	Unit	城镇 Cities& Towns	农村 Rural
一、人口就业情况	**Population employment**				
1. 住户数	Household number	户	Households	1790	1160
2. 期内住户常住成员数	Resident membership of the period	人	person	4994	2987
3. 劳动力人数	Labor force	人	person	3917	2504
4. 常住成员从业人数	Number of permanent members employed	人	person	2789	1914
二、可支配收入	**Disposable income**	元	**yuan**	**76690**	**45487**
（一）工资性收入	Wages Income	元	yuan	42390	26031
（二）经营净收入	Net operating income	元	yuan	13019	9313
1. 第一产业经营净收入	Net income of the first industry operation	元	yuan	170	2945
2. 第二产业经营净收入	Net income of the second industry operation	元	yuan	5033	2122
3. 第三产业经营净收入	Net income of the third industry operation	元	yuan	7816	4246
（三）财产净收入	Net income of property	元	yuan	9385	1705
（四）转移净收入	Net income of transfer	元	yuan	11896	8438
三、总支出	**Total expenditure**	元	**yuan**	**75098**	**44797**
1. 生产经营费用支出	Production and operating expenses	元	yuan	12984	6383
2. 财产性支出	Property Expenditure	元	yuan	712	120
3. 转移性支出	Transfer Expenditure	元	yuan	4326	3599
4. 部分商业保险支出	Part of commercial insurance expenses	元	yuan	241	98
5. 购置资产及非经常性转移支出	Acquisition of assets and non recurrent transfer expenses	元	yuan	6053	3808
6. 借贷性支出	Borrowing expenses	元	yuan	2865	1274
四、消费支出	**Consumption expenditure**	元	**yuan**	**47916**	**29514**
（一）食品烟酒	Food alcohol and tobacco	元	yuan	13671	9997
（二）衣着	Garments	元	yuan	2567	1518
（三）居住	Residence	元	yuan	12842	7548
（四）生活用品及服务	Daily necessities and services	元	yuan	2835	1606
（五）交通通信	Transportation and Communication	元	yuan	7552	3848
1. 交通	Transportation	元	yuan	6271	2890
2. 通讯	Communication	元	yuan	1281	958
（六）教育文化娱乐	Recreation,Education and Culture	元	yuan	4320	2679
1. 教育	Education	元	yuan	3147	2143
2. 文化娱乐	Cultural recreation	元	yuan	1173	536
（七）医疗保健	Medical Care	元	yuan	2651	1770
（八）其他用品和服务	Other supplies and services	元	yuan	1478	548

表5-10 各地城镇居民收入与支出（2022年）
Income and Expenditure of Urban Residents（2022）

指标	Indicators	单位	Unit	全市 Total	海曙区 Haishu
可支配收入	**Disposable income**	**元**	**yuan**	**76690**	**81600**
（一）工资性收入	Wages Income	元	yuan	42390	43796
（二）经营净收入	Net operating income	元	yuan	13019	13111
（三）财产净收入	Net income of property	元	yuan	9385	11597
（四）转移净收入	Net income of transfer	元	yuan	11896	13096
消费支出	**Consumption expenditure**	**元**	**yuan**	**47916**	**50842**
（一）食品烟酒	Food alcohol and tobacco	元	yuan	13671	13245
（二）衣着	Garments	元	yuan	2567	2156
（三）居住	Residence	元	yuan	12842	16529
（四）生活用品及服务	Daily necessities and services	元	yuan	2835	3071
（五）交通通信	Transportation and Communication	元	yuan	7552	6558
（六）教育文化娱乐	Recreation,Education and Cultural	元	yuan	4320	4270
（七）医疗保健	Medicine and Medical Articles	元	yuan	2651	4015
（八）其他用品和服务	Other supplies and services	元	yuan	1478	998

江北区 Jiangbei	镇海区 Zhenhai	北仑区 Beilun	鄞州区 Yinzhou	奉化区 Fenghua	余姚市 Yuyao	慈溪市 Cixi	宁海县 Ninghai	象山县 Xiangshan
79480	**81078**	**78474**	**84630**	**67490**	**73749**	**73385**	**72549**	**69478**
40475	53669	53257	49846	43282	39813	43060	36644	36657
12281	9489	12291	6756	5722	13957	13642	20141	14258
10933	9076	6461	13762	7941	10898	7406	9790	10720
15791	8844	6465	14266	10545	9081	9277	5974	7843
46179	**51369**	**46790**	**58949**	**47896**	**46729**	**48163**	**47601**	**40378**
13373	15051	12758	14796	14273	13761	13858	12496	11139
2549	3147	2349	3311	2760	3143	2640	2927	3078
13022	10515	12416	16911	12485	10991	10155	13127	10855
2902	2947	4102	4342	2568	2846	2614	3590	2158
6535	10643	7833	8365	7407	7858	10121	6565	4857
3714	4162	4179	5320	4666	4429	4648	4984	4527
2436	3041	2023	3073	2501	3014	2743	2447	2659
1648	1863	1130	2831	1236	687	1384	1465	1105

表5-11 各地农村居民收入与支出（2022年）
Income and Expenditure of Rural Residents（2022）

指标	Indicators	单位	Unit	全市 Total	海曙区 Haishu
可支配收入	**Disposable income**	**元**	**yuan**	**45487**	**46504**
（一）工资性收入	Wages Income	元	yuan	26031	25208
（二）经营净收入	Net operating income	元	yuan	9313	9033
（三）财产净收入	Net income of property	元	yuan	1705	3654
（四）转移净收入	Net income of transfer	元	yuan	8438	8609
消费支出	**Consumption expenditure**	**元**	**yuan**	**29514**	**30736**
（一）食品烟酒	Food alcohol and tobacco	元	yuan	9997	9052
（二）衣着	Garments	元	yuan	1518	1045
（三）居住	Residence	元	yuan	7548	9874
（四）生活用品及服务	Daily necessities and services	元	yuan	1606	1415
（五）交通通信	Transportation and Communication	元	yuan	3848	3135
（六）教育文化娱乐	Recreation,Education and Cultural	元	yuan	2679	2718
（七）医疗保健	Medicine and Medical Articles	元	yuan	1770	2866
（八）其他用品和服务	Other supplies and services	元	yuan	548	631

江北区 Jiangbei	镇海区 Zhenhai	北仑区 Beilun	鄞州区 Yinzhou	奉化区 Fenghua	余姚市 Yuyao	慈溪市 Cixi	宁海县 Ninghai	象山县 Xiangshan
48088	**47027**	**47397**	**50333**	**41007**	**45665**	**47142**	**42165**	**41578**
27747	30255	31658	26818	21111	28209	29489	18562	15608
3831	6693	9815	14602	11743	10701	8687	16381	16011
4822	2964	2826	2126	610	1040	1007	2226	1982
11688	7115	3098	6787	7543	5715	7959	4996	7977
34834	**31346**	**30355**	**34115**	**25649**	**31338**	**31793**	**32491**	**27524**
12941	10501	10207	9962	8926	11454	10599	10804	9070
1618	1818	1362	1838	1080	1712	1463	1683	1595
8964	7054	6722	9882	7884	6218	7408	6981	7786
1821	1687	2258	2127	1127	1818	1537	1613	1117
4534	4459	5855	4824	2886	3743	5229	5434	3445
2126	2539	1385	2377	1126	2667	2819	2815	1913
1846	2392	1647	2322	1997	2441	1921	2612	2227
984	896	919	783	623	1285	817	549	371

表5-12　分城乡居民耐用消费品拥有量（2022年）
The Amount of Consumer Durable Goods of Urban and Rural Areas（2022）

指标	Indicators	单位	Unit	城镇 Cities& Towns	农村 Rural
家用汽车拥有量	Homeuse Cars Ownership	辆/百户	car/hundred families	65	44
洗衣机拥有量	Washing Machines Ownership	台/百户	set/hundred families	101	94
电冰箱(柜)拥有量	Refrigerators Ownership	台/百户	set/hundred families	106	113
彩色电视机拥有量	Color TV Sets Ownership	台/百户	set/hundred families	190	198
空调拥有量	Air－conditioners Ownership	台/百户	set/hundred families	242	200
固定电话拥有量	Fixed phone Ownership	线/百户	line/hundred families	25	23
移动电话拥有量	Mobile Phone Ownership	部/百户	set/hundred families	240	233
计算机拥有量	Computer Ownership	台/百户	set/hundred families	83	47

表5-13　按收入等级分的城乡居民人均可支配收入
Disposable Income of Urban and Rural Residents by Income Levels

指标 Indicators	年份 Year	按人均可支配收入五等分组（元） Grouped by Level of Disposable Income(Yuan)				
		低20%收入户 Lower Income Households (20%)	次低20%收入户 Low Income Households (20%)	中等20%收入户 Middle Income Households (20%)	次高20%收入户 High Income Households (20%)	高20%收入户 Higher Income Households (20%)
城镇 Town	2022	30701	48546	63428	84205	168605
农村 Rural	2022	17248	27600	35855	47138	102813
城镇 Town	2021	30266	45596	60147	81615	162404
农村 Rural	2021	16426	25667	33841	44149	97442

主要统计指标解释

【居民消费价格指数】居民消费价格，是指城乡居民支付生活消费品和服务项目消费的价格，是社会产品和服务项目的最终价格。居民消费价格指数，就是反映一定时期内居民消费价格变动趋势和变动程度的相对数。利用居民消费价格指数，可以全面观察居民消费价格变动对居民生活的影响。居民消费价格指数还是反映通货膨胀程度的重要指标。

【商品零售价格指数】商品的零售价格是商品在流通过程中的最后一个环节的价格，是工业、商业、餐饮业和其他零售企业向城乡居民、机关团体出售生活消费品和办公用品的价格。因此，商品零售价格指数是全面反映市场零售物价总水平变动趋势和程度的相对数。其目的在于掌握零售商品的价格变动状况，为国家制定经济政策、研究城乡市场流通和为国民经济核算提供科学依据。

【工业生产者出厂价格指数】工业生产者出厂价格，是指工业企业向商业（物资）部门或商业企业、其他生产单位、个人出售的或调拨产品的价格，亦称工业生产者价格。它是工业品进入流通领域的最初价格。工业生产者出厂价格指数是指反映一定时期内工业品出厂价格水平变动趋势及变动程度的相对数，是国民经济核算和计算工业发展速度的一个重要参考指标。

【工业生产者购进价格指数】是反映工业企业作为生产投入，而从物资交易市场和能源、原材料生产企业购买原材料、燃料、动力产品时，所支付的价格水平变动趋势和程度的统计指标，是扣除工业企业物质消耗成本中价格变动影响的重要依据。

【住宅销售价格指数】住宅销售价格指数（简称HPI），是反映房地产价格水平总体变化趋势和变化幅度的相对数，是房地产价格变动趋势定量分析的指标。

【可支配收入】 指调查户在调查期内获得的、可用于最终消费支出和储蓄的总和，即调查户可以用来自由支配的收入。可支配收入既包括现金，也包括实物收入。按照收入的来源，可支配收入包含四项，分别为：工资性收入、经营净收入、财产净收入和转移净收入。

【生活消费支出】是指住户用于满足家庭日常生活消费需要的全部支出，包括用于消费品的支出和用于服务性消费的支出。根据用途不同，消费支出可划分为食品烟酒、衣着、居住、生活用品及服务、交通通信、教育文化娱乐、医疗保健、其他用品及服务八大类。

Explanatory Notes on Main Statistical Indicators

【Consumer Price Index】 Consumer price refers to the price that urban and rural residents pay for consumption of consumer goods and services, and the final price of social goods and services. Consumer price index is the relative number that reflects the trend and degree of change of consumer price in a certain period. By using the consumer price index, we can observe the influence of the change of consumer price on residents' life. Consumer price index is also an important indicator of the degree of inflation.

【Retail Price Index】 The retail price of commodities is the price of the last link in the circulation of commodities. It is the price of industrial, commercial, catering and other retail enterprises selling consumer goods and office supplies to urban and rural residents, agencies and groups. Therefore, the retail price index is the relative number that reflects the changing of the trend and degree of the total retail price level in the market. Its purpose is to grasp the price change of retail commodities, to make economic policies for the country, to study the circulation of urban and rural markets and to provide scientific basis for national economic accounting.

【Producer Price Indices for Industrial Producers】 The price of an industrial producer is the price at which an industrial enterprise sells or allocates a product to a commercial (material) department or a commercial enterprise, other production units, or an individual, and is also known as the price of an industrial producer. It is the initial price at which industrial goods enter circulation at the first time. The ex–factory price index of industrial producers refers to the relative number that reflects the changing trend and degree of the price level of industrial products in a certain period of time. It is an important reference index for national economic accounting and calculating the speed of industrial development.

【Purchasing Price Indices for Industrial Producers】 It is a statistical indicator that reflects the trend and extent of price changes paid by industrial enterprises as production inputs when purchasing raw materials, fuels and power products from material trading markets and energy and raw materials manufacturing enterprises. It is the important basis of deducting the price change influence in the industrial enterprise material consumption cost.

【The housing price index】 The housing price index (HPI) is the relative number reflecting the overall change trend and change range of the real estate price level, and is the index of quantitative analysis of the change trend of real estate price.

【Disposable Income】 Refers to the sum of the final consumer spending and savings available to the survey household during the survey period, that is, the disposable income available to the survey household. Disposable income includes both cash and physical income. According to the source of income, disposable income includes four items: wage income, net operating income, net property income and transfer income.

【Living Consumption Expenditure】 It refers to the total expenditure required by households to meet the needs of household daily life, including expenditures for consumer goods and expenditures for service consumption. According to the different uses, consumption expenditure can be divided into 8 categories, including food tobacco, clothing, living, living goods and services, traffic communication, education and cultural entertainment, health care, other supplies and services.

NINGBO 2023 Statistical Yearbook

6 CHAPTER

第六篇

农业

AGRICULTURE

农业
Agriculture

主要统计指标
Major Statistics Indicators

2022年农林牧渔业总产值	Total Output Value of Agriculture	589. 82	亿元	100 million yuan
比上年增长（现价）	Increase Over Last Year	6. 35	%	
2022年粮食总产量	Total Yield of Grain Grops	715965	吨	ton
比上年增长	Increase Over Last Year	5. 61	%	
2022年油料总产量	Yield of Oil – bearing Crops	31380	吨	ton
比上年增长	Increase Over Last Year	9. 19	%	
2022年肉类产量	Output of Meat	93593. 7	吨	ton
比上年增长	Increase Over Last Year	9. 18	%	
2022年水产品总产量	Total Aquatic Products	1122779	吨	ton
比上年增长	Increase Over Last Year	4. 58	%	
2022农业机械总动力	Total Power of Agricultural Machinery	2360754	千瓦	kW
比上年增长	Increase Over Last Year	2. 03	%	

表6-1 历年农林牧渔业总产值
Gross Output Value of Farming,Forestry,Animal Husbandry and Fishery Over the Years

单位：亿元(100 million yuan)

年份 Year	农林牧渔业总产值 Gross Output Value	其中 Of Which				
		农业 Farming	林业 Forestry	牧业 Animal Husbandry	渔业 Fishery	服务业 Services
1978	8.83					
1979	10.93					
1980	11.70					
1981	11.07					
1982	14.79					
1983	14.81					
1984	19.68					
1985	21.89	15.40	0.83	3.53	2.13	
1986	24.31	16.85	0.93	4.26	2.27	
1987	28.99	19.47	1.13	5.71	2.68	
1988	36.23	23.41	1.28	7.53	4.01	
1989	40.98	27.37	1.52	8.31	3.78	
1990	40.68	26.94	1.30	8.30	4.14	
1991	45.86	29.35	1.74	8.42	6.35	
1992	51.47	31.51	1.57	9.59	8.80	
1993	69.89	40.29	2.40	11.75	15.45	
1994	96.40	51.60	3.00	17.26	24.54	
1995	123.95	67.22	4.18	20.71	31.84	
1996	138.65	75.77	3.92	22.85	36.11	
1997	129.44	67.19	4.22	21.65	36.38	
1998	136.36	71.92	4.09	20.53	39.82	
1999	142.82	73.04	4.34	20.16	45.28	
2000	148.37	71.57	4.59	20.45	51.76	
2001	156.43	74.31	5.14	22.21	54.77	
2002	163.31	73.65	4.92	24.25	60.49	
2003	173.75	77.42	5.03	26.03	63.10	2.17
2004	193.13	86.94	5.01	29.61	69.18	2.39
2005	207.40	91.14	5.31	32.93	75.31	2.71
2006	207.93	97.14	6.01	32.20	68.97	3.60
2007	236.43	106.83	6.77	46.31	72.29	4.22
2008	261.23	118.44	7.32	48.38	82.40	4.69
2009	284.74	133.15	8.85	48.01	89.41	5.32
2010	336.20	165.06	9.83	51.94	103.43	5.94
2011	392.86	188.14	10.86	62.85	124.37	6.65
2012	413.49	196.79	11.43	65.08	132.49	7.71
2013	421.05	197.12	11.64	60.96	142.95	8.38
2014	423.66	203.42	12.51	53.75	144.52	9.47
2015	437.15	208.21	13.24	49.61	155.03	11.07
2016	463.31	219.37	14.08	48.14	167.71	14.01
2017	464.51	226.83	15.31	37.37	169.60	15.41
2018	473.81	229.14	15.54	34.86	177.16	17.12
2019	507.05	240.17	16.39	43.12	188.19	19.18
2020	534.08	245.72	16.90	51.24	197.90	22.32
2021	554.58	261.02	16.36	40.56	212.04	24.60
2022	589.82	275.58	17.20	41.71	228.49	26.84

表6-2 部分年份农林牧渔业分项产值
Gross Output Value of Farming,Forestry,Animal Husbandry and Fishery by Branch in Partial Years

单位：万元(10000 yuan)

指标	Indicators	2019	2020	2021	2022
合计	**Gross Output Value**	**5070459**	**5340826**	**5545844**	**5898235**
农业产值	**Farming**	**2401649**	**2457205**	**2610193**	**2755790**
粮食作物	Grain	236954	251924	257439	276893
谷物	Cereal	184694	210458	214487	230778
豆类	Beans	21874	23293	17436	19610
薯类	Tubers	30386	18173	25516	26505
油料	Oil Plants	25395	25454	27391	29855
棉花	Cotton	4918	4009	3705	3364
麻类	Fiber Crops				
甘蔗	Sugarcane	2582	2895	2117	1864
中草药材	Chinese medicinal materials	75331	64156	60506	55502
蔬菜	Vegetables	809734	826918	914391	1005157
食用菌	Edible Mushroom	12220	14639	17253	18653
花卉园艺	Flower & Horticulture	330390	328877	335887	293307
茶、桑、水果、坚果	Tea,Mulberry & Fruits	874052	906511	960990	1050987
其他农作物	Others	30073	31822	30513	20206
林业产值	**Forestry**	**163907**	**168950**	**163633**	**171992**
林木的培育和种植	Cultivation and Planting of Trees	25911	39118	26409	11961
林产品	Forest Products	106077	105512	113695	137697
竹木采运	Cut Lumbering	28011	20658	23530	22334
牧业产值	**Animal Husbandry**	**431229**	**512375**	**405619**	**417144**
牲畜	Livestock Raising	301961	387531	282439	288530
家禽饲养	Poultry Raising	34948	37324	33549	32518
活的畜禽产品	Livestock Products	64897	61613	71076	71855
其他畜牧业	Other Animal Husbandry	29423	25907	18555	24240
渔业产值	**Fishery**	**1881905**	**1979038**	**2120401**	**2284883**
海水产品	Seawater Aquatic Products	1636277	1731696	1854274	2009327
淡水产品	Freshwater Aquatic Products	245628	247342	266127	275556
农林牧渔专业及辅助性活动产值	**Agriculture, Forestry, Animal Husbandry and Fishery Specialty and Auxiliary Activities**	**191769**	**223258**	**245998**	**268426**

注：本表按现行价格计算。
Note : Data in this table are calculated at current prices.

表6-3 历年主要农作物播种面积及产量
Sown Areas and Yield of Major Farm Crops Over the Years

单位：千公顷（1000 hectares）

年份 Year	农作物播种面积 Sown Area	其中 of Which 粮食 Grain 面积 Area	产量（万吨） Yield(10000 tons)	棉花 Cotton 面积 Area	产量（万吨） Yield(10000 tons)	油料 Oil Plants 面积 Area	产量（万吨） Yield(10000 tons)	蔬菜 Vegetables 面积 Area	产量（万吨） Yield(10000 tons)
1980	625.37	413.95	171.60						
1981	622.19	396.91	153.88						
1982	626.41	402.19	191.11						
1983	624.95	410.17	166.30	51.88	4.79	40.21	5.97		
1984	616.76	410.39	213.70	51.36	6.98	32.96	5.99		
1985	612.90	380.39	188.52	48.13	3.91	44.45	7.99	34.57	143.97
1986	596.50	361.81	188.65	41.39	3.66	48.70	8.41	36.09	158.75
1987	595.54	372.05	185.23	34.27	2.95	45.09	7.77	42.89	166.61
1988	580.01	369.58	189.98	34.65	1.80	46.70	8.47	41.01	161.74
1989	579.97	360.69	183.84	31.30	2.07	49.44	7.55	47.79	151.00
1990	591.03	368.77	189.06	34.55	3.34	52.51	9.50	48.79	135.64
1991	587.53	372.02	205.63	33.84	3.84	52.08	9.19	44.58	135.36
1992	572.68	357.66	181.62	33.03	2.59	49.15	8.62	46.82	126.89
1993	522.02	317.08	175.44	27.37	2.36	32.28	6.13	52.73	152.20
1994	504.73	308.04	172.51	26.93	2.07	30.17	4.84	56.37	162.65
1995	512.08	316.57	172.76	27.59	2.48	40.29	7.34	50.04	144.62
1996	519.48	318.99	190.30	27.14	2.73	40.37	8.00	54.20	164.26
1997	502.21	316.44	173.73	24.19	1.53	35.27	6.81	51.86	158.10
1998	510.73	317.76	180.39	25.81	2.69	34.21	5.05	58.01	174.67
1999	504.82	308.98	173.67	14.75	1.59	36.16	7.37	69.73	207.62
2000	445.90	246.79	132.51	9.69	1.05	32.58	6.59	82.16	243.70
2001	406.64	200.16	112.17	10.20	1.18	27.28	5.59	99.25	299.22
2002	386.85	172.34	94.89	6.85	0.80	24.51	4.76	104.71	291.67
2003	348.64	136.73	75.61	6.55	0.76	19.98	4.21	98.86	275.04
2004	338.09	145.12	83.73	6.53	0.74	17.67	4.04	91.80	286.76
2005	332.53	145.27	80.12	6.77	0.72	17.71	4.01	93.36	274.86
2006	317.17	141.01	81.30	6.21	0.73	14.91	3.62	88.75	264.73
2007	307.01	135.32	73.49	5.70	0.65	14.18	3.46	86.88	251.97
2008	310.62	135.98	78.43	5.62	0.65	13.66	3.43	89.49	272.92
2009	302.77	131.83	77.86	5.30	0.61	16.40	4.10	86.76	274.42
2010	292.84	128.75	77.06	5.10	0.58	15.44	3.80	83.59	265.73
2011	285.45	125.79	78.50	4.58	0.58	13.62	3.47	82.13	269.09
2012	274.80	117.92	71.10	3.95	0.47	13.05	3.32	80.73	261.20
2013	266.41	111.30	60.79	3.28	0.37	12.41	3.18	80.05	248.79
2014	269.26	114.41	63.76	2.57	0.30	10.97	2.82	77.44	244.17
2015	259.98	110.92	61.69	2.04	0.24	11.57	3.00	76.84	244.95
2016	254.76	106.11	61.50	1.68	0.19	10.40	2.69	79.21	249.68
2017	261.48	109.74	63.70	1.32	0.15	10.47	2.82	82.60	260.70
2018	258.37	109.40	66.59	2.35	0.30	12.22	3.16	81.06	255.81
2019	259.31	109.87	66.33	2.10	0.27	11.43	3.06	82.47	261.01
2020	237.83	111.29	67.44	1.74	0.22	11.39	3.10	86.44	268.01
2021	238.17	112.82	67.79	1.58	0.20	11.77	2.87	88.78	271.33
2022	239.78	114.96	71.60	1.40	0.19	12.31	3.14	90.09	285.15

注：2007年年报开始，马铃薯作为粮食，不算蔬菜。从2014年年报开始数据实行“下管一级”，省级核定。2007到2017年数据已根据三农普数据进行调整。从2019年起粮食数据来自国家统计局宁波调查队。根据2020年年报制度要求，农作物播种面积不再包含花卉苗木，蔬菜产量含食用菌。

Note: Potato is classified as food, not vegetable from 2007. Starting from 2014 annual report data "down level", approved by the provincial. Data from the year 2007 to 2017 have been amended according to the last census of agriculture. From 2019, data of grain are obtained from the State Statistical Bureau Ningbo Investigation team. According to the requirements of the 2020 annual report system, the planting area of crops no longer includes flower seedlings, Vegetable yield inchding edible mushrooms.

表6-4 各区（县、市）农林牧渔业总产值(2022年)

Gross Output Value of Farming,Forestry,Animal Husbandry and Fishery by Region（2022）

指标	Indicators	全市 Total	市区 Urban District	海曙区 Haishu
合计	**Gross Output Value**	**5898235**	**1683738**	**240604**
农业产值	**Farming**	**2755790**	**1008686**	**197826**
粮食作物	Grain	276893	107477	26746
谷物	Cereal	230778	91898	22923
豆类	Beans	19610	4059	783
薯类	Tubers	26505	11520	3040
油料	Oil Plants	29855	5764	1529
棉花	Cotton	3364	91	31
麻类	Fiber Crops			
甘蔗	Sugarcane	1864	528	280
中草药材	Chinese medicinal materials	55502	36424	18337
蔬菜	Vegetables	1005157	334977	75508
食用菌	Edible Mushroom	18653	16015	234
花卉园艺	Flower & Horticulture	293307	187687	7395
茶、桑、水果、坚果	Tea,Mulberry & Fruits	1050987	301430	53180
其他农作物	Others	20206	18295	14587
林业产值	**Forestry**	**171992**	**81052**	**11240**
林木的培育和种植	Cultivation and Planting of Trees	11961	6725	686
林产品	Forest Products	137697	63459	9565
竹木采运	Cut Lumbering	22334	10868	989
牧业产值	**Animal Husbandry**	**417144**	**90923**	**6765**
牲畜	Livestock Raising	288530	62795	6112
家禽饲养	Poultry Raising	32518	5012	295
活的畜禽产品	Livestock Products	71855	21150	342
其他畜牧业	Other Animal Husbandry	24240	1966	17
渔业产值	**Fishery**	**2284883**	**406173**	**10853**
海水产品	Seawater Aquatic Products	2009327	361930	
淡水产品	Freshwater Aquatic Products	275556	44242	10853
农林牧渔专业及辅助性活动产值	**Agriculture, Forestry, Animal Husbandry and Fishery Specialty and Auxiliary Activities**	**268426**	**96904**	**13920**

注：本表按现行价格计算。
Note: Data in this table are calculated at current prices.

单位：万元(10000 yuan)

江北区 Jiangbei	镇海区 Zhenhai	北仑区 Beilun	鄞州区 Yinzhou	奉化区 Fenghua	余姚市 Yuyao	慈溪市 Cixi	宁海县 Ninghai	象山县 Xiangshan
140509	**106682**	**131349**	**451270**	**613323**	**842629**	**987992**	**766972**	**1616905**
59240	**85970**	**107466**	**324137**	**234048**	**585368**	**657443**	**239211**	**265081**
7961	7786	3452	36710	24822	65339	36349	37591	30138
7282	6347	2338	33486	19523	61897	24478	29897	22608
200	424	231	547	1874	2277	9918	1630	1727
479	1015	883	2678	3425	1164	1953	6065	5803
118	403	355	2096	1264	5491	13625	2213	2763
		1	59		16	2218	1035	5
85	10		92	61	258	367	160	551
2899	4972	374	8461	1380	4289	8491	2030	4268
16629	46131	20814	159799	16096	242839	304431	44704	78206
258	299	506	731	13987	132	2001	447	59
1708	12117	59285	14029	93153	55366	26908	5825	17522
29581	13976	22127	99878	82687	211395	261450	145192	131521
1	277	552	2281	598	244	1604	15	48
2445	**3265**	**2115**	**9013**	**52974**	**46962**	**3956**	**21996**	**18025**
356	1155	490	1355	2682	1859	7	523	2846
1798	2052	1317	5721	43005	41153	3736	16954	12395
291	57	308	1936	7286	3950	213	4519	2784
16462	**11958**	**10879**	**6089**	**38769**	**87536**	**106109**	**50424**	**82152**
3963	7515	9368	5186	30652	59658	69360	38260	58458
51	992	424	153	3096	6584	5899	4835	10189
12448	3380	317	405	4258	10395	22429	5219	12663
	71	770	345	763	10900	8422	2110	842
53940	**917**	**2535**	**72871**	**265058**	**79988**	**181386**	**420740**	**1196596**
53178		1656	48217	258880	5357	88671	399885	1153484
762	917	879	24654	6178	74631	92715	20855	43112
8422	**4572**	**8354**	**39160**	**22476**	**42775**	**39098**	**34600**	**55050**

表6-5　各区（县、市）农作物播种面积和产量(2022年)
Total Sown Area and Yield of Major Farm Crops by Region（2022）

指标	Indicators	全市 Total	市区 Urban District	
				海曙区 Haishu
农作物播种面积总计	**Sown Area of Farm Crops**	**239785**	**73912**	**17514**
经济作物播种面积	**Sown Area of Cash Crops**	**124820**	**32211**	**7291**
粮食作物播种面积	**Sown Area of Grain**	**114965**	**41701**	**10223**
总产量（吨）	**Total Yield of Grain(ton)**	**715965**	**269972**	**66141**
油料播种面积	**Sown Area of Oil Plants**	**12315**	**2202**	**490**
总产量（吨）	**Yield of Oil Plants(ton)**	**31381**	**5397**	**1310**
花生面积	Sown Area of Peanuts	3324	719	185
总产量（吨）	Yield of Rapeseeds(ton)	11185	2706	774
油菜籽面积	Sown Area of Rapeseeds	8478	1435	294
总产量（吨）	Yield of Peanuts(ton)	19271	2603	517
芝麻面积	Sown Area of Sesame	463	49	12
总产量（吨）	Yield of Sesame(ton)	839	88	18
棉花（皮棉）播种面积	Sown Area of Cotton	1401	26	9
棉花（皮棉）总产量（吨）	Yield of Cotton(ton)	1863	34	13
甘蔗播种面积	Sown Area of Sugarcane	166	43	16
甘蔗总产量（吨）	Yield of Sugarcane(ton)	7528	1825	953
中草药材类播种面积	**Sown Area of Medicinal Material**	**1398**	**622**	**360**
中草药材类总产量（吨）	**Yield of Medicinal Material(ton)**	**4957**	**2847**	**1619**

注：粮食数据来自国家统计局宁波调查队。
Note: Data of grain are obtained from the State Statistical Bureau Ningbo Investigation team.

单位：公顷 (hectare)

江北区 Jiangbei	镇海区 Zhenhai	北仑区 Beilun	鄞州区 Yinzhou	奉化区 Fenghua	余姚市 Yuyao	慈溪市 Cixi	宁海县 Ninghai	象山县 Xiangshan
5013	**7348**	**3503**	**25940**	**14592**	**49648**	**67536**	**25886**	**22630**
1729	**4130**	**2174**	**12728**	**4158**	**22064**	**48941**	**10029**	**11403**
3284	**3218**	**1329**	**13212**	**10434**	**27584**	**18595**	**15858**	**11227**
21759	**20418**	**7684**	**89741**	**64229**	**182094**	**95744**	**94551**	**73605**
79	**161**	**134**	**736**	**602**	**1898**	**5611**	**1167**	**1436**
145	**392**	**314**	**2046**	**1191**	**5292**	**14878**	**2333**	**3481**
1	1	41	219	272	331	1380	504	391
3	6	145	1090	687	1285	4195	1162	1837
78	160	90	498	314	1546	3903	576	1017
142	386	165	916	477	3962	10061	1047	1598
		3	18	16	21	278	87	27
		3	40	27	45	536	124	46
			16		7	1002	363	2
			21		9	1325	492	3
3			14	9	16	49	24	35
235	38		370	229	1034	2635	614	1421
39	**40**	**7**	**93**	**82**	**131**	**438**	**79**	**128**
70	**329**	**11**	**553**	**265**	**359**	**1218**	**338**	**196**

表6–5 续表 continued

指标	Indicators	全市 Total	市区 Urban District	海曙区 Haishu
浙贝播种面积	Sown Area of Zhebeinine	333	305	305
总产量（吨）	Yield of Zhebeinine(ton)	1496	1406	1406
铁皮石斛播种面积	Sown Area of Dendrobium Candidum	310	91	1
总产量（吨）	Yield of Dendrobium Candidum(ton)	540	321	4
蔬菜类播种面积	**Sown Area of Vegetables**	**90087**	**23263**	**4562**
蔬菜类总产量（吨）	Yield of Vegetables(ton)	2851515	665758	104606
食用菌产量（吨）	Yield of Edible Mushroom(ton)	19654	16871	94
瓜果类播种面积	**Sown Area of Melon and Fruits**	**16582**	**3877**	**750**
总产量（吨）	Yield of Melon and Fruits(ton)	481862	127602	25237
西瓜播种面积	Sown Area of Watermelon	10032	2744	579
总产量（吨）	Yield of Watermelon(ton)	322809	99841	21396
香瓜播种面积	Sown Area of Muskmelon	3813	389	43
总产量（吨）	Yield of Muskmelon(ton)	100036	11297	990
草莓面积	Sown Area of Strawberry	1170	448	114
总产量（吨）	Yield of Strawberry(ton)	20379	8328	2546
其他农作物播种面积	**Sown Area of Other Crops**	**2871**	**2177**	**1103**
青饲料	Green feed	279	18	6

单位：公顷 (hectare)

江北区 Jiangbei	镇海区 Zhenhai	北仑区 Beilun	鄞州区 Yinzhou	奉化区 Fenghua	余姚市 Yuyao	慈溪市 Cixi	宁海县 Ninghai	象山县 Xiangshan
						18	9	1
						59	24	7
11	22	6	23	28	102	10	6	101
56	122	8	53	80	61	43	41	75
1535	**3430**	**1697**	**9486**	**2554**	**18824**	**34537**	**5160**	**8302**
39958	97627	46096	316165	61307	728288	1127109	132807	197552
193	203	395	737	15249	135	2039	547	63
65	**498**	**335**	**1725**	**503**	**1117**	**6805**	**3179**	**1603**
1808	11854	8263	69828	10612	37984	178857	94373	43045
42	181	252	1352	338	813	4250	1106	1118
1336	5313	6776	57194	7826	29911	123949	35709	33399
6	111	35	159	34	111	1064	2015	233
131	2587	651	6384	555	2982	23292	57533	4933
10	94	36	64	131	107	438	58	119
173	1855	609	915	2232	1812	7690	1131	1417
8	**1**	**1**	**657**	**408**	**70**	**498**	**57**	**69**
1			11		1	224		36

表6-6 各区（县、市）粮食作物播种面积和产量（2022年）
Sowing Area and Yield of Grain Crops by Region（2022）

指标	Indicators	全市 Total	市区 Urban District	海曙区 Haishu
粮食作物播种面积	**Sown Area of Grain Crops**	**114965**	**41701**	**10223**
总产量（吨）	**Total Output(ton)**	**715965**	**269972**	**66141**
一、谷物面积	Sown Area of Grain	98318	37031	9067
总产量（吨）	Total Output(ton)	654219	250462	61209
其中：稻谷面积	Among:Rice	73285	28635	6236
总产量（吨）	Total Output(ton)	547337	214988	49577
1. 早稻面积	Sowing Area of Early Rice	15142	7677	1044
总产量（吨）	Total Output(ton)	95863	50109	7111
2. 中稻和一季晚稻面积	Sowing Area of Middle Season Rice and One Season Late Rice	44332	13367	4123
总产量（吨）	Total Output(ton)	358545	112952	35188
3. 双季晚稻面积	Sowing Area of Double Cropping Late	13811	7591	1068
总产量（吨）	Total Output(ton)	92929	51926	7277
其中：小麦面积	Sowing Area of Wheat	18351	6645	2120
总产量（吨）	Total Output(ton)	80290	28580	8555
二、豆类面积	Sowing Area of Peas and Beans	10014	2175	458
总产量（吨）	Total Output(ton)	28306	6040	1306
其中：大豆面积	Sowing Area of Soybean	4985	1159	229
总产量（吨）	Total Output(ton)	13583	2894	558
三、薯类面积	Sowing Area of Tubers	6632	2495	698
总产量（吨）	Total Output(ton)	33439	13470	3627
其中：马铃薯面积	Sowing Area of Potato	3488	1119	305
总产量（吨）	Total Output(ton)	14650	4987	1164

注：本表数据来自国家统计局宁波调查队。
Note: Data in this table are obtained from the State Statistical Bureau Ningbo Investigation team.

单位：公顷 (hectare)

江北区 Jiangbei	镇海区 Zhenhai	北仑区 Beilun	鄞州区 Yinzhou	奉化区 Fenghua	余姚市 Yuyao	慈溪市 Cixi	宁海县 Ninghai	象山县 Xiangshan
3284	**3218**	**1329**	**13212**	**10434**	**27584**	**18595**	**15858**	**11227**
21759	**20418**	**7684**	**89741**	**64229**	**182094**	**95744**	**94551**	**73605**
3119	2838	1064	12478	8465	25927	13339	12900	9121
21119	18593	6534	86421	56586	176440	78803	84851	63664
2378	2192	822	10493	6514	19727	7420	9831	7672
17750	15987	5424	77331	48920	147868	53049	73038	58394
564	689	171	3653	1556	5037	993	580	854
3939	4457	1015	24160	9427	31667	5562	3021	5503
1208	883	466	3355	3331	9719	6000	9002	6244
9996	7306	3289	28708	28466	82861	44748	68537	49447
606	620	185	3485	1626	4971	427	249	575
3815	4224	1120	24463	11027	33340	2739	1480	3444
697	489	191	1783	1365	4466	3865	2115	1260
3225	2057	860	8240	5643	20734	17425	9001	4550
85	164	119	262	1086	1040	4751	1233	815
277	553	317	747	2839	3162	14391	2422	2291
52	67	39	80	692	681	2088	491	566
156	203	110	216	1651	2059	6090	1013	1528
80	215	147	471	884	617	505	1725	1290
363	1271	833	2572	4804	2492	2550	7278	7650
52	115	96	251	300	527	298	1126	417
209	603	503	1117	1391	1984	1285	4491	1903

表6-7 各区（县、市）林业生产情况（2022年）
Basic Statistics on Forestry by Region（2022）

指标	Indicators	全市 Total	市区 Urban District	海曙区 Haishu
林业用地面积（亩）	Area of Forestry Land (mu)	6174142	2639003	411861
森林面积（公顷）	Area of Forest (hectare)	437954	180101	28839
森林覆盖率(%)	Forest Coverage (%)	44. 67		48. 45
活立木总蓄积量(万立方米)	Total Standing Tree Stock (10000cu.m)	2617. 76	1041. 31	170. 71
森林蓄积量(万立方米)	Forest Stock (10000 cu.m)	2520. 72	1010. 83	166. 84
森林抚育面积(公顷)	Area of Forest Conservation (hectare)	5953	2653	411
湿地面积（公顷）	Area of Wetland (hectare)	231656	39273	2820
湿地保护率（%）	Wetland Conservation Rate (%)	66. 08		/
营造林情况(公顷)	Afforestation (hectare)	1846. 07	908. 87	156. 80
造林面积按方式分	By Way of Afforestation			
当年人工造林面积(公顷)	Area of Afforest artificially in this Year (hectare)	1846. 07	908. 87	156. 80
造林面积按用途分	By Use of Afforestation			
森林抚育面积(公顷)	Forest Tending area(hectare)	5953	2653	411
林木种苗	Tree Seedlings			
育苗面积(公顷)	Area of Growing Seedings(hectare)	19435	12659	1714
主要林产品产量(吨)	Output of Major Forest Products (ton)			
油茶籽产量（吨）	Yield of Oil–tea Camellia Seed (ton)	275	25	
油茶产量（吨）	Yield of Oil–tea Camellia (ton)	62		

注：本表数据来自宁波市自然资源和规划局。
Note:Data in this tables are obtained from Ningbo Bureau of Natural Resources and Planning.

江北区 Jiangbei	镇海区 Zhenhai	北仑区 Beilun	鄞州区 Yinzhou	奉化区 Fenghua	余姚市 Yuyao	慈溪市 Cixi	宁海县 Ninghai	象山县 Xiangshan
66330	70586	349048	473545	1267633	852580	200023	1523879	958655
5187	5310	23643	34091	83031	57902	19544	108150	72257
24.93	21.62	38.29	42.49	64.95	40.04	14.63	58.11	51.07
20.94	35.97	165.40	237.13	411.16	343.56	99.14	722.62	411.13
16.84	33.40	160.58	229.95	403.22	320.71	86.65	702.49	400.04
33	76	486	718	929	909	227	962	1202
1273	11433	9287	7107	7353	26647	51643	33560	80533
100.00	74.64	100.00	75.88	56.11	89.27	57.25	53.63	79.55
15.53	101.20	14.93	136.73	483.67	268.53	43.47	129.67	495.53
15.53	101.20	14.93	136.73	483.67	268.53	43.47	129.67	495.53
33	76	486	718	929	909	227	962	1202
300	43	4410	137	6054	3596	1728	565	887
				25			250	
							62	

表6-8 各区（县、市）茶叶生产情况（2022年）
Basic Statistics on Tea and Edible Nuts by Region（2022）

指标	Indicators	全市 Total	市区 Urban District	海曙区 Haishu
茶叶生产	**Tea Production**			
茶园总面积(公顷)	**Tea Field Area(hectare)**	**11006**	**2975**	**655**
本年采摘	Pluck in This Year	9710	2611	557
茶叶总产量（吨）	**Total Tea Output (ton)**	**10585**	**3443**	**873**
按品种分类	**Classified by Variety**			
绿茶	Green Tea	10230	3123	755
青茶	Oolong Tea			
红茶	Black Tea	222	199	19
黑茶	Dark Tea			
黄茶	Yellow Tea	1		
白茶	White Tea	133	120	99
其他茶叶	Other Tea			

江北区 Jiangbei	镇海区 Zhenhai	北仑区 Beilun	鄞州区 Yinzhou	奉化区 Fenghua	余姚市 Yuyao	慈溪市 Cixi	宁海县 Ninghai	象山县 Xiangshan
224	**78**	**351**	**883**	**785**	**3933**	**240**	**3091**	**767**
220	78	302	822	633	3826	239	2492	542
53	**70**	**323**	**1194**	**930**	**2856**	**47**	**3826**	**414**
52	70	305	1012	930	2848	45	3800	414
		17	163				23	
					1			
1		1	19		8	2	3	

表6-9 各区（县、市）果园水果生产情况（2022年）
Basic Statistics on Fruits Production by Region（2022）

指标	Indicators	全市 Total	市区 Urban District	海曙区 Haishu
果园面积合计（公顷）	**Area of Orchards(hectare)**	**44251**	**8693**	**910**
柑橘园	Citrus	9626	1626	93
梨园	Pears	1937	335	85
桃园	Peaches	4152	2623	126
猕猴桃园	Kiwi Fruit	536	143	24
葡萄园	Grapery	6121	1334	250
其他果园	Others	21880	2634	331
园林水果产量（吨）	**Output of Fruits(ton)**	**788146**	**170170**	**18520**
柑橘	Citrus	270989	42188	2677
柑	Mandarin Orange	119019	3464	339
橘	Mandarin	138028	31882	2291
橙	Orange	681	268	17
柚	Shaddock	126	58	30
梨	Pears	62012	8890	2284
桃	Peaches	70715	45047	2862
猕猴桃	Kiwi Fruit	6562	1670	405
葡萄	Grapes	166808	38442	6944

江北区 Jiangbei	镇海区 Zhenhai	北仑区 Beilun	鄞州区 Yinzhou	奉化区 Fenghua	余姚市 Yuyao	慈溪市 Cixi	宁海县 Ninghai	象山县 Xiangshan
915	**492**	**872**	**2149**	**3356**	**7500**	**11535**	**7042**	**9481**
77	140	358	649	309	154	277	2767	4803
107	16	17	84	25	419	741	283	159
27	23	64	168	2213	198	536	591	205
7		5	43	65	85	14	274	20
402	110	80	400	90	713	3738	81	255
293	203	347	805	653	5932	6230	3046	4039
19429	**10083**	**16827**	**54810**	**50500**	**112978**	**213058**	**127159**	**164781**
1558	3742	10294	18409	5508	2993	6281	94144	125384
80	713	1061	1177	95	1341	1420	63	112731
266	100	9169	15383	4673	435	2827	94066	8817
1		18	74	158	8	58		347
		1		27	2	48	15	3
2169	442	299	3357	339	14479	32140	3547	2956
602	629	1023	4470	35462	4950	13102	4810	2806
86		40	808	331	944	204	3441	303
12227	2500	1751	13263	1757	23950	97305	1596	5515

表6-10 各区（县、市）畜牧业生产情况（2022年）
Basic Statistics on Animal Husbandry By Region（2022）

指标	Indicators	全市 Total	海曙区 Haishu
生猪(万只)	**Hogs (10000 heads)**		
年末存栏头数(含未断奶小猪)	Being Raised at Year－end	64.48	1.95
#能繁殖的母猪	Reproducable	7.11	0.21
年内生猪出栏头数	Slaughtered Fattened Hogs	93.06	1.65
牛(万头)	**Cattles & Buffaloes(10000 heads)**		
年末存栏头数	Being Raised at Year－end	1.55	0.04
年内出栏头数	Slaughtered Cattles & Buffaloes of the Year	0.65	0.02
羊(万只)	**Sheep & Goat(10000 heads)**		
年末存栏只数	Being Raised at Year－end	6.73	0.09
年内出栏只数	Slaughtered Sheep & Goat of the Year	5.68	0.08
家禽（万只）	**Poultry(10000 heads)**		
年末存栏只数	Being Raised at Year－end	498.81	5.82
年内出栏只数	Slaughtered Poultry of the Year	622.48	4.71
主要畜禽产品产量(万吨)	**Output of Main Livestock Production(10000 tons)**		
猪肉	Pork	8.04	0.14
牛肉	Beef	0.10	
羊肉	Mutton	0.10	
禽肉	Poultry Meat	1.08	0.01

注：本表数据来自国家统计局宁波调查队。
Note:Data in this table are obtained from the State Statistical Bureau Ningbo Investigation team.

江北区 Jiangbei	镇海区 Zhenhai	北仑区 Beilun	鄞州区 Yinzhou	奉化区 Fenghua	余姚市 Yuyao	慈溪市 Cixi	宁海县 Ninghai	象山县 Xiangshan
1. 42	2. 14	1. 71	0. 88	6. 84	12. 24	15. 74	10. 14	11. 41
0. 09	0. 21	0. 15	0. 27	1. 17	1. 46	1. 40	1. 02	1. 13
1. 30	2. 25	2. 84	1. 35	10. 86	17. 78	26. 65	12. 04	16. 35
0. 37	0. 07	0. 04	0. 05	0. 05	0. 43	0. 06	0. 33	0. 10
0. 10	0. 04	0. 02	0. 05	0. 04	0. 18	0. 03	0. 12	0. 05
	0. 03	0. 16	0. 01	0. 54	1. 16	2. 69	0. 75	1. 30
	0. 01	0. 06		0. 50	0. 76	2. 68	0. 34	1. 25
0. 88	11. 48	8. 95	2. 56	47. 23	79. 39	179. 19	37. 69	125. 61
1. 06	13. 83	8. 16	1. 87	55. 36	122. 59	155. 16	93. 96	165. 78
0. 10	0. 24	0. 24	0. 11	0. 86	1. 69	2. 25	1. 02	1. 40
0. 01	0. 01		0. 01		0. 03	0. 01	0. 02	0. 01
				0. 01	0. 02	0. 05	0. 01	0. 02
	0. 03	0. 01	0. 00	0. 07	0. 24	0. 25	0. 11	0. 35

表6-11 各区（县、市）水产品产量及养殖面积(2022年)
Output and Area of Artificially Cultured of Aquatic Production by Region（2022）

指标	Indicators	全市 Total	市区 Urban District	海曙区 Haishu
水产品总产量(吨)	**Total Aquatic Products (ton)**	**1122779**	**221708**	**2133**
海水产品产量(吨)	**Seawater Aquatic Products (ton)**	**1031493**	**204886**	
按生产性质分	**By Production Character**			
海洋捕捞	Catching in Ocean	513723	136388	
鱼类	Fish	389577	123732	
甲壳类	Shrimps.Prawns and Crabs	76323	2426	
贝类	Shell－Fish	7072	623	
其他类	Others	5370	4047	
海水养殖	Seawater Aquiculture	398496	36624	
鱼类	Fish	19729	5128	
甲壳类	Shrimps.Prawns and Crabs	46731	6029	
贝类	Shell－Fish	303730	23088	
其他类	Others	3737	110	
远洋渔业产品产量(吨)	**Pelagic Fishery (ton)**	**119274**	**31874**	
淡水产品产量(吨)	**Freshwater Aquatic Products (ton)**	**91286**	**16822**	**2133**
按生产性质分	**By Production Character**			
淡水捕捞	Catching in Freshwater	25732	7806	782
淡水养殖	Freshwater Aquiculture	65554	9016	1351
按类别分	By Category			
鱼类	Fish	37223	8023	1057
甲壳类	Shrimps.Prawns and Crabs	25599	684	122
贝类	Shell－Fish	721	106	6
其他类	Others	1991	203	166
海水养殖面积（公顷)	**Seawater Aquiculture Area(hectare)**	**32145**	**2729**	
淡水养殖面积（公顷)	**Freshwater Aquiculture Area(hectare)**	**9109**	**1214**	**185**

注：本表数据来自宁波市农业农村局。
Note:Date in this table are obtained from Ningbo Agricultural and rural Bureau.

江北区 Jiangbei	镇海区 Zhenhai	北仑区 Beilun	鄞州区 Yinzhou	奉化区 Fenghua	余姚市 Yuyao	慈溪市 Cixi	宁海县 Ninghai	象山县 Xiangshan
32373	**283**	**979**	**18708**	**167232**	**26565**	**45918**	**178468**	**650120**
31874		**548**	**8933**	**163531**	**1409**	**21873**	**171475**	**631850**
		372	2545	133471	1409	2756	5540	367630
		174	2109	121449	799	497	1035	263514
		198	297	1931	458	348	1154	71937
				623	140	1393	2891	2025
			10	4037	12	514		797
		176	6388	30060		19117	165935	176820
				5128		3196	2575	8830
		63	4473	1493		2386	16140	22176
		113	915	22060		13020	144860	122762
				110		515	880	2232
31874								**87400**
499	**283**	**431**	**9775**	**3701**	**25156**	**24045**	**6993**	**18270**
415		173	4718	1718	6667	8636	443	2180
84	283	258	5057	1983	18489	15409	6550	16090
74	277	258	4480	1877	13586	6629	3150	5835
	6		488	68	3254	8191	3400	10070
			62	38	503	67		45
10			27		1146	522		120
		34	**1367**	**1328**		**5937**	**12266**	**11213**
22	**249**	**14**	**557**	**187**	**1656**	**2847**	**2012**	**1380**

表6-12 各区（县、市）农业机械拥有量(2022年末)
Possession of Agricultural Machinery by Region (End of 2022)

指标	单位	Indicators	Unit	全市 Total	市区 Urban District	海曙区 Haishu
农业机械总动力	千瓦	**Total Power of Agricultural Machinery**	**kW**	**2360754**	**631622**	**138834**
柴油发动机动力	千瓦	Power of Diesel Engine	kW	1648215	411748	96759
汽油发动机动力	千瓦	Power of Gasoline Engine	kW	137785	31124	5689
电动机动力	千瓦	Power of Motors	kW	574754	188750	36386
拖拉机及配套机械		**Tractors and Supporting Machinery**				
其中：拖拉机动力合计	台	Total Power of Tractors	set	6163	2272	240
	千瓦		kW	199137	61543	9610
小型拖拉机	台	Mini－tractors	set	3056	1429	49
	千瓦		kW	34300	17728	607
中型拖拉机	台	Medium Sized Tractors	set	2760	758	173
	千瓦		kW	134761	37079	7510
大型拖拉机	台	Large Sized Tractors	set	347	85	18
	千瓦		kW	30076	6736	1493
种植业机械		**Plantation Machinery**				
耕整机	台	Cultivators	set	2568	519	154
	千瓦		kW	12592	2179	755
水稻插秧机	台	Rice Transplanters	set	4664	2055	359
	千瓦		kW	50742	16694	4342
谷物联合收割机	台	Grain Combine Harvesters	set	2057	543	119
	千瓦		kW	107155	26927	6727
设施农业设备－温室面积	万平方米	Facility Agricultural Equipment－Greenhouse Area	10000 cu.m	7390	2340	607
农产品初加工机械		**Agricultural Pre－processing Machinery**				
农产品初加工机械动力合计	台	Mechanical Power of Agricultural Primary Processing	set	28742	10136	2789
	千瓦		kW	157624	52163	14484
畜牧机械		**Livestock Machinery**				
畜牧机械动力合计	台	Mechanical Power of Livestock	set	5753	1000	192
	千瓦		kW	35007	5375	1579
水产机械		Aquatic Machinery				
水产机械动力合计	台	Mechanical Power of Aquatic Production	set	61405	11467	434
	千瓦		kW	704124	50866	1797
农田基本建设机械		**Agricultural Capital Construction Machinery**				
农田基本建设机械动力合计	台	Mechanical Power of Agricultural Capital Construction	set	2605	1165	170
	千瓦		kW	237136	102139	13741
农用航空器	架	Agricultural Aircrafts	unit	1086	315	130

注：本表数据来自宁波市农业农村局。
Note:Date in this table are obtained from Ningbo Agricultural and rural Bureau.

江北区 Jiangbei	镇海区 Zhenhai	北仑区 Beilun	鄞州区 Yinzhou	奉化区 Fenghua	余姚市 Yuyao	慈溪市 Cixi	宁海县 Ninghai	象山县 Xiangshan
33444	**40605**	**96653**	**140272**	**181814**	**461441**	**308486**	**226120**	**733085**
16390	25669	65192	82456	125282	265221	156430	151213	663603
324	2604	10936	4510	7061	33689	47808	15564	9600
16730	12332	20525	53306	49471	162531	104248	59343	59882
60	212	158	879	723	1882	948	420	641
3280	5603	3914	16490	22646	62287	38940	15913	20454
4	145	107	716	408	836	378	117	296
60	1622	1166	7944	6329	7984	3689	1574	3325
43	59	48	121	314	950	461	298	293
2155	3325	2498	5348	16243	46459	24761	13945	12517
13	8	3	42	1	96	109	5	52
1065	656	250	3198	74	7844	10490	394	4612
46	20	48	122	129	11	1438	488	112
134	74	174	514	528	44	7264	2435	670
62	201	27	1057	349	1325	420	453	411
810	1232	375	5499	4436	20533	5002	4270	4243
18	21	8	229	148	602	146	267	499
1190	1555	630	8265	8560	35346	7901	14207	22774
567	139	211	172	644	688	1505	467	2390
402	253	1213	1929	3550	11228	2295	3376	1707
3899	1578	2285	9622	20295	61104	20547	12222	11588
341	129	62	19	257	1460	1397	208	1688
1087	608	237	256	1608	8117	15955	1491	4069
88	141	488	9123	1193	4556	17801	15279	12302
5990	1319	1394	15253	25113	22487	37175	46483	547113
37	87	533	39	299	359	329	462	290
2000	8999	44462	4617	28320	41412	16034	46570	30981
9	17	7	110	42	378	169	93	131

表6-13 各区（县、市）灌溉和水利情况(2022年)
Irrigation and Water Conservancy Facilities of Farmland by Region（2022）

指标	Indicators	全市 Total	市区 Urban District	海曙区 Haishu
水库年末累计(座)	**Total Number of Reservoirsat the Year－end(set)**	**397**	**186**	**24**
总库容量（万立方米)	**Total Capacity of Reservoirs at the Year－end(10000cu.m)**	**189589**	**86757**	**28373**
大型水库（座)	Large－sized Reservoirs(set)	6	4	2
总库容(万立方米)	Capacity(10000 cu.m)	78527	49415	23185
中型水库(座)	Medium-sized Reservoirs(set)	26	7	1
总库容(万立方米)	Capacity(10000 cu.m)	77617	21923	2838
小型水库(座)	Small－sized Reservoirs(set)	365	175	21
总库容(万立方米)	Capacity(10000 cu.m)	33445	15419	2350
水电站数量(座)	Hydropower Station(set)	133	46	14
泵站数量(处)	Pumping Station(unit)	3979	1928	28
灌溉面积总计(千公顷)	Total Irrigated Area(1000 hectares)	163.66	63.49	10.12
有效灌溉面积(千公顷)	Effective Irrigated Area(1000 hectares)	141.18	48.78	10.12
有效实灌面积(千公顷)	Effective Fact Irrigated Area(1000 hectares)	135.13	46.84	9.87
除涝面积(千公顷)	Drainage Area(1000 hectares)	84.80	36.62	
水土流失综合治理面积(千公顷)	Area of Soil Erosion under Control(1000 hectares)	270.91	113.83	1.34
水闸座数(座)	Sluice(set)	2136	579	48
堤防长度(公里)	Total Length of Dikes(km)	2849	1372	55
全部供水工程总供水量(万立方米)	**Annually Water Supply of Water Conservancy(10000cu.m)**	**221764**	**125077**	**17286**
地表水源工程供水(万立方米)	Water supply for surface water source project(10000 cu.m)	216666	121068	17238
地下水源工程供水(万立方米)	Water supply for underground water source project(10000cu.m)	74	63	48
其他水源工程供水(万立方米)	Water supply of other water source projects(10000 cu.m)	5024	3946	

注：本表数据来自宁波市水利局。
Note:Data in this tables are obtained from Ningbo Municipal Bureau of Water Conservancy.

江北区 Jiangbei	镇海区 Zhenhai	北仑区 Beilun	鄞州区 Yinzhou	奉化区 Fenghua	余姚市 Yuyao	慈溪市 Cixi	宁海县 Ninghai	象山县 Xiangshan
5	**5**	**33**	**30**	**89**	**55**	**18**	**62**	**76**
2189	**3787**	**4414**	**16452**	**31541**	**25635**	**17297**	**42432**	**17468**
				2	1		1	
				26230	12272		16840	
	1	1	4		3	5	6	5
	2441	1474	15170		9149	13592	22677	10277
5	4	32	26	87	51	13	55	71
2189	1346	2940	1282	5311	4214	3705	2915	7191
				32	64		23	
431	627	236	11	595	285	68	612	1086
4. 33	4. 21	7. 57	14. 12	23. 14	28. 65	34. 11	21. 41	16. 00
3. 24	3. 78	6. 37	12. 93	12. 34	27. 64	33. 10	18. 20	13. 46
3. 24	3. 49	6. 37	11. 53	12. 34	27. 64	30. 49	16. 70	13. 46
3. 70	14. 36	8. 66	1. 11	8. 79	8. 37	5. 94	15. 65	18. 22
0. 10	2. 26	15. 71	31. 29	63. 14	32. 30	10. 03	66. 21	48. 53
103	47	142	95	144	456	212	372	517
96	84	134	160	843	211	74	927	265
7560	**23452**	**32661**	**27608**	**16510**	**31826**	**31205**	**17992**	**15664**
7560	21064	31105	27603	16498	31644	30388	17981	15585
			3	12			11	
	2388	1556	2		182	817		79

主要统计指标解释

【农林牧渔业总产值】农林牧渔业总产值是以货币表现的农林牧渔业的全部产品总量和对农林牧渔业生产活动进行的各种支持性服务活动的价值。它反映一定时期内农林牧渔业生产总规模和总成果，是观察农林牧渔业生产水平和发展速度，研究农林牧渔业内部比例关系、农林牧渔业与工业、农林牧渔业与国家建设、人民生活比例关系的重要指标，同时也是计算农林牧渔业劳动生产率和农林牧渔业增加值的基础资料。

【经济作物播种面积】经济作物播种面积是指农业生产经营者应在日历年度内收获的经济作物在全部土地（耕地或非耕地）上的播种或移植面积。凡是本年内收获的经济作物，无论是本年还是上年播种，都算为本年播种面积，但不包括本年播种，下年收获的作物面积。移植的作物面积按移植后的面积计算，不计算移植前在育苗田、棚等的面积。多年生作物，即播种后可连续生长多年的缩根性草本植物，如有些麻类、中药等作物的播种面积，按本年新增面积加往年的连续累计面积计算。如果因灾害等原因，应该收获却未能收获，也要按原播种面积计算，新补或改种，并在本年收获的，要按复种作物计算面积。间种、混种的作物面积按比例折算各个作物的面积，如果完全混合、同步生长、收获的作物，按混合面积平均分配。复种、套种的作物，按次数计算面积，每种一次计算一次。再生烟等，因其没有经过播种或移植，不计入播种面积。莲藕等水生蔬菜类生长在湖泊、水塘等水域的面积占比重较大，不仅难以统计，而且因非耕地面积过大对统计口径产生影响，因此在湖泊、水塘等水域的莲藕等水生蔬菜无论是野生还是人工种植均不计算面积，只计算其在耕地上种植的面积。

【经济作物总产量】经济作物总产量是指本年度内生产的各种经济作物总产量，不论计划内外，数量多少，耕地上与非耕地上的经济作物产量，都应该统计在内，不得遗漏。经济作物产量应统计全社会的产量。不仅要把国有农场等国有经济和乡、村集体经济以及农民家庭经营的经济作物产量统计在内，还要把工矿企业职工家属办的农场和其他单位生产的农作物产量统计在内；不仅要把卖给国家的农作物产量统计在内，还要把生产单位自产自用的农作物产量统计在内。经济作物产量原则上应以晒干入仓的产量为统计标准，由于经济作物产品繁多，个别农产品产量规定按鲜品统计。

【茶叶产量】指本年度内生产的全部茶叶产量。包括从成片茶园和零星种植的茶树以及荒芜未垦复的茶树上所采摘的全部产量。不论自食的或出售的，都应统计在内。茶叶的产量按经过初步加工的干毛茶的重量计算。根据制造方法的不同和品质上的差异，将茶叶分为绿茶、青茶、红茶、黑茶、黄茶、白茶、其他茶等。

【园林水果产量】指农业生产经营者日历年度内在专业性果园、林地及零星种植果树（藤）上生产的水果产量。包括苹果、梨、柑橘类、热带水果和其他园林水果五类，不包括采集的野生水果。按实收的鲜果计算产量。经脱水、晾干等处理的干果，如干枣、葡萄干、柿饼、桔饼等一律折合成鲜果计算。

Explanatory Notes on Main Statistical Indicators

【Gross Output Value of Farming, Forestry, Animal Husbandry and Fishery】 The total output value of agriculture, forestry, animal husbandry and fishery is the total amount of all products of agriculture, forestry, animal husbandry and fishery in currency and the value of various supporting service activities for the production activities of agriculture, forestry, animal husbandry and fishery. It reflects the total scale and achievements of agriculture, forestry, animal husbandry and fishery production in a certain period of time. It is an important indicator to observe the production level and development speed of agriculture, forestry, animal husbandry and fishery, to study the internal proportion relationship between agriculture, forestry, animal husbandry and fishery, industry, national construction, and people's living ratio. It is also the basis for calculating the labor productivity and added value of agriculture, forestry, animal husbandry and fishery.

【Sown area of cash crops】 The sown area of cash crops refers to the planting or transplanting area of cash crops on all land (cultivated land or non cultivated land) that agricultural producers and operators should harvest in the calendar year. All economic crops harvested in the current year, whether sown this year or last year, are counted as the sown area of this year, but excluding the crop area sown in this year and harvested in the next year. The area of transplanted crops is calculated according to the area after transplantation, and the area in nursery field and shed before transplantation is not calculated. Perennial crops, i.e. the planting area of shrunk root herbaceous plants that can continuously grow for many years after sowing, such as some hemp and traditional Chinese medicine crops, shall be calculated according to the newly increased area of this year plus the continuous accumulated area of previous years. If the crop should be harvested but failed to be harvested due to disasters and other reasons, the area shall be calculated according to the original sown area, and the area shall be calculated according to the multiple cropping crops. The crop area of intercropping and mixed planting is converted into the area of each crop in proportion. If the crops are completely mixed, grow synchronously and harvest, they are evenly distributed according to the mixed area. For multiple cropping and interplanting crops, the area is calculated according to the number of times, and each kind is calculated once. Because it has not been seeded or transplanted, it is not included in the sowing area. Lotus root and other aquatic vegetables growing in lakes, ponds and other waters account for a large proportion of the area, which is not only difficult to count, but also has an impact on the statistical caliber due to the large area of non cultivated land. Therefore, the area of lotus root and other aquatic vegetables in lakes, ponds and other waters, whether wild or artificial, is not calculated, but only the area planted on cultivated land.

【Total output of cash crops】 The total output of cash crops refers to the total output of various kinds of cash crops produced in the current year. No matter how much the quantity is inside or outside the plan, the economic crop yields on cultivated land and non cultivated land should be counted, and should not be omitted. The output of economic crops should be counted for the whole society. We should include not only the output of state–owned economy such as state–owned farms, the collective economy of townships and villages, and the production of cash crops run by peasant families, but also the output of crops produced by farms run by the families of workers and staff members of industrial and mining enterprises and other units. We should not only include the output of agricultural products sold to the state, but also the output of crops produced and used by production units. In principle, the output of cash crops should be based on the output of drying in the warehouse. Due to the variety of cash crops, the output of individual agricultural products should be counted according to fresh products.

【Tea production】 Tea production refers to the total tea production in the current year, including the total output picked from tea plantations, scattered tea trees and barren tea trees.Whether eaten or sold, they should be counted.The output of tea is calculated according to the weight of dry tea after preliminary processing.According to the differences in manufacturing methods and quality, tea is divided into green tea, oolong tea, black tea, black tea, yellow tea, white tea and other teas.

【Garden fruit output】 Garden fruit output refers to the fruit output produced by agricultural producers and operators in professional orchards, woodlands and sporadically planted fruit trees (vines) in the calendar year.It includes apple, pear, citrus, tropical fruits and other garden fruits, excluding the collected wild fruits.The output is calculated according to the fresh fruits.Dried fruits such as dried jujubes, raisins, persimmons and orange cakes that have been dehydrated and dried shall be converted into fresh fruits.

NINGBO 2023 Statistical Yearbook

CHAPTER 7

第七篇

工业、能源消费和电力

INDUSTRY,ENERGY CONSUMPTION AND ELECTRICITY

工业、能源消费和电力
Industry, Energy Consumption and Electricity

主要统计指标
Major Statistics Indicators

2022年规模以上工业企业数	Number of Industrial Enterprises Above The Set Scale	10342	个	unit
比上年增长	Increase Over Last Year	5.2	%	
2022年规模以上工业总产值	Output Value of Industrial Enterprises Above The Set Scale	242051716	万元	10000 yuan
比上年增长	Increase Over Last Year	7.3	%	
2022年规模以上工业实现利税	Total Profits and Taxes of Industrial Enterprises Above The Set Scale	23361205	万元	10000 yuan
比上年增长	Increase Over Last Year	-11.2	%	
2022年规模以上工业实现利润	Total Profits of Industrial Enterprises Above The Set Scale	14180052	万元	10000 yuan
比上年增长	Increase Over Last Year	-19.3	%	
2022年规模以上应交增值税	Value - added Taxes Payable of Industrial Enterprises Above The Set Scale	4236988	万元	10000 yuan
比上年增长	Increase Over Last Year	2.1	%	

表7-1 部分年份规模以上工业企业单位数
Number of Industrial Enterprises Above Designated Size in Partial Years

单位：个(unit)

指标	Indicators	2018	2019	2020	2021	2022
工业企业单位数	**Number of Industrial Enterprises**	**7602**	**8242**	**8571**	**9831**	**10342**
按轻重工业分	**By Light and Heavy Industry**					
轻工业	Light Industry	3177	3418	3542	4030	4188
重工业	Heavy Industry	4425	4824	5029	5801	6154
按注册登记类型分	**By Registered Type**					
国有企业	State－owned Enterprises	6	5	5	5	7
集体企业	Collective－owned Enterprises	6	6	5	6	5
股份合作企业	Share Cooperative Enterprises	29	35	28	31	30
有限责任公司	Limited Liability Corporations	575	323	334	389	435
股份有限公司	Share－holding Corporations Ltd.	163	96	82	88	94
私营企业	Private Enterprises	5449	6409	6783	7991	8466
港澳台商投资企业	Hongkong, Macao and Taiwan Funded	727	681	648	631	616
外商投资企业	Enterprises with Foreign Investment	647	687	686	690	689
在总计中：国有控股企业	In Total:State－owned holding enterprises	125	123	133	153	164
按规模分	**By Enterprises Size**					
大型企业	Large－Sized	132	139	144	155	150
中型企业	Medium－Sized	890	851	882	914	863
小型企业	Small－Sized	6354	6981	7203	8310	8748

注：2011年起，规模以上工业企业为年主营业务收入2000万元及以上的企业，下表同。

Note: From 2011,Industrial enterprises above designated size are those with annual revenue from principal business over 20 million yuan.The other tables are the same.

表7-2 部分年份规模以上工业企业总产值
Gross Output Value of Industrial Enterprises Above Designated Size in Partial Years

单位：万元 (10000 yuan)

指标	Indicators	2018	2019	2020	2021	2022
工业总产值	**Gross Industrial Output Value**	**170152550**	**178520996**	**181036619**	**225538127**	**242051716**
按轻重工业分	**By Light and Heavy Industry**					
轻工业	Light Industry	43416853	46499923	47825457	55412360	54339576
重工业	Heavy Industry	126735697	132021073	133211163	170125767	187712141
按注册登记类型分	**By Registered Type**					
国有企业	State－owned Enterprises	75608	68152	81892	188181	450505
集体企业	Collective－ owned Enterprises	28591	30105	29766	38870	24729
股份合作企业	Share Cooperative Enterprises	239980	293405	262967	301812	274355
有限责任公司	Limited Liability Corporations	38669903	30904053	29607993	34952646	36545977
股份有限公司	Share－holding Corporations Ltd.	19711647	19531190	16824212	21332574	24522424
私营企业	Private Enterprises	59933644	73578331	81868174	107822615	114816098
港澳台商投资企业	Hongkong, Macao and Taiwan Funded	33701391	34911190	32519170	38001562	38278168
外商投资企业	Enterprises with Foreign Investment	17791787	19204570	19842445	22899868	27139461
在总计中: 国有控股企业	In Total: State－owned holding enterprises	33546877	33560416	31357332	39907381	47903544
按规模分	**By Enterprises Size**					
大型企业	Large－Sized	61049480	66621968	70448773	85412426	79250700
中型企业	Medium－Sized	47579713	49340107	48043690	60373109	68727294
小型企业	Small－Sized	54373734	57869883	60420332	75221870	79826064

注：工业总产值按现行价格计算。
Note: Gross industrial output value are calculated at current prices.

表7-3 历年工业企业主要经济指标
Main Economic Indicators of Industrial Enterprises Over the Years

单位：亿元(100 million yuan)

年份 Year	总产值（当年价）Gross Industrial Output Value (current prices)	固定资产原值 Original Value of Fixed Assets	固定资产净值 Net Value of Fixed Assets	主营业务收入 Prime Operating Revenue	利税总额 Total Profits and Taxes	利润总额 Total Profits	全部从业人员年平均人数（万人）Annual Average Employees (10000 persons)
1978	15.79	7.07			4.29	2.59	
1979	18.11	8.25	6.28	18.71	4.73	2.86	
1980	23.73	9.59	7.35	24.89	6.17	3.93	
1981	29.67	11.38	8.76	30.05	6.94	4.26	
1982	29.99	13.53	10.49	32.36	7.99	4.86	
1983	35.23	15.84	12.17	38.98	9.07	5.57	
1984	50.93	21.09	16.67	54.57	11.30	6.53	
1985	68.63	32.55	26.43	76.16	14.62	7.65	65.48
1986	81.96	38.43	30.49	86.67	15.86	7.94	68.69
1987	102.16	52.61	41.79	110.96	18.54	9.92	71.29
1988	132.17	62.81	48.85	147.85	23.24	12.00	72.06
1989	159.41	74.80	56.60	162.81	23.64	11.47	69.05
1990	200.00	89.31	64.39	167.35	20.99	8.21	67.71
1991	261.62	107.17	79.45	218.15	25.27	11.79	72.02
1992	341.42	128.57	95.03	282.90	31.65	14.82	73.15
1993	491.07	192.06	147.38	430.65	45.15	22.68	73.94
1994	642.18	276.98	225.18	480.46	53.56	26.06	71.53
1995	837.80	357.05	281.28	664.70	62.61	29.46	66.08
1996	843.48	407.73	312.70	722.15	66.57	28.63	64.60
1997	842.62	496.05	374.92	747.51	78.60	33.32	55.88
1998	940.59	567.09	423.50	835.24	88.00	37.52	50.78
1999	1062.29	668.71	490.07	985.32	118.65	61.21	52.38
2000	1427.70	829.69	601.93	1350.52	163.26	88.11	58.42
2001	1629.66	926.49	648.50	1538.70	213.72	115.95	66.90
2002	2000.16	1058.90	727.01	1945.02	267.09	152.34	77.22
2003	2630.29	1251.24	854.79	2604.90	322.01	189.30	91.96
2004	3815.04	1602.75	1113.37	3660.69	417.63	241.31	128.94
2005	4890.97	1926.51	1337.30	4698.16	446.13	262.36	140.82
2006	6187.91	2469.35	1755.66	5930.59	525.65	312.63	159.64
2007	7789.01	2886.87	2013.56	7456.24	639.84	387.31	174.24
2008	8746.36	3422.49	2363.23	8283.18	489.32	221.25	178.59
2009	8272.85	3908.81	2633.33	7824.88	867.35	462.11	168.67
2010	10853.55	4431.40	2920.36	10396.63	1160.55	657.77	181.09
2011	12044.77	4543.83		11803.24	1193.21	631.66	152.25
2012	12155.08	4792.65		11795.98	1112.86	553.21	147.06
2013	13010.09	5092.25		12594.24	1315.94	701.68	147.50
2014	14028.05	5595.92		13254.65	1347.42	688.25	151.84
2015	13869.46	5989.39		12911.27	1525.33	776.28	147.43
2016	14500.24	6467.45		13639.11	1787.44	1016.89	146.82
2017	15850.89	6866.73		15643.88	2158.61	1287.46	148.69
2018	17015.25	7368.90		16861.05	2116.21	1259.50	150.53
2019	17852.10	7904.97		17482.25	2129.72	1339.87	151.29
2020	18103.66	8531.20		17790.51	2312.07	1502.74	150.58
2021	22553.81	9625.69		22513.83	2632.14	1757.68	165.11
2022	24205.17	10639.05		24373.36	2336.12	1418.01	166.99

注：1997年以前为乡及乡以上独立核算工业企业。1998年及以后为规模以上工业企业。

Note: Data in this table refer to all industrial enterprises with annual revenue from principal business over 5 million yuan, before 1997 to enterprises with independent accounting at townships and above level.

表7-4 全市及各区（县、市）规模以上工业企业总产值(现行价格、2022年)

Gross Output Value of Industrial Enterprises Above Designated Size by Region (at Current Price、2022)

指标	Indicators	全市 Total	市区 Urban District	海曙区 Haishu
工业总产值	**Gross Industrial Output Value**	**242051716**	**149239322**	**14452875**
按轻重工业分	**Grouped by Light and Heavy Industry**			
轻工业	Light Industry	54339576	27271507	4270234
重工业	Heavy Industry	187712141	121967815	10182641
按注册登记类型分	**Grouped by Registered Type**			
国有企业	State-owned Enterprises	450505	247289	
集体企业	Collective-owned Enterprises	24729	14376	
股份合作企业	Share Cooperative Enterprises	274355	190298	19325
有限责任公司	Limited Liability Corporations	36545977	24137417	5584450
股份有限公司	Share-holding Corporations Ltd.	24522424	21474770	276227
私营企业	Private Enterprises	114816098	56411664	6258371
港澳台商投资企业	Hong Kong. Macao & Taiwan Funded	38278168	30243027	1828055
外商投资企业	Foreign Funded Enterprises	27139461	16520482	486447
在总计中：国有控股企业	In Total: State-owned holding enterprises	47903544	41291721	5248057
按规模分	**Grouped by Enterprises Size**			
大型企业	Large-Sized	79250700	55354489	5763578
中型企业	Medium-Sized	68727294	43547431	2955663
小型企业	Small-Sized	79826064	41746096	5454693
按工业行业分	**Grouped by Sector**			
非金属矿采选业	Non-metallic Mining Industry	332384	187627	42198
农副食品加工业	Farm and Sideline Products Processing	1392383	641061	152754
食品制造业	Food Manufacturing	709370	435097	64327
酒、饮料和精制茶制造业	Wine, Beverages and Refined Tea Manufacturing	333698	248224	36681
纺织业	Textile Industry	3510122	2219653	190491
纺织服装、服饰业	Clothing, Apparel Industry	8023280	7014691	2188151
皮革、毛皮、羽毛及其制品和制鞋业	Leather, Fur, Feather and Its Products and Footwear Industry	198436	79415	20525

单位：万元 (10000 yuan)

江北区 Jiangbei	镇海区 Zhenhai	北仑区 Beilun	鄞州区 Yinzhou	奉化区 Fenghua	余姚市 Yuyao	慈溪市 Cixi	宁海县 Ninghai	象山县 Xiangshan
11042016	**38038425**	**54704355**	**21490439**	**9511213**	**23963352**	**47637782**	**12864034**	**8347226**
1534231	1930730	8861537	5990596	4684178	6967931	12887451	5288756	1923931
9507785	36107694	45842818	15499843	4827035	16995421	34750331	7575278	6423295
	158356	20316	68618				6935	196281
	14376				4516	3601	2237	
13443	8193	32448	116889		8054	59718	11954	4332
1202490	4866181	7509125	1708246	3266926	1483793	7040446	2409815	1474507
788600	15949456	1369466	2971640	119382	718230	926755	1091791	310879
7234640	11077100	15778989	11318225	4744340	14580104	30192998	8384933	5246399
567019	2546548	21881889	2467331	952186	4086437	3081720	451666	415318
1235825	3418216	8112123	2839491	428381	3082218	6332546	504705	699510
433441	20077997	11316575	1498044	2717608	1181475	2039120	1966363	1424865
2581294	17590394	23953331	4330671	1135222	5983928	11854665	5226358	831260
4615319	12147529	14141682	5871541	3815697	7569315	12345062	2429434	2836052
3566046	7727967	10489089	10152900	4355402	10117838	18682385	5070844	4208902
	23919		116201	5309	53435	56780		34543
2764	4847	411053	69344	300	181451	225610	29493	314767
77910	73483	119865	27638	71876	155112	5445	24826	88890
		131801	28389	51354	74199		4981	6294
231446	409698	944927	332265	110827	188550	837158	98655	166106
92391	130226	3349538	751469	502916	32555	79115	23820	873099
3270	12597	6459	17332	19232	15967	79521	23533	

表 7 －4 续表 Continued

指标	Indicators	全市 Total	市区 Urban District	海曙区 Haishu
木材加工和木、竹、藤、棕、草制品业	Timber Processing, Bamboo, Rattan, Cane Palm, and Straw Products	126808	55119	6845
家具制造业	Furniture Manufacturing	1491596	481201	66636
造纸和纸制品业	Paper－making and Paper Products Manufacturing	2104405	1505934	60372
印刷和记录媒介复制业	Printing and Record Duplicating	1234726	717552	152977
文教、工美、体育和娱乐用品制造业	Culture, Art, Sports and Recreation Supplies Manufacturing	5729087	1771602	253637
石油、煤炭及其他燃料加工业	Petroleum, Coal & other Fuel Processing	18797717	18786539	7044
化学原料和化学制品制造业	Raw Chemical Materials and Chemical Products	30659919	29875036	118930
医药制造业	Medicines Manufacturing	1025043	832354	105188
化学纤维制造业	Chemical Fiber Manufacturing	1911059	262538	15959
橡胶和塑料制品业	Rubber and Plastic Products Industry	6522937	2492254	287180
非金属矿物制品业	Nonmetal Mineral Products	4473009	2755152	747171
黑色金属冶炼和压延加工业	Smelting and Pressing of Ferrous Metals	4417401	3206631	82665
有色金属冶炼和压延加工业	Smelting and Pressing of Nonferrous Metals	9860977	4038002	117090
金属制品业	Metal Products Manufacturing	9554176	5870475	442624
通用设备制造业	General Purpose Equipment Manufacturing	14363207	8465572	721584
专用设备制造业	Special Purpose Equipment Manufacturing	8479983	5104740	429860
汽车制造业	Automobile Manufacturing	31705986	14372317	732002
铁路、船舶、航空航天和其他运输设备制造业	Railroad, Marine, Aviation and Other Transport Equipment Manufacturing	1892154	499549	94868
电气机械和器材制造业	Electric Equipment and Machinery Manufacturing	29343446	10315109	977484
计算机、通信和其他电子设备制造业	Computer, Communications and Other Electronic Equipment Manufacturing	21416403	12833704	815618
仪器仪表制造业	Instrument Manufacturing	4382660	1839643	209262
其他制造业	Other Manufacturing	557464	199223	45232
废弃资源综合利用业	Waste Comprehensive Utilization of Resources Industry	209860	108254	21253
金属制品、机械和设备修理业	Metal Products, Machinery and Equipment Repair Industry	122088	35350	
电力、热力生产和供应业	Production and Supply Electric Power and Thermal Power	13102153	8649937	4754333
燃气生产和供应业	Production and Supply Gas	1276671	754385	491935
水的生产和供应业	Production and Supply Tap Water	445671	239942	

单位：万元 (10000 yuan)

江北区 Jiangbei	镇海区 Zhenhai	北仑区 Beilun	鄞州区 Yinzhou	奉化区 Fenghua	余姚市 Yuyao	慈溪市 Cixi	宁海县 Ninghai	象山县 Xiangshan
5861	2132		29131	11149	24957	30676		16057
27436	15475	58548	249405	63701	448218	533629	20879	7669
5476	18637	1137861	139446	144141	44699	415070	137751	951
28735	62092	202633	183637	87478	248183	238253	7550	23189
343783	88089	737460	182782	165852	193437	738555	2999841	25653
	14514116	4227736	6250	31393		2440	7210	1528
59102	15778467	13220617	560888	137032	326222	150150	172612	135898
88511	129670	250898	172956	85130	48270	82191	35965	26264
	163962	75220	7398		514271	1134250		
233528	392878	508395	756086	314188	1807059	1568242	461888	193493
221004	363817	431962	727520	263677	500543	442711	419784	354821
1417	6607	2948714	150338	16891	548274	370890	169004	122601
2939891	451881	175379	200954	152808	1797492	3693682	261949	69852
150889	605785	2024726	1991276	655176	1335700	1652563	387980	307458
490456	1643225	1859698	2405568	1345040	1181196	2745352	960024	1011065
336226	523437	2812451	760287	242479	1095213	1310771	545296	423963
1313189	324701	9117963	2333493	550969	2121829	12852672	1037803	1321363
42756	19147	190846	131162	20770	78232	808105	7927	498341
2803759	655268	1960026	3072747	845826	3963865	11359963	2739987	964522
774000	572943	5504514	4314572	852058	3752605	3991235	541704	297154
740297	71301	180203	592579	46001	1935042	538556	43779	25640
	34226	15089	79875	24800	118709	171170	56293	12069
	20971	23799	42232		34541	9295	31992	25779
	9542	25809					8516	78221
	884055	1900530	798685	312333	1024016	1053770	1520983	853447
		131139	108704	22607	49074	382020	50897	40295
27921	31234	18497	149832	12459	70438	77944	31114	26234

表7-5 全市规模以上工业企业主要经济指标(2022年，按2017年国民经济新行业分类)
Main Economic Indicators of Industrial Enterprises Above Designated Size（2022）

指标	Indicators	企业个数（个）Number of Enterprises (unit)	#亏损企业 Loss Making
总计	**Total**	**10342**	**2141**
按轻重工业分	**Grouped by Light and Heavy Industry**		
轻工业	Light Industry	4188	1007
重工业	Heavy Industry	6154	1134
按注册登记类型分	**Grouped by Registered Type**		
国有企业	State–owned Enterprises	7	
集体企业	Collective–owned Enterprises	5	2
股份合作企业	Share Cooperative Enterprises	30	2
有限责任公司	Limited Liability Corporations	435	99
股份有限公司	Share–holding Corporations Ltd.	94	13
私营企业	Private Enterprises	8466	1726
港澳台商投资企业	Hong Kong, Macao & Taiwan Funded	616	131
外商投资企业	Foreign Funded Enterprises	689	168
在总计中：国有控股企业	In Total: State–owned holding enterprises	164	24
按规模分	**Grouped by Enterprises Size**		
大型企业	Large–Sized	150	15
中型企业	Medium–Sized	863	93
小型企业	Small–Sized	8748	1841
按工业行业分	**Grouped by Sector**		
非金属矿采选业	Non–metallic Mining Industry	13	3
农副食品加工业	Farm and Sideline Products Processing	72	24
食品制造业	Food Manufacturing	55	20
酒、饮料和精制茶制造业	Wine, Beverages and Refined Tea Manufacturing	19	8
纺织业	Textile Industry	260	88
纺织服装、服饰业	Clothing, Apparel Industry	520	182
皮革、毛皮、羽毛及其制品和制鞋业	Leather, Fur, Feather and Its Products and Footwear Industry	40	11

单位：万元(10000 yuan)

工业总产值（现价） Gross Industrial Output Value (Current Prices)	资产合计 Total Asset	流动资产小计 Current Assets	固定资产净额 net fixed assets	固定资产原价 Original Value of Fixed Assets
242051716	**260064653**	**154747887**	**54424635**	**106390475**
54339576	57159132	37213212	10257897	19510466
187712141	202905521	117534676	44166738	86880009
450505	951855	501841	206647	411205
24729	25761	14276	9137	22708
274355	283058	207287	55043	124245
36545977	40181248	18549266	13577614	28846320
24522424	26743156	13336891	3797841	8411648
114816098	112742137	74992545	21946057	37253255
38278168	46258461	28195871	9227157	18611226
27139461	32878977	18949911	5605140	12709869
47903544	38437316	14328235	14696857	33800539
79250700	85944768	46555036	18771874	35133007
68727294	73311007	41753136	16524545	30835463
79826064	83985666	53098150	17350906	34832327
332384	1733802	550151	62441	98633
1392383	1189642	829299	241680	497377
709370	854484	516958	206584	434556
333698	429399	273851	94126	279934
3510122	4949479	3202086	809341	1680826
8023280	9272979	6776405	1173409	2157386
198436	177581	113823	41913	73267

表 7 －5 续表 1 Continued 1

指标	Indicators	企业个数（个）Number of Enterprises (unit)	#亏损企业 Loss Making
木材加工和木、竹、藤、棕、草制品业	Timber Processing, Bamboo, Rattan, Cane Palm, and Straw Products	24	7
家具制造业	Furniture Manufacturing	145	36
造纸和纸制品业	Paper－making and Paper Products Manufacturing	99	36
印刷和记录媒介复制业	Printing and Record Duplicating	155	39
文教、工美、体育和娱乐用品制造业	Culture, Art, Sports and Recreation Supplies Manufacturing	375	83
石油、煤炭及其他燃料加工业	Petroleum, Coal & other Fuel Processing	21	4
化学原料和化学制品制造业	Raw Chemical Materials and Chemical Products	248	57
医药制造业	Medicines Manufacturing	56	10
化学纤维制造业	Chemical Fiber Manufacturing	69	22
橡胶和塑料制品业	Rubber and Plastic Products Industry	759	144
非金属矿物制品业	Nonmetal Mineral Products	331	90
黑色金属冶炼和压延加工业	Smelting and Pressing of Ferrous Metals	84	28
有色金属冶炼和压延加工业	Smelting and Pressing of Nonferrous Metals	158	47
金属制品业	Metal Products Manufacturing	936	166
通用设备制造业	General Purpose Equipment Manufacturing	1383	217
专用设备制造业	Special Purpose Equipment Manufacturing	680	118
汽车制造业	Automobile Manufacturing	847	148
铁路、船舶、航空航天和其他运输设备制造业	Railroad, Marine, Aviation and Other Transport Equipment Manufacturing	136	34
电气机械和器材制造业	Electric Equipment and Machinery Manufacturing	1651	309
计算机、通信和其他电子设备制造业	Computer, Communications and Other Electronic Equipment Manufacturing	714	140
仪器仪表制造业	Instrument Manufacturing	242	32
其他制造业	Other Manufacturing	90	12
废弃资源综合利用业	Waste Comprehensive Utilization of Resources Industry	18	7
金属制品、机械和设备修理业	Metal Products, Machinery and Equipment Repair Industry	8	2
电力、热力生产和供应业	Production and Supply Electric Power and Thermal Power	80	8
燃气生产和供应业	Production and Supply Gas	23	5
水的生产和供应业	Production and Supply Tap Water	30	4

单位：万元(10000 yuan)

工业总产值（现价）Gross Industrial Output Value (Current Prices)	资产合计 Total Asset	流动资产小计 Current Assets	固定资产净额 net fixed assets	固定资产原价 Original Value of Fixed Assets
126808	128634	79284	26585	51517
1491596	1513431	1023898	309763	537347
2104405	3632069	2108129	603256	1090255
1234726	2044143	897875	359678	774678
5729087	4748995	3173647	749425	1460611
18797717	8262744	3007859	2451806	6234379
30659919	27318873	11988953	9857433	16962272
1025043	2036847	912515	391184	661531
1911059	1463946	925359	357128	820030
6522937	6311990	3779454	1568763	2832255
4473009	5580082	3930495	853532	1607003
4417401	3353170	1831913	1108281	3108490
9860977	4025685	2941950	543747	1058770
9554176	9698696	5962135	2036733	3646345
14363207	17813731	11094427	3447377	6558118
8479983	12180916	8270248	2041263	3821380
31705986	45604663	29875148	6465510	11686171
1892154	2027336	1531455	279507	527637
29343446	28935333	20175983	4074312	7260857
21416403	27680704	17328293	4187339	7544775
4382660	7021673	4366110	1089513	1823594
557464	507319	326032	116016	221449
209860	222129	105770	66697	105780
122088	244488	166301	50783	91256
13102153	12301606	2994255	7050782	17017600
1276671	1746483	849449	632855	1029253
445671	3179106	1440973	853030	2031495

表 7 －5 续表 2 Continued 2

指标	Indicators	本年折旧 Depreciation in this year	负债小计 Total Liabilities
总计	**Total**	**6378431**	**143769275**
按轻重工业分	**Grouped by Light and Heavy Industry**		
轻工业	Light Industry	1208598	32134913
重工业	Heavy Industry	5169833	111634362
按注册登记类型分	**Grouped by Registered Type**		
国有企业	State－owned Enterprises	21335	626793
集体企业	Collective－owned Enterprises	1668	12221
股份合作企业	Share Cooperative Enterprises	6706	106809
有限责任公司	Limited Liability Corporations	1501882	24192407
股份有限公司	Share－holding Corporations Ltd.	454077	11289286
私营企业	Private Enterprises	2538168	70221148
港澳台商投资企业	Hong Kong, Macao & Taiwan Funded	1065636	20686103
外商投资企业	Foreign Funded Enterprises	788960	16634508
在总计中：国有控股企业	In Total: State－owned holding enterprises	1672526	19936126
按规模分	**Grouped by Enterprises Size**		
大型企业	Large－Sized	2157491	43600193
中型企业	Medium－Sized	1850856	38356357
小型企业	Small－Sized	2086075	49113802
按工业行业分	**Grouped by Sector**		
非金属矿采选业	Non－metallic Mining Industry	9859	1028126
农副食品加工业	Farm and Sideline Products Processing	27071	565724
食品制造业	Food Manufacturing	24776	481146
酒、饮料和精制茶制造业	Wine, Beverages and Refined Tea Manufacturing	11998	271281
纺织业	Textile Industry	96201	2180476
纺织服装、服饰业	Clothing, Apparel Industry	107553	5836834
皮革、毛皮、羽毛及其制品和制鞋业	Leather, Fur, Feather and Its Products and Footwear Industry	5595	124584

单位：万元(10000 yuan)

所有者权益 Creditors' Equity	实收资本 Paid-in Capital	营业收入 Operating Revenue	营业成本 Operating Costs	税金及附加 Tax and Extra Charge	销售费用 Sales Expenses	管理费用 Administrative Expenses	财务费用 Finance Charge
116295315	**46106343**	**254064101**	**218554853**	**4944165**	**4477768**	**8500435**	**789228**
25024196	8987072	57175774	46907203	1782776	1929235	2861768	85924
91271119	37119271	196888327	171647650	3161389	2548533	5638667	703304
325062	200274	487175	421057	3909	810	24274	7241
13540	163	24476	21422	106	533	1611	7
176249	27634	271476	215892	1508	7459	15712	2320
15988838	9052310	39722108	34720109	1644616	351699	736877	197584
15453871	5325633	27653039	23616552	1689381	271228	579072	-15825
42520934	15584545	117691379	101102882	708720	2618029	4864084	738884
25572355	9223340	39615402	34623016	560779	753373	1097927	-50685
16244466	6692446	28599046	23833924	335145	474639	1180878	-90298
18501190	10521568	50876040	44282827	3671029	179433	632058	114289
42344575	13961357	84856202	73633694	2387509	1251655	1868833	-231245
34954645	13695665	72883664	62639741	1775220	1314380	2155296	281287
34871811	15922793	81618615	69650285	353236	1852779	4189831	634956
705676	374560	322667	203888	9793	7610	19520	38099
623918	249076	1508820	1391188	4715	30909	37138	8850
373339	154786	706190	572151	3563	33869	40278	7946
158117	92941	365513	299173	12793	15239	14262	1894
2769003	961723	3637637	3079188	20750	71134	168704	21487
3436144	1492780	8362224	7403905	36871	497868	386279	-69559
52997	54052	194918	163316	968	7325	12970	2797

表 7 －5 续表 3 Continued 3

指标	Indicators	本年折旧 Depreciation in this year	负债小计 Total Liabilities
木材加工和木、竹、藤、棕、草制品业	Timber Processing, Bamboo, Rattan, Cane Palm, and Straw Products	3067	76108
家具制造业	Furniture Manufacturing	37252	1084345
造纸和纸制品业	Paper－making and Paper Products Manufacturing	71584	2243590
印刷和记录媒介复制业	Printing and Record Duplicating	46502	957733
文教、工美、体育和娱乐用品制造业	Culture, Art, Sports and Recreation Supplies Manufacturing	94005	2675182
石油、煤炭及其他燃料加工业	Petroleum, Coal & other Fuel Processing	310306	3266527
化学原料和化学制品制造业	Raw Chemical Materials and Chemical Products	969980	15010256
医药制造业	Medicines Manufacturing	42363	1004156
化学纤维制造业	Chemical Fiber Manufacturing	41038	1037677
橡胶和塑料制品业	Rubber and Plastic Products Industry	196172	3451347
非金属矿物制品业	Nonmetal Mineral Products	106818	3614579
黑色金属冶炼和压延加工业	Smelting and Pressing of Ferrous Metals	142477	1546155
有色金属冶炼和压延加工业	Smelting and Pressing of Nonferrous Metals	66119	2724832
金属制品业	Metal Products Manufacturing	230743	5030849
通用设备制造业	General Purpose Equipment Manufacturing	414818	8922190
专用设备制造业	Special Purpose Equipment Manufacturing	242693	6184205
汽车制造业	Automobile Manufacturing	887848	27317294
铁路、船舶、航空航天和其他运输设备制造业	Railroad, Marine, Aviation and Other Transport Equipment Manufacturing	33787	1446470
电气机械和器材制造业	Electric Equipment and Machinery Manufacturing	479378	17189646
计算机、通信和其他电子设备制造业	Computer, Communications and Other Electronic Equipment Manufacturing	527954	14187337
仪器仪表制造业	Instrument Manufacturing	144390	3149693
其他制造业	Other Manufacturing	15810	363505
废弃资源综合利用业	Waste Comprehensive Utilization of Resources Industry	6570	105081
金属制品、机械和设备修理业	Metal Products, Machinery and Equipment Repair Industry	3889	136933
电力、热力生产和供应业	Production and Supply Electric Power and Thermal Power	816236	7636920
燃气生产和供应业	Production and Supply Gas	50343	858389
水的生产和供应业	Production and Supply Tap Water	81653	1831480

单位：万元(10000 yuan)

所有者权益 Creditors' Equity	实收资本 Paid-in Capital	营业收入 Operating Revenue	营业成本 Operating Costs	税金及附加 Tax and Extra Charge	销售费用 Sales Expenses	管理费用 Administrative Expenses	财务费用 Finance Charge
52527	35828	129964	106832	632	2525	10012	1213
429086	284544	1542602	1271894	8629	77332	99494	17227
1388480	576997	2194091	1875556	9618	56976	63075	-8267
1086409	522754	1396183	1203858	6404	39433	80927	15313
2073810	614623	5581586	4808158	24746	212209	284965	12571
4996217	3095012	19798317	17254304	2056094	27373	161002	-6707
12308616	7661074	33047825	30410709	174020	197796	479665	353504
1032691	387177	952857	507449	7843	146046	94096	7361
426269	442897	1948307	1845305	4951	13123	40798	20279
2860639	896991	6538901	5351219	29473	190454	387906	38246
1965500	2457736	4460828	3785142	22921	145806	187965	49416
1807014	1638451	4532532	4271407	13290	19353	77581	-7082
1300852	552698	10802343	10480512	21185	40732	104308	39448
4667840	1380165	9337594	7729619	47373	208784	510670	36057
8891532	2602381	14410122	11462252	74879	453463	815547	19339
5996708	1828899	8493664	6698635	47376	286881	538356	18802
18287364	5520471	33258218	28208592	507640	388840	1124567	68968
580865	297166	1851481	1593137	9012	25865	84593	4583
11745675	3115380	32048329	27601570	114928	617854	1278176	-5893
13493361	3698224	22259056	18710289	77564	373216	858215	43523
3871977	963852	4381939	3268563	21271	157758	214250	-47547
143814	73789	586641	488301	2923	17566	38768	4464
117048	45189	211873	164742	1091	4102	11188	2733
107555	81028	127172	112290	462	464	15036	458
4664686	2932954	13497320	12927218	42358	13243	93630	86147
888093	554409	1314518	1161171	3999	34604	20600	4410
1347625	428648	558839	412034	4752	30832	36295	17401

表 7 －5 续表 4 Continued 4

指标	Indicators	营业利润 Business Profits	利润总额 Total Profits
总计	**Total**	**13579864**	**14180052**
按轻重工业分	**Grouped by Light and Heavy Industry**		
轻工业	Light Industry	2660208	2841646
重工业	Heavy Industry	10919657	11338406
按注册登记类型分	**Grouped by Registered Type**		
国有企业	State－owned Enterprises	23397	24347
集体企业	Collective－owned Enterprises	767	673
股份合作企业	Share Cooperative Enterprises	18545	20822
有限责任公司	Limited Liability Corporations	1947057	1975349
股份有限公司	Share－holding Corporations Ltd.	1797593	1803025
私营企业	Private Enterprises	4946844	5305609
港澳台商投资企业	Hong Kong, Macao & Taiwan Funded	2179453	2328483
外商投资企业	Foreign Funded Enterprises	2666211	2721745
在总计中：国有控股企业	In Total: State－owned holding enterprises	2256614	2263907
按规模分	**Grouped by Enterprises Size**		
大型企业	Large－Sized	5540917	5608160
中型企业	Medium－Sized	3452873	3589316
小型企业	Small－Sized	3267211	3649062
按工业行业分	**Grouped by Sector**		
非金属矿采选业	Non－metallic Mining Industry	44010	44112
农副食品加工业	Farm and Sideline Products Processing	78319	82157
食品制造业	Food Manufacturing	28829	32252
酒、饮料和精制茶制造业	Wine, Beverages and Refined Tea Manufacturing	13743	14082
纺织业	Textile Industry	262715	279819
纺织服装、服饰业	Clothing, Apparel Industry	196301	209456
皮革、毛皮、羽毛及其制品和制鞋业	Leather, Fur, Feather and Its Products and Footwear Industry	4946	4593

单位：万元(10000 yuan)

#应交所得税 Income Tax Payable	亏损企业亏损总额 Total Loss	利税总额 Total Profits and Taxes	本年应付职工薪酬 Employee Compensation Payable The Year	本年应交增值税 Value-added Taxes Payable the Year	本年进项税额 Withholdings on VAT the Year	本年销项税额 Substituted Money on VAT the Year	全部从业人员年平均人数(人) Annual Average Employees (person)
1614112	**2083296**	**23361205**	**18113005**	**4236988**	**27009053**	**27622522**	**1669898**
394082	387342	5844106	6256926	1219684	5553320	5295078	684304
1220030	1695955	17517100	11856079	3017305	21455734	22327444	985594
-1204	0	37636	37610	9379	46529	47051	1678
156	156	1628	5210	850	1935	2781	758
1871	195	29616	28464	7287	26585	32291	3151
289711	696086	4537529	1527357	917563	3852959	4793105	91706
216854	12411	3747300	1033837	254894	3234136	3210380	60355
580813	768826	8067912	10501804	2053583	12717773	12523105	1117439
319556	223434	3393192	2790943	503930	4366743	4260203	221275
206357	382189	3546392	2187780	489502	2762394	2753606	173536
357411	564317	6813781	1273795	878845	5191477	6123737	49670
674282	263948	9120075	4838117	1124407	9114461	9457184	343502
422868	896266	6551773	5075249	1187237	8070211	7886395	446192
492521	862216	5602854	8069249	1600556	8280974	8485182	862859
14532	7575	63482	8699	9578	3328	6782	685
17465	5747	100756	71225	13884	103245	92002	8215
4687	8701	48859	86175	13043	62658	48361	10013
1877	3458	39459	21154	12584	45488	35657	1740
37406	25603	390983	452483	90415	365232	396068	41872
40525	41350	398491	1120298	152164	876989	854616	121083
511	2829	10674	34448	5113	16967	18554	4758

表 7 －5 续表 5 Continued 5

指标	Indicators	营业利润 Business Profits	利润总额 Total Profits
木材加工和木、竹、藤、棕、草制品业	Timber Processing, Bamboo, Rattan, Cane Palm, and Straw Products	6235	8635
家具制造业	Furniture Manufacturing	-467	18778
造纸和纸制品业	Paper-making and Paper Products Manufacturing	142231	152168
印刷和记录媒介复制业	Printing and Record Duplicating	41947	47241
文教、工美、体育和娱乐用品制造业	Culture, Art, Sports and Recreation Supplies Manufacturing	195533	216134
石油、煤炭及其他燃料加工业	Petroleum, Coal & other Fuel Processing	456884	457401
化学原料和化学制品制造业	Raw Chemical Materials and Chemical Products	1301970	1303135
医药制造业	Medicines Manufacturing	117580	125379
化学纤维制造业	Chemical Fiber Manufacturing	37981	19460
橡胶和塑料制品业	Rubber and Plastic Products Industry	373795	399930
非金属矿物制品业	Nonmetal Mineral Products	212702	219124
黑色金属冶炼和压延加工业	Smelting and Pressing of Ferrous Metals	30030	43609
有色金属冶炼和压延加工业	Smelting and Pressing of Nonferrous Metals	55371	64879
金属制品业	Metal Products Manufacturing	584862	619637
通用设备制造业	General Purpose Equipment Manufacturing	1094286	1174115
专用设备制造业	Special Purpose Equipment Manufacturing	659387	728099
汽车制造业	Automobile Manufacturing	2699060	2767084
铁路、船舶、航空航天和其他运输设备制造业	Railroad, Marine, Aviation and Other Transport Equipment Manufacturing	75660	86455
电气机械和器材制造业	Electric Equipment and Machinery Manufacturing	1779316	1875360
计算机、通信和其他电子设备制造业	Computer, Communications and Other Electronic Equipment Manufacturing	1524393	1588003
仪器仪表制造业	Instrument Manufacturing	661971	686101
其他制造业	Other Manufacturing	18871	20138
废弃资源综合利用业	Waste Comprehensive Utilization of Resources Industry	23084	23276
金属制品、机械和设备修理业	Metal Products, Machinery and Equipment Repair Industry	120	177
电力、热力生产和供应业	Production and Supply Electric Power and Thermal Power	399654	398438
燃气生产和供应业	Production and Supply Gas	96934	98589
水的生产和供应业	Production and Supply Tap Water	68054	81441

单位：万元(10000 yuan)

#应交所得税 Income Tax Payable	亏损企业亏损总额 Total Loss	利税总额 Total Profits and Taxes	本年应付职工薪酬 Employee Compensation Payable The Year	本年应交增值税 Value-added Taxes Payable the Year	本年进项税额 Withholdings on VAT the Year	本年销项税额 Substituted Money on VAT the Year	全部从业人员年平均人数(人) Annual Average Employees (person)
1049	995	16205	18226	6938	12813	10241	2016
4129	35576	61696	248797	34289	142332	122069	25676
24076	12892	199823	122865	38037	223137	241261	11149
4648	9733	82712	168138	29067	147772	157151	18279
22101	15801	339178	606871	98297	588902	513813	68972
104620	46164	2625654	315909	112159	2347504	2353690	8250
160304	657876	1880262	709714	403107	4312254	4099436	35095
9682	18659	171214	141767	37991	75095	98891	9659
5644	59543	47703	79115	23292	228068	236029	8634
40375	35035	551132	809517	121729	645523	636007	87707
41702	41887	387819	287009	145773	394917	509958	26519
4239	22434	104342	152157	47443	549475	581620	10170
17578	44732	144747	204123	58682	1330526	1302168	17080
91328	34767	849191	1123807	182181	919879	833899	121499
126625	54368	1547076	1844893	298082	1431195	1426866	177887
76337	67496	977493	1179861	202017	821687	883529	95084
135683	251573	3966587	2094358	691864	3731370	4114703	181832
8244	14440	132528	173804	37061	192593	194674	19660
175103	121788	2408520	2732625	418232	3468259	3005656	302544
194069	239323	1930597	2072020	265029	2184158	2088868	170840
51181	24265	779017	556120	71646	451340	439624	46427
2595	2967	35652	95462	12591	52090	41574	12411
2878	2795	30181	17555	5814	18440	23307	1409
538	2817	4212	40178	3574	2591	6150	2317
77674	157237	735661	382970	294864	924342	1626710	13767
27556	12576	128382	36367	25794	103238	123011	1949
14730	296	101331	60738	15138	13152	17937	3707

表7-6 各区(县、市)规模以上工业企业主要财务指标(2022年)
Main Financial Indicators of Industrial Enterprises Above Designated Size by Region（2022）

指标	Indicators	全市 Total	市区 Urban District	海曙区 Haishu
企业单位数（个）	Number of Enterprises(unit)	10342	5149	836
#亏损企业	Deficits Enterprises	2141	1144	196
工业总产值（现价）	Gross Industrial Output Value(Current Prices)	242051716	149239322	14452875
资产合计	Total Asset	260064653	163115128	14894333
流动资产小计	Current Assets	154747887	94010728	8363790
固定资产净额	net fixed assets	54424635	33973152	3955627
本年折旧	Depreciation in this year	6378431	3838360	463944
负债合计	Total Liabilities	143769275	86503416	9735726
流动负债小计	Current Liabilities	124003814	73942385	8884083
所有者权益合计	Total Owner' Equity	116295315	76611688	5158604
#实收资本	Paid-in Capital	46106343	33563381	2549231
营业收入	Operating Revenue	254064101	158739009	14919031
营业成本	Operating Costs	218554853	137318817	13094047
税金及附加	Tax & Extra Charge	4944165	4356585	63091
销售费用	Sales Expenses	4477768	2617973	574503
管理费用	Administrative Expenses	8500435	4693054	545169
财务费用	Finance charge	789228	438560	91036
#利息费用	Interest charge	1918460	1208883	117235
营业利润	Business Profits	13579864	7799972	450956
利润总额	Total Profits	14180052	8199390	488671
所得税费用	Income Tax Payable	1614112	1098703	53289
亏损企业亏损总额	Total Loss	2083296	1375272	81036
利税总额	Total Profits and Taxes	23361205	15017282	824869
本年应付职工薪酬	Employee Compensation Payable in this Year	18113005	9819097	1182132
本年应交增值税	Value-added Taxes Payable in this Year	4236988	2461308	273106
本年进项税额	Withholdings on VAT in this Year	27009053	16952463	1076516
本年销项税额	Substituted Money on VAT in this Year	27622522	17525851	1658473
全部从业人员年平均人数(人)	Annual Average Employees(person)	1669898	821194	119479

单位：万元 (10000 yuan)

江北区 Jiangbei	镇海区 Zhenhai	北仑区 Beilun	鄞州区 Yinzhou	奉化区 Fenghua	余姚市 Yuyao	慈溪市 Cixi	宁海县 Ninghai	象山县 Xiangshan
380	668	1039	1473	753	1581	2167	755	690
81	157	217	330	163	266	354	171	206
11042016	38038425	54704355	21490439	9511213	23963352	47637782	12864034	8347226
10857774	29708330	69644095	28244610	9765987	27314576	42198204	15075031	12361714
7123245	13397574	42032742	17019868	6073509	17609368	27391153	8909174	6827465
1739617	9298238	12586912	4224086	2168673	5649860	9047372	3084576	2669674
201605	941123	1426924	538041	266722	767367	1162135	363853	246717
5812978	16372093	34860830	14714481	5007308	15855111	24846687	9313390	7250672
4948167	11744299	30650432	13071315	4644089	13261788	22459978	8546133	5793529
5044793	13336235	34783260	13530120	4758677	11459453	17351507	5761631	5111036
1656528	7954417	14016885	5698428	1687891	3171305	5920939	1674987	1775731
12321740	41016529	56895965	22685042	10900702	24063644	48792113	14402056	8067279
10840594	36534549	50226319	18932136	7691173	20323667	41388706	12568017	6955646
42998	1812167	773564	98719	1566046	102517	401306	50910	32847
262254	306451	635526	636935	202304	470351	895902	318172	175370
371353	825961	1350372	1087449	512750	1101294	1816233	558703	331151
29016	284054	-60449	48600	46303	59864	156333	68543	65928
77854	338920	419723	185184	69968	203268	270372	140268	95669
545902	998619	3713261	1444253	646980	1328064	3402822	557469	491539
612591	1058372	3811892	1549341	678523	1365924	3503835	591144	519759
58378	150797	550798	164627	120814	133579	287714	66807	27311
59338	595783	444802	146082	48232	226598	278070	88358	114998
804328	3285420	5388484	2059093	2655088	1819753	4890272	918225	715673
816959	1524264	3226577	2115690	953475	2408066	3890059	1231308	764474
148739	414881	803029	411033	410519	351312	985131	276170	163067
1409841	5094299	6129583	2312306	929918	2455581	5182576	1575258	843175
1366524	4772719	6220562	2329900	1177673	2269061	5368131	1606216	853264
64864	100771	242271	192926	100883	248597	403230	121463	75414

表7-7 各区（县、市）国有控股工业企业主要财务指标(2022年)

Main Financial Indicators of State Holding Shares Industrial Enterprises by Region(2022)

指标	Indicators	全市 Total	市区 Urban District	海曙区 Haishu
企业单位数（个）	Number of Enterprises(unit)	164	97	9
#亏损企业	Deficits Enterprises	24	15	1
工业总产值（现价）	Gross Industrial Output Value(Current Prices)	47903544	41291721	5248057
资产合计	Total Asset	38437316	30694460	3320693
流动资产小计	Total Current Assets	14328235	11279606	580089
固定资产原价	Original Value of Fixed Assets	33800539	26567151	4817400
#累计折旧	Accumulative Depreciation	18900020	14994578	2572491
负债合计	Total Liabilities	19936126	15418396	2759695
流动负债小计	Current Liabilities	13118980	10704626	2638197
所有者权益合计	Total Owners' Equity	18501190	15276064	560998
#实收资本	Paid-in Capital	10521568	8780817	317314
营业收入	Operating Revenue	50876040	44091850	5285013
营业成本	Operating Costs	44282827	37939154	5174390
税金及附加	Tax & Extra Charge	3671029	3647940	12511
销售费用	Sales Expenses	179433	146810	22610
管理费用	Administrative Expenses	632058	569798	36447
财务费用	Finance Charge	114289	59066	-6772
营业利润	Business Profits	2256614	2002516	73989
利润总额	Total Profits	2263907	1992875	66439
亏损企业亏损总额	Total Loss	564317	491174	1272
本年应付职工薪酬	Employee Compensation Payable in this Year	1273795	1024589	114774
本年应交增值税	Value-added Taxes Payable in this Year	878845	737379	81611
本年进项税额	Withholdings on VAT in this Year	5191477	4517079	94803
本年销项税额	Substituted Money on VAT in this Year	6123737	5356362	673858
全部从业人员年平均人数(人)	Annual Average Employees(person)	49670	35438	6081

单位：万元 (10000 yuan)

江北区 Jiangbei	镇海区 Zhenhai	北仑区 Beilun	鄞州区 Yinzhou	奉化区 Fenghua	余姚市 Yuyao	慈溪市 Cixi	宁海县 Ninghai	象山县 Xiangshan
7	27	24	17	13	12	18	16	21
1	7	2	1	3	3	2		4
433441	20077997	11316575	1498044	2717608	1181475	2039120	1966363	1424865
570666	13240760	8967615	2212381	2382346	1684694	1597643	1695049	2765470
398224	4090789	3798475	847590	1564439	886970	727072	452176	982411
255486	9393935	8948423	2043140	1108767	1216381	1049698	2648123	2319186
133676	4679743	5786671	1177005	644991	651254	532422	1547945	1173821
338972	6528833	3908784	1244301	637811	1064129	683852	746973	2022776
286570	3327089	3227331	712571	512869	318337	481470	579206	1035341
231694	6711928	5058831	968080	1744535	620565	913791	948076	742694
100145	4828118	2795244	647380	92617	386109	375371	467914	511358
474312	20896282	11754981	1575951	4105312	1189687	2141547	1991850	1461108
402411	18720783	10133569	1398527	2109474	1152549	2052031	1730639	1408454
2146	1655906	447290	9298	1520790	5615	4584	8178	4712
8921	16075	26370	36479	36355	3326	12656	8097	8544
16532	259331	108115	32593	116780	9374	13855	19436	19596
-40	86710	-26646	13326	-7512	5807	5879	13057	30480
26334	269510	1238888	86775	307020	14167	53378	200727	-14173
26370	269715	1237331	88274	304747	15151	55590	206203	-5912
349	410248	77701	92	1512	1971	4850		66322
24323	436822	317452	67231	63988	32665	53905	88302	74333
10544	136171	201622	38209	269222	27351	29651	49491	34974
53487	2703582	1291756	138997	234455	112566	253524	177128	131180
62861	2515744	1463051	140968	499880	130606	250667	241699	144403
1178	11533	11212	3469	1965	1890	3370	4917	4055

表7-8 各区(县、市)规模以上私营工业企业主要财务指标(2022年)
Main Financial Indicators of Private Industrial Enterprises Above Designated Size by Region (2022)

指标	Indicators	全市 Total	市区 Urban District	海曙区 Haishu
企业单位数（个）	Number of Enterprises(unit)	8466	3979	704
#亏损企业	Deficits Enterprises	1726	904	170
工业总产值（现价）	Gross Industrial Output Value(Current Prices)	114816098	56411664	6258371
资产合计	Total Asset	112742137	58387855	6373127
流动资产小计	Total Current Assets	74992545	39349604	4383339
固定资产原价	Original Value of Fixed Assets	37253255	17769038	1733898
#累计折旧	Accumulative Depreciation	15021828	6922589	820685
负债合计	Total Liabilities	70221148	36483892	3864707
流动负债小计	Current Liabilities	64822455	33383641	3553707
所有者权益合计	Total Owners' Equity	42520934	21903942	2508417
#实收资本	Paid-in Capital	15584545	9445839	942266
营业收入	Operating Revenue	117691379	59081488	6362772
营业成本	Operating Costs	101102882	51432465	5297646
税金及附加	Tax & Extra Charge	708720	471851	25685
销售费用	Sales Expenses	2618029	1185583	245055
管理费用	Administrative Expenses	4864084	2214820	357934
财务费用	Finance Charge	738884	456150	55897
营业利润	Business Profits	4946844	2118500	242710
利润总额	Total Profits	5305609	2336891	274212
亏损企业亏损总额	Total Loss	768826	439171	55847
本年应付职工薪酬	Employee Compensation Payable in this Year	10501804	4546626	698275
本年应交增值税	Value-added Taxes Payable in this Year	2053583	967206	126502
本年进项税额	Withholdings on VAT in this Year	12717773	6625770	651990
本年销项税额	Substituted Money on VAT in this Year	12523105	6511274	654377
全部从业人员年平均人数(人)	Annual Average Employees(person)	1117439	458142	78514

单位：万元 (10000 yuan)

江北区 Jiangbei	镇海区 Zhenhai	北仑区 Beilun	鄞州区 Yinzhou	奉化区 Fenghua	余姚市 Yuyao	慈溪市 Cixi	宁海县 Ninghai	象山县 Xiangshan
261	489	629	1245	651	1348	1925	641	573
56	117	142	279	140	214	293	143	172
7234640	11077100	15778989	11318225	4744340	14580104	30192998	8384933	5246399
5195232	9967243	19674768	12097868	5079617	13683113	26068716	8217408	6385045
3352936	5307965	14977227	8090983	3237155	8781188	17160704	5437945	4263104
1517377	4629792	4181578	3800445	1905949	5560188	9571156	2481616	1871255
658425	1340795	1533108	1725807	843770	2380090	3987883	1039196	692071
2846553	6444260	13806992	6242996	3278385	8439309	16403608	5226640	3667699
2367852	5605527	12843632	5901539	3111384	7754864	15497368	4808969	3377613
2348677	3522982	5867773	5854863	1801230	5243793	9665098	2990759	2717342
717406	1727417	2059767	2857890	1141093	1609539	3078596	641780	808792
8327741	12333844	15912047	11405302	4739782	14585454	30596933	8456634	4970871
7588379	11050571	14153105	9446160	3896603	12299394	26100458	7159230	4111335
22499	127294	222173	51131	23069	61165	122398	33919	19387
124495	157066	186832	345512	126624	331187	702352	266705	132202
205924	304808	394409	641610	310135	747129	1252215	412213	237707
24679	160056	117810	51275	46434	76619	119903	64239	21972
259807	261720	612449	558735	183079	691198	1500842	326013	310292
277720	302854	633082	635979	213045	708896	1584714	350652	324455
38932	105522	101189	104676	33007	108432	149708	44573	26943
429813	656404	866190	1266524	629420	1563125	2934543	927161	530350
82978	186712	222013	242952	106049	250492	549360	189108	97418
978867	1612465	1804760	1104373	473315	1451268	3209611	892407	538717
939448	1458056	1818293	1168793	472309	1397319	3170637	916931	526944
35854	60338	80461	129767	73208	177288	329092	96988	55929

表7-9 各区(县、市)规模以上大中型工业企业主要财务指标(2022年)

Main Financial Indicators of Large and Medium Size Industrial Enterprises Above Designated Size by Region（2022）

指标	Indicators	全市 Total	市区 Urban District	海曙区 Haishu
企业单位数（个）	Number of Enterprises(unit)	1013	479	57
#亏损企业	Deficits Enterprises	108	51	7
工业总产值（现价）	Gross Industrial Output Value(Current Prices)	147977994	98901921	8719241
资产合计	Total Asset	159255774	105392594	9221115
流动资产小计	Total Current Assets	88308172	54184608	4452422
固定资产原价	Original Value of Fixed Assets	65968470	46608986	6292015
#累计折旧	Accumulative Depreciation	31879562	23312170	3202292
负债合计	Total Liabilities	81956550	51901254	6183199
流动负债小计	Current Liabilities	69804855	42960824	5597062
所有者权益合计	Total Owners' Equity	77299220	53491338	3037916
#实收资本	Paid–in Capital	27657022	21339190	1707762
营业收入	Operating Revenue	157739866	106199564	8988103
营业成本	Operating Costs	136273435	91581172	8063176
税金及附加	Tax & Extra Charge	4162729	3967117	34337
销售费用	Sales Expenses	2566035	1604518	434038
管理费用	Administrative Expenses	4024129	2379876	202379
财务费用	Finance Charge	50042	58684	40113
营业利润	Business Profits	8993789	5934957	264350
利润总额	Total Profits	9197475	6069080	261671
亏损企业亏损总额	Total Loss	1160214	820428	11751
本年应付职工薪酬	Employee Compensation Payable in this Year	9913366	5561488	565893
本年应交增值税	Value–added Taxes Payable in this Year	2311644	1494195	150929
本年进项税额	Withholdings on VAT in this Year	17184672	11526088	484868
本年销项税额	Substituted Money on VAT in this Year	17343579	11927688	1071332
全部从业人员年平均人数(人)	Annual Average Employees(person)	789694	393342	47288

单位：万元 (10000 yuan)

江北区 Jiangbei	镇海区 Zhenhai	北仑区 Beilun	鄞州区 Yinzhou	奉化区 Fenghua	余姚市 Yuyao	慈溪市 Cixi	宁海县 Ninghai	象山县 Xiangshan
42	63	149	112	56	150	273	73	38
3	11	13	11	6	17	23	9	8
7196613	29737924	38095012	10202212	4950920	13553243	24199726	7655792	3667313
6599892	21036409	47306683	16350624	4877870	16299427	23135884	9230187	5197684
4090413	8214202	25167955	9181622	3077994	10305946	15210923	5456113	3150582
1844032	12851433	20314186	3296943	2010377	5876452	7521322	3374865	2586846
729061	5569968	10540594	2362491	907764	2458486	2947132	1744873	1416901
3247100	11306864	21419373	7979446	1765272	8873483	12685373	5478001	3018438
2541597	7776707	18243381	7130971	1671107	7350285	11699649	5141171	2652926
3352792	9729544	25887309	8371178	3112598	7425942	10450510	3752185	2179246
919259	5848701	10031501	2390390	441577	1681215	3118448	909404	608766
8148823	31686224	39632916	11467259	6276239	13637896	25167048	9203352	3532007
7274471	28223411	34754425	9454496	3811192	11702869	21660374	8286746	3042276
26014	1779320	541618	51543	1534285	51815	102338	28553	12906
160133	179524	387814	353629	89381	183063	500939	195239	82276
172981	489756	828705	458104	227951	452853	839954	243756	107690
5325	200711	-154483	-30798	-2185	-29675	12033	2571	6429
381399	730924	3048153	1019947	490185	877548	1681773	310682	188829
398509	736305	3127596	1051249	493751	882134	1730339	322503	193420
21978	458858	301068	21822	4950	156101	69814	42129	71742
450668	916146	2243980	982100	402701	1198479	2190135	637906	325358
78133	252412	525275	186740	300708	143829	455873	158216	59531
970755	4127512	4216359	1238427	488166	1462115	2721615	1076683	398172
920317	3767325	4224685	1227493	716536	1295048	2676382	1074342	370119
33181	45844	153777	74526	38726	106189	209711	54425	26027

表7-10 各区(县、市)规模以上外商和港澳台投资工业企业主要财务指标(2022年)
Main Financial Indicators of Foreign Funded and Hongkong,Macao,Taiwan Funded Industrial Enterprises Above Designated Size by Region (2022)

指标	Indicators	全市 Total	市区 Urban District	海曙区 Haishu
企业单位数（个）	Number of Enterprises(unit)	1305	835	84
#亏损企业	Deficits Enterprises	299	177	18
工业总产值（现价）	Gross Industrial Output Value(Current Prices)	65417628	46763509	2314502
资产合计	Total Asset	79137438	58965249	3128214
流动资产小计	Total Current Assets	47145782	34056098	1896764
固定资产原价	Original Value of Fixed Assets	31321095	22785012	1492458
#累计折旧	Accumulative Depreciation	16144063	11959619	696978
负债合计	Total Liabilities	37320611	26354231	1735594
流动负债小计	Current Liabilities	31237844	22221663	1580947
所有者权益合计	Total Owners' Equity	41816821	32611016	1392620
#实收资本	Paid-in Capital	15915786	13153868	853671
营业收入	Operating Revenue	68214449	49157527	2313901
营业成本	Operating Costs	58456940	43053449	1827319
税金及附加	Tax & Extra Charge	895924	602450	19571
销售费用	Sales Expenses	1228012	960258	287769
管理费用	Administrative Expenses	2278805	1483202	102378
财务费用	Finance Charge	-140983	-154071	12243
营业利润	Business Profits	4845664	2899431	80410
利润总额	Total Profits	5050228	3070793	86555
亏损企业亏损总额	Total Loss	605623	382178	21595
本年应付职工薪酬	Employee Compensation Payable in this Year	4978723	3451692	286083
本年应交增值税	Value-added Taxes Payable in this Year	993432	624914	45736
本年进项税额	Withholdings on VAT in this Year	7129137	5145125	221709
本年销项税额	Substituted Money on VAT in this Year	7013809	5009192	219633
全部从业人员年平均人数(人)	Annual Average Employees(person)	394811	264278	27757

单位：万元 (10000 yuan)

江北区 Jiangbei	镇海区 Zhenhai	北仑区 Beilun	鄞州区 Yinzhou	奉化区 Fenghua	余姚市 Yuyao	慈溪市 Cixi	宁海县 Ninghai	象山县 Xiangshan
73	123	336	165	54	182	157	70	61
13	31	60	41	14	43	43	20	16
1802844	5964764	29994012	5306822	1380566	7168656	9414266	956370	1114828
2873896	5275115	39070250	7163222	1454552	9919406	7626828	1193200	1432755
1846044	2942581	21917525	4749865	703320	6636629	4778667	748958	925430
784695	2992396	14994845	1692090	828528	3116715	4329425	523199	566745
375592	1721381	8003872	858324	303472	1368833	2327038	226211	262362
1410047	2396789	16391873	3829849	590079	5501160	3916786	705116	843318
1173823	1612764	13920682	3368707	564742	4457248	3192099	606500	760334
1463848	2878326	22678376	3333373	864473	4418245	3710041	488083	589437
436470	1538586	9033715	1013773	277653	958848	1235468	284061	283541
1907651	6155208	31657806	5720128	1402833	7259983	9762064	916209	1118665
1555034	5418164	28315043	4795016	1142872	6123141	7551891	759450	969010
9479	23256	509170	21651	19323	29466	253245	4844	5919
63142	111444	342158	131454	24292	105059	119094	21727	21875
80860	219109	777068	242842	60946	281713	411877	57426	44586
-4302	30289	-169666	-24816	2181	-19305	13714	9900	8780
148481	356473	1717230	473705	123133	477444	1389975	34204	44609
190748	374938	1793608	494571	130373	494939	1399354	37182	47959
10974	92583	210165	39296	7565	114097	87433	9227	12688
199016	329588	1920256	519521	197227	702069	606833	109614	108514
25391	87368	383579	66580	16260	61213	280719	8538	18048
191257	656301	3306078	618773	151007	799375	976064	95902	112671
174064	676058	3265936	549788	123713	663701	1158209	70097	112609
16094	21612	138944	41446	18425	59680	48111	11386	11356

表7-11 部分年份工业主要产品产量
Output of Major Industrial Products in Partial Years

主要工业产品生产量	单位	Output of Major Industrial Products	Unit	2019	2020	2021	2022
大米	万吨	Rice	10000 tons	11. 19	13. 65	13. 49	17. 15
精制食用植物油	万吨	Edible Vegetable Oil	10000 tons	10. 02	10. 77	10. 24	8. 96
冷冻水产品	万吨	Frozen Aquatic Products	10000 tons	18. 89	17. 19	16. 42	15. 69
啤酒	千万升	Beer	ten million liters	34. 55	31. 66	38. 08	38. 18
精制茶	万吨	Refined Tea	10000 tons	2. 34	2. 60	3. 00	3. 09
卷烟	亿支	Cigarette	100 million	419. 55	414. 06	423. 01	417. 99
纱	万吨	Yarn	10000 tons	14. 75	12. 02	13. 92	8. 54
布	万米	Cloth	10000 m	42857. 10	33864. 80	40815. 70	35907. 80
服装	万件	Garment	10000 units	109122. 90	113898. 40	120552. 30	110386. 60
梭织服装	万件	Shuttle Woven Garment	10000 units	13897. 30	11625. 80	10976. 80	11778. 30
西服套装	万件	Western-style Suit	10000 units	1643. 70	1288. 10	1551. 50	1777. 50
衬衫	万件	Shirt	10000 units	4075. 50	2845. 80	2929. 50	3915. 40
羽绒服装	万件	Eiderdown Garment	10000 units	78. 10	56. 00	78. 10	85. 20
针织服装	万件	Knitting Garment	10000 units	95225. 60	102272. 60	109575. 60	98608. 30
机制纸及纸板（外购原纸加工除外）	万吨	Paper-making and Paperboard	10000 tons	345. 60	229. 78	225. 96	250. 26
纸制品	万吨	Paper Products	10000 tons	96. 50	107. 05	102. 05	69. 71
原油加工量	万吨	Crude Oil Processed	10000 tons	2897. 65	2704. 02	2860. 58	2979. 64
汽油	万吨	Gasoline	10000 tons	351. 69	347. 19	384. 47	429. 74
煤油	万吨	Kerosene	10000 tons	290. 33	184. 35	209. 97	195. 65
柴油	万吨	Diesel	10000 tons	600. 34	561. 73	557. 17	568. 37
石油沥青	万吨	Asphalt	10000 tons	371. 11	377. 16	357. 13	326. 40
液化石油气	万吨	Liquefied Petroleum Gas	10000 tons	140. 79	131. 17	149. 68	164. 08
硫酸（折100%）	万吨	Sulphuric Acid(100%)	10000 tons	45. 50	38. 10	42. 23	36. 30
盐酸（氯化氢，含量31%）	万吨	Hydrochloric Acid(above31%percent)	10000 tons	24. 29	22. 60	18. 24	14. 29
烧碱(折100%)	万吨	Caustic Soda(100%)	10000 tons	78. 97	86. 71	94. 30	98. 21
合成氨(无水氨)	万吨	Synthetic Ammonia	10000 tons	9. 36	10. 75	13. 46	12. 91
纯苯	万吨	Pure Benzene	10000 tons	36. 09	35. 51	38. 29	51. 47
初级形态塑料	万吨	Primary Form Plastic	10000 tons	622. 26	630. 13	627. 95	719. 55
塑料制品	万吨	Plastic Products	10000 tons	119. 02	115. 71	130. 90	155. 11
水泥	万吨	Cement	10000 tons	1924. 94	1898. 16	1653. 49	1595. 73
粗钢	万吨	Rural Steel	10000 tons	433. 43	450. 36	459. 52	439. 44
钢材	万吨	Rolled-steel Final Products	10000 tons	706. 28	698. 74	674. 63	668. 13
精炼铜（电解铜）	万吨	Copper	10000 tons	8. 46	4. 93	8. 18	7. 16
铜材	万吨	Copper Material	10000 tons	165. 92	170. 09	155. 99	151. 32

表 7 －11 续表 Continued

主要工业产品生产量	单位	Output of Major Industrial Products	Unit	2019	2020	2021	2022
铝材	万吨	Aluminium	10000 tons	36. 40	38. 05	38. 13	32. 50
液压元件	万件	Hydraulic Pressure Element	10000 units	1958. 18	2729. 82	3170. 56	3885. 17
气动元件	万件	Pneumatic Element	10000 units	5880. 21	5650. 12	8140. 08	8243. 54
粉末冶金零件	万吨	Powder Metallurgy Products	10000 tons	5. 35	5. 28	5. 98	6. 32
中型拖拉机	台	Lager and Medium－sized Tractor	unit	17071	15103	10716	9547
汽车	万辆	Motor Vechicle	10000 units	43. 75	42. 89	46. 33	42. 14
基本型乘用车（轿车）	万辆	Car	10000 units	43. 49	42. 43	25. 99	14. 38
新能源汽车	辆	New energy vehicle	unit	2609	4680	14722	132811
摩托车整车	万辆	Motorcycle	10000 units	10. 71	12. 76	15. 18	13. 88
两轮脚踏自行车	万辆	Bicycle	10000 units	137. 29	25. 46	20. 92	18. 70
电动自行车	万辆	Electric Bicycles	10000 units	110. 07	155. 50	183. 37	172. 02
民用钢质船舶	载重吨	Civil Steel Ship	DWT	615369	380748	659288	528136
交流电动机	万千瓦	Alternating Current Motor	10000 kW	373. 36	340. 86	291. 15	201. 85
变压器	万千伏安	Transformer	10000 kev	1857. 92	1883. 95	1936. 33	1599. 08
电力电缆	万公里	Power Cable	10000 km	26. 89	10. 29	9. 02	3. 65
原电池及原电池组（非扣式）	万只	Primary Cellsand Batterices	10000 units	742128. 70	865939. 20	869274. 40	784157. 80
家用洗衣机	万台	Household Washing Machine	10000 units	818. 26	674. 74	596. 90	676. 67
家用吸尘器	万台	Dust Catcher	10000 units	1453. 69	1763. 99	2682. 01	1934. 47
家用电风扇	万台	Electric Fan	10000 units	863. 89	1068. 55	1543. 20	1132. 64
房间空气调节器	万台	Home Air Conditioner	10000 units	1605. 40	1132. 38	1038. 78	1132. 69
家用吸排油烟机	万台	Range Hood	10000 units	338. 91	364. 55	433. 00	417. 11
移动通信手持机（手机）	万部	Mobile Phone	10000 units	876. 41	1404. 95	1579. 56	1566. 16
智能手机	万台	Intelligent mobile phone	10000 units	583. 02	1191. 65	1432. 46	1445. 36
光学仪器	万台	Optical Instrument	10000 units	343. 04	674. 80	315. 85	213. 12
稀土磁性材料	吨	Rare earth magnetic materials	ton	6380	7881	9821	12239
工业机器人	套	Industrial robot	set	5137	8159	9867	7922
城市轨道车辆	辆	Urban rail vehicle	unit	170	159	195	86
光纤	千米	Optical fiber	km	20629	5720	6867	4198
光缆	芯千米	Optical cable	core km	41772	35677	33842	31106
锂离子电池	万只	Lithium ion battery	10000 units	13154. 83	19233. 49	19793. 99	13666. 86
太阳能电池（光伏电池）	千瓦	Solar cell (photovoltaic cell)	kW	1534317. 60	988593. 60	1124265. 60	1683314. 80
集成电路	万块	Integrated circuit	10000 units	159861. 20	200087. 10	363478. 60	347947. 10
发电量	亿千瓦小时	Generating Capacity	100 million kW·h	769. 13	761. 91	957. 80	970. 40

表7-12 历年各区(县、市)规模以上工业增加值能耗绝对量及增速

Comprehensive Energy Consumption of Industrial Enterprises Above Designated Size by Region in All Districts Over the Years

年份 Year	增加值能耗绝对量（吨标煤/万元）				
	全市 Total	海曙 Haishu	江东 Jangdong	江北区 Jiangbei	镇海区 Zhenhai
2016	0.9434	0.4730	0.1760	0.3788	2.5998
2017	0.9192	0.4220		0.3608	2.3247
2018	0.7594	0.3803		0.3263	1.6075
2019	0.7403	0.3877		0.3484	1.7219
2020	0.7228	0.2858		0.3238	2.0890
2021	0.6380	0.2870		0.2757	1.6410
2022	0.6539	0.3059		0.2766	1.6146

表 7 －12 续表 Continued

年份 Year	增加值能耗增速(%)				
	全市 Total	海曙 Haishu	江东 Jangdong	江北区 Jiangbei	镇海区 Zhenhai
2016	0.77	-5.98	-16.64	-2.30	6.86
2017	-3.99	-6.87		-2.05	-3.59
2018	-4.91	-6.24		0.35	-5.70
2019	-3.05	-6.11		1.82	-0.25
2020	-4.72	2.00		-0.03	-3.46
2021	-5.20	-0.38		-5.99	-3.13
2022	6.49	3.31		-3.89	17.60

Absolute energy consumption of added value (Ton of SCE/10000 yuan)						
北仑区 Beilun	鄞州区 Yinzhou	奉化区 Fenghua	余姚市 Yuyao	慈溪市 Cixi	宁海县 Ninghai	象山县 Xiangshan
1. 6638	0. 3423	0. 1510	0. 5415	0. 4348	0. 4630	0. 4577
1. 5461	0. 3224	0. 2013	0. 5412	0. 3929	0. 4366	0. 4504
1. 1657	0. 3805	0. 1799	0. 5240	0. 3182	0. 4151	0. 4861
1. 1022	0. 3578	0. 1642	0. 5014	0. 3177	0. 4059	0. 4996
1. 0481	0. 3361	0. 1646	0. 4224	0. 2786	0. 3908	0. 4811
0. 8887	0. 2038	0. 1664	0. 3737	0. 2630	0. 3900	0. 4458
0. 8457	0. 2650	0. 1674	0. 3871	0. 2648	0. 3822	0. 4403

Added value energy consumption growth(%)						
北仑区 Beilun	鄞州区 Yinzhou	奉化区 Fenghua	余姚市 Yuyao	慈溪市 Cixi	宁海县 Ninghai	象山县 Xiangshan
-2. 66	-5. 92	-10. 51	-4. 62	-6. 46	-1. 05	-4. 51
-2. 45	-7. 19	8. 75	-4. 26	-7. 08	-5. 97	-2. 70
-4. 12	4. 47	1. 47	7. 33	-5. 84	-5. 87	-3. 49
-7. 56	-3. 56	-8. 66	-4. 50	-1. 71	-4. 34	-1. 09
-5. 93	-2. 92	4. 53	-4. 36	-6. 45	-4. 17	1. 35
-6. 66	-4. 18	5. 67	-8. 03	-0. 95	-0. 48	-2. 50
-4. 31	-7. 48	-1. 53	-3. 27	-8. 35	-2. 93	-1. 14

表7-13 按工业行业分组的主要能源消费量(2022年)
Comprehensive Energy Consumption by Industrial Sector（2022）

指标	Indicators	能源合计 吨标准煤 Total Ton of SCE	原煤 Raw Coal	焦炭 Coke
合计	**amount to**	**115155729**	**43037764**	**1485177**
非金属矿采选业	Non-metallic Mining Industry	18951		
农副食品加工业	Farm and Sideline Products Processing	89819		
食品制造业	Food Manufacturing	74567		
酒、饮料和精制茶制造业	Wine, Beverages and Refined Tea Manufacturing	44482		
烟草制品业	Tobacco Manufacturing	10460		
纺织业	Textile Industry	621547	59625	
纺织服装、服饰业	Clothing, Apparel Industry	89727		74
皮革、毛皮、羽毛及其制品和制鞋业	Leather, Fur, Feather and Its Products and Footwear Industry	3846		
木材加工及木、竹、藤、棕、草制品业	Timber Processing, Bamboo, Rattan, Cane Palm, and Straw Products	8762		
家具制造业	Furniture Manufacturing	39135		
造纸及纸制品业	Paper-making and Paper Products Manufacturing	623860	456060	
印刷和记录媒介复制业	Printing and Record Duplicating	49716		
文教、工美、体育和娱乐用品制造业	Culture, Art, Sports and Recreation Supplies Manufacturing	89859		
石油加工、炼焦和核燃料加工业	Petroleum Processing. Coking & Nuclear Fuel Processing	60715860	1754046	
化学原料和化学制品制造业	Raw Chemical Materials and Chemical Products	13973107	1417999	
医药制造业	Medicines Manufacturing	57314		
化学纤维制造业	Chemical Fiber Manufacturing	390653	84373	
橡胶和塑料制品业	Rubber and Plastic Products Industry	402103	23721	
非金属矿物制品业	Nonmetal Mineral Products	385560	5797	
黑色金属冶炼和压延加工业	Smelting and Pressing of Ferrous Metals	5042217	628683	1455082
有色金属冶炼和压延加工业	Smelting and Pressing of Nonferrous Metals	238476	27	
金属制品业	Metal Products Manufacturing	618932		14289
通用设备制造业	General Purpose Equipment Manufacturing	438962		15729
专用设备制造业	Special Purpose Equipment Manufacturing	208897		
汽车制造业	Automobile Manufacturing	680350		
铁路、船舶、航空航天和其他运输设备制造业	Railroad, Marine, Aviation and Other Transport Equipment Manufacturing	52010		
电气机械和器材制造业	Electric Equipment and Machinery Manufacturing	441068		3
计算机、通信和其他电子设备制造业	Computer, Communications and Other Electronic Equipment Manufacturing	481392		
仪器仪表制造业	Instrument Manufacturing	109549		
其他制造业	Other Manufacturing	14825		
废弃资源综合利用业	Waste Comprehensive Utilization of Resources Industry	14810		
金属制品、机械和设备修理业	Metal Products, Machinery and Equipment Repair Industry	6592		
电力、热力的生产和供应业	Production and Supply Electric Power and Thermal Power	29071559	38607434	
燃气生产和供应业	Production and Supply Gas	15918		
水的生产和供应业	Production and Supply Tap Water	30841		

单位：吨(ton)

原油 Crude Oil	汽油 Gasoline	煤油 Kerosene	柴油 Diesel Oil	燃料油 Fuel Oil	液化石油气 LPG	其他油制品 Other Petroleum Products	热力 （百万千焦） Heat million kilo－jou	电力 （万千瓦时） Electricity 10000 kW·h
29796446	**29518**	**4519**	**86771**	**620336**	**617799**	**6846632**	**134516957**	**5617819**
			7328					6613
	194		413		27		761315	21391
	115		874		68	7953	856206	13841
	22		42		19		815305	9289
							53998	4260
	447		391		780	32	7247391	132718
	1370		1807		128	9	727418	34940
	47		38					2467
	52	2	11				62531	4613
	420		546		132	7	2399	19369
	761	1	1434		116		1488700	167656
	610	3	1700		94	69	87980	17606
	748	1	715		339	11	238448	54006
29796446	75	1355	2151	605034	403671	3869271	34350369	436243
	954		3856	2266	204242	2953464	75341830	1256203
	190		187				597138	19440
	6		349				4733278	104503
	1404	267	2111	43	3441	5595	1390878	218438
	387	2	29237	9047	9	2052	1456425	107942
	187	10	713	135	43	80	321014	253931
	178	27	1441	608	287	157	98422	107170
	2579	52	6445	58	1371	285	1951630	293758
	4272	2499	4852	166	1141	3750	126408	276089
	3672	13	2651	4	352	666	46241	130352
	2667	4	3797	1	305	1116	801956	367766
	245	71	1174	1636	54	10	5619	27567
	3748	16	4636	279	798	770	70734	295439
	1705		1181		123	97	514427	347718
	675	195	653	29	131	39	35448	84087
	184		123		130			10652
	19		1292	487		1198	14022	5996
	73	1	331					4874
	1192		4205	543			317920	745273
	178		63				1509	10714
	143		22					24897

表7-14 各区（县、市）规模以上工业企业等价综合能源消费量(2022年)

Equivalent Comprehensive Energy Consumption of Industrial Enterprises Above Designated Size by Region（2022）

指标	Indicators	全市 Total	市区 Urban District	海曙区 Haishu
综合能源消费量总计（吨标准煤）	**Final energy comprehensive consumption per million (Tons of standard coal)**	**34912180**	**27710049**	**743342**
非金属矿采选业	Non-metallic Mining Industry	29608	15489	3613
农副食品加工业	Farm and Sideline Products Processing	124293	45084	5311
食品制造业	Food Manufacturing	96873	20732	3555
酒、饮料和精制茶制造业	Wine, Beverages and Refined Tea Manufacturing	59452	46773	6303
烟草制品业	Tobacco Manufacturing	17325		
纺织业	Textile Industry	820985	371959	8129
纺织服装、服饰业	Clothing, Apparel Industry	146037	99420	29960
皮革、毛皮、羽毛及其制品和制鞋业	Leather, Fur, Feather and Its Products and Footwear Industry	7823	1822	967
木材加工及木、竹、藤、棕、草制品业	Timber Processing, Bamboo, Rattan, Cane Palm, and Straw Products	16196	5063	766
家具制造业	Furniture Manufacturing	70350	18730	2810
造纸及纸制品业	Paper-making and Paper Products Manufacturing	712268	638172	3069
印刷和记录媒介复制业	Printing and Record Duplicating	78089	36684	8603
文教、工美、体育和娱乐用品制造业	Culture, Art, Sports and Recreation Supplies Manufacturing	176895	63556	10081
石油加工、炼焦和核燃料加工业	Petroleum Processing. Coking & Nuclear Fuel Processing	9112901	9111202	33
化学原料和化学制品制造业	Raw Chemical Materials and Chemical Products	9821618	9751255	12560
医药制造业	Medicines Manufacturing	88644	58797	8304
化学纤维制造业	Chemical Fiber Manufacturing	559071	157498	2243
橡胶和塑料制品业	Rubber and Plastic Products Industry	740020	233497	24709
非金属矿物制品业	Nonmetal Mineral Products	559519	288580	71816
黑色金属冶炼和压延加工业	Smelting and Pressing of Ferrous Metals	2664996	2409613	8465
有色金属冶炼和压延加工业	Smelting and Pressing of Nonferrous Metals	411192	207616	4269
金属制品业	Metal Products Manufacturing	1092353	592822	34003
通用设备制造业	General Purpose Equipment Manufacturing	883907	379382	23396
专用设备制造业	Special Purpose Equipment Manufacturing	418972	221008	12631
汽车制造业	Automobile Manufacturing	1273041	556287	46740
铁路、船舶、航空航天和其他运输设备制造业	Railroad, Marine, Aviation and Other Transport Equipment Manufacturing	96437	39093	3654
电气机械和器材制造业	Electric Equipment and Machinery Manufacturing	917197	245589	34420
计算机、通信和其他电子设备制造业	Computer, Communications and Other Electronic Equipment Manufacturing	1041775	570737	43383
仪器仪表制造业	Instrument Manufacturing	245064	38993	10782
其他制造业	Other Manufacturing	31992	8938	2318
废弃资源综合利用业	Waste Comprehensive Utilization of Resources Industry	24473	14624	1505
金属制品、机械和设备修理业	Metal Products, Machinery and Equipment Repair Industry	14448	12493	
电力、热力的生产和供应业	Production and Supply Electric Power and Thermal Power	2456195	1393083	306980
燃气生产和供应业	Production and Supply Gas	31209	30280	7961
水的生产和供应业	Production and Supply Tap Water	70964	25178	

江北区 Jiangbei	镇海区 Zhenhai	北仑区 Beilun	鄞州区 Yinzhou	奉化区 Fenghua	余姚市 Yuyao	慈溪市 Cixi	宁海县 Ninghai	象山县 Xiangshan
525270	**15239051**	**9887535**	**1314851**	**633501**	**2049422**	**2695303**	**1067104**	**756802**
	39		11837		8582	3419		2119
125	216	34890	4542	14	15857	23457	657	39225
4922	4429	5731	2096	5588	61081	576	2632	6264
		39896	574	9276	1759		1641	3
				17325				
2881	42945	282780	35224	5890	117928	231359	17429	76420
1286	4795	50296	13083	14105	5399	2349	285	24479
42	237	204	372	510	720	3001	1769	
353	851	197	2896	2721	826	7107		479
642	520	3788	10971	3096	19718	27362	599	845
78	1700	594622	38702.6	13508	3719	40654	16205	11
1410	4366	11576	10728	3621	16777	18620	663	1724
11423	3943	31665	6445	6050	14879	40678	49316	2417
	8242136	868905	128	839		15	809	36
2053	6119667	3600153	16823	10172	33031	11013	10032	6115
7871	13178	23804	5640	8338	5351	3094	8677	4387
	109869	44451	935		103983	297569		20
12218	58900	69431	68239	34461	261378	154063	43756	12865
16122	38630	55242	106770	19932	63670	32643	100730	53963
1212	32550	2316758	50628	649	167305	63410	23637	382
156434	25949	14702	6261	8029	71472	97541	24094	2441
17383	90190	200584	250662	140164	141905	147825	48806	20833
16967	160154	107277	71589	120946	80792	172292	40345	90149
12598	15544	156190	24045	12093	74441	56400	34564	20466
114449	24700	245758	124639	47800	105242	421353	85519	56841
938	575	29756	4171	849	4332	30183	755	21224
56861	22547	60134	71626	42043	162890	371398	80396	14882
68590	22690	214656	221418	26288	154997	233844	24324	31585
12930	1696	4056	9529	3939	177487	22909	1604	131
	1160	1169	4292	1411	6566	12404	2368	305
	4745	1941	6434		1045	325		8479
	16	12477					5	1950
	184402	780537	121163	72078	154020	148399	440258	248357
		22045	273	91	146	504	97	92
5483	5712	1864	12118	1679	12122	19536	5136	7314

表7-15 全市规模以上工业企业能源购、消、存情况(2022年)

Purchases,Sales and Inventory of Energy of Industrial Enterprises Above Designated Size（2022）

指标	单位	Indicators	Unit	年初库存 Stock (Year-head)	购进量 Purchases	
					实物量 Material Amount	购自省外 Purchase from outside the
原煤	吨	Raw Coal	ton	1830447	42817764	22855427
洗精煤	吨	Clenedcoal	ton	162914	1147154	1089796
煤制品	吨	Coal Products	ton			
焦炭	吨	Coke	ton	43459	667493	366240
天然气（气态）	万立方米	Natural Gas(Gas)	10000 Cubic Meters	42	407851	
液化天然气(液态)	吨	Liquefied Natural Gas(Liquid)	ton	498	166675	582
原油	吨	Crude Oil	ton	1063167	29905713	29905709
汽油	吨	Gasoline	ton	150	41405	573
煤油	吨	Kerosene	ton	209	3141	70
柴油	吨	Diesel Oil	ton	3722	92241	409
燃料油	吨	Fuel Oil	ton	16490	497486	409545
液化石油气	吨	Liquefied Petroleum Gas	ton	28520	343379	
炼厂干气	吨	Refinery Dry Gas	ton		592268	
石油焦	吨	Petroleum Coke	ton	18265	267913	63276
其他石油制品	吨	Other Petroleum Products	ton	33912	3344069	727542
热力	百万千焦	Heat	million kilo-joule		107510699	
电力	万千瓦时	Electricity	10000 kW·h		4921904	
余热余压	百万千焦	Residual Heat and Pressure	million kilo-joule		50272	
能源合计	吨标准煤	Total	Ton of SCE			

工业生产消费 Consumptiop of Industrial Production	年末库存 Stock (Year-ead)	能源转出量 Energy Producing	能源投入 Energy Input	火力发电 Generation of Electric Power by Thermal Power	供热 Heat Supply	炼油投入 Input of Oil Refining
43037764	1656000		40579070	35611995	4967076	
1344949	89866		1344949			
1485177	38803	1046373				
245424	45		125849	107037	18812	
166364	406		1538	1175	363	
29796446	1048420		29796446			29796446
29518	144	4297391				
4519	165	1956515	1355			1355
86771	4056	5683664	800	799	2	
620336	26240	2400561	605577		543	472419
617799	27499	1640774	600447	2271	44387	553789
2372572		1826350	420425	2671	57841	359913
1058177	12501	977598	820540	328101	445213	
6846632	48346	13418090	2941846	1266	28176	2912404
134516957		126018602				
5617819		9356499				
10385357			4146904	4146904		
115155729		72468225	89413051	26553546	4874089	55136367

表7-16 各区（县、市）全社会用电量（2022年）
Total Electricity Consumption by Region（2022）

指标	Indicators	全市 Total	为上年（%） The Preceding Year=100(%)	市区 Urban District
总计	**Total**	**9726637**	**103.7**	**5352764**
全行业用电量	Electricity Consumption for Non－Living Electricity	8384542	101.3	4718268
农林牧渔业	Farming, Forestry, Animal Husbandry, Fishery	51942	117.5	14237
#排灌	Irrigation and Drainage	9398	116.0	2709
①农业	Farming	18577	119.1	6239
②林业	Forestry	497	106.3	225
③畜牧业	Animal Husbandary	8294	125.2	1727
④渔业	Fishery	11705	117.2	1389
⑤其他	Others	12868	111.5	4658
工业	Industry	6746670	100.0	3718299
轻工业	Light Industry			
重工业	Heavy Industry			
建筑业	Construction	136945	103.5	56856
交通运输、仓储和邮政业	Transportation, Storage and Post	181687	102.5	144169
交通运输	Transportation	138977	100.9	109185
仓储业	Warehousing Industry	39379	108.7	32570
邮政	Post	3331	100.5	2414
信息传输、计算机服务和软件业	Information Transmission,Computer Service and Soft	100101	120.2	48037
商业、住宿和饮食业	Trade, Hotel and Catering Trade	436550	105.3	265325
金融、房地产、商务及居民服务业	Financial, Real Estate, Business and Resident Serv	314893	110.1	224862
公共事业及管理组织	Public Service and Management Organizations	415754	105.5	245965
城乡居民生活用电量	**Electricity Consumption for Urban and Rural Resid**	**1342095**	**121.3**	**634495**
城市	Urban Residents	481427	95.8	317813
乡村	Rural Residents	860669	142.4	316681

单位：万千瓦时(10000 kW·h)

海曙区 Haishu	江北区 Jiangbei	镇海区 Zhenhai	北仑区 Beilun	鄞州区 Yinzhou	奉化区 Fenghua	余姚市 Yuyao	慈溪市 Cixi	宁海县 Ninghai	象山县 Xiangshan
611167	**391308**	**1418670**	**1796813**	**1134806**	**471974**	**1246323**	**1876017**	**469449**	**342515**
476610	321417	1348811	1691810	879620	391023	1072232	1607419	361301	266702
3833	1521	2207	1777	4899	4883	8547	10559	7279	6436
1171	312	490	6	730	651	2637	1117	611	1673
1522	892	1024	1145	1656	1977	1675	5735	1506	1445
76	16	3	85	45	34	67	43	90	39
430	201	599	349	148	1680	2146	1221	885	635
156	6	17	40	1170	349	1636	2088	3887	2355
1650	406	564	158	1880	842	3023	1472	909	1963
283217	196236	1235755	1508321	494770	295875	926341	1358840	284349	195373
8826	6492	10109	11089	20340	16534	10900	39891	7959	4805
22342	12208	25196	54516	29907	10461	15072	6094	3105	2785
20428	9557	21837	29775	27588	8386	13069	3976	2228	2132
811	2223	3248	24644	1644	1913	1742	1799	791	564
1103	428	111	97	675	162	261	319	85	89
8342	6922	7695	5137	19941	4885	8882	29927	4698	3672
59353	31682	29713	50393	94184	18349	48507	53694	24875	25800
41142	25846	12462	23341	122071	15894	18637	40794	9135	5050
49556	39989	25674	37237	93509	24144	35346	67621	19898	22780
134557	**69891**	**69859**	**105002**	**255186**	**80950**	**174091**	**268598**	**108147**	**75813**
60824	34830	31644	17858	172657	9093	57567	52694	17219	27040
73733	35061	38215	87144	82528	71858	116524	215905	90927	48773

表7-17 历年全社会用电量
Total Electricity Consumption Over the Years

年份 Year	总计 Total	比上年增长 Growth Rate over Preceding Year(%)	全行业用电 总计 Total	农业 Agriculture	工业 Industry
1978	70905				43704
1979	89023	25.6			56404
1980	106695	19.9			66886
1981	119606	12.1			72878
1982	129011	7.9			78879
1983	147338	14.2			91251
1984	164071	11.4			93618
1985	185167	12.9			98512
1986	223048	20.5			123033
1987	253457	13.6			140978
1988	279914	10.4			148756
1989	285460	2.0			218247
1990	314858	10.3	271855	16657	233766
1991	365090	16.0	315484	17682	273333
1992	421441	15.4	363939	18601	316558
1993	482578	14.5	416063	18680	359972
1994	552044	14.4	467366	20325	400080
1995	619447	12.2	517935	21262	439498
1996	670281	8.2	551953	22039	457688
1997	718416	7.2	595479	21339	496127
1998	799300	11.3	667837	20470	560624
1999	914936	14.5	778181	21063	664623
2000	1134811	24.0	983475	25777	840125
2001	1266535	11.6	1107317	30111	943788
2002	1520751	20.1	1333570	26115	1146566
2003	1890027	24.3	1651392	22305	1416625
2004	2189528	15.8	1967731	20410	1703126
2005	2684887	22.6	2421555	19142	2110735
2006	3135530	16.8	2833457	17176	2490873
2007	3671231	17.1	3321752	19856	2934498
2008	3849407	4.9	3453560	20562	3027597
2009	4002520	4.0	3577500	21990	3101523
2010	4590431	14.7	4092098	24240	3542660
2011	5053017	10.1	4517125	27067	3886156
2012	5140915	1.7	4547780	28724	3845918
2013	5593943	8.8	4932666	33422	4149789
2014	5767787	3.1	5159482	33393	4352456
2015	5850658	1.4	5203327	34053	4348960
2016	6465408	10.5	5716247	36769	4767430
2017	7092306	9.7	6285915	39288	5254029
2018	7752759	9.3	6864798	41489	5717293
2019	8079226	4.2	7131897	40205	5901652
2020	8321517	3.0	7308252	40935	6031659
2021	9384110	12.8	8277711	44173	6746731
2022	9726637	3.7	8384542	51942	6746670

单位：万千瓦时(10000 kW·h)

Production Consumption				生活用电 Living Consumption		
其中 of Which		建筑业 Construction	第三产业 Tertiary Industry	总计 Total	其中 of Which	
轻工业 Light Industry	重工业 Heavy Industry				城市 Urban	农村 Rural
				4325		
				4835		
				5355		
				6315		
				6734		
				7500		
				9313		
				12603		
				17662		
				22881		
				29510		
				33088		
103301	130465	3770	21432	43003	11926	31077
122714	150619	3179	24469	49606	13406	36200
146272	170286	3898	28780	57502	15499	42003
171383	188589	5870	37412	66515	18972	47543
186145	213935	8016	46961	84678	26002	58677
209890	229608	9855	57175	101512	31626	69886
209606	248082	13586	72226	118328	40536	77792
240220	255907	12132	78013	122937	43257	79680
262246	298378	10589	86743	131463	48670	82793
305906	358717	9745	92495	136755	50740	86015
394760	445365	12559	117573	151336	59557	91779
402840	540948	14234	133418	159218	65054	94164
483275	663292	15523	160889	187188	74294	112886
574100	842525	21672	212462	238635	95616	143019
647516	1055610	31570	244195	221797	105639	116158
775922	1334813	34520	257158	263332	135827	127505
897750	1593123	36255	289154	302073	152348	149725
1013214	1921284	42460	324937	349479	174873	174606
1016912	2010684	44590	360812	395847	198536	197311
1045023	2056500	52322	401664	425020	216319	208701
1182101	2360559	62833	462365	498333	249932	248401
1260629	2625527	74231	529671	535891	271889	264003
1242699	2603219	79121	594017	593135	301647	291489
1303187	2846603	81823	667632	661277	334887	326389
1322290	3030166	81207	692426	608304	310525	297779
1301772	3047187	70725	749589	647332	331335	315997
1392371	3375059	67962	844086	749161	382824	366338
1511697	3742332	73846	918751	806391	408297	398094
		83753	1043679	887961	450944	437016
		95539	1115547	947328	486838	460490
		104202	1153669	1013265	519942	493324
		132344	1377043	1106399	502154	604245
		136945	1472350	1342095	481427	860669

表7-18　2022年主营业务收入前20位工业企业
The Top 20 Enterprises on Annual Revenue from Principal Business in 2022

序号 No.	企业名称 Name of Enterprises	注册类型 Registered Type
1	中国石油化工股份有限公司镇海炼化分公司 Sinopec Zhenhai Refining & Chemical Co., Ltd.	股份有限公司 Share–holding Corporations Ltd.
2	浙江吉利汽车有限公司 Zhejiang Geely Automobile Co., Ltd	私营有限责任公司 Private Limited Liability Company
3	国网浙江省电力有限公司宁波供电公司 State Grid Ningbo Power Supply Co.,Ltd.	其他有限责任公司 Other Limited Liability Corporations
4	上汽大众汽车有限公司宁波分公司 Saic Volkswagen Automobile Co., Ltd. Ningbo branch	中外合资经营 Chinese–foreign Equity Joint Ventures Enterprises
5	中海石油宁波大榭石化有限公司 CNOOC Petrochemical Ningbo Daxie Co., Ltd.	与港澳台商合资经营 Equity Joint Ventures with HongKong, Macao & Taiwan
6	浙江逸盛新材料有限公司 Zhejiang Yisheng New Material Co., Ltd.	私营有限责任公司 Private Limited Liability Company
7	宁波中金石化有限公司 Ningbo CICC Petrochemical Co., Ltd.	私营有限责任公司 Private Limited Liability Company
8	浙江中烟工业有限责任公司宁波卷烟厂 China Tobacco Zhejiang Industrial Co., Ltd., Ningbo Cigarette Factory	国有独资公司 State – owned Company
9	浙江逸盛石化有限公司 Zhejiang Yisheng Petrochemical Co., Ltd.	与港澳台商合资经营 Equity Joint Ventures with HongKong, Macao & Taiwan
10	台化兴业（宁波）有限公司 Taihua Xingye (Ningbo) Co., Ltd.	港澳台商独资 HongKong, Macao & Taiwan Funded Sole
11	得力集团有限公司 Deli Group Co., Ltd.	私营有限责任公司 Private Limited Liability Company
12	宁波申洲针织有限公司 Ningbo Shenzhou Weaving Co., Ltd.	港澳台商独资 HongKong, Macao & Taiwan Funded Sole
13	中石化宁波镇海炼化有限公司 Ningbo Zhenhai Petrochemical Co., LTD	其他有限责任公司 Other Limited Liability Corporations
14	东方日升新能源股份有限公司 Risen Energy Co., Ltd.	股份有限公司 Share–holding Corporations Ltd.
15	宁波舜宇光电信息有限公司 Ningbo Sunny Optoech Co., Ltd.	与港澳台商合资经营 Equity Joint Ventures with HongKong, Macao & Taiwan
16	宁波金田新材料有限公司 Ningbo Jintian Electric Material Co., Ltd.	私营有限责任公司 Private Limited Liability Company
17	宁波杭州湾吉利汽车部件有限公司 Ningbo Hangzhou Bay Geely Auto Parts Co., Ltd.	其他有限责任公司 Other Limited Liability Corporations
18	宁波钢铁有限公司 Ningbo Steel Co., Ltd.	其他有限责任公司 Other Limited Liability Corporations
19	万华化学(宁波)有限公司 Wanhua Chemical (Ningbo) Co., Ltd	其他有限责任公司 Other Limited Liability Corporations
20	奥克斯空调股份有限公司 Oakes Air Conditioning Co., Ltd.	股份有限公司 Share–holding Corporations Ltd.

主要统计指标解释

【工业总产值】是以货币形式表现的，工业企业在一定时期内生产的工业最终产品或提供工业性劳务活动的总价值量。 它是反映一定时期内工业生产总规模和总水平的指标。

工业总产值包括:本期生产的成品价值、对外加工费收入和在制品半成品期末期初差额价值三部分。

【工业销售产值】是以货币形式表现的，工业企业在一定时期内销售的本企业生产的工业产品或提供工业性劳务活动的价值总量。它是反映一定时期内工业企业产品销售总规模和总水平的重要指标。

【工业增加值】是指工业企业在报告期内以货币形式表现的工业生产活动的最终成果，是企业全部生产活动的总成果扣除了在生产过程中消耗或转换的物质产品和劳务价值后的余额，是企业生产过程中新增加的价值。

【固定资产原价】固定资产原值指企业在建造、购置、安装、改建、扩建、技术改造某项固定资产时所支出的全部货币总额。它一般包括买价、包装费、运杂费和安装费等。

【流动资产】流动资产是指可以在一年或者超过一年的一个生产周期内变现或者耗用的资产，包括现金及各种存款、短期投资、应收及预付货款、存货等。

【主营业务收入】指企业在销售商品（不一定是本企业生产）、提供劳务及让渡资产使用权等日常活动中所产生的收入

【主营业务成本】指企业在销售商品、提供劳务及让渡资产使用权等日常活动而发生的实际成本。

【主营业务税金及附加】指企业日常活动应负担的税金及附加，包括营业税、消费税、城市维护建设税、资源税、土地增值税和教育费附加等。

【利润总额】指企业在生产经营过程中各种收入扣除各种耗费后的盈余，反映企业在报告期内实现的亏盈总额，包括营业利润、补贴收入、投资净收益和营业外收支净额。

【利税总额】指企业利润总额、主营业务税金及附加和本年应交增值税之和。

【资产总计】指企业拥有或控制的能以货币计量的经济资源，包括各种财产、债权和其他权利。资产按其流动性（即资产的变现能力和支付能力）划分为：流动资产、长期投资、固定资产、无形资产、递延资产和其他资产。

【负债合计】指企业所承担的能以货币计量，将以资产或劳务偿付的债务，偿还形式包括货币、资产或提供劳务。负债一般按偿还期长短分为流动负债和长期负债。

【所有者权益】指企业投资人对企业净资产的所有权。企业净资产等于企业全部资产减去全部负债后的余额，其中包括投资者对企业的最初投入，以及资本公积金、盈余公积金和未分配利润，对股份制企业即为股东权益。

【实收资本】指投资者按照企业章程，或合同、协议的约定，实际投入企业的资本。企业实收资本按照投资主体划分为国家资本、集体资本、法人资本、个人资本、港澳台资本和外商资本六种。根据“资产负债表”中的“实收资本”项填列。实收资本中如有以外币形式投入的资本，需折合成人民币形式填写。

【综合能源消费量】指一定时期、一定地域内工业企业在工业生产活动中实际消费的各种能源的总和净值。计算综合能源消费量时，需要先将使用的各种能源折算成标准燃料后再进行计算。

Explanatory Notes on Main Statistical Indicators

【**Gross Industrial Output Value**】is in a form of currency. Total value of end–products or industrial services activities industrial enterprises provide in the period. It reflects the total achievements and overall scale of industrial production during a given period.

It includes the value of the finished products in a given period, the value of industrial services rendered to other units and the changes in the value of the semi finished products and products in process between the beginning and closing of the period.

【**Industrial Sales Output Value**】is in a form of currency. Is the total volume of industrial products sold in value terms of an industrial enterprise and Industrial services activities, which reflects the total achievements and overall sales scale of industrial production during a given period.

【**Value Added of Industry**】refers to the final results of industrial production in money terms during the reporting period. Is the total business results of all production activities deducted consumption in the production process and converted the value of material goods and services. Is the production process to increase the value of new.

【**Original Value of Fixed Assets**】refers to the original value of all fixed assets owned by industrial enterprises, calculated at the cost paid at the time of purchase, installation, reconstruction, expansion, and technical innovation and transformation of the said assets, which includes expenses on purchase, package, transportation, and installation, etc.

【**Liquid Assets**】is assets that can be turned into cash or consumed in more than one year or in a year, including cash and deposits, short–term investments, accounts receivable and prepaid inventories.

【**Main Business Income**】refers to the enterprises in selling products (not necessarily in this enterprises' production), providing services and transferring assets, daily activities such as the right to the revenue that generated.

【Main Business Cost】refers to the actual incurred costs the enterprises sell products, provide services, transfer assets, and other daily activities.

【**Main Business Taxes and Surcharges**】refers to taxes and surcharges in the enterprises' daily production activities, including sales tax, consumption tax, urban maintenance and construction tax, resource tax, land tax and education surcharge, etc.

【**Total Profits**】refers to the Surplus an enterprise products in the process of production and business activities after deducting all cost, reflecting the company's profit and loss during the reporting period, including operating profit, subsidy income, net investment income and the net non–operating income and expenditure.

【**Total Profits and Taxes**】refer to total corporate profits taxes, business taxes and surcharges, and the sum of VAT of this year.

【**Total Assets**】refer to all assets which are owned or controlled by enterprises, including circulating assets, long–term investment, fixed assets, intangible assets and deferred assets, other long–term assets, and defertaxes, etc. The summation of above items is equal to total assets shown in the balance sheets of the enterprises.(1) Circulating assets (working capital) refer to assets which can be cashed in or spent or consumed in an operating cycle of one year or over one year, including cash, all kinds of deposits, short term investment, receivables, advance payment, stock,etc.(2) Fixed assets refer to the net value of fixed assets, clearance of fixed assets, project under construction, fixed assets losses in suspense. These are corporations' fund holdings.(3) Intangible assets refer to the assets without material form used by enterprises over a long time, such as patents, non–patent technologies, trade marks, copyright, land use right, business reputation, etc

【**Total Liabilities**】refer to the debts that enterprises are responsible for repayment, including liquid liabilities, long term liabilities and deferred taxes, etc. Total liabilities correspond to the summation item of liabilities shown in the balance sheets of the enterprises. Liabilities include short term loans and long–term loans.

【**Creditors' Equity**】refers to equity investment in an enterprise net assets of the enterprise ownership. Net assets equal total assets minus total liabilities of business the balance, including the investor's initial investment in the enterprise, and capital reserve, surplus reserve and undistributed profits of the joint–stock company is the shareholders' equity.

【**Paid–in capital**】refers to the investors in accordance with corporate charter, or contract, to the agreement, the actual capital invested enterprises. Business investment in paid–in capital in accordance with the main division of the state capital, collective capital, corporate capital, personal capital, Hong Kong, Macao, Taiwan capital and foreign capital six. Filled according to the "paid–up capital" items in the "balance sheet". Paid–up capital in any foreign currency in the form of capital investment required to fill out

【**Comprehensive Energy Consumption**】in a certain period, certain areas of industrial enterprises in the industrial production activities in the actual consumption of energy is the sum of net. Calculation of comprehensive energy consumption, need to be used in a variety of energy conversion to standard fuel after calculation.

NINGBO

2023

Statistical Yearbook

8

CHAPTER

第八篇

固定资产投资和建筑业

INVESTMENT IN FIXED ASSETS AND CONSTRUCTION

固定资产投资和建筑业
Investment Fixed Assets and Construction

主要统计指标
Major Statistics Indicators

2022年固定资产投资额	Value of Investment Fixed Assets			
比上年增长	Increase Over Last Year	10.4	%	
2022年房地产开发投资额	Value of Investment in Real Estate Development	2131.7	亿元	100 million yuan
比上年增长	Increase Over Last Year	2.7	%	
2022年房屋竣工面积	Floor Space of Building Completed	16284059	平方米	sq.m
比上年增长	Increase Over Last Year	8.6	%	
2022年商品房销售面积	Floor Space of Commercial Building Sold	11287960	平方米	sq.m
比上年增长	Increase Over Last Year	-29.7	%	
2022年商品房实际销售额	Sales Volume of Commercial Buildings	19375751	万元	10000 yuan
比上年增长	Increase Over Last Year	-35.8	%	
2022年商品房待售面积	Floor Space of Sale Building	4199634	平方米	sq.m
比上年增长	Increase Over Last Year	6.3	%	
2022年建筑业总产值	Gross Output Value of Construction	34261106	万元	10000 yuan
比上年增长	Increase Over Last Year	8.0	%	

表8-1 历年固定资产投资情况
Total Investment in Fixed Assets Over the Years

单位:亿元(100 million yuan)

年份 Year	总计 Total	其中 of Which 限额以上项目投资 Above Designated Size	工业投资 Industrial Investment	基础设施投资 Infrastructure Investment	房地产开发投资 Real Estate Development
1978	5.02				
1979	5.79				
1980	6.50				
1981	6.39				
1982	8.57				
1983	7.69				
1984	10.95				
1985	18.08				
1986	22.01				
1987	29.46				
1988	35.81				
1989	32.79				
1990	39.28				2.49
1991	51.42				3.00
1992	76.25				7.36
1993	129.27				25.44
1994	184.60				50.46
1995	264.19				71.59
1996	309.97				65.90
1997	300.57				51.92
1998	309.81				43.87
1999	318.93				46.54
2000	360.75				59.71
2001	470.28				87.08
2002	601.27				125.97
2003	740.92	556.66			184.26
2004	1026.64	782.38			244.26
2005	1268.55	1009.05			259.50
2006	1413.00	1099.42			313.58
2007	1486.54	1153.65			332.89
2008	1610.86	1303.11			307.75
2009	1860.45	1485.93	709.45	620.32	374.51
2010	2034.99	1477.72	619.01	610.87	557.27
2011	2385.50	1630.56	668.36	697.25	754.94
2012	2901.42	2017.07	817.24	845.71	884.35
2013	3422.95	2299.81	1061.90	846.70	1123.14
2014	3989.46	2661.32	1263.22	971.03	1328.14
2015	4506.58	3277.74	1499.86	1290.14	1228.84
2016	4961.39	3691.06	1469.95	1631.53	1270.33
2017	5009.58	3635.11	1356.48	1720.46	1374.47
2018	3.6	-4.9	-0.3	1.6	15.5
2019	8.1	8.7	10.5	7.5	7.3
2020	5.5	4.4	10.0	8.4	6.8
2021	11.0	8.2	20.4	-9.9	14.1
2022	10.4	17.6	14.5	14.1	2.7

注：（1）自2003年以后总计数为限额以上固定资产投资口径（即限额以上项目投资与房地产开发投资之和）。
（2）自2018年起，各项指标数据均为该指标的同比增速。

Notes:（1）The norm of the total count of fixed asset investment excessing the quota since 2003. That is the sum of real estate development investments and projects investments excessing the quota.
（2）Sice 2018,the data of all indicators are the year-on-year growth rate of the indicator.

表8-2 各区（县、市）固定资产投资完成情况（2022年）
Total Investment in Fixed Assets by Region（2022）

指标	Indicators	全市 Total	市区 Urban District	海曙区 Haishu
固定资产投资比上年增长（按经营地）	**Increased over the previous year(By Place of Business)**	**10.4**	**10.8**	**13.3**
固定资产投资比上年增长（按建设地）	**Increased over the previous year(By Place of Building)**	**10.4**	**10.8**	**13.3**
限额以上项目投资比上年增长	**Investment in Fixed Assets Above Designed Size**	**17.6**	**18.1**	**31.1**
按行业分	**Group by Sector**			
农林牧渔业	Framing, Forestry, Animal Husbandry and Fishery	-22.2	-28.3	
采矿业	Mining and Quarrying	79.6	-57.7	-100.0
制造业	Manufacturing	14.8	4.2	26.2
电力、燃气及水的生产和供应业	Electric Power, Gas and Water Production and Supply	6.7	50.6	4.9
建筑业	Construction	-94.3	-29.5	
批发和零售业	Wholesale and Retail Trade	-27.4	7.3	-38.0
交通运输、仓储和邮政业	Transportation, Storage and Post	4.3	17.8	44.5
住宿和餐饮业	Hotel and Catering Services	11.5	31.5	9.8
信息传输、软件和信息技术服务业	Information Transmission, Software and Information Technology Service	34.9	0.6	167.1
金融业	Financial Industries	-27.5	-51.5	-82.8
房地产业	Real Estate Industries	46.2	53.9	75.1
租赁和商务服务业	Leasing and Business Service Industries	77.8	91.5	211.9
科学研究和技术服务业	Scientific Research and Technology Service	32.0	33.0	12.4
水利、环境和公共设施管理业	Water Conservancy, Environment and Public Facility Management	25.3	19.6	6.7
居民服务、修理和其他服务业	Residential Service, Repairing & Maintenance and Other Service	322.5	332.4	
教育	Education	10.1	22.5	51.0
卫生和社会工作	Health Care and Social Work	72.0	78.4	283.2
文化、体育和娱乐业	Culture, Sports and Entertainment	38.1	56.8	-71.5
公共管理、社会保障和社会组织	Public Management, Social Security and Social Organizations	64.4	138.0	35.0
房地产开发投资完成额比上年增长（按经营地）	**Real Estate Development(By Place of Business)**	**2.7**	**4.9**	**5.3**
#住宅	Residential Buildings	2.4	5.4	5.3
房地产开发投资完成额比上年增长（按建设地）	**Real Estate Development(By Place of Building)**	**2.7**	**4.9**	**5.3**
#住宅	Residential Buildings	2.4	5.4	5.3

注：本表按2011年修订的国民经济行业标准统计。
Note: Statistics in this table are classified as the national economic category that was modified in 2011.

单位：万元（10000 yuan）

江北区 Jiangbei	镇海区 Zhenhai	北仑区 Beilun	鄞州区 Yinzhou	奉化区 Fenghua	余姚市 Yuyao	慈溪市 Cixi	宁海县 Ninghai	象山县 Xiangshan
10.7	**9.5**	**14.5**	**7.2**	**13.7**	**13.7**	**14.4**	**9.3**	**5.8**
10.7	**9.5**	**14.5**	**7.2**	**13.7**	**13.7**	**14.4**	**9.3**	**5.8**
55.7	**7.7**	**13.1**	**14.6**	**24.4**	**17.9**	**33.4**	**24.9**	**11.4**
-82.9	-58.3		1894.9	-54.3		-18.5	-41.8	-7.5
			-13.7		4.9	31.4	1223.7	
19.6	-8.8	2.7	18.5	31.0	19.2	39.5	35.5	32.3
164.2	49.5	103.8	28.9	27.9	-1.5	-25.1	15.7	-9.7
		-29.5					-98.8	
6.2		-48.1	11.6	571.5	-48.4	-80.5	7.0	-73.1
142.8	-27.4	51.9	-3.8	-13.3	5.5	43.1	4.0	-13.5
124.6	491.3	100.1	-30.0	2187.5	88.7		59.3	-33.1
	34250.0		-57.3		-97.3	245.5	-100.0	
-44.1			-100.0		210.7			-16.2
197.4	45.9	287.5	32.0	36.3	48.8	23.0	-0.3	110.3
56.7		1338.1	89.3	42.0		43.2	-59.8	130.6
	122.9	1.5	4.1	-15.8	-78.4	33.1	161.3	
109.9	117.0	9.4	-6.4	16.3	45.8	37.6	40.1	31.2
		-39.8	5.2	749.7		-100.0		
8.1	136.2	39.1	5.5	-9.5	44.1	-5.4	-48.8	9.3
-2.3	48.8	12.1	40.6	92.2	84.0	1874.4	-32.2	22.4
-77.4	1096.5	-28.9	28.1	149.0	-68.8	11.7	172.3	82.9
		119.6	19.9	333.9	-21.4	129.0	-6.4	13.3
-5.2	**18.0**	**18.6**	**3.8**	**7.0**	**8.5**	**-2.2**	**-14.1**	**-10.9**
-6.0	21.5	10.1	7.8	4.1	-0.3	-4.3	-10.8	-4.5
-5.2	**18.0**	**18.6**	**3.8**	**7.0**	**8.5**	**-2.2**	**-14.1**	**-10.9**
-6.0	21.5	10.1	7.8	4.1	-0.3	-4.3	-10.8	-4.5

表8-3 部分年份分产业固定资产投资完成额
Total Fixed Assets Investment by Industry in Partial Years

单位：万元（10000 yuan）

指标	Indicators	2018	2019	2020	2021	2022
总计	**Total**	**3.6**	**8.1**	**5.5**	**11.0**	**10.4**
第一产业	Primary Industry	-26.7	-15.9	405.4	-13.3	-38.9
第二产业	Secondary Industry	-0.1	10.4	10.2	20.6	14.0
第三产业	Tertiary Industry	4.8	7.4	3.9	8.1	9.3
限额以上项目投资	**Investment in Fixed Assets Above Designed Size**	**-4.9**	**8.7**	**4.4**	**8.2**	**17.6**
第一产业	Primary Industry	-26.7	-15.9	405.4	-13.3	-38.9
第二产业	Secondary Industry	-0.1	10.4	10.2	20.6	14.0
第三产业	Tertiary Industry	-7.9	7.6	-0.3	-1.5	21.4
城镇限额以下投资	**Investment in Fixed Assets Below Designed Size in Town**					
第一产业	Primary Industry					
第二产业	Secondary Industry					
第三产业	Tertiary Industry					
农村非农户限额以下投资	**Investment in Fixed Assets about Non-peasant Households & Below Designed Size in Rural Area**					
第一产业	Primary Industry					
第二产业	Secondary Industry					
第三产业	Tertiary Industry					
房地产开发	**Real Estate Development**	**15.5**	**7.3**	**6.8**	**14.1**	**2.7**
#住宅建设	Residential Buildings	18.1	9.1	0.2	16.2	2.4
农村私人固定资产投资	**Private Investment in Rural Areas**					

注：自2018年起，各项指标数据均为该指标的同比增速。
Note: Since 2018, the data of all indicators are the year-on-year growth rate of the indicator.

表8-4 部分年份新增固定资产及房屋建筑面积
Newly Increase Fixed Assets and Floor Space of Buildings in Partial Years

单位：万平方米(10000 sq.m)

年份	本年新增固定资产额（万元）Newly Increase Fixed Assets in This Year(10000 yuan)	房屋施工面积 Floor Space of Buildings Under Construction	#住宅 Residential Buildings	房屋竣工面积 Floor Space of Buildings Completed	#住宅 Residential Buildings
1990	179769	308.76	137.73	180.48	77.30
1991	289108	362.09	175.07	182.28	88.11
1992	253780	518.29	254.60	209.38	91.38
1993	516881	906.08	501.36	383.28	224.91
1994	908056	1205.39	615.30	528.40	285.92
1995	1007217	1386.64	760.99	515.02	312.26
1996	1433274	1395.46	681.71	579.60	332.59
1997	1758309	1264.97	543.00	442.76	232.08
1998	1685871	1156.62	467.16	506.87	232.26
1999	1915400	1050.10	519.91	499.65	233.31
2000	2464806	1208.39	681.38	446.70	227.64
2001	2776661	1626.01	886.08	622.64	341.45
2002	2382537	2342.77	1132.48	745.33	365.88
2003	3292041	3401.43	1744.41	971.64	550.62
2004	3603854	4062.61	2225.05	996.97	546.09
2005	5708349	4600.43	2225.51	1562.32	680.51
2006	7321849	4542.09	2186.55	1427.87	671.66
2007	7166189	5715.13	2190.54	1452.22	535.06
2008	7523565	6505.64	2447.55	1746.09	712.79
2009	11797353	6741.74	2352.59	1669.41	500.54
2010	9781355	7679.59	2741.93	1486.97	470.94
2011	12296942	9792.22	3532.76	2232.56	672.49
2012	10643686	10925.24	4037.87	2025.64	615.75
2013	18423979	12227.39	4422.44	2558.33	666.48
2014	20319735	11798.76	4694.56	2780.58	880.96
2015	32252559	14486.60	4998.62	4263.26	958.79
2016	37141826	11331.58	4709.24	3410.80	1198.08
2017	27772141	12506.71	4622.02	2632.61	938.26
2018	-33.8	-14.9	3.7	-41.9	-44.1
2019	-24.5	7.1	10.2	-5.6	10.9
2020	73.6	26.7	28.5	139.7	155.2
2021	11.8	1.9	1.5	-12.1	-12.6
2022	27.5	-10.4	-10.9	8.6	14.8

注：（1）2015年始本表口径为计划总投资500万及以上项目投资与房地产开发投资合计数，2014年之前口径为计划总投资500万及以上城镇以上项目投资与房地产开发投资合计数。
（2）自2018年起，各项指标数据均为该指标的同比增速。
（3）2020年始本表房屋竣工面积和房屋施工面积及其中数仅为房地产开发投资的增速。

Notes:（1）From 2015 table caliber plans a total investment of 5 million and above number of projects total investment in real estate development and investment, caliber before 2014 plans a total investment of 5 million over and above the town in project investment and real estate development investment totals.
（2）Since 2018, the data of all indicators are the year-on-year growth rate of the indicator.
（3）From 2020, the completed area and construction area of houses in this table are only the growth rate of real estate development investment.

表8-5 固定资产投资完成情况(2022年)
Investment in Fixed Assets（2022）

指标	Indicators	计划总投资比上年增长 Total Investment of Project	累计完成投资比上年增长 Accumulative Finish Total Investment
总计	**Total**	**24.0**	**17.8**
按登记类型	**By Registered Type**		
内资	Domestic-investment Enterprises	26.8	17.9
国有	State-owned	40.7	16.7
港澳台投资	Hongkong, Macao and Taiwan Funded	-2.9	6.0
外资	Foreign Funded Enterprises	20.2	38.0
按隶属关系	**By Subordination**		
中央	Central	359.7	197.7
地方	Local	18.1	13.0
按建筑性质	**By type of Construction**		
#新建	New Construction	23.4	12.5
扩建	Expansion	38.7	36.3
改建	Reconstruction	8.7	13.0
按国民经济行业分组	**By Sector**		
农林牧渔业	Framing, Forestry, Animal Husbandry and Fishery	80.1	25.1
采矿业	Mining and Quarrying	41.3	50.6
制造业	Manufacturing	17.9	25.2
电力、燃气及水的生产和供应业	Electric Power, Gas and Water Production and Supply	72.8	37.7
建筑业	Construction	-34.1	-23.5
批发和零售业	Wholesale and Retail Trade	-41.8	-61.5
交通运输、仓储和邮政业	Transportation, Storage and Post	38.5	11.9
住宿和餐饮业	Hotel and Catering Services	9.6	18.9
信息传输、软件和信息技术服务业	Information Transmission, Software and Information Technology Service	-0.1	26.7
金融业	Financial Industries	-5.1	-25.6
房地产业	Real Estate Industries	19.6	16.1
租赁和商务服务业	Leasing and Business Service Industries	48.4	105.5
科学研究和技术服务业	Scientific Research and Technology Service	25.5	30.8
水利、环境和公共设施管理业	Water Conservancy, Environment and Public Facility Management	12.3	5.0
居民服务、修理和其他服务业	Residential Service, Repairing & Maintenance and Other Service	43.7	207.7
教育	Education	15.2	29.9
卫生和社会工作	Health Care and Social Work	38.4	45.8
文化、体育和娱乐业	Culture, Sports and Entertainment	26.9	21.0
公共管理、社会保障和社会组织	Public Management, Social Security and Social Oorganizations	33.7	15.5

注：2015年始本表口径为计划总投资500万及以上项目投资，2014年之前口径为计划总投资500万及以上城镇以上项目投资。
Note: beginning in 2015 in this table are project plans a total investment of 5 million and above caliber, caliber before 2014 plans a total investment of 5 million over and above the town in project investments.

单位：%

本年完成投资比上年增长 Investment Completed of The Year	按构成分 by Composition					本年新增固定资产比上年增长 Newly Increased Fixed Assets of The Year
	建筑工程比上年增长 Construction	安装工程比上年增长 Installation	设备工器具购置比上年增长 Purchase of Equipment and Instruments	其他费用比上年增长 Others	#土地购置费比上年增长 Purchase of Land	
17.6	**22.0**	**-25.5**	**3.1**	**36.5**	**46.0**	**29.0**
18.6	22.2	-25.4	2.0	37.6	46.2	28.9
14.3	13.6	28.3	-38.6	26.3	39.2	134.6
-3.2	9.1	-31.4	-8.4	6.1	8.5	4.4
35.0	35.1	-12.7	35.0	45.6	82.4	109.5
130.3	216.9	29.2	84.3	390.0	487.2	-57.8
13.5	19.1	-35.9	-2.2	29.6	44.6	33.2
13.7	18.7	-55.2	-10.6	25.0	42.3	36.2
34.9	38.9	9.8	4.6	80.8	54.6	36.8
12.5	18.5	-3.3	5.3	48.5	83.4	-0.8
-22.2	-38.2	-84.7	2.7	71.9	10992.1	50.5
79.6	44.4	4400.0	-5.1	88.7		73738.2
14.8	36.4	-37.7	3.1	38.1	26.4	34.0
6.7	-4.2	10.3	13.8	25.5	255.6	96.8
-94.3		-100.0	-94.0	-97.7		-93.9
-27.4	-21.7	33.2	173.8	-38.8	-30.2	-89.5
4.3	6.4	-26.0	-23.1	16.0	50.0	-34.3
11.5	9.8	-5.6	126.7	18.5	15.0	886.9
34.9	33.7	278.4	-24.8	50.3	26.9	-98.9
-27.5	-33.1	-100.0	-90.3	16.6	111.2	-4.1
46.2	36.0	40.9	106.1	87.8	102.2	15.6
77.8	56.0	53.6	-56.3	210.2	135.1	2988.1
32.0	13.5	115.4	102.8	37.3	329.9	344.7
25.3	18.5	127.4	50.5	37.6	46.4	49.8
322.5	212.2		4285.7	766.4	1835.0	904.7
10.1	7.0	70.6	18.2	17.8	19.3	105.7
72.0	76.4	193.9	146.9	17.6	6.3	-47.8
38.1	43.4	-97.8	197.9	63.2	105.8	53.6
64.4	64.9	29.3	230.9	46.0	0.3	248.8

表8-6 各区（县、市）固定资产投资主要指标（2022年）
Main Indicators of Investment in Fixed Assets by Region（2022）

指标	Indicators	全市 Total	市区 Urban District	海曙区 Haishu
计划总投资比上年增长	**Total Investment of Plan increased over the previous year**	**24.0**	**13.8**	**0.8**
本年完成投资比上年增长	Finished Investment increased over the previous year	17.6	18.1	31.1
按经济注册类型分	**By Registration Status**			
国有经济	State－Owned Units	14.3	22.6	25.0
集体经济	Collective－owned Units	87.0	107.6	157.7
其他有限责任公司	Share－holding Corporation Units	19.2	29.8	25.6
股份有限公司	Other Limited Liability Corporations	-2.9	-6.6	141.1
港澳台投资经济	HongKong, Macao and Taiwan Funded	-3.2	-4.8	-33.7
外商投资经济	Foreign Funded	35.0	13.3	-33.4
按隶属关系分	**By Administrative Relationship**			
中央	Central	130.3	194.6	-100.0
地方	Province	274.1	286.0	288.8
其他	Others	-39.0	-45.0	-51.2
按建设性质分	**By Type of Construction**			
新建	New Construction	13.7	9.7	31.3
扩建	Expansion	34.9	43.3	26.0
改建	Reconstruction	12.5	13.7	32.2
按构成分	**By Use of Funds**			
建筑工程	Construction	22.0	28.3	33.5
安装工程	Installation	-25.5	-33.3	-0.6
设备工器具购置	Purchase of Equipment and Instruments	3.1	-0.2	9.4
其他费用	Others	36.5	43.0	40.4
按国民经济行业分	**By Sector**			
农林牧渔业	Framing, Forestry, Animal Husbandry and Fishery	-22.2	-28.3	

单位：%

江北区 Jiangbei	镇海区 Zhenhai	北仑区 Beilun	鄞州区 Yinzhou	奉化区 Fenghua	余姚市 Yuyao	慈溪市 Cixi	宁海县 Ninghai	象山县 Xiangshan
31.7	**23.4**	**13.0**	**7.7**	**12.8**	**24.2**	**22.8**	**38.4**	**20.8**
55.7	7.7	13.1	14.6	24.4	17.9	33.4	24.9	11.4
123.4	147.5	-23.8	-1.2	71.1	52.4	27.1	18.5	-18.3
	228.6	87.3	61.1	14.7	89.4	326.5	10.7	-56.1
68.2	4.6	52.3	28.3	67.8	49.3	8.1	25.0	-22.0
289.8	-34.5	20.0	-0.3	-64.9	89.6	13.2	-4.0	-58.3
-54.9	-47.9	-1.1	-29.0	40.9	-9.1	49.6	-11.1	54.6
27.5	19.8	-6.1	18.7	254.6	95.7	8.3	1.3	244.5
106.3	270.1	-23.7	83.7	416.7	26.4	0.5	17.0	389.5
654.6	259.7	333.4	195.9	307.3	102.3	1235.4	690.6	707.5
-42.6	-61.2	-30.7	-43.6	-45.9	-2.4	-12.7	-18.3	-47.4
82.1	-35.9	16.5	17.8	27.3	25.2	34.9	36.6	15.6
58.0	103.2	10.8	11.5	8.3	45.6	29.8	-6.2	27.6
-7.6	37.8	10.9	5.5	15.6	-9.6	38.9	23.0	1.6
65.9	60.8	21.6	19.2	11.9	21.9	36.0	22.5	7.5
46.7	-58.5	9.6	6.5	174.9	-9.0	0.7	21.7	92.3
43.3	-20.9	-0.1	-0.8	57.5	-1.0	35.2	10.3	0.2
51.8	88.0	31.4	13.2	51.4	39.2	29.4	48.5	34.1
-82.9	-58.3		1894.9	-54.3		-18.5	-41.8	-7.5

表8-6续表 Continued

指标	Indicators	全市 Total	市区 Urban District	海曙区 Haishu
采矿业	Mining and Quarrying	79.6	-57.7	-100.0
制造业	Manufacturing	14.8	4.2	26.2
电力、燃气及水的生产和供应业	Electric Power, Gas and Water Production and Supply	6.7	50.6	4.9
建筑业	Construction	-94.3	-29.5	
批发和零售业	Wholesale and Retail Trade	-27.4	7.3	-38.0
交通运输、仓储和邮政业	Transportation, Storage and Post	4.3	17.8	44.5
住宿和餐饮业	Hotel and Catering Services	11.5	31.5	9.8
信息传输、软件和信息技术服务业	Information Transmission, Software and Information Technology Service	34.9	0.6	167.1
金融业	Financial Industries	-27.5	-51.5	-82.8
房地产业	Real Estate Industries	46.2	53.9	75.1
租赁和商务服务业	Leasing and Business Service Industries	77.8	91.5	211.9
科学研究和技术服务业	Scientific Research and Technology Service	32.0	33.0	12.4
水利、环境和公共设施管理业	Water Conservancy, Environment and Public Facility Management	25.3	19.6	6.7
居民服务、修理和其他服务业	Residential Service, Repairing & Maintenance and Other Service	322.5	332.4	
教育	Education	10.1	22.5	51.0
卫生和社会工作	Health Care and Social Work	72.0	78.4	283.2
文化、体育和娱乐业	Culture, Sports and Entertainment	38.1	56.8	-71.5
公共管理、社会保障和社会组织	Public Management, Social Security and Social Organizations	64.4	138.0	35.0
本年新增固定资产比上年增长	**Newly Increased Fixed Assets increased over the previous year**	**29.0**	**39.4**	**-20.7**
按资金来源分	**By Source of Funds**			
#国家预算资金	State Budget	32.5	34.9	45.4
国内贷款	Domestic Loans	2.7	4.2	-74.6
利用外资	Foreign Investment	-69.7	-77.9	-100.0
自筹资金	Fund Raising	21.0	16.6	26.8

注：（1）从2012年开始国家预算内资金改成国家预算资金。
（2）本表按2011年修订的国民经济行业标准统计。
（3）2015年始本表口径为计划总投资500万及以上项目投资，2014年之前口径为计划总投资500万及以上城镇以上项目投资。

Notes:（1）Starting from 2012 national budget funds into State budget funds.
（2）Statistics in this table are classified as the national economic category that was modified in 2011.
（3）Beginning in 2015 in this table are project plans a total investment of 5 million and above caliber, caliber before 2014 plans a total investment of 5 million over and above the town in project investments.

单位：%

江北区 Jiangbei	镇海区 Zhenhai	北仑区 Beilun	鄞州区 Yinzhou	奉化区 Fenghua	余姚市 Yuyao	慈溪市 Cixi	宁海县 Ninghai	象山县 Xiangshan
			-13.7		4.9	31.4	1223.7	
19.6	-8.8	2.7	18.5	31.0	19.2	39.5	35.5	32.3
164.2	49.5	103.8	28.9	27.9	-1.5	-25.1	15.7	-9.7
		-29.5					-98.8	
6.2		-48.1	11.6	571.5	-48.4	-80.5	7.0	-73.1
142.8	-27.4	51.9	-3.8	-13.3	5.5	43.1	4.0	-13.5
124.6	491.3	100.1	-30.0	2187.5	88.7		59.3	-33.1
	34250.0		-57.3		-97.3	245.5	-100.0	
-44.1			-100.0		210.7			-16.2
197.4	45.9	287.5	32.0	36.3	48.8	23.0	-0.3	110.3
56.7		1338.1	89.3	42.0		43.2	-59.8	130.6
	122.9	1.5	4.1	-15.8	-78.4	33.1	161.3	
109.9	117.0	9.4	-6.4	16.3	45.8	37.6	40.1	31.2
		-39.8	5.2	749.7		-100.0		
8.1	136.2	39.1	5.5	-9.5	44.1	-5.4	-48.8	9.3
-2.3	48.8	12.1	40.6	92.2	84.0	1874.4	-32.2	22.4
-77.4	1096.5	-28.9	28.1	149.0	-68.8	11.7	172.3	82.9
		119.6	19.9	333.9	-21.4	129.0	-6.4	13.3
3.9	**10.8**	**145.8**	**57.2**	**66.5**	**47.8**	**-2.7**	**-37.0**	**-0.5**
56.8	93.3	212.1	-1.1	71.0	345.7	140.7	2.4	-35.9
55.8	87.4	30.5	-31.5	-18.8	17.1	7.2	5.7	-17.2
	-76.7	-91.8	-76.5	-89.0	52.8	-13.1	-97.8	866.9
46.5	0.1	12.3	21.7	33.2	20.2	42.0	30.6	22.0

表8-7 部分年份固定资产投资主要指标
Main Indicators of Investment in Fixed Assets in Partial Years

单位：%

指标	Indicators	2018	2019	2020	2021	2022
计划总投资	**Total Investment of Plan**	**7.4**	**6.0**	**2.3**	**11.8**	**24.0**
累计完成投资	Accumulative Finished Investment	-6.2	10.9	1.5	22.7	17.8
本年完成投资	**Finished Investment of This Year**	**-4.9**	**8.7**	**4.4**	**8.2**	**17.6**
按经济注册类型分	**By Registration Status**					
国有经济	State - Owned Units	-15.1	2.4	-9.0	-4.5	14.3
集体经济	Collective - owned Units	-24.5	66.0	20.8	39.9	87.0
股份有限公司	Share-holding Corporation Units	-16.8	25.6	36.5	24.0	19.2
其他有限责任公司	Other Limited Liability Corporations	54.9	-7.4	-37.3	58.5	-2.9
外商投资经济	Foreign Investment	-1.7	20.3	3.9	7.3	-3.2
港澳台投资经济	HongKong, Macao and Taiwan Funded	40.8	-10.3	12.4	39.8	35.0
其他经济	Others					
按隶属关系分	**By Administrative Relationship**					
中央	Central Government	10.8	-6.6	-21.7	-1.2	130.3
地方	Province	-11.1	-39.8	5.7	-29.0	274.1
其他	Others	-0.5	53.0	5.8	21.5	-39.0
按建设性质分	**By Type of Construction**					
新建	New Construction	-2	10.1	1.6	8.2	13.7
扩建	Expansion	-1.5	10.9	6.4	-7.2	34.9
改建	Reconstruction	-14.5	0.7	11.5	29.9	12.5
其他	Others				29.9	12.5
按构成分	**By Use of Funds**					
建筑工程	Construction	-6.2	15.5	1.4	1.0	22.0
安装工程	Installation	0.9	-15.0	43.4	59.9	-25.5
设备工器具购置	Purchase of Equipment and Instruments	-1.5	-4.8	18.2	18.1	3.1
其他费用	Others	-10.5	8.4	0.7	7.0	36.5
按资金来源分	**By Source of Funds**					
#国家预算资金	State Budget	-45.3	-7.0	-16.8	4.6	32.5
国内贷款	Domestic Loans	-14.5	14.7	9.6	21.9	2.7
利用外资	Foreign Investment	60.0	-18.3	-43.7	208.4	-69.7
自筹资金	Self-Financed Capital	-47.6	3.9	15.4	29.6	21.0

注：（1）从2012年开始国家预算内资金改成国家预算资金。
（2）2015年始本表口径为计划总投资500万及以上项目投资，2014年之前口径为计划总投资500万及以上城镇以上项目投资。
（3）自2018年起，各项指标数据均为该指标的同比增速。

Notes: (1) Starting from 2012 national budget funds into State budget funds.
(2) Beginning in 2015 in this table are project plans a total investment of 5 million and above caliber, caliber before 2014 plans a total investment of 5 million over and above the town in project investments.
(3) Since 2018, the data of all indicators are the year-on-year growth rate of the indicator.

表8-8 新增生产能力或效益（2022年）
Newly Increase Production Capacity or Benefit（2022）

指标	单位	Indicators	Unit	本年新增 Added at This Year
铜加工材	吨/年	Copper processing material	tons/year	39000
太阳能发电	万千瓦	solar power	10-thousand kW	3004
输电线路长度(11万伏及以上)	公里	Transmission line length (110000V and above)	km	30
裂化设备能力	处理万吨/年	Capacity of cracking equipment	10-thousand tons/year	61
塑料树脂及共聚物	吨/年	Plastic resin and copolymer	Ton/year	
轿车制造	辆/年	Car manufacturing	Vehicle/year	25000
新建公路	公里	new highway	km	101
其中：高速公路	公里	Including: Expressway	km	67
一级公路	公里	second-class highway	km	28
改建公路	公里	reconstruction highway	km	75
一级公路	公里	first-class highway	km	23
二级公路	公里	second-class highway	km	49
新（扩）建公路客、货运站	个	newly-expanded highway passenger, cargo terminal	Unit	2
新（扩）建公路客、货运站	平方米	newly-expanded highway passenger, cargo terminal	Square meter	31000
城市自来水供水能力	万吨/日	city water supply capacity	10-thousand tons/day	35
城市污水处理能力	万吨/日	city waste water treatment capacity	10-thousand tons/day	90

表8-9 全市房地产企业开发投资情况（2022年）
Develop and Investment of Enterprises for Real Estate Development（2022）

指标	Indicators	总计 Total	按控股情况分	
			国有 State－owned	集体 Colloective－owned
计划总投资	**Total Investment of Plan**	**113724611**	**17203407**	**290995**
本年完成投资	**Investment Made of the Year**	**21316845**	**3145681**	**15546**
土地购置费	Purchase of Land	10629986	1328728	
配套工程投资	Ancillary Works			
按构成分	**By Composition**			
建筑工程	Construction	9118321	1547615	14453
安装工程	Installation	80299	13859	
设备工器具购置	Purchase of Equipment and Instruments	54221	14420	
其他费用	Others	12064004	1569787	1093
按工程用途分	**By Purpose**			
住宅	Residential Buildings	14328468	2143725	2667
办公楼	Office Buildings	840052	103095	1403
商业营业用房	Buildings for Commercial Business	1671453	176276	10713
其他	Others	4476872	722585	763
本年新增固定资产	Newly Increased Fixed Assets in the Year	11252481	1459979	18278
待开发土地面积(平方米)	Land Space Needed Development (sq.m)	2120773	481642	
本年购置土地面积(平方米)	Land Space Purchased in the Year (sq.m)	1250566	387159	
本年土地成交价款	Actual Land Price of the Year	2264848	512254	

单位：万元（10000 yuan）

By Holding Status				按资质等级分 By the Qualification Score					
私人 Private	港澳台商 Hongkong,Macao &Taiwan Funded	外商 Foreign Funds	其他 Others	一级 First Class	二级 Second Class	三级 Third Class	四级 Fourth Class	暂定 Tentative Class	其他 Others
85133340	**1501192**	**2989246**	**6606431**	**2027170**	**6655123**	**29029282**	**760894**	**35444853**	**39807289**
16311166	**278460**	**486052**	**1079940**	**395494**	**975041**	**4327639**	**111462**	**7592021**	**7915188**
8554182	106635	175399	465042	186233	383049	1627803	30429	4059061	4343411
6625158	142442	267050	521603	192348	484135	2306611	67238	3057694	3010295
65367	10		1063	143	4504	32787	137	24786	17942
34022	1503		4276	2394	6665	20255	283	12430	12194
9586619	134505	219002	552998	200609	479737	1967986	43804	4497111	4874757
11061223	126539	268748	725566	240115	669916	2827986	68999	4987759	5533693
608109	39391	42581	45473	8499	46094	240671	8789	313755	222244
1316792	38592	56072	73008	11055	59104	398187	11714	617338	574055
3325042	73938	118651	235893	135825	199927	860795	21960	1673169	1585196
8309974	228758	428648	806844	1043784	441048	3406139	68469	2148054	4144987
1621047	18084				86422	269048		492460	1272843
833755			29652		195091	110937		62591	881947
1619043			133551		50892	60835		138352	2014769

表8-10 全市房地产企业房屋施工及竣工情况（2022年）

Buildings Construction and the Completed of Enterprises for Real Estate Development（2022）

指标	Indicators	总计 Total	按控股情况分	
			国有 State-owned	集体 Colloective-owned
房屋施工面积	**Floor Space of Buildings Under Construction**	**96607722**	**15608573**	**434548**
1. 住宅	Residential Buildings	56354852	8771106	97223
2. 办公楼	Office Buildings	5343596	853624	95960
3. 商业营业用房	Buildings for Commercial Business	7959371	874372	96372
4. 其他	Others	26949903	5109471	144993
本年新开工房屋施工面积	**Floor Space of Newly Started of The Year**	**11491930**	**3437168**	
1. 住宅	Residential Buildings	6810175	1842060	
2. 办公楼	Office Buildings	467942	141393	
3. 商业营业用房	Buildings for Commercial Business	819313	260691	
4. 其他	Others	3394500	1193024	
房屋竣工面积	**Floor Space of Buildings Completed**	**16284059**	**2999046**	**39094**
#不可销售面积	Floor Space for Con not	2269758	387142	5842
1. 住宅	Residential Buildings	10782000	2037130	22557
2. 办公楼	Office Buildings	453417	31170	7436
3. 商业营业用房	Buildings for Commercial Business	529580	49708	4038
4. 其他	Others	4519062	881038	5063
商品住宅竣工套数（套）	**Completed Residential House (flat)**	**88139**	**17050**	**121**
竣工房屋价值（万元）	**Value of Buildings Completed(10000 yuan)**	**9905874**	**1366675**	**18278**
1. 住宅	Residential Buildings	7186888	1001148	11256
2. 办公楼	Office Buildings	288040	14344	4717
3. 商业营业用房	Buildings for Commercial Business	396976	50541	1799
4. 其他	Others	2033970	300642	506
出租房屋面积	**Floor Space of Lease House**	**25658**		
1. 住宅	Residential Buildings			
2. 办公楼	Office Buildings	3180		
3. 商业营业用房	Buildings for Commercial Business	22478		
4. 其他	Others			
待售面积	**Floor Space of Vacant Building**	**4199634**	**1134312**	**48997**
1. 住宅	Residential Buildings	962373	427003	7906
2. 办公楼	Office Buildings	655233	123688	12226
3. 商业营业用房	Buildings for Commercial Business	1129286	257479	15967
4. 其他	Others	1452742	326142	12898

单位:平方米(sq.m)

By Holding Status				按资质等级分 By the Qualification Score					
私人 Private	港澳台商 Hongkong,Macao &Taiwan Funded	外商 Foreign Funds	其他 Others	一级 First Class	二级 Second Class	三级 Third Class	四级 Fourth Class	暂定 Tentative Class	其他 Others
72000701	**1455230**	**2728771**	**4379899**	**2056432**	**6022959**	**26279560**	**1126272**	**30020915**	**31101584**
42944188	483589	1442811	2615935	1271685	3254901	14684566	676821	17260783	19206096
3675638	210913	243372	264089	45372	445609	1814656	55679	1909449	1072831
5973787	272430	326166	416244	50153	666196	2679060	149015	2223980	2190967
19407088	488298	716422	1083631	689222	1656253	7101278	244757	8626703	8631690
6956835	**102437**	**561741**	**433749**	**310494**	**1036752**	**2374065**	**176875**	**874539**	**6719205**
4298072	63731	361991	244321	202055	612087	1283798	97940	472473	4141822
302168	1115	17250	6016		30624	133010	16920	59390	227998
479086	6902	22723	49911	4452	48533	134724	4912	161301	465391
1877509	30689	159777	133501	103987	345508	822533	57103	181375	1883994
11609864	**200046**	**504434**	**931575**	**1475650**	**779699**	**4755573**	**163965**	**3873532**	**5235640**
1581254	64027	82804	148689	334669	44447	731210	23760	335059	800613
7756922		282815	682576	898467	554712	3284485	109188	2455366	3479782
258785	81761	53959	20306	39523	32359	145739	21116	179146	35534
367660	47219	42621	18334	37408	13954	106770	8861	170676	191911
3226497	71066	125039	210359	500252	178674	1218579	24800	1068344	1528413
63868		**2361**	**4739**	**7723**	**4185**	**26520**	**707**	**19199**	**29805**
7386187	**208556**	**384229**	**541949**	**1027853**	**426323**	**2610065**	**61110**	**1935178**	**3845345**
5479018		234982	460484	635910	322019	2035351	42409	1414399	2736800
130036	113557	15918	9468	17531	32523	147937	8638	58515	22896
217118	21338	69947	36233	22600	15259	91249	4394	91397	172077
1560015	73661	63382	35764	351812	56522	335528	5669	370867	913572
25658						**25658**			
3180						3180			
22478						22478			
2415629	**257074**	**122360**	**221262**	**179795**	**187291**	**2067149**	**117406**	**997154**	**650839**
450845	35611	10077	30931	54240	81653	407979	31003	126197	261301
353664	128874	30539	6242	15474	39881	434467	25778	122684	16949
678770	59790	43946	73334	49510	20845	519523	36952	405669	96787
932350	32799	37798	110755	60571	44912	705180	23673	342604	275802

表8-11 全市房地产企业房屋销售情况（2022年）
Building Sale Situation of Enterprises for Real Estate Development（2022）

指标	Indicators	总计 Total	按控股情况分 国有 State－owned	集体 Colloective－owned
商品房销售面积（平方米）	**Floor Space of Building Sold（sp.m）**	**11287960**	**1754923**	**7192**
1. 住宅	Residential Buildings	8351535	1254880	1611
2. 办公楼	Office Buildings	1006714	327101	
3. 商业营业用房	Buildings for Commercial Business	996285	80059	5196
4. 其他	Others	933426	92883	385
现房销售面积	Floor Space of Completed Building	2042578	660579	1429
1. 住宅	Residential Buildings	1047419	462693	1262
2. 办公楼	Office Buildings	284410	121264	
3. 商业营业用房	Buildings for Commercial Business	370959	41746	145
4. 其他	Others	339790	34876	22
期房销售面积	Floor Space of Forward Delivery Building	9245382	1094344	5763
1. 住宅	Residential Buildings	7304116	792187	349
2. 办公楼	Office Buildings	722304	205837	
3. 商业营业用房	Buildings for Commercial Business	625326	38313	5051
4. 其他	Others	593636	58007	363
商品房销售额（万元）	**Sales Volume of Commercial Buildings（10000yuan）**	**19375751**	**2677052**	**8485**
1. 住宅	Residential Buildings	15981551	2050164	1352
2. 办公楼	Office Buildings	1273996	357548	
3. 商业营业用房	Buildings for Commercial Business	1423836	181170	6984
4. 其他	Others	696368	88170	149
现房销售额	Sales Volume of Completed Building	2340269	671988	1249
1. 住宅	Residential Buildings	1380692	454187	1049
2. 办公楼	Office Buildings	333472	116509	
3. 商业营业用房	Buildings for Commercial Business	416676	90456	159
4. 其他	Others	209429	10836	41
期房销售额	Sales Volume of Forward Delivery Building	17035482	2005064	7236
1. 住宅	Residential Buildings	14600859	1595977	303
2. 办公楼	Office Buildings	940524	241039	
3. 商业营业用房	Buildings for Commercial Business	1007160	90714	6825
4. 其他	Others	486939	77334	108

By Holding Status				按资质等级分 By the Qualification Score					
私人 Private	港澳台商 Hongkong,Macao &Taiwan Funded	外商 Foreign Funds	其他 Others	一级 First Class	二级 Second Class	三级 Third Class	四级 Fourth Class	暂定 Tentative Class	其他 Others
8598812	**99485**	**263578**	**563970**	**225937**	**450543**	**2391864**	**309393**	**3758467**	**4151756**
6457705	55241	173122	408976	157580	355501	1315320	227963	2724798	3570373
617617	5197	36778	20021	16606	67993	364518	2885	434302	120410
788200	22891	41011	58928	13053	12998	404843	15975	293156	256260
735290	16156	12667	76045	38698	14051	307183	62570	306211	204713
1163640	40287	88859	87784	47738	45417	929597	72142	463729	483955
540555	2057	9512	31340	25117	14494	412452	50489	154710	390157
114067	5197	36778	7104	2243	16683	159459	1047	103700	1278
230327	22891	34606	41244	9831	4683	168082	13356	129774	45233
278691	10142	7963	8096	10547	9557	189604	7250	75545	47287
7435172	59198	174719	476186	178199	405126	1462267	237251	3294738	3667801
5917150	53184	163610	377636	132463	341007	902868	177474	2570088	3180216
503550			12917	14363	51310	205059	1838	330602	119132
557873		6405	17684	3222	8315	236761	2619	163382	211027
456599	6014	4704	67949	28151	4494	117579	55320	230666	157426
15091429	**188310**	**434386**	**976089**	**336507**	**815804**	**3173103**	**220604**	**7145393**	**7684340**
12635594	125973	330962	837506	268830	695664	1961406	192301	5808688	7054662
818258	17516	42884	37790	26513	81940	503515	3247	557354	101427
1089223	28542	47845	70072	17063	23369	534126	15074	494663	339541
548354	16279	12695	30721	24101	14831	174056	9982	284688	188710
1406101	59745	91397	109789	68625	51834	881876	49016	527814	761104
856619	2073	7276	59488	45856	12188	404754	33176	202552	682166
146455	17516	42884	10108	2231	26005	185565	1298	117023	1350
231421	28542	34138	31960	11253	4289	196994	11739	158069	34332
171606	11614	7099	8233	9285	9352	94563	2803	50170	43256
13685328	128565	342989	866300	267882	763970	2291227	171588	6617579	6923236
11778975	123900	323686	778018	222974	683476	1556652	159125	5606136	6372496
671803			27682	24282	55935	317950	1949	440331	100077
857802		13707	38112	5810	19080	337132	3335	336594	305209
376748	4665	5596	22488	14816	5479	79493	7179	234518	145454

表8-12 全市房地产企业经营情况（2022年）
Main Economy Indicators of Real Estate Development（2022）

指标	Indicators	总计 Total	按控股情况分	
			国有 State-owned	集体 Colloective-owned
本年资金来源合计	**Total Capital Source in This Year**	**39723894**	**5238027**	**10367**
上年末结余资金	Balance at End of Previous Year	13682248	1771518	5581
本年资金来源小计	Subtotal Capital of This Year	26041646	3466509	4786
1. 国内贷款	Domestic Loans	3015423	436965	
2. 利用外资	Foreign Investment	25193		
3. 自筹资金	Self-Financed Capital	8637934	1272502	830
4. 其他资金来源	Others	713189	141421	344
本年各项应付款合计	Total Account Payable This Year	4898359	754158	10805
年末资产负债情况	**Assets and Liabilities of Year-end**			
资产总计	Total Assets	150392141	52992442	687853
#本年固定资产折旧	Depreciation of Fixed Assets in This Year	67423	13697	103
负债总计	Total Liabilities	118617202	39978462	667019
所有者权益合计	Creditors' Equity	31774939	13013981	20834
实收资本合计	Total Capital Hold	19061780	5086918	25018
损益情况	**Expenditure and Income**			
主营业务收入	Prime Operating Revenue	21752807	3238385	3308
土地转让收入	Land Transferred	10406	7659	
商品房屋销售收入	Commercial Buildings Sold	21049551	2997672	3132
房屋出租收入	Buildings Leased	86097	35903	28
其他收入	Others	595826	191790	148
主营业务成本	Prime Operating Costs	17564720	2645396	1456
业务税金及附加	Sales Taxes and Extra Charges	765112	91752	339
其他业务利润	Other Operating Profits	13102	6040	21
销售费用	Sales Expenses	664195	81739	1697
管理费用	Manage Expenses	500476	93769	1552
财务费用	Finance Expenses	188468	98291	1126
营业利润	Business Profits	2571737	330893	-2468
利润总额	Total Profits	2560309	329140	-2162
应付职工薪酬	Employee Compensation Payable	367869	78009	622

单位：万元（10000 yuan）

By Holding Status				按资质等级分 By the Qualification Score					
私人 Private	港澳台商 Hongkong,Macao &Taiwan Funded	外商 Foreign Funds	其他 Others	一级 First Class	二级 Second Class	三级 Third Class	四级 Fourth Class	暂定 Tentative Class	其他 Others
30598662	**621357**	**984785**	**2270696**	**396561**	**2028007**	**7140764**	**258865**	**14086928**	**15812769**
10139216	303224	429012	1033697	4417	710562	2554640	62974	5484413	4865242
20459446	318133	555773	1236999	392144	1317445	4586124	195891	8602515	10947527
2089369	121135	234000	133954	6722	346256	464233	4570	661626	1532016
2299	3185	19709				3185		19709	2299
6755824	117498	63388	427892	51386	384855	1882817	51314	1795104	4472458
552526	2975	11304	4619	185	57464	244026	21	202640	208853
3720000	43051	115452	254893	18044	88722	1419400	25935	1834074	1512184
84941745	3709994	5131159		6400425	27457744	34695100	1267369	41390392	36252163
45873	2922	1861		4344	1784	24297	-1443	27476	7998
68667264	2734535	4063371		2943037	21644227	27091153	1001612	33260279	30170342
16274482	975459	1067788		3457388	5813516	7603947	265758	8130114	6081821
11744256	888571	1022485		710509	2881292	5528203	182693	5500447	3964105
17537614	76986	469887		1373815	1527104	6840267	192515	5872821	5519658
2747					7659	-15		2762	
17096763	61460	468281		1320824	1291606	6592886	181575	5819867	5420551
40711	6425	670		13900	10723	38059	1832	7601	11620
391939	9043	936		39092	213532	206841	9108	37838	87444
14141870	72224	355356		825089	1050917	5669046	147683	4903848	4619718
616152	27780	13701		99499	116380	164226	11660	195138	162820
6178	-20	524			1836	2619	24	11587	349
540609	9449	20696		10746	70194	131948	3535	252717	185050
346240	12543	30440		35389	47495	145414	8130	147386	100730
47909	6695	15449		303	27169	44223	3122	38264	56390
2257133	-99108	78809		607163	132266	804204	8784	495114	517729
2245872	-98510	78467		607380	135146	793714	9879	492358	514329
260280	8343	14834		20931	51323	101803	4311	104246	79471

表8-13 各区（县、市）房地产企业开发投资情况（2022年）
Develop and Investment of Enterprises for Real Estate Development（2022）

指标	Indicators	全市 Total	海曙区 Haishu
计划总投资	**Total Investment of Plan**	**113724611**	**13138696**
本年完成投资	**Investment Made of the Year**	**21316845**	**2476611**
土地购置费	Purchase of Land	10629986	1473974
按构成分	**By Composition**		
建筑工程	Construction	9118321	863485
安装工程	Installation	80299	5265
设备工器具购置	Purchase of Equipment and Instruments	54221	6096
其他费用	Others	12064004	1601765
按工程用途分	**By Purpose**		
住宅	Residential Buildings	14328468	1612831
办公楼	Office Buildings	840052	83672
商业营业用房	Buildings for Commercial Business	1671453	250039
其他	Others	4476872	530069
本年新增固定资产	**Newly Increased Fixed Assets in the Year**	**11252481**	**1713273**
待开发土地面积（平方米）	Land Space Needed Development (sq.m)	2120773	104758
本年购置土地面积（平方米）	Land Space Purchased in the Year (sq.m)	1250566	148105
本年土地成交价款	Actual Land Price of the Year	2264848	225103
本年资金来源合计	**Total Funding Sources**	**39723894**	**4765195**
上年末结余资金	At the End of the Balance of Funds	13682248	1687251
本年资金来源小计	Total Fund Source of the Year	26041646	3077944
1. 国内贷款	1.Domestic Loans	3015423	138487
2. 利用外资	2.Use of Foreign Capital	25193	
3. 自筹资金	3.Self – Financing	8637934	1174539
4. 其他资金来源	4.Other Sources	713189	139473
本年各项应付款合计	**The Total Payment of the Year**	**4898359**	**311839**

单位：万元（10000 yuan）

江北区 Jiangbei	镇海区 Zhenhai	北仑区 Beilun	鄞州区 Yinzhou	奉化区 Fenghua	余姚市 Yuyao	慈溪市 Cixi	宁海县 Ninghai	象山县 Xiangshan
10980824	**4200643**	**6109783**	**32390683**	**13176920**	**8072375**	**19329594**	**3360928**	**2964165**
2111271	**705223**	**1241958**	**5930854**	**2597205**	**1645252**	**3331457**	**804920**	**472094**
1327787	366762	621277	3145427	1124481	677627	1383603	349467	159581
670937	297331	520996	2387549	1231352	791164	1698325	408939	248243
2682	968	3521	9811	31377	1958	15007	669	9041
1753	4353	7031	6927	14782	764	7021	3295	2199
1435899	402571	710410	3526567	1319694	851366	1611104	392017	212611
1300441	484021	822514	3850765	1965513	1149407	2271775	495035	376166
152910	16817	40803	336583	100097	36640	57813	13150	1567
183396	50904	85578	443235	122488	103097	354702	63308	14706
474524	153481	293063	1300271	409107	356108	647167	233427	79655
787999	**595715**	**742482**	**3033009**	**1244670**	**640936**	**1263042**	**965935**	**265420**
223629	13455	154653	213928	361797	405815	300374	280109	62255
201355	71350	65944	512298	132724		32939	68724	17127
336983	73622	39401	1427588	103401		4801	38049	15900
3078138	**965680**	**2582123**	**13115650**	**4094766**	**3115894**	**6139656**	**1022139**	**844653**
664285	121738	757457	4023561	1413269	1649972	3036583	96651	231481
2413853	843942	1824666	9092089	2681497	1465922	3103073	925488	613172
168200	131184	245426	1457859	252306	107700	319649	98449	96163
			22894			2299		
1070906	300496	333655	3174537	1086850	224099	875856	204447	192549
20951	64060	24208	230036	100999	10201	101865	12830	8566
534910	**198277**	**286604**	**1242159**	**513789**	**347516**	**1183767**	**137116**	**142382**

表8-14 各区（县、市）房地产企业房屋施工及竣工情况（2022年）
Buildings Construction and the Completed of Enterprises for Real Estate Development（2022）

指标	Indicators	全市 Total	海曙区 Haishu
房屋施工面积（平方米）	**Floor Space of Buildings Under Construction（sq.m）**	**96607722**	**8167485**
1. 住宅	Residential Buildings	56354852	4913627
2. 办公楼	Office Buildings	5343596	427499
3. 商业营业用房	Buildings for Commercial Business	7959371	545452
4. 其他	Others	26949903	2280907
本年新开工房屋施工面积	**Floor Space of Newly Started of The Year**	**11491930**	**680308**
1. 住宅	Residential Buildings	6810175	473765
2. 办公楼	Office Buildings	467942	2726
3. 商业营业用房	Buildings for Commercial Business	819313	20809
4. 其他	Others	3394500	183008
房屋竣工面积	**Floor Space of Buildings Completed**	**16284059**	**1662068**
#不可销售面积	Floor Space for Con not	2269758	349263
1. 住宅	Residential Buildings	10782000	1103533
2. 办公楼	Office Buildings	453417	
3. 商业营业用房	Buildings for Commercial Business	529580	26204
4. 其他	Others	4519062	532331
商品住宅竣工套数（套）	**Completed Residential House (flat)**	**88139**	**8498**
竣工房屋价值（万元）	**Value of Buildings Completed(10000 yuan)**	**9905874**	**1684069**
1. 住宅	Residential Buildings	7186888	1240998
2. 办公楼	Office Buildings	288040	
3. 商业营业用房	Buildings for Commercial Business	396976	41676
4. 其他	Others	2033970	401395
出租房屋面积	**Floor Space of Lease House**	**25658**	
1. 住宅	Residential Buildings		
2. 办公楼	Office Buildings	3180	
3. 商业营业用房	Buildings for Commercial Business	22478	
4. 其他	Others		
待售面积	**Floor Space of Vacant Building**	**4199634**	**221313**
1. 住宅	Residential Buildings	962373	6484
2. 办公楼	Office Buildings	655233	46843
3. 商业营业用房	Buildings for Commercial Business	1129286	85141
4. 其他	Others	1452742	82845

江北区 Jiangbei	镇海区 Zhenhai	北仑区 Beilun	鄞州区 Yinzhou	奉化区 Fenghua	余姚市 Yuyao	慈溪市 Cixi	宁海县 Ninghai	象山县 Xiangshan
7470507	**4067090**	**5978737**	**17580655**	**11921157**	**10015253**	**23232759**	**4385525**	**3788554**
3534763	2603594	3693658	8395831	7595987	6385829	14151735	2563667	2516161
898817	129854	251909	1991030	416561	319074	769615	98721	40516
734672	301702	184206	2035518	648087	678404	2126384	464554	240392
2302255	1031940	1848964	5158276	3260522	2631946	6185025	1258583	991485
1797203	**686351**	**283927**	**4013779**	**1484592**	**725614**	**862887**	**633380**	**323889**
962448	420685	221434	2441516	816374	472759	372426	410544	218224
77044	13440		260901	92729		4120		16982
106701	74106	311	207837	132140	66629	169895	37943	2942
651010	178120	62182	1103525	443349	186226	316446	184893	85741
1167615	**1012127**	**1603310**	**2879565**	**1662820**	**1490482**	**3219223**	**1285788**	**301061**
173473	192969	146959	453150	190993	51498	347070	294133	70250
660071	676545	984176	1675416	1248507	1085317	2346625	798105	203705
103070	27277	24899	240097	14358	32789		9660	1267
61070	65263	21779	100323	45315	44477	90946	39602	34601
343404	243042	572456	863729	354640	327899	781652	438421	61488
5798	**5243**	**7596**	**13601**	**12243**	**7991**	**18097**	**7095**	**1977**
497262	**421796**	**664374**	**2491830**	**1222205**	**629236**	**1164240**	**944771**	**186091**
351303	281665	495423	1688577	1009279	461962	933992	585418	138271
35749	9686	8991	205768	8805	14356		4223	462
33502	46175	33193	112277	34007	27771	22696	26624	19055
76708	84270	126767	485208	170114	125147	207552	328506	28303
25658								
3180								
22478								
396683	**296993**	**400603**	**667611**	**318979**	**472001**	**464058**	**507858**	**453535**
12755	41555	191647	98258	167738	47432	77170	156164	163170
77964	40580	30399	243677	7351	4827	86018	26826	90748
165227	139341	61326	76573	41455	209257	92253	124405	134308
140737	75517	117231	249103	102435	210485	208617	200463	65309

表8-15 各区（县、市）房地产企业房屋销售情况（2022年）
Building Sale Situation of Enterprises for Real Estate Development（2022）

指标	Indicators	全市 Total	海曙区 Haishu
商品房销售面积（平方米）	**Floor Space of Building Sold(sq.m)**	**11287960**	**1252873**
1. 住宅	Residential Buildings	8351535	1106379
2. 办公楼	Office Buildings	1006714	67539
3. 商业营业用房	Buildings for Commercial Business	996285	51146
4. 其他	Others	933426	27809
现房销售面积	Floor Space of Completed Building	2042578	51043
1. 住宅	Residential Buildings	1047419	11707
2. 办公楼	Office Buildings	284410	14368
3. 商业营业用房	Buildings for Commercial Business	370959	16335
4. 其他	Others	339790	8633
期房销售面积	Floor Space of Forward Delivery Building	9245382	1201830
1. 住宅	Residential Buildings	7304116	1094672
2. 办公楼	Office Buildings	722304	53171
3. 商业营业用房	Buildings for Commercial Business	625326	34811
4. 其他	Others	593636	19176
商品房销售额（万元）	**Sales Volume of Commercial Buildings(10000 yuan)**	**19375751**	**2908856**
1. 住宅	Residential Buildings	15981551	2724570
2. 办公楼	Office Buildings	1273996	77529
3. 商业营业用房	Buildings for Commercial Business	1423836	68800
4. 其他	Others	696368	37957
现房销售额	Sales Volume of Completed Building	2340269	91144
1. 住宅	Residential Buildings	1380692	38549
2. 办公楼	Office Buildings	333472	20883
3. 商业营业用房	Buildings for Commercial Business	416676	21231
4. 其他	Others	209429	10481
期房销售额	Sales Volume of Forward Delivery Building	17035482	2817712
1. 住宅	Residential Buildings	14600859	2686021
2. 办公楼	Office Buildings	940524	56646
3. 商业营业用房	Buildings for Commercial Business	1007160	47569
4. 其他	Others	486939	27476

江北区 Jiangbei	镇海区 Zhenhai	北仑区 Beilun	鄞州区 Yinzhou	奉化区 Fenghua	余姚市 Yuyao	慈溪市 Cixi	宁海县 Ninghai	象山县 Xiangshan
1089991	**344747**	**883641**	**2312566**	**1178632**	**1578158**	**1511506**	**597207**	**538639**
486809	230268	710484	1598421	970400	1266961	1032957	515484	433372
314480	29105	55415	398195	46166	15931	55167	7153	17563
216595	55768	32987	123084	34919	138140	287103	8999	47544
72107	29606	84755	192866	127147	157126	136279	65571	40160
163357	92623	296836	484445	271298	156339	169941	155588	201108
3012	500	233498	208986	204692	53780	81143	129275	120826
75939	29105	2471	136383	636	2805	3862	1278	17563
60004	41370	24103	63461	1379	76488	42314	6282	39223
24402	21648	36764	75615	64591	23266	42622	18753	23496
926634	252124	586805	1828121	907334	1421819	1341565	441619	337531
483797	229768	476986	1389435	765708	1213181	951814	386209	312546
238541		52944	261812	45530	13126	51305	5875	
156591	14398	8884	59623	33540	61652	244789	2717	8321
47705	7958	47991	117251	62556	133860	93657	46818	16664
2104314	**524117**	**1486218**	**5721125**	**1431357**	**1943915**	**1981401**	**704354**	**570094**
1080535	421827	1326346	4778282	1287163	1694678	1537772	643240	487138
511597	25655	57809	501300	32139	14160	29569	7694	16544
440527	59085	41931	206077	48791	153360	340351	14171	50743
71655	17550	60132	235466	63264	81717	73709	39249	15669
238316	81848	239601	829062	252187	130466	125810	176533	175302
5374	1055	201388	516385	213407	58694	75637	154745	115458
102342	25655	2429	159052	610	2078	2529	1350	16544
115991	41032	22738	83511	2696	52748	29118	9112	38499
14609	14106	13046	70114	35474	16946	18526	11326	4801
1865998	442269	1246617	4892063	1179170	1813449	1855591	527821	394792
1075161	420772	1124958	4261897	1073756	1635984	1462135	488495	371680
409255		55380	342248	31529	12082	27040	6344	
324536	18053	19193	122566	46095	100612	311233	5059	12244
57046	3444	47086	165352	27790	64771	55183	27923	10868

表8-16 建筑业企业生产情况（2022年）

Basic Statistics on Production of Construction Enterprises（2022）

指标	Indicators	企业个数（家）Number of Enterprises (unit)	建筑业总产值 Gross Output Value of Construction	在外省完成的产值 Output Value of Other Province
总　　计	**Total**	**1520**	**34261106**	**6268485**
按登记注册类型分组	**By Registered Type**			
内资企业	Domestic Funded Enterprises	1515	33850482	6158219
国有企业	State – owned Enterprises	2	5766	
集体企业	Collective – owned Enterprises			
股份合作企业	Share–holding Cooperative Enterprises	1	687	
有限责任公司	Limited Liability Corporations	85	6697392	1286436
股份有限公司	Share–holding Corporations Ltd.	7	1312176	185351
私营企业	Private Enterprises	1420	25834462	4686432
港、澳、台商投资企业	HongKong, Macro and Taiwan Funded	4	352065	110266
外商投资企业	Enterprises with Foreign Investment	1	58559	
按建筑业行业分组	**By Sector**			
房屋工程建筑	Building	515	21103028	4063608
土木工程建筑	Civil Engineering	540	9478967	1767124
建筑安装业	Construction Installation	139	1276526	147756
建筑装饰、装修和其他建筑业	Construction Decoration and Other Construction	326	2402585	289996
按控股情况分组	**By Holding Status**			
国有控股	State–holding	42	5343773	1249594
集体控股	Collective–holding	11	798349	
私人控股	Private–holding	1465	27732114	4918239
港澳台控股	Hong Kong, Macao and Taiwan Holdings	1	328311	100652
外商控股	Foreign–holding	1	58559	
其他	Others			
按企业资质等级分组	**By Qualification Criteria**			
施工总承包	Construc General Contractor	1036	30397837	5781804
特级	Special Class	19	12985321	3574253
一级	First Class	126	10541350	1738054
二级	Second Class	192	3082824	191640
三级	Third Class	699	3788342	277857
专业承包	Special General Contractor	484	3863269	486681
一级	First Class	128	2374342	387505
二级	Second Class	261	982065	86337
三级	Third Class	95	506862	12839

单位：万元（10000 yuan）

建筑业总产值按构成分 Oross Output of Construction by constitute			承包工程完成产值 Gross Output Value of Contract Pro			竣工产值 Output Value of Buildings Completed
1. 建筑工程 Construction	2. 安装工程 Installation	3. 其他 Others	1. 直接从建设单位承揽工程 Contract Project from Construction Unit Directly	其中 of Which 自行完成 Finish by Oneself	2. 从建设单位以外承揽工程 Contract Project Outside Construction Unit	
30193700	**3324480**	**742926**	**33060602**	**32233242**	**2027864**	**17298461**
29797654	3311353	741476	32660666	31833305	2017177	17105282
5766			2420	2420	3345	4803
687			449	449	238	490
5383031	1168741	145620	6621304	6049746	647646	2418609
974662	337514		1200598	1200598	111579	1089152
23433508	1805097	595856	24835895	24580094	1254368	13592228
337487	13127	1451	341377	341377	10688	106380
58559			58559	58559		86799
19731967	995969	375092	20779121	20351893	751135	10949976
7986657	1301943	190366	9207368	8854920	624046	4927847
404935	846289	25302	1138880	1106219	170307	539740
2070141	180278	152166	1935232	1920209	482376	880897
4508411	697416	137946	5370901	4809841	533932	1644938
187008	611341		789979	785822	12527	578283
25111411	2015722	604981	26522088	26259945	1472169	14900578
328311			319075	319075	9237	87863
58559			58559	58559		86799
27644945	2213965	538926	29988529	29211305	1186532	15853166
11991426	715795	278100	13408327	12847727	137593	7714994
9883271	569378	88702	10013770	9940960	600389	4536056
2883613	171359	27853	3000354	2981686	101139	1544449
2886635	757434	144273	3566077	3440932	347410	2057666
2548755	1110514	204000	3072073	3021936	841333	1445295
1663373	582781	128188	1769772	1763066	611277	677285
509207	434536	38322	879010	839018	143047	569037
376174	93198	37490	423291	419853	87009	198973

表8–16续表 Continued

指标	Indicators	房屋建筑施工面积（平方米）Floor Space Under Construction (sq.m)	其中 of Which #本年新开工 Newly Operating Projects in this Year
总　　计	**Total**	**247644314**	**59837649**
按登记注册类型分组	**By Registered Type**		
内资企业	Domestic Funded Enterprises	247121056	59650444
国有企业	State – owned Enterprises		
集体企业	Collective – owned Enterprises		
股份合作企业	Share–holding Cooperative Enterprises		
有限责任公司	Limited Liability Corporations	33462333	7149676
股份有限公司	Share–holding Corporations Ltd.	4320309	1635643
私营企业	Private Enterprises	209338414	50865125
港、澳、台商投资企业	HongKong, Macro and Taiwan Funded	523258	187205
外商投资企业	Enterprises with Foreign Investment		
按建筑业行业分组	**By Sector**		
房屋工程建筑	Building	232090532	55311299
土木工程建筑	Civil Engineering	13415802	3368900
建筑安装业	Construction Installation	197002	49371
建筑装饰、装修和其他建筑业	Construction Decoration and Other Construction	1940978	1108079
按控股情况分组	**By Holding Status**		
国有控股	State–holding	24221237	5657378
集体控股	Collective–holding	2144	2144
私人控股	Private–holding	222897675	53990922
港澳台控股	Hong Kong, Macao and Taiwan Holdings	523258	187205
外商控股	Foreign–holding		
其他	Others		
按企业资质等级分组	**By Qualification Criteria**		
施工总承包	Construc General Contractor	241728956	57204864
特级	Special Class	120944364	20127696
一级	First Class	76609725	20657465
二级	Second Class	27885306	8948091
三级	Third Class	16289561	7471612
专业承包	Special General Contractor	5915358	2632785
一级	First Class	3405790	1504990
二级	Second Class	1888540	810517
三级	Third Class	621028	317278

签订的合同额（万元）Signed Contract Amount (10000 yuan)	其中 of Which # 本年新签 Newly Signed this year	年末自有机械设备总台数（台）Number of Machinery and Equipment (year-end) (set)	年末自有机械设备总功率（千瓦）Total Power of Machinery and Equipment (kW)	年末自有机械设备净值（万元）Net Value of Machinery and Equipment (10000yuan)	年末人数（人）Employed Persons at Year-end (person)	从事建筑业活动的平均人数（人）Average number of People Engaged in Construction Activities(person)
71536454	**35674283**	**54806**	**1338370**	**355702**	**639781**	**855478**
70583766	35044295	54804	1338220	355695	629819	841450
6295	2436	30	80	4	442	317
963	663	61	112	8	37	33
15176902	8250035	7962	105805	42202	40441	139266
2916842	1255383	1386	19609	577	5347	28576
52482764	25535778	45365	1212614	312904	583552	673258
876477	610734	2	150	8	9875	10124
76211	19255				87	3904
43592389	20551801	30096	659278	134692	422927	533128
22967457	11673020	15564	537901	170379	150207	224279
1839793	1207507	3867	23529	12886	17659	27390
3136815	2241955	5279	117662	37746	48988	70681
13563683	7096037	7396	86734	28585	23510	106846
1409031	853318	1403	11625	4712	2946	17720
55650144	27121298	46007	1240011	322405	603610	717149
837386	584376				9628	9859
76211	19255				87	3904
65960568	32184289	44271	1187135	272847	567532	749973
32950569	13366813	9794	241220	67918	170101	313568
20940529	11471364	18295	523795	87482	234949	256246
6397101	3579156	8266	191085	50520	72523	81747
5672368	3766957	7916	231035	66926	89959	98412
5575886	3489993	10535	151235	82855	72249	105505
3203185	1987447	4631	88213	31306	47280	56875
1685713	986411	4777	29247	44450	17008	38374
686988	516136	1127	33775	7099	7961	10256

表8-17 部分年份建筑业生产经营及主要财务指标
Basic Statistics and Main Financial Indicators of Construction Enterprises in Partial Years

单位：万元（10000 yuan）

指标	Indicators	2021	2022
企业个数（家）	**Number of Enterprises (unit)**	**1353**	**1520**
建筑业总产值	**Gross Output Value of Construction**	**32990222**	**34261106**
1. 建筑工程	Construction	28743047	30193700
2. 安装工程	Installation	3595425	3324480
3. 其他	Building Repair and Maintenance	651750	742926
竣工产值	Output Value of Buildings Completed	15424138	17298461
房屋建筑施工面积 （万平方米）	Floor Space of Buildings Under Construction (10000 sq.m)	23796	24764
房屋建筑竣工面积（万平方米）	Floor Space of Buildings Completed (10000 sq.m)	4514	4736
年末自有机械设备总台数（台）	Number of Machinery and Equipment (year – end) (set)	62324	54806
年末自有机械设备总功率（万千瓦）	Total Power of Machinery and Equipment (10000kW)	156	134
年末自有机械设备净值	Net Value of Machinery and Equipment	445398	355702
从事建筑业活动的平均人数（万人）	Average number of People Engaged in Construction Activities (10000 person)	89	86
年末资产负债	**Asset and Liabilities at Year – end**		
流动资产	Circulating Assets	25377317	27785344
固定资产小计	Fixed Assets		
固定资产原价	Original Value of Fixed Assets	2343714	2384352
本年折旧	Depreciation in This Year	133686	141287
资产总计	Total Assets	30364091	32868565
流动负债	Liquid Liabilities	20658816	22800448
所有者权益	Creditors' Equity	9190321	9700829
损益及分配	**Expenditure, Income and Distribution**		
主营业务收入	Prime Operating Revenue	29367373	29065878
主营业务成本	Prime Operating Costs	27275641	27074377
主营业务税金及附加	Taxes and Surcharge for Main Operations	79749	83627
利润总额	Total Profit	873774	697275

表8-18 本年完成建筑业总产值前20位企业（2022年）
The Top 20 Enterprises of Completed Total Output Value for Construction Industry（2022）

企业名称 Name of Enterprises	资质等级 Grade of Natural Endowments
龙元建设集团股份有限公司 Longyuan Construction Group Co.,Ltd.	房屋建筑工程施工总承包特级 Whole Contract To Project of Building Construction by Special Grade
宁波建工工程集团有限公司 Ningbo Construction And Industry Group Co.,Ltd.	房屋建筑工程施工总承包特级 Whole Contract To Project of Building Construction by Special Grade
浙江省二建建设集团有限公司 Zhejiang No.2 Construction Group Co.,Ltd.	房屋建筑工程施工总承包特级 Whole Contract To Project of Building Construction by Special Grade
浙江欣捷建设有限公司 Zhe Jiang Xinjie Construction Co.,Ltd.	房屋建筑工程施工总承包特级 Whole Contract To Project of Building Construction by Special Grade
宁波市建设集团股份有限公司 Ningbo Construction Group Co.,Ltd.	房屋建筑工程施工总承包特级 Whole Contract To Project of Building Construction by Special Grade
华锦建设集团股份有限公司 Huajing Construction Co.,Ltd.	房屋建筑工程施工总承包特级 Whole Contract To Project of Building Construction by Special Grade
宁波市政工程建设集团股份有限公司 Ningbo Municipal Engineering Construction Group Co.,Ltd.	市政公用工程施工总承包特级 Whole Contract To Municipal Engineering Construction by Special Grade
宏润建设集团股份有限公司 Hongrun Construction Group Co.,Ltd.	市政公用工程施工总承包特级 Whole Contract To Municipal Engineering Construction by Special Grade
海达建设集团有限公司 Haida construction group co. Ltd.	房屋建筑工程施工总承包特级 Whole Contract To Project of Building Construction by Special Grade
浙江新中源建设有限公司 Zhejiang New Zhongyuan Construction Co.,Ltd.	房屋建筑工程施工总承包特级 Whole Contract To Project of Building Construction by Special Grade
九峰海洋生态建设集团有限公司 Ningbo Jiufeng Municipal Engineering Co., Ltd.	市政公用工程施工总承包壹级 Whole Contract To Municipal Engineering Construction by First Grade
华恒建设集团有限公司 Huaheng construction group co., ltd.	房屋建筑工程施工总承包特级 Whole Contract To Project of Building Construction by Special Grade
宁波建工建乐工程有限公司 Ningbo Jianle Engineering Co., Ltd.	房屋建筑工程施工总承包壹级 Whole Contract To Project of Building Construction by First Grade
中和华丰建设集团有限公司 Zhonghe Huafeng Construction Co., Ltd.	房屋建筑工程施工总承包特级 Whole Contract To Project of Building Construction by Special Grade
宁波交通工程建设集团有限公司 Ningbo Communications Engineering Construction Group Co.,Ltd.	公路工程施工总承包特级 Qualification of the General Contracting of The National Highway Engineering Construction by Special Grade
宁波住宅建设集团股份有限公司 Ningbo Residential Construction Group Co.,Ltd.	房屋建筑工程施工总承包壹级 Whole Contract To Project of Building Construction by First Grade
中科盛博建设集团有限公司 Zhongke shengbo construction group co., ltd.	房屋建筑工程施工总承包特级 Whole Contract To Project of Building Construction by Special Grade
中交水利水电建设有限公司 CCCC water conservancy and Hydropower Construction Co., Ltd	港口与航道工程施工总承包特级 General Contracting of Construction of Harbor and Waterway Works by Special Grade
浙江万华建设有限公司 Zhejiang wanhua construction co., ltd.	房屋建筑工程施工总承包壹级 Whole Contract To Project of Building Construction by First Grade
浙江良和交通建设有限公司 Zhejiang lianghe communications construction co., ltd.	公路工程施工总承包壹级 Qualification of the General Contracting of The National Highway Engineering Construction by First Grade

主要统计指标解释

【固定资产投资】固定资产投资是社会固定资产再生产的主要手段。通过建造和购置固定资产的活动，国民经济不断采用先进技术装备，建立新兴部门，进一步调整经济结构和生产力的地区分布，增强经济实力，为改善人民物质文化生活创造物质条件。这对我国的社会主义现代化建设具有重要意义。

固定资产投资额是以货币表现的建造和购置固定资产活动的工作量，它是反映固定资产投资规模、速度、比例关系和使用方向的综合性指标。固定资产投资按经济类型可分为国有、集体、个体、联营、股份制、外商、港澳台商、其他等。按照管理渠道，固定资产投资总额分为基本建设、更新改造、房地产开发投资和其他固定资产投资四个部分。

【房地产开发投资】指房地产开发公司、商品房建设公司及其他房地产开发法人单位和附属于其他法人单位实际从事房地产开发或经营的活动单位统一开发的包括统代建、拆迁还建的住宅、厂房、仓库、饭店、宾馆、度假村、写字楼、办公楼等房屋建筑物和配套的服务设施，土地开发工程（如道路、给水、排水、供电、供热、通讯、平整场地等基础设施工程）的投资；不包括单纯的土地交易活动。

【农村非农户投资】农村非农户建造和购置固定资产投资计划固定资本形成总额在500万元以上的项目，农村非农户包括以下二大类：

第一类为企业单位，分成（1）集体企业，包括集体直接经营及集体所有租赁给个人的企业；（2）股份合作企业；（3）联营企业；（4）有限责任公司（5）股份有限公司；（6）私营企业（7）与港澳台商合资、合作企业；（8）中外合资、合作企业；（9）其他企业。

联营和合资企业按其是否由农村集体与个人相对控股或绝对控股，或由农村集体、个人实际管理来确定是否纳入农村固定资产投资统计范围，其投资额按实际发生额全额统计；个体工商户外雇从业人员8人以上（含8人）的按企业统计。

第二类为乡镇行政事业单位及社会群众团体。

【新增固定资产】指通过投资活动所形成的新的固定资产价值。包括已经建成投入生产或交付使用的工程价值和达到固定资产标准的设备、工具、器具的价值及有关应摊入的费用。它是以价值形式表示的固定资产投资成果的综合性指标，可以综合反映不同时期、不同部门、不同地区的固定资产投资成果。

【新增生产能力（或工程效益）】指通过固定资产投资活动而增加的设计能力或工程效益，它是用实物形态表示的固定资产投资的成果。新增生产能力的计算，是以能独立发挥生产能力或工程效益的单项工程(或项目)为对象。当单项工程(或项目)建成，经有关部门鉴定合格，正式移交投入生产，即可计算新增生产能力。

新增生产能力或工程效益有以下几种表现形式：

⑴以建设项目或单项工程建成后的年产能力表示，如煤炭开采、石油开采等。

⑵以建设项目或单项工程建成后处理原料的能力表示，如选矿工程的年处理矿石能力、洗煤厂年洗原煤能力等。

⑶以新增的主要设备数量或容量表示，如棉纺锭锭数、发电机组容量等。

⑷以建筑物容积、容量、面积或长度表示，如水库容量、铁路公路里程等。

新增生产能力的数量一般按设计能力计算。设计能力是指设计文件中规定的在正常情况下能够达到的生产能力，而不论投产后的实际产量如何。以设备数量、建筑物容积、面积、长度等表示的新增生产能力或工程效益，则按建成的实际数量计算。

【建筑业统计单位】指从事房屋、构筑物建造和设备安装活动的法人企业。建筑业法人企业应同时具备的条件是：①依法成立，有自己的名称、组织机构和场所，能够承担民事责任；②独立拥有和使用资产，承担负债，有权与其他单位签订合同；③独立核算盈亏，能够编制资产负债表。

【建筑业总产值（即自行完成施工产值）】指建筑业企业或附属施工单位自行完成的按工程进度计算的建筑安装生产总值。施工产值包括：

①建筑工程产值：指列入建筑工程预算内的各种工程价值。

②设备安装工程产值：指设备安装工程价值。

③房屋、构筑物修理产值：指房屋、构筑物修理所完成的价值，但不包括被修理房屋、构筑物本身的价值和生产设备的修理价值。

④非标准设备制造产值：指加工制造没有定型的、非标准的生产设备的加工费和原材料价值，不论是现场还是附属加工厂为本单位承建工程制造的非标准设备的价值，都应计算产值。

【房屋建筑施工面积】指报告期内施工的全部房屋建筑面积。包括本期新开工的面积、上期跨入本期继续施工的房屋面积、上期停缓建在本期恢复施工的房屋面积、本期竣工的房屋面积及本期施工后又停缓建的房屋面积。

【房屋建筑竣工面积】指在报告期内房屋建筑按照设计要求已全部完工，达到住人和使用条件，经验收鉴定合格，正式移交使用单位的建筑面积。

【自有机械设备年末总台数】指归本企业(或单位)所有，属于本企业固定资产的生产性机械设备年末总台数。包括施工机械、生产设备、运输设备以及其他设备。

【自有机械设备年末总功率】指本企业(或单位)自有施工机械、生产设备、运输设备以及其他设备等列为在册固定资产的生产性机械设备年末总功率，按设定能力或查定能力计算。包括机械本身的动力和为该机械服务的单独动力设备，如电动机等。计算单位用千瓦，动力换算可按1马力=0.735千瓦折合成千瓦数。电焊机、变压器、锅炉不计算动力。

【工程结算收入】指企业(或单位)按工程的分部分项自行完成的建筑产品价值并已与甲方在报告期内办理结算手续的工程价款收入，以及向甲方收取的除工程价款以外的按规定列作营业收入的各种款项，如临时设施费、劳动保险费、施工机械调迁费等以及向甲方收取的各种索赔款。

【工程结算利润】指已结算工程实现的利润。如为亏损以“－”号表示。其计算公式为：　工程结算利润＝工程结算收入－工程结算成本－工程结算税金及附加

Explanatory Notes on Main Statistical Indicators

【Investment in Fixed Assets】 Investment in fixed assets is the essential means for social reproduction of fixed assets. By means of construction and purchase of fixed assets, more advanced technologies and equipment are adopted in the national economy, and new sectors are established, which promote the adjustment of economic structure and the regional distribution of productive forces and enhance the economic strengths so as to provide the material conditions for improving people' s livelihood. This is significant for speeding up the drive of socialist modernization in China.

Amount of investment in fixed assets refers to the volume of activities in construction and purchases of fixed assets in monetary terms. It is a comprehensive indicator which shows the size, pace, proportional relations and use orientation of the investment in fixed assets. Investment in fixed assets includes, by registration type of ownership, the investment by the state–owned units, collective units, individuals, joint ownership units, share–holding units, as well as investment by businessmen from foreign countries and from Hong Kong, Macao and Taiwan, and by other units. According to China' s current management system, the investment in fixed assets is classified into the following four parts: investment in capital construction, investment in innovation, investment in real estates development and other investment in fixed assets.

【Investment in Real Estate Development】 It includes the investment by the real estate development companies, commercial buildings construction companies and other real estate development units of various types of ownership in the construction of house buildings, such as residential buildings, factory buildings, warehouses, hotels, guesthouses, holiday villages, office buildings, and the complementary service facilities and land development projects, such as roads, water supply, water drainage, power supply, heating, telecommunications, land leveling and other projects of infrastructure. It excludes the activities in simple land transactions.

【Individual Investment in Rural Areas】 The individual investment in the rural areas includes the investment in house construction and purchase of productive fixed assets by the individuals in the rural areas.

【non–agricultural investment in rural areas】 refers to the project which the estimated total investment amount of its fixed assets built or bought by the non–agriculture units in rural areas is over 5 million yuan. The non–agricultural units include two kinds as below:

I.enterprises. 1.Collective Co. (including companies both directly managed by collective leadership and rent to the private),2.Stock–hoiding cooperation,3.Joint Ownership Enterprises,4.Limited liability Corporations,5.Share–holding corporations Ltd.,6.Private enterprises,7.Joint ventures or Cooperative Operation with Hong kong, Macao and Taiwan,8.Foreign joint ventures or Cooperative Operation Enterprises,9.other Enterprises

whether the associated companies and the joint ventures should be considered as the rural fixed assets depends on whether they are actually possessed or managed by rural communities or privates. Their investment amounts refer to the capital which had been actually invested into the enterprises. Private businesses which employ 8 or more workers should be considered as enterprises in statistics

II. public undertakings and public communities in rural areas.

【Newly Increased Fixed Assets】 refer to the newly increased value of fixed assets through investment, including the value of projects completed and put into production, the value of equipment, tools, and vessels considered as fixed assets, as well as the relevant expenses as investment in fixed assets . This is a comprehensive indicator of investment in fixed assets, reflecting the achievements of investment in fixed assets in different periods, different sect ors, and different regions.

【Newly Increased Production Capacity】 refers to the increase of designed capacity and project efficiency through investment in fixed assets, which reflects the accomplishment of investment in fixed assets in kind. The calculation of newly increased production capacity is based on individual project which operates independently and efficiently. When an individual project is completed and checked and accepted and put into production, it is counted as newly increased production capacity.

The newly increased production capacity and project efficiency are usually expressed in one of the following forms:

(1)annual production capacity, such as extraction of coal and petroleum;

(2)raw material processing capacity, such as ore dressing capacity of ore dressing projects, the dressing capacity of a coal washery;

(3)number or capacity of major equipment increased, such as the number of cotton spindles increased and the capacity of generating sets increased;

(4)physical measures of construction, such as volume, capacity, area, and length, for instance, the capacity of reservoirs, the length of railways or highways.

Newly increased production capacity in terms of quantity is calculated in designed capacity in general, which refers to the production capacity of a project under normal conditions designed in construction documents regardless of the actual output.

【Statistical units in construction industries】 refers to the legal enterprises which build architectures or install equipments. The legal enterprises should meet all the demands as follows, 1. being formed legally with own name, organizational structure and working place.

Can fully bear civil responsibilities. 2. possessing and using its own assets independently, which means it should be able to incur liabilities and has right to make contracts with other enterprises. 3. should be an independent accounting unit which can draw balance sheet.

【Gross Output Value of Construction(Output Value of Projects Under Construction)】 refers to total of construction products, expressed in money terms,completed by construction and installation enterprises during a given period of time. It includes:

(1)Output value of construction projects, that is the value of projects covered by the project budgets;

(2)Output value of installation projects, that is the value of the installation of equipment,(excluding the value of the equipment to be installed);

(3)Output value of repair of buildings and structures, that is the value created through the repairs of buildings or structures, but does not include the value of buildings or structures being repaired and the value of the repair of production equipment;

(4)Output value of manufactured non–standard equipment, that is the value of no standard production equipment(including raw materials and manufacturing cost)made for the construction project, and the equipment manufactured by subsidiary workshops.

【Floor Space under Construction】 refers to total floor space of all buildings under construction during the reference period, including floor space of newly started buildings during the reference period, floor space of construction extended from the previous period to the current period, floor space of construction suspended during the previous period and resumed in the current period, floor space of construction completed in the current period, and floor space of construction started and then suspended in the current period.

【Floor Space of Buildings Completed】 refers to the floor space of buildings completed in the reference period, which have come up to the designed standards and have been put into use.

【Total Number of Machinery and Equipment Owned by the Construction Enterprises】 refers to the number of machines and equipment owned by the enterprises (or units, and listed as the fixed assets of the enterprises(or units) by the end of the year, including machinery and equipment for construction, production and transportation.

【Total Power of Machinery and Equipment Owned by the Construction Enterprises】 refer to the total power of machinery and equipment owned by the enterprises(or units), and listed as the fixed assets of the enterprises (or units) by the end of the year, including machinery and equipment for construction, production and transportation. The power of the machinery is calculated on basis of the designed or verified capacity, covering the power of the machinery/equipment and the separate power equipment serving the machinery/equipment (such as electric motors), but excluding welders, transformers and boilers. The unit use for the calculation of power is kilowatt, with horsepower converted to kilowatt by 1horsepower=0.735 kilowatt.

【Income from Settlement of Projects】 refers to the income received by the construction enterprise/unit from the completed portion of the project through settlement procedures with the contracted during the reference period, and other charges to the contracted as operational costs, such as facility fee, labor insurance premium, moving cost of construction unit, as well as various types of claims to the contracted.

【Profit from Settlement of Projects】 refers to profit realized through settled projects. It is calculated with the following formula: Profit from Settlement of Projects=Income from Settlement of projects–Settled Cost–Settled Taxes and Other Cost.

9

第九篇

港口、交通、运输、邮电

PORT,TRANSPORTATION,POST AND TELECOMMUNICATION SERVICE

港口、交通、运输、邮电
Port, Transportations, Post and Telecommunications

主要统计指标
Major Statistics Indicators

2022年全社会客运量	Total Passenger Traffic	4822	万人	10000 persons
比上年增长	Increase Over Last Year	-32.7	%	
2022年全社会货运量	Total Freight Traffic	80100	万吨	10000 tons
比上年增长	Increase Over Last Year	1.7	%	
2022年宁波港域货物吞吐量	Cargo Handled at Ports	63722	万吨	10000 tons
比上年增长	Increase Over Last Year	2.2	%	
2022年宁波港域集装箱吞吐量	Container Handled at Ports	3077.8	万标箱	10000 TEU
比上年增长	Increase Over Last Year	4.8	%	
2022移动电话用户	Number of Mobile Telephone Subscribers	1385.4	万户	10000 subcribers
比上年增长	Increase Over Last Year	0.7	%	
2022年固定电话用户	Number of Local Telephone Subscribers	207.77	万户	10000 subcribers
比上年增长	Increase Over Last Year	-4.5	%	

表9-1 历年港口、交通、邮电基本情况
Basic Statistics on Port,Transportation and Telecommunications Over the Years

年份 Year	宁波港域货物吞吐量（万吨）Cargo at Throughput Ports (10000 tons)	宁波港域集装箱吞吐量（万标箱）Container Throughput (10000 TEU)	货运量（万吨）Freight Traffic (10000 tons)	客运量（万人）Passenger Traffic (10000 persons)	固定电话用户（万户）Number of Local Telephone Subscribers (10000 subscribers)
1978	214		1385	2966	1.07
1979	236		1430	3369	1.19
1980	326		1562	4156	1.36
1981	349		1496	4654	1.53
1982	371		1617	5192	1.71
1983	483		1641	5652	1.86
1984	597		1810	6026	2.22
1985	1040		2015	6527	2.60
1986	1797		3204	7373	2.91
1987	1940		3745	7473	3.55
1988	2002		5408	7277	4.64
1989	2209		4570	7686	5.37
1990	2554	2.2	4763	7378	6.19
1991	3390	3.6	5070	8757	8.05
1992	4367	5.3	6492	9773	12.22
1993	5321	7.9	7583	11224	18.59
1994	5850	12.5	8711	17776	27.86
1995	6853	16.0	9577	19705	41.78
1996	7638	20.2	10460	21152	53.33
1997	8220	25.7	10547	21719	67.75
1998	8707	35.3	10317	21736	83.74
1999	9660	60.1	10344	22211	104.13
2000	11547	90.2	10819	22736	130.15
2001	12852	121.3	11283	23225	163.21
2002	15398	185.9	12429	23752	203.58
2003	18543	277.2	13919	24938	242.00
2004	22586	400.5	16026	27291	296.72
2005	26881	520.8	17664	28412	339.41
2006	30969	706.8	22238	29146	345.08
2007	34519	935.0	24363	30693	334.98
2008	36185	1084.6	27508	32250	338.24
2009	38385	1042.3	29028	33791	301.41
2010	41217	1300.4	30553	33911	317.39
2011	43339	1451.2	31228	28745	312.45
2012	45303	1567.1	32616	28053	308.00
2013	49592	1677.4	35409	24793	298.00
2014	52646	1870.0	40407	16508	270.00
2015	51005	1982.4	42083	14230	269.00
2016	49619	2069.6	46258	10450	238.00
2017	55151	2356.6	52520	10609	224.00
2018	57652	2510.0	61454	10965	207.00
2019	58413	2617.0	68407	11451	250.20
2020	60098	2705.4	71898	7513	241.82
2021	62340	2937.3	78747	7169	217.63
2022	63722	3077.8	80100	4822	207.77

表9-2 港口吞吐情况（2022年）
Basic Statistics on Cargo at Ports Throughput（2022）

单位：吨(ton)

指标	Indicators	吞吐量 Capacity 合计 Total	吞吐量 Capacity 外贸 Foreign Trade	其中 of Which 出口量 Export 合计 Total	其中 of Which 出口量 Export 外贸 Foreign Trade	其中 of Which 进口量 Import 合计 Total	其中 of Which 进口量 Import 外贸 Foreign Trade
货物吞吐量	**Cargo at Throughput Ports**	**637215201**	**379945065**	**252667291**	**158579668**	**384547910**	**221365397**
#转口货物	Cargo of Transfer	116309494	54115721	58154747		58154747	54115721
货物分类	**Type of Cargo**						
煤炭及制品	Coal And Its Products	63805241	3202277	5771400		58033841	3202277
石油及制品	Petroleum And Its Products	94094459	60100674	16725099	1626225	77369360	58474449
金属矿石	Metal Ores	105065931	60594470	44308039		60757892	60594470
钢铁	Steel and Iron	12660509	24945	1529946	10971	11130563	13974
矿建材料	Mineral Building Materials	21086865	2739	2566387	2739	18520478	
水泥	Cement	15821279		3098918		12722361	
木材	Timber	814940	249402			814940	249402
非金属矿石	Nonmetal Ores	5400343	223439	215147	215147	5185196	8292
化肥及农药	Chemical Fertilizers and Pesticides						
盐	Salt	1460382	1215698			1460382	1215698
粮食	Grain	1992987	1275965	452131		1540856	1275965
机械设备	Machinery Equipment	89573	2051	52671		36902	2051
化工原料及制品	Industrial Chemicals And Its Products	19236609	9984661	3305698	518985	15930911	9465676
轻工、医药	Products of Light Industry and Medicine	718289	52899	74090		644199	52899
农林牧渔业产品	Products of Farming, Forestry, Animal Husbandry And Fishery	9027	4027			9027	4027
其他	Others	294958767	243011818	174567765	156205601	120391002	86806217
旅客吞吐量(万人次)	**Number of Passenger In-And Out (10000 person.times)**	**74.1**					

表9-3 港口集装箱吞吐量（2022年）
International Container Throughput at Ports（2022）

航线	Shipping Lines	箱数（箱）Number of Containers	重量（吨）Weigh(ton)	
			合计 Total	货重 Weight of Cargo
总计	**Total**	**30777647**	**291425098**	**228908751**
国际航线合计	International Lines	25474410	229021688	177402180
非洲合计	Africa	998999	10633853	8603626
亚洲合计	Asia	10711141	113992709	92120261
欧洲合计	Europe	5186499	41815500	31346007
北美洲合计	North America	6415352	43299697	30469830
南美洲合计	South America	1296797	12384792	9724068
大洋洲及太平洋岛屿合计	Oceania	600241	4845333	3627732
世界其他	Others	265382	2049804	1510656
内支线合计	Total of Domestic Sub – Line	1272801	13777757	11192622
天津	Tianjin	18533	239363	200532
大连	Dalian	506	4012	2992
上海	Shanghai	26	52	
江苏	Jiangsu	238627	3178723	2688361
浙江	Zhejiang	881783	8957725	7175500
福建	Fujian	115073	1118406	883494
青岛	Qingdao	8883	146846	128446
中国其他	Others	2767005	34980526	29234624
国内航线合计	Total of Domestic Lines	4030436	48625653	40313949

表9-4 历年客运量
Passenger Capacity Over the Years

单位：万人(10000 persons)

年份 Year	合计 Total	其中 of Which			
		铁路 Railway	公路 Highway	水路 Waterway	航空 Civil Aviation
1978	2966	105	2311	550	
1979	3369	122	2692	555	
1980	4156	317	3241	598	
1981	4654	351	3714	598	
1982	5192	366	4277	549	
1983	5652	411	4737	504	
1984	6026	480	5073	473	
1985	6527	502	5575	450	
1986	7373	482	6472	418	1
1987	7473	497	6536	438	2
1988	7277	536	6339	399	3
1989	7686	527	6790	366	3
1990	7378	462	6611	299	6
1991	8757	445	8006	295	11
1992	9773	414	9076	268	14
1993	11224	435	10523	245	21
1994	17776	486	16993	265	32
1995	19705	506	18870	283	45
1996	21152	405	20432	262	53
1997	21719	342	21101	222	55
1998	21736	300	21199	182	55
1999	22211	278	21734	146	53
2000	22736	288	22255	133	60
2001	23225	349	22700	115	61
2002	23752	393	23160	135	64
2003	24938	438	24320	115	65
2004	27291	567	26510	119	95
2005	28412	607	27570	113	122
2006	29146	745	28120	121	160
2007	30693	842	29541	130	180
2008	32250	1770	30130	152	198
2009	33791	1700	31545	142	403
2010	33911	1012	32340	107	452
2011	28745	2186	25960	97	501
2012	28053	1119	26285	123	527
2013	24793	1273	22850	124	546
2014	16508	3556	12144	171	636
2015	14229	3954	9430	160	685
2016	10450	4687	4813	170	779
2017	10609	5183	4302	185	939
2018	10965	5745	3858	190	1172
2019	11451	6198	3829	183	1241
2020	7513	4052	2426	138	897
2021	7169	4621	1427	175	946
2022	4822	2964	1105	136	617

注：自2011年起，客运量为营业性客运量。
Note: From 2011,passenger volume is a business volume of passenger.

表9-5 历年货运量
Freight Traffic Over the Years

单位：万吨(10000 tons)

年份 Year	合计 Total	其中 of Which 铁路 Railway	公路 Highway	水路 Waterway	航空（吨） Civil Aviation(ton)
1978	1385	45	625	715	
1979	1430	67	681	682	
1980	1562	167	709	686	
1981	1496	170	714	612	
1982	1617	186	788	643	
1983	1641	217	810	614	
1984	1810	234	883	693	
1985	2015	284	955	776	
1986	3204	310	1910	984	237
1987	3745	337	2576	832	371
1988	5408	380	4196	832	567
1989	4570	398	3443	729	500
1990	4763	355	3800	608	800
1991	5070	302	4143	625	1600
1992	6492	429	5328	710	2200
1993	7583	428	6255	868	3262
1994	8711	455	7113	1112	4000
1995	9577	527	7843	1173	4900
1996	10460	573	8509	1233	5200
1997	10547	551	8642	1314	5400
1998	9952	569	8195	1143	6900
1999	10344	609	8154	1534	9000
2000	10819	682	8219	1829	11000
2001	11283	725	8300	2156	10000
2002	12429	980	8630	2716	12500
2003	13919	1158	9070	3568	13812
2004	16026	1210	9890	4734	18725
2005	17664	1207	10480	5619	23450
2006	22238	1238	11725	7349	23505
2007	24363	1274	12889	8706	23608
2008	27508	2171	13550	9993	24549
2009	29028	2377	15594	11050	68700
2010	30553	2060	16220	12265	81200
2011	34385	2960	15280	13771	90000
2012	32616	1924	16570	14113	90800
2013	35409	2168	17790	15441	94900
2014	40407	2364	21918	16113	114000
2015	42083	2395	22906	16771	117000
2016	46258	2379	25635	18229	151000
2017	52520	2446	29002	21054	170000
2018	61454	2689	32424	26325	167000
2019	68407	2835	35757	29798	171000
2020	71898	2978	38860	30045	119000
2021	78747	3298	43923	31511	113000
2022	80100	3503	45310	31279	85000

表9-6 历年全社会旅客周转量和货物周转量
Total Turnover Volume of Passengers and Turnover Volume of Freight Traffic Over the Years

年份 Year	旅客周转量（万人公里）Turnover Volume of Passengers(10000 Persons-km)			货物周转量（万吨公里）Turnover Volume of Freight Traffic(10000 tons-km)		
	总计 Total	其中 of Which 公路 Highway	其中 of Which 水路 Waterway	总计 Total	其中 of Which 公路 Highway	其中 of Which 水路 Waterway
1985	147863	135273	12590	132890	34369	98521
1986	176321	163351	12970	219594	86541	133053
1987	182877	168280	14597	294320	130907	163413
1988	191911	176853	15058	271187	89321	181865
1989	193779	180061	13718	319319	135845	183474
1990	202868	190057	12811	308099	134299	173800
1991	229727	215573	14154	438528	187032	251496
1992	270125	258068	12057	608363	242989	365157
1993	324919	314471	10448	777570	262057	515229
1994	623257	610761	12496	1243892	448457	795435
1995	699514	685120	14394	1450892	495929	954674
1996	735912	721653	14259	1742582	523495	1218722
1997	755941	740381	15560	1853782	533382	1320018
1998	752757	741848	10909	1887113	491380	1395325
1999	771393	764287	7106	2311376	481555	1829381
2000	800193	794858	5335	2367484	482518	1884241
2001	822326	818704	3622	2727939	492170	2231435
2002	870546	867830	2716	3342614	521700	2844927
2003	921901	919900	2001	4559749	553005	4002654
2004	992957	990870	2087	5545297	608310	4932308
2005	1042307	1040410	1897	7478890	644800	6806210
2006	1060134	1058100	2034	10361127	719114	8696860
2007	1213443	1211162	2281	11298162	812007	9775967
2008	1235559	1232691	2868	12470705	856713	10745112
2009	1245586	1242710	2876	13216223	1351300	10999544
2010	1362007	1360600	1407	15753422	2465250	13288172
2011	1383064	1382100	963	20903442	2815110	16884961
2012	1431814	1430930	884	20710458	3025860	17684598
2013	1242765	1242030	735	22307108	3254460	19052648
2014	780393	779567	826	20615264	3355532	17259732
2015	650747	649976	771	21677517	3677986	17999531
2016	553473	552732	741	22976464	3952549	19023915
2017	499421	498688	733	27135184	4317400	22817784
2018	466973	466171	802	35971951	4717941	31254010
2019	434829	434149	680	39769328	4970802	34798526
2020	251654	251154	501	41705480	5625885	36079595
2021	207497	206791	706	43951165	6577087	37374078
2022	127317	126782	536	47389881	7133771	40256110

表9-7 公路运输工具拥有量（2022年）
Number of Means of Transportation Through Highway（2022）

指标	单位	Indicators	Unit	营业性 Business
载客汽车	辆	**Buses And Cars**	**unit**	**1963**
	客位		seat	78026
#大型	辆	Large-Sized	unit	1550
	客位		seat	70162
中型	辆	Middle-Sized	unit	392
	客位		seat	7588
载货汽车	辆	**Trucks**	**unit**	**58921**
	吨位		ton	1509914
①普通载货汽车	辆	Ordinary Trucks	unit	24618
	吨位		ton	453223
#大型	辆	Large-Space	unit	24351
	吨位		ton	452467
重型	辆	Heavy	unit	22853
	吨位		ton	443721
中型	辆	Middle	unit	132
	吨位		ton	492
②专用载货汽车	辆	Trucks for Special Purpose	unit	34303
	吨位		ton	1056691
#集装箱车	辆	Container Trucks	unit	26903
	TEU		TEU	53619

表9-8 水路运输工具拥有量（2022年）
Number of Means of Transportation Through Waterway（2022）

指标	单位	Indicators	Unit	总计 Total	其中 of Which 内河 Freshwater	沿海 Coastal	远洋 Ocean
总计	艘	**Total**	**unit**	**532**	**54**	**478**	
机动船	艘	**Motor Vessels**	**unit**	**532**	**54**	**478**	
净载重量	吨位	Dead Weight	ton	10358326	15676	10342650	
载客量	客位	Passenger Capacity	seat	2271	1300	971	
标准箱位	TEU	Standard Container Space	TEU	40470	108	40362	
功率	千瓦	Power	kW	1866646	7282	1859363	
机动船按类别分		**Group by Type of Motor Vessels**					
客船	艘	Passenger Ships	unit	34	29	5	
载客量	客位	Passenger Capacity	seat	1878	1300	578	
功率	千瓦	Power	kW	8518	3456	5062	
客货船	艘	Passenger－cargo Vessels	unit	4		4	
净载重量	吨位	Dead Weight	ton				
载客量	客位	Passenger Capacity	seat	393		393	
功率	千瓦	Power	kW	1468		1468	
货船	艘	Cargo Ships	unit	452	25	468	
净载重量	吨位	Dead Weight	ton	9661880	15676	10339846	
标准箱位	TEU	Standard Container Space	TEU	9014	108	40362	
功率	千瓦	Power	kW	1627889	3827	1843833	
#①油船	艘	Tanker	unit	107		107	
净载重量	吨位	Dead Weight	ton	573926		573926	
功率	千瓦	Power	kW	172973		172973	
②集装箱船	艘	Container Ships	unit	27		27	
净载重量	吨位	Dead Weight	ton	517673		517673	
标准箱位	TEU	Standard Container Space	TEU	35443		35443	
功率	千瓦	Power	kW	192127		192127	
拖船	艘	Tugboats	unit	1		1	
功率	千瓦	Power	kW	9000		9000	
驳船	艘	**Barges**	**unit**				
净载重量	吨位	Dead Weight	ton				

表9-9 部分年份运输线路里程长度
Length of Transportation Routes in Partial Years

单位：公里(km)

指标	Indicators	2018	2019	2020	2021	2022
公路总里程	**Overall Length of Highway**	**11295**	**11375**	**11433**	**11523**	**11470**
按技术等级分:	**Divided by Grade**					
①等级公路	Highway Grade	11295	11375	11433	11523	11470
高速公路	Express Way	567	567	567	584	584
一级公路	Highway Grade 1	1297	1342	1378	1402	1431
二级公路	Highway Grade 2	826	835	848	857	830
三级公路	Highway Grade 3	1586	1598	1566	1568	1587
四级公路	Highway Grade 4	7019	7033	7074	7113	7038
准四级公路	Near Highway Grade 4					
②等外公路	Highway Without Grade					
按路面等级分	**Divided by Road Surface**					
高级路面	High Grade Road Surface	10926	11040	11106	11288	11247
次高级路面	Sub-High Grade Road Surface	287	286	279	222	216
中级路面	Medium Grade Road Surface	82	49	49	13	7
低级路面	Lower Grade Road Surface					
按行政等级分	**Divided by Administrative Level**					
国道	State Way	818	821	823	818	818
省道	Province Way	701	701	689	707	701
县道	County Way	2966	3018	3042	3074	3060
乡道	Township Way	2203	2189	2186	2166	2180
专用道	Special Use Way	32	31	30	25	19
村道公路里程	Village Way	4574	4614	4662	4734	4694
内河通航里程	**Length of Navigable Inland Waterways**	**932**	**932**	**932**	**932**	**932**

表9-10 历年电信业主要指标
Main Indicators of Telecommunications Services Over the Years

年份 Year	固定电话用户 (万户) Number of Local Telephone Subscribers (10000 subcribers)	#农话 (万户) Rural Telephone Subscribers (10000 subscribers)	移动电话 (万户) Number of Subscribers of Mobile Telephone (10000 subscribers)	国际互联网用户 (户) Number of Users of International Computer Network (user)
1978	1.07	0.49		
1979	1.19	0.53		
1980	1.36	0.58		
1981	1.53	0.64		
1982	1.71	0.70		
1983	1.86	0.76		
1984	2.22	0.89		
1985	2.60	1.05		
1986	2.91	1.14		
1987	3.55	1.35		
1988	4.64	1.68		
1989	5.37	1.92		
1990	6.19	2.15		
1991	8.05	2.88		
1992	12.22	4.92	0.14	
1993	18.59	7.49	0.80	
1994	27.86	11.60	1.92	
1995	41.78	17.80	4.71	
1996	53.33	23.10	9.05	
1997	67.75	31.14	16.44	
1998	83.74	41.40	25.72	4248
1999	104.13	54.39	56.75	37334
2000	130.15	72.69	117.92	70928
2001	163.21	90.13	195.65	93208
2002	203.58	91.52	256.86	104293
2003	242.00	107.20	379.31	835674
2004	296.72	94.79	421.00	1040127
2005	339.41		467.10	1705300
2006	345.08		514.70	908123
2007	334.98		757.70	1737851
2008	338.24		821.58	1027689
2009	301.41		866.87	1360000
2010	317.39		845.50	1720000
2011	312.45		1029.46	1900000
2012	308.00		1088.00	2360500
2013	298.00		1228.00	2500000
2014	270.00		1267.00	2810000
2015	269.00		1257.00	3020000
2016	238.00		1209.83	3360000
2017	224.00		1218.85	3840000
2018	207.00		1258.86	4196600
2019	250.20		1358.16	4255100
2020	241.82		1335.91	4383400
2021	217.63		1375.24	4711100
2022	207.77		1385.40	5181265

注：2008年起，国际互联网用户不含移动用户。
Note: From 2008, the datum of international Internet users excludes China mobile users.

表9-11 部分年份邮政业务情况
Basic Statistics on Post Services in Partial Years

指标	单位	Indicators	unit	2019	2020	2021	2022
邮政局、所数	处	Number of Post Offices	unit	271	270	270	270
邮路总长度（单程）	公里	Length of Postal Routes	km	31369	34045	30082	32418
农村投递路线	公里	Rural Delivery Routes	km	41841	40615	55882	57520
邮政业务量	万元	Business volume of Post Services	10000 yuan	300374	284478	162355	171438
函件	万件	Number of Letters	10000 pcs	1612. 54	857. 78	662. 02	664. 29
#国际函件	万件	International Letters	10000 pcs	692. 51	157. 10	27. 75	4. 00
国内函件	万件	Domestic Letters	10000 pcs	920. 02	700. 68	634. 27	660. 29
报纸期发份数	万份	Newspaper Issued	10000 copies	91. 88	66. 98		69. 74
杂志期发份数	万份	Magazine Issued	10000 copies	35. 24	29. 74		32. 77
订销报纸累计份数	万份	Number of Newspaper Circulation	10000 copies	20635	20093	20018	19436
订销杂志累计份数	万份	Number of Magazine Circulation	10000 copies	512. 72	475. 86	478. 75	503. 53

表9-12 各县（市）邮政业务基本情况（2022年）
Basic Statistics on Post Services by Region（2022）

指标	单位	Indicators	Unit	全市 Total	市区 Urban Districts	余姚 Yuyao
邮政局、所数	处	Number of Post Offices	unit	270	151	42
邮路总长度（单程）	公里	Length of Postal Routes	km	32418	26520	952
农村投递路线	公里	Rural Delivery Routes	km	57520	15725	14816
邮政业务量	万元	Business volume of Post Services	10000 yuan	171438	76571	26869
函件	万件	Number of Letters	10000 pcs	664.29	566.16	25.93
国际函件	万件	International Letters	10000 pcs	4.00	3.68	0.07
国内函件	万件	Domestic Letters	10000 pcs	660.29	562.48	25.86
订销报纸累计份数	万份	Number of Newspaper Circulation	10000 copies	19436.02	10964.39	2036.83
订销杂志累计份数	万份	Number of Magazine Circulation	10000 copies	503.53	332.95	47.98

表9－12 续表 Continued

指标	单位	Indicators	Unit	慈溪 Cixi	宁海 Ninghai	象山 Xiangshan
邮政局、所数	处	Number of Post Offices	unit	34	19	24
邮路总长度（单程）	公里	Length of Postal Routes	km	3396	1096	454
农村投递路线	公里	Rural Delivery Routes	km	22333	2312	2334
邮政业务量	万元	Business volume of Post Services	10000 yuan	41774	18958	7266
函件	万件	Number of Letters	10000 pcs	38.14	13.10	20.96
国际函件	万件	International Letters	10000 pcs	0.23	0.02	
国内函件	万件	Domestic Letters	10000 pcs	37.91	13.08	20.96
订销报纸累计份数	万份	Number of Newspaper Circulation	10000 copies	3686.94	1716.01	1031.85
订销杂志累计份数	万份	Number of Magazine Circulation	10000 copies	51.64	38.72	32.24

主要统计指标解释

【公路里程】指在一定时期内实际达到《公路工程技术标JTJ01-88》规定的等级公路，并经公路主管部门正式验收交付使用的公路里程数。其计算单位为：公里。它包括大中城市的郊区公路以及通过小城镇街道部分的公路里程，也包括桥梁、渡口的长度，但不包括大中城市的街道、厂矿、林区生产用道和农业生产用道的里程。两条或多条公路共同经由同一路段，只计算一次，不得重复计算里程长度。公路里程是反映公路建设发展规模的重要指标，也是计算运输网密度等指标的基础资料。

【货(客)运量】指在一定时期内，各种运输工具实际运送的货物(旅客)数量。是反映运输业为国民经济和人民生活服务的数量指标，也是制定和检查运输生产计划，研究运输发展规模和速度的重要指标。货运按吨计算，客运按人计算。货物不论运输距离长短，货物类别，均按实际重量统计；旅客不论行程远近或票价多少，均按一人一次作为客运量统计。半价票、小孩票也按一人统计。

【货物(旅客)周转量】指在一定时期内，由各种运输工具运送的货物(旅客)数量与其相应运输距离的乘积之总和，是反映运输业生产总成果的重要指标，也是编制和检查运输生产计划，计算运输效率、劳动生产率以及核算运输单位成本的主要基础资料。通常以吨公里和人公里为计算单位。计算货物周转量通常按发出站与到达站之间的最短距离，也就是计费距离计算。

【港口货物吞吐量】指由水运进出港区范围，并经过装卸的货物数量，包括邮件及办理托运手续的行李、包裹以及补给运输船舶的燃、物料和淡水。其计量单位为吨。货物吞吐量的货种分类及其主要流向流量，反映了港口在国内外物资交流和对外贸易运输中的地位和作用。吞吐量可以分为进口、出口，又可以分为国内贸易和对外贸易。

【邮电业务总量】指以货币表现的邮电部门用于传递信息和提供其他邮电服务的总数量。它综合反映了一定时期邮电工作的总成果，是研究邮电业务量构成和发展趋势的重要指标。根据邮电管理体制不同，分为中央国营业务总量和地方国营业务总量。它用各种邮电分类业务量，如函件件数、电报份数、长话张数、市内电话和农村电话的年均户数、订销报刊累计份数等，分别乘以相应的平均单价(不变价)，加总后再加上出租电路和设备的收入、代用户维护电话交换机和线路等设备的收入、其他业务收入求得。

Explanatory Notes on Main Statistical Indicators

【Length of Highways】 refers to the length of highways which are built in conformity with the grades specified by the highway engineering standard formulated by the Ministry of Communications, and have been formally checked and accepted by the departments of highways and put into use. The length of highways includes that of the suburb highways at large and medium sized cities, highways passing through streets at small cities and towns, and also the length of bridges and ferries. It does not include the length of streets in big and medium sized cities and highways built for the production purpose at factories, mines, forest areas and agricultural areas, If two or more highways go the same section of the way, the length of the section is only calculated for once and no duplication is allowed. The length of highways is an important indicator to show the development of the highway construction and to provide essential information to calculate the transport network density.

【Freight(Passenger) Traffic】 refers to the volume of freight (passenger) transported with various means. Freight transport is calculated in to ns and passenger traffic is calculated in the number of persons. Despite the type of freight and traveling distance, the freight transport is calculated by the principle that one person can be counted only once in one travel. The passenger who travel with a half price ticket or a child ticket is also calculated as one person. The freight (passenger) traffic provides a quantitative measure to show how the transport industry serves the national economy and people, and is also an important indicator for planning the transport industry and for studying the development scale and speed of the transport industry.

【Freight Ton–kilometers(Passenger–kilometers)】 refers to the sum of the products of the volume of transported cargo(passengers) multiplying by the transport distance, usually using ton kilometer and passenger kilometer as units for measurement. Normally, the shortest distance between the departure station and the destination station(i.e., the payable distance) is the basis to calculate the freight ton–kilometers. This is an important indicator to show the total results of the transport industry, to prepare and examine the transport plan and to measure the efficiency, the labor productivity and the unit cost of transport.

【Volume of Freight Handled】 refers to the volume of cargo passing in and out the harbor area of the major coastal ports and having been loaded and unloaded. The volume includes that of the coastal matters, registered luggage and fuels, materials and fresh water as supplies of the ships. The volume of freight dandled maybe classified as import, export, or as domestic trade and foreign trade. The volume of freight handled by type of cargo and by main flow direction reflects he position and function of the ports in the inflow of Chinese and foreign commodities and in the transportation of foreign trade.

【Business Volume of Post and Telecommunications】 refers to the total amount of the information delivered and other post and telecommunications services provided by the post and telecommunications departments for the customers. It is derived by first multiplying the business volume of different types, such as number of letters, telegrams, long distance calls, city and rural telephone subscribers and accumulated number of newspapers and journals subscribed and sold, etc. by their respective average unit price (fixed price) and then adding these products together: plus the income from maintenance of telephone exchanges and lines, and the income from other business operations. The business volume of post and telecommunications indicates the total achievements made by the post and telecommunications department during a given period of time in a comprehensive way, and is an important indicator to study the composition and development of the post and telecommunications business.

NINGBO 2023 Statistical Yearbook

10 CHAPTER

第十篇

国内贸易、餐饮业

DOMESTIC TRADE AND CATERING TRADE

国内贸易、餐饮
Domestic Trade and Catering Trade

主要统计指标
Major Statistics Indicators

				总计 Total	比上年增长 (%) Increase Over Last Year(%)
2022年社会消费品零售总额	万元	Total Retail Sales of Consumer Goods	10000 yuan	48967202	5. 3
#批发零售贸易业	万元	Wholesale and Retail Sale	10000 yuan	44493695	5. 2
住宿及餐饮业	万元	Hoteling and Catering Trade	10000 yuan	4473508	6. 2
限额以上批发业主要指标		Main Indicators of Wholesales Trade Above Designated Size			
企业数	个	Number of Enterprises	unit	7616	5. 9
从业人员数	人	Number of Employees	person	151332	1. 1
销售总额	万元	Total Sales Value	10000 yuan	467997863	20. 1
资产总计	万元	Total Assets	10000 yuan	136094034	21. 1
利润总额	万元	Total Profits	10000 yuan	5005983	-4. 6
限额以上零售业主要指标		Main Indicators of Retail Trade Above Designated Size			
企业数	个	Number of Enterprises		1257	17. 1
从业人员数	人	Number of Employees	person	65137	1. 9
销售总额	万元	Total Sales Value	10000 yuan	18839027	17. 9
资产总计	万元	Total Assets	10000 yuan	9077708	10. 4
利润总额	万元	Total Profits	10000 yuan	277364	-1. 8
2022年住宿餐饮业从业人员数	人	Number of Employees in Catering Trade and Hoteling	person	47219	4. 2

表10-1 历年社会消费品零售总额
Total Retail Sales of Consumer Goods Over the Years

单位：万元(10000 yuan)

年份 Year	全市 Total	其中 of Which 市区 Urban District	县(市)合计 Total County
1978	70935	26276	44659
1979	87965	32510	55454
1980	112223	40523	71699
1981	130682	47338	83344
1982	140346	50248	90098
1983	157516	55556	101960
1984	188598	66829	121769
1985	254279	99591	154688
1986	305758	118303	187455
1987	356069	133957	222112
1988	492338	192732	299606
1989	530188	216597	313591
1990	551863	233148	318715
1991	636277	274217	362060
1992	797058	337059	459999
1993	1186690	524131	662559
1994	1675988	683129	992858
1995	2283888	925771	1358117
1996	2658572	1037517	1621055
1997	2947318	1179134	1768184
1998	3204653	1238474	1966179
1999	3503525	1339024	2164501
2000	3838584	1439165	2399419
2001	4096038		
2002	4517436		
2003	5080886		
2004	6390600		
2005	7285896	3465806	3820090
2006	8457083	4009477	4447605
2007	9916042	4671247	5244795
2008	11849656	5549233	6300423
2009	13513330	7191448	6321883
2010	16176783	6607837	9568946
2011	19279842	10401180	8878662
2012	21904469	11716089	10188379
2013	24337157	12998452	11338704
2014	27383085	14824076	12559009
2015	30501774	18792810	11708964
2016	33376097	21815159	11560939
2017	36729099	23736483	12992615
2018	39643854	24972403	14671451
2019	42685582	26846947	15838634
2020	42382625	27179447	15203178
2021	46491010	29611285	16879725
2022	48967202	31430383	17536819

注：本表数据已根据四经普数据修订，表10-2同。
Note：The data in this table have been adjusted according to the 4th economic census，the same as Table 10-2.

表10-2 部分年份分行业社会消费品零售总额
Total Retail Sales of Consumer Goods by Sector in Partial Years

单位：万元(10000 yuan)

年份 Year	社会消费品零售总额 Total Retail Sales of Consumer Goods	#市的零售额 City	按行业分 Grouped by Sector 批发和零售贸易业 Wholesale and Retail Sale Trades	住宿及餐饮业 Hoteling and Catering Trade	其他 Others
1990	551863				
1991	636277				
1992	797058				
1993	1186690				
1994	1675988				
1995	2283888	1329556	1639823	126310	517756
1996	2658572	1596024	1979393	163706	515474
1997	2947318	1740245	2149181	203939	594198
1998	3204653	1833442	2409463	191378	603812
1999	3503525	2044941	2634476	280564	588485
2000	3838584	2216324	2924422	372849	541313
2001	4096038	2374484	3090271	437158	568609
2002	4517436	2671965	3359373	556520	601544
2003	5080886	3005234	4320085	654720	106081
2004	6390600	3783030	5602768	739701	48130
2005	7285896	4489352	6374032	877449	34414
2006	8457083	5210222	7488284	964097	4702
2007	9916042	6099658	8814648	1099116	2277
2008	11849656	7412445	10518737	1328479	2439
2009	13513330	8674121	12036940	1473791	2600
2010	16176783	12088231	14674020	1502763	
2011	19279842	13059336	17517858	1761985	
2012	21904469	18384081	19898818	2005651	
2013	24337157	20438759	22205524	2131633	
2014	27383085	22596145	24986091	2396994	
2015	30501774	25084979	27951141	2550633	
2016	33376097	27229564	30039451	3336647	
2017	36729099	29740811	32535582	4193517	
2018	39643854	33758410	34620714	5023140	
2019	42685582	36182897	37022681	5662900	
2020	42382625	37011458	39197492	3185133	
2021	46491076	41116341	42276946	4214130	
2022	48967202	43311546	44493695	4473508	

注：（1）2004年以前，住宿及餐饮业统计数据仅包含餐饮业。
（2）2010年零售额的计算方法根据报表制度有所调整。

Notes:（1）Hoteling and catering trade statistics only include the catering trade, before 2004.
（2）Calculation of retail sales in 2010 had been adjusted according to the reporting system.

表10-3 零售业态（2022年）
Status of Retail Sale（2022）

指标	Indicators	法人单位数（个）Number of Corporation (unit)	销售合计（万元）Total Sale (10000 yuan)	其中 of Witch	
				批发 Wholesale	零售 Retail
零售企业合计	**Total Retail Enterprise**	**1257**	**18836538**	**2910022**	**15926516**
按经营方式分：	**Grouped by Management Method**				
独立店	Sole Shop	989	13444175	1615255	11828919
连锁商店总店	Chain General Shop	23	1129668	351617	778051
连锁直营店	Regular Chain Store	24	1127806	298684	829121
连锁加盟店	Franchise Chain Store	8	19031	956	18075
其他	Others	213	3115859	643510	2472349
按零售业态分：	**Grouped by Retail Sale Line**				
百货商店	Department Store	16	938939	35492	903447
超级市场	Supermarket	46	1316028	296344	1019685
专业(专卖)店	Special (exclusive) Shop	854	11915941	1806785	10109155
其他	Others	46	471220	95038	376182

表10-4 限额以上批发贸易业单位数和从业人员数（2022年）

Number of Units and Employees of Wholesale Trade Above Designed Size（2022）

指标	Indicators	法人企业数（个） Number of Corporations(unit)	从业人数（人） Number of Employees(person)
批发业合计	**Wholesale Trade**	**7616**	**151332**
#国有控股	State－holding	158	6385
按注册类型分	**Grouped by Registration Type**		
内资企业	Domestic Funded Enterprises	7340	131829
国有企业	State－Owned Enterprises	11	1361
集体企业	Collective－Owned Enterprises		
股份合作企业	Share Cooperative Enterprises	6	60
有限责任公司	Limited Liability Corporations	545	24862
股份有限公司	Share－holding Corporations Ltd.	22	2149
私营企业	Private Enterprises	6753	103373
港、澳、台商投资企业	Hong Kong, Macao and Taiwan Funded Enterprises	94	4865
外商投资企业	Foreign Funded Enterprises	182	14638
按行业分	**Grouped by Sector**		
农畜产品批发	Agricultural and Livestock Products	125	1311
食品、饮料及烟草制品批发	Food, Beverages and Tobaccos	244	9320
#烟草制品批发	Tobacco	1	1277
纺织、服装及日用品批发	Textile, Garments and Daily Necessities	1189	48508
#服装批发	Garments	254	10812
家用视听设备批发	Household audio－visual equipment	17	1758
日用家电批发	Household appliances	174	13733
文化、体育用品及器材批发	Culture, Sports Appliances and Equipments	289	10000
医药及医疗器材批发	Medicines and Medical Appliance	157	5111
矿产品、建材及化工产品批发	Mineral Products, Building Materials, Chemical Products	4370	39153
#石油及制品批发	Petroleum and Related Products	298	4634
金属及金属矿批发	Metal and Metallic Ore	1942	13960
机械设备、五金交电及电子产品批发	Machine Equipments, Hardware, Electric Appliances, Electronic Equipment	1084	31816
#汽车及零配件批发	Motor Vehicles and Parts	176	9593
摩托车及零配件批发	Motorcycles and Parts	4	63
贸易经纪与代理	Trade brokerage and agency	18	529
其他批发	Others	140	5584

表10-5 限额以上零售贸易业单位数和从业人员数（2022年）
Number of Units and Employees of Retail Trade Above Designed Size（2022）

指标	Indicators	法人企业数（个）Number of Corporations(unit)	从业人数（人）Number of Employees(person)
零售业总计	**Total**	**1257**	**65137**
#国有控股	State – holding	95	3663
按注册类型分	**Grouped by Registration Type**		
内资企业	Domestic Funded Enterprises	1173	56719
国有企业	State – Owned Enterprises	5	389
集体企业	Collective – Owned Enterprises	4	69
股份合作企业	Share Cooperative Enterprises	6	136
联营企业	Joint – owned Enterprises	3	38
有限责任公司	Limited Liability Corporations	199	11107
股份有限公司	Share–holding Corporations Ltd.	4	342
私营企业	Private Enterprises	952	44638
港、澳、台商投资企业	Hong Kong, Macao and Taiwan Funded Enterprises	26	4811
外商投资企业	Foreign Funded Enterprises	58	3607
按行业分	**Grouped by Sector**		
综合零售	Comprehensive Retail	59	12669
#百货零售	General Merchandise	13	1455
超级市场零售	Supermarket	39	10842
食品、饮料及烟草制品专门零售	Food, Beverages and Tobaccos	107	4366
纺织、服装及日用品专门零售	Textile, Garments and Articles for Daily Use	56	4820
#服装零售	Garments	27	3663
文化、体育用品及器材专门零售	Culture, Sports Appliances and Equipments	45	3093
#图书、报刊零售	Books	14	926
医药及医疗器材专门零售	Medicines and Medical Appliance	54	3850
汽车、摩托车、零配件和燃料及其他动力销售	Automobile, Motorcycles,Fuels and Parts	531	21834
#汽车新车零售	New Automobiles	385	18443
汽车旧车零售	Used Automobiles	5	1452
家用电器及电子产品专门零售	Household Appliances and Electronic Products	101	2953
#家用视听设备零售	Household Audiovisual Equipment	10	269
日用家电零售	Household Appliances	47	1020
通信设备零售	Communication Equipment	19	828
五金、家具及室内装饰材料专门零售	Hardware, Furniture and Decoration Materials	33	868
货摊、无店铺及其他零售业	Non– shop and Others	271	10684
#互联网零售	Internet	246	10211

表10-6 限额以上批发贸易业购进、销售、库存总额（2022年）
Total Purchases,Sale and Inventory of Wholesale Trade Above Designated Size（2022）

指标	Indicators	购进总额 Total Purchases	进口 Imports
批发业	**Wholesale Trade**	**449718722**	**24100394**
#国有控股	State－holding	61350394	2959659
按注册类型分	**Grouped by Registration Type**		
内资企业	Domestic Funded Enterprises	395900270	21925245
国有企业	State－Owned Enterprises	3403531	464
集体企业	Collective－Owned Enterprises		
股份合作企业	Share Cooperative Enterprises	42732	
有限责任公司	Limited Liability Corporations	107237314	5979090
股份有限公司	Share－holding Corporations Ltd.	8745094	2747936
私营企业	Private Enterprises	275594551	13179663
港、澳、台商投资企业	Hong Kong, Macao and Taiwan Funded Enterprises	8614007	384461
外商投资企业	Foreign Funded Enterprises	28079704	1036344
按行业分	**Grouped by Sector**		
农畜产品批发	Agricultural and Livestock Products	7176810	173713
食品、饮料及烟草制品批发	Food, Beverages and Tobaccos	8018140	496919
#烟草制品批发	Tobacco	1401374	
纺织、服装及日用品批发	Textile, Garments and Daily Necessities	27996812	1494851
#服装批发	Garments	7111918	928800
家用视听设备批发	Household audio－visual equipment	1343631	
日用家电批发	Household appliances	6080299	4444
文化、体育用品及器材批发	Culture, Sports Appliances and Equipments	7874608	145447
医药及医疗器材批发	Medicines and Medical Appliance	2839594	147443
矿产品、建材及化工产品批发	Mineral Products, Building Materials, Chemical Products	330702781	18236743
#石油及制品批发	Petroleum and Related Products	23675626	763743
金属及金属矿批发	Metal and Metallic Ore	163012231	9597227
机械设备、五金交电及电子产品批发	Machine Equipments, Hardware, Electric Appliances, Electronic Equipment	36755168	1506028
#汽车及零配件批发	Motor Vehicles and Parts	15335697	565225
摩托车及零配件批发	Motorcycles and Parts	768733	
贸易经纪与代理	Trade brokerage and agency	509302	30848
其他批发	Others	10720766	1114058

单位：万元(10000 yuan)

销售总额 Total Sales	其中 of Which					年末库存总额 Inventory (year – end)
	通过网络实现的销售额 Sales through network	批发 Wholesale	出口 Exports	零 售 Retail Sale	通过网络实现的零售额 Sales through network	
467997863	**23817941**	**447892092**	**31009349**	**18565223**	**5183451**	**11771534**
65033089	5596288	64376591	2253492	633984	100	1699318
408812775	17772442	405715207	28498178	1567206	654404	8681523
4059816	2058887	4056869		706	100	97702
43671		43671				2750
111152967	5102518	110805984	6274603	312280	140418	2827849
9648549	250248	9638452	1720600	10097		237526
283028337	10360790	280290796	20500586	1244123	513887	5496756
9053967	244991	8899588	396667	150249	58477	235285
31292095	1267218	30367275	2099309	921252	317652	977401
7241491	26053	7239020	7717	2471		126053
8768489	2228505	8528643	849676	228478	25968	516410
2059827	2058787	2059827				66178
30986860	1202766	29990803	12170579	974759	634957	1204668
7892768	179425	7697595	3891406	194600	142575	243010
1493578	1552	1489404	145942	3462	489	27427
6950125	709838	6590520	1432955	342427	308703	110940
8460494	391330	8279280	2508371	177776	133579	301565
3377511	228963	3334640	272447	33249		339553
339765441	8487126	337524713	6497072	781634	219	5715469
26264624	417	25464884	98738	667177	219	589595
165744613	4528715	164590600	2799592	45347		2276048
38731881	407153	38449687	8045171	248954	47558	1428152
15915821	51929	15850635	1657495	63499	25616	510290
780968		780968	23378			63
519427		519427	290636			66859
11307243	6312755	11115858	352484	191386	188252	195481

表10-7 限额以上零售贸易业购进、销售、库存总额（2022年）
Total Purchases, Sale and Inventory of Retail Trade Above Designed Size（2022）

指标	Indicators	购进总额 Total Purchases	进口 Imports
零售业合计	**Retail Trade**	**17124741**	**754344**
#国有控股	State-holding	1305577	20244
按注册类型分	**Grouped by Registration Type**		
内资企业	Domestic Funded Enterprises	13803796	382090
国有企业	State-Owned Enterprises	16968	
集体企业	Collective-Owned Enterprises	56839	
股份合作企业	Share Cooperative Enterprises	43610	
联营企业	Joint-owned Enterprises	15293	
有限责任公司	Limited Liability Corporations	3553995	203847
股份有限公司	Share-holding Corporations Ltd.	493384	
私营企业	Private Enterprises	9623709	178243
港、澳、台商投资企业	Hong Kong, Macao and Taiwan Funded Enterprises	1867779	119831
外商投资企业	Foreign Funded Enterprises	1453166	252423
按行业分	**Grouped by Sector**		
综合零售	Comprehensive Retail	2035061	28
#百货零售	General Merchandise	788090	
超级市场零售	Supermarket	1204151	28
食品、饮料及烟草制品专门零售	Food, Beverages and Tobaccos	480024	
纺织、服装及日用品专门零售	Textile, Garments and Articles for Daily Use	778853	310
#服装零售	Garments	578839	310
文化、体育用品及器材专门零售	Culture, Sports Appliances and Equipments	218638	
#图书、报刊零售	Books	77197	
医药及医疗器材专门零售	Medicines and Medical Appliance	569178	
汽车、摩托车、零配件和燃料及其他动力销售	Automobile, Motorcycles, Fuels and Parts	9343978	594738
#汽车新车零售	New Automobiles	7761494	594738
汽车旧车零售	Used Automobiles	264342	
家用电器及电子产品专门零售	Household Appliances and Electronic Products	801423	
#家用视听设备零售	Household Audiovisual Equipment	33087	
日用家电零售	Household Appliances	436422	
通信设备零售	Communication Equipment	241600	
五金、家具及室内装饰材料专门零售	Hardware, Furniture and Decoration Materials	88955	1421
货摊、无店铺及其他零售业	Non-shop and Others	2808633	157848
#互联网零售	Internet	2738866	157043

单位：万元(10000 yuan)

销售总额 Total Sales	其中 of Which 通过网络实现的销售额 Sales through network	批发 Wholesale	出口 Exports	零售 Retail Sale	通过网络实现的零售额 Sales through network	年末库存总额 Inventory (year-end)
18839027	**4533291**	**2910022**	**15195**	**15926516**	**4152917**	**1877324**
1409312	12691	355336		1053977	8708	78456
15238779	3905077	2464991	15195	12773163	3535526	1495787
17864	5839	5346		12517	1856	399
63526		3607		59919		838
44974	1982	7754		37220	1670	1044
17246		2681		14565		485
3945560	1183527	626631	935	3318929	1075578	426057
500237		283124		217113		9200
10649372	2713729	1535848	14260	9112900	2456422	1057764
1979498	417675	229870		1749627	411874	140293
1620750	210539	215161		1403726	205517	241245
2201042	255865	309389	485	1891653	213946	165288
881756	72057	4856		876900	72057	29133
1274070	182858	293965		980104	140939	131964
546837	17774	92070		454767	17070	56724
945337	63370	336172		609165	61146	250816
692814	56480	236362		456452	54257	213055
304072	54041	39112	797	264960	53475	64222
87941	267	2499		85442	267	28203
625415	35943	205018		420397	31044	63326
9501894	815619	1034084		8467800	727819	790658
7788142	805249	569030		7219102	718642	717221
271504	125	37522		233981	125	46232
872147	124154	159152		712995	122896	59261
38244	780	2406		35838	780	10131
484751	117048	46013		438738	116165	34025
246311	4931	102227		144084	4931	8826
109379	4324	12329		97050	4324	14273
3732904	3162201	722697	13913	3007728	2921196	412756
3661939	3145593	701141	13913	2958320	2914313	409738

表10-8 限额以上批发贸易业主要财务指标（2022年）
Main Financial Indicators of Wholesale Trade Above Designed Size（2022）

指标	Indicators	年末资产负债 流动资产合计 Current Funds	#存货 Inventories	固定资产原价 Original Value of Fixed Assets
批发业合计	**Wholesale Trade**	**117587294**	**10870125**	**3370941**
#国有控股	State – holding	13979563	2252993	625830
按注册类型分	**Grouped by Registration Type**			
内资企业	Domestic Funded Enterprises	100155242	9081977	3015289
国有企业	State – Owned Enterprises	989994	108029	108091
集体企业	Collective – Owned Enterprises			
股份合作企业	Share Cooperative Enterprises	8188	2487	1374
有限责任公司	Limited Liability Corporations	29994859	3351590	816360
股份有限公司	Share–holding Corporations Ltd.	2531410	214032	105099
私营企业	Private Enterprises	66189118	5389075	1984327
港、澳、台商投资企业	Hong Kong, Macao and Taiwan Funded Enterprises	4601267	220357	114833
外商投资企业	Foreign Funded Enterprises	12830785	1567792	240819
按行业分	**Grouped by Sector**			
农畜产品批发	Agricultural and Livestock Products	3048596	158915	89715
食品、饮料及烟草制品批发	Food, Beverages and Tobaccos	2758529	425863	306133
#烟草制品批发	Tobacco	692481	66178	106420
纺织、服装及日用品批发	Textile, Garments and Daily Consumer Articles	11364816	1154288	504906
#服装批发	Garments	3614984	212845	151062
家用视听设备批发	Household Audiovisual Equipment	347667	22627	1921
日用家电批发	Household Appliances	1849456	132729	38298
文化、体育用品及器材批发	Culture, Sports Appliances and Equipments	2940990	276500	175639
医药及医疗器材批发	Medicines and Medical Appliance	1796910	329790	162359
矿产品、建材及化工产品批发	Mineral Products, Building Materials, Chemical Products	74917413	6282932	1510752
#石油及制品批发	Petroleum and Related Products	4982153	624123	229121
金属及金属矿批发	Metal and Metallic Ore	35384072	2449943	641823
机械设备、五金交电及电子产品	Machine Equipments, Hardware, Electric Appliances, Electronic Equipment	17827529	2045930	523949
#汽车及零配件批发	Automobile and Parts	7840863	1132366	118515
摩托车及零配件批发	Motorcycle and Parts	351770	63	614
其他批发	Others	2762883	179681	90485

单位：万元(10000 yuan)

Total Assets and Liabilities at the Year－end				损益与分配 Profit, Loss and Distribution	
本年折旧 Depreciation in This year	资产合计 Total Asset	负债合计 Total Liabilities	所有者权益 Creditors' Equity	营业收入 Business Revenue	营业成本 Business Costs
222694	**136094034**	**109383532**	**27379890**	**401913824**	**389722547**
27612	16097488	11502228	4551418	56560037	55023656
201367	114944006	92525182	23088977	367056273	356465774
5569	1051947	432451	616620	3595230	2999619
90	8438	4130	4308	38756	36137
39666	33533367	26887365	7453819	99984255	96934868
3404	3904194	2330244	1573950	8833133	8628856
152630	76004337	62437533	13432015	253824901	247085894
6559	5305156	4129218	1175933	8100832	7738040
14768	15844872	12729133	3114979	26756720	25518732
3088	4068419	3050396	1018023	6575466	6528850
17254	3338281	2236176	1052662	8043055	7135151
5452	751971	167508	584464	1823958	1236168
30960	14114189	10753184	3356245	29033603	26129473
8537	5567964	3819371	1748520	7457627	6687804
425	350264	342051	8214	1339461	1201496
3287	2008927	1735962	268434	6407474	5653538
11099	3229739	2300351	929148	7837457	7214783
13499	2084844	1413573	670280	3045059	2521128
95963	86471568	71426171	15779975	301085713	296469890
10792	5708969	4397482	1310313	21840284	21474114
39108	42278936	34278476	7895467	147307714	145988669
42096	19685508	15967303	3708450	35512600	33535507
10017	8555020	7769641	784930	14532861	13965893
30	353255	318457	34798	693726	679619
8284	2924240	2078449	845790	10278223	9712851

表 10－8 续表 Continued

指标	Indicators	损益与分配	
		税金及附加 Tax and Extra Charge	管理费用 Management Cost
批发业合计	**Wholesale Trade**	**527374**	**2369774**
#国有控股	State－holding	301413	145879
按注册类型分	**Grouped by Registration Type**		
内资企业	Domestic Funded Enterprises	495006	2108175
国有企业	State－Owned Enterprises	246354	47427
集体企业	Collective－Owned Enterprises		
股份合作企业	Share Cooperative Enterprises	30	892
有限责任公司	Limited Liability Corporations	96532	340735
股份有限公司	Share－holding Corporations Ltd.	5269	59085
私营企业	Private Enterprises	146545	1659672
港、澳、台商投资企业	Hong Kong, Macao and Taiwan Funded Enterprises	7455	75062
外商投资企业	Foreign Funded Enterprises	24914	186538
按行业分	**Grouped by Sector**		
农畜产品批发	Agricultural and Livestock Products	3961	27307
食品、饮料及烟草制品批发	Food, Beverages and Tobaccos	251466	115028
#烟草制品批发	Tobacco	245411	46062
纺织、服装及日用品批发	Textile, Garments and Daily Consumer Articles	30708	560389
#服装批发	Garments	8692	140201
家用视听设备批发	Household Audiovisual Equipment	1507	6335
日用家电批发	Household Appliances	9167	84000
文化、体育用品及器材批发	Culture, Sports Appliances and Equipments	8403	142971
医药及医疗器材批发	Medicines and Medical Appliance	8090	86031
矿产品、建材及化工产品批发	Mineral Products, Building Materials, Chemical Products	180678	898174
#石油及制品批发	Petroleum and Related Products	31176	74563
金属及金属矿批发	Metal and Metallic Ore	63674	320902
机械设备、五金交电及电子产品	Machine Equipments, Hardware, Electric Appliances, Electronic Equipment	34603	462098
#汽车及零配件批发	Automobile and Parts	13319	124953
摩托车及零配件批发	Motorcycle and Parts	476	983
其他批发	Others	9292	69138

单位：万元(10000 yuan)

Profit, Loss and Distribution			工资福利与税金 Wages, Welfare and Tax	
财务费用 Financial Expenses	营业利润 Business Profits	利润总额 Total Profits	本年应付职工薪酬总额 Total Employee Compensation Payable	本年应交增值税总额 Total Value-added Taxes Payable
608497	**4474150**	**5005983**	**2512116**	**1565544**
-11331	1175605	1223291	163180	381955
551759	4080226	4557077	2034446	1363134
3	614	636	564	592
45963	1915341	2011614	497673	521616
27307	28297	36119	58441	13093
504456	1832769	2202859	1421519	752565
12927	-54695	-49723	95428	21215
43811	448618	498630	382242	181196
36249	-28909	-19338	22349	11720
-8925	382669	414445	130077	117828
-26906	300010	300280	54841	73971
96344	613584	698812	732517	187646
50415	366174	386392	149657	48698
-3625	10993	10635	26643	10037
-4292	47317	48428	233961	53326
4730	224504	236687	155268	49376
16272	150716	166174	89576	71993
473895	2173832	2458238	692552	865747
280641	638422	746365	239488	214617
-29459	669344	746918	612584	224025
-25640	-28151	18	267696	94981
475	7007	7600	1849	1370
19329	282936	297791	68377	36776

表10-9 限额以上零售贸易业主要财务指标（2022年）
Main Financial Indicators of Retail Trade Above Designated Size（2022）

指标	Indicators	年末资产负债		
		流动资产合计 Current Funds	#存货 Inventories	固定资产原价 Original Value of Fixed Assets
零售业总计	**Total**	**6481150**	**1729993**	**1592886**
#国有控股	State – holding	363931	71714	113573
按注册类型分	**Grouped by Registration Type**			
内资企业	Domestic Funded Enterprises	5433624	1407250	965777
国有企业	State – Owned Enterprises	13072	364	1508
集体企业	Collective – Owned Enterprises	6204	797	818
股份合作企业	Share Cooperative Enterprises	7636	1056	5877
联营企业	Joint – owned Enterprises	1979	438	938
有限责任公司	Limited Liability Corporations	1519402	372477	209753
股份有限公司	Share – holding Corporations Ltd.	77147	8497	25290
私营企业	Private Enterprises	3808184	1023622	721593
港、澳、台商投资企业	Hong Kong, Macao and Taiwan Funded Enterprises	584663	112373	259037
外商投资企业	Foreign Funded Enterprises	462863	210370	368073
按行业分	**Grouped by Sector**			
综合零售	Comprehensive Retail	1131207	112509	709301
#百货零售	General Merchandise	408637	27131	366220
超级市场零售	Super Market	705838	82860	338400
食品、饮料及烟草制品专门零售	Food, Beverages and Tobaccos	319994	62803	56115
纺织、服装及日用品专门零售	Textile, Garments and Articles for Daily Use	431660	235275	34693
文化、体育用品及器材专门零售	Culture, Sports Appliances and Equipments	191021	60080	40172
医药及医疗器材专门零售	Medicines and Medical Appliance	214990	67103	13383
汽车、摩托车、燃料及零配件专	Automobile, Motorcycles, Fuels and Parts	2269405	740940	595226
#汽车新车零售	New Automobiles	1949366	671555	483283
汽车旧车零售	Used Automobiles	107562	43685	33
家用电器及电子产品专门零售	Household Appliances and Electronic Products	384806	62152	18741
五金、家具及室内装修材料专门	Hardware, Furniture and Decoration Materials	58578	13148	62949
无店铺及其他零售	Non – shop and Others	1479490	375984	62306
按经营方式分组	**Grouped by Management Method**			
#独立商店	Sole Shop	4224417	1251635	1120413
连锁商店总店	Chain General Shop	632421	87248	196509
连锁直营店	Regular Chain Store	391609	53690	99719
连锁加盟店	Franchise Chain Store	2814	1400	336
按零售业态分组	**Grouped by Retail Sale Line**			
超市	Supermarket	724902	85729	340951
百货店	Special Shop	482892	33274	376801
购物中心	Shopping Mall	14445	5331	1390
专业店	Special Sale Shop	2016674	646176	487440
便利店	Convenience Shop	22338	6131	4751

单位：万元(10000 yuan)

Total Assets and Liabilities at the Year – end				损益与分配 Profit, Loss and Distribution	
本年折旧 Depreciation in This year	资产合计 Total Asset	负债合计 Total Liabilities	所有者权益 Creditors' Equity	营业收入 Business Revenue	营业成本 Business Costs
93456	**9077708**	**6429850**	**2656194**	**17363811**	**14972474**
5195	871414	402659	468755	1281694	1153414
63674	7304222	5328417	1976258	13944674	11998187
59	25326	22172	3154	14547	12660
45	6630	3463	3167	56218	53777
300	26120	12182	13938	39543	33420
61	3059	662	2397	15263	13485
14428	2317123	1544986	772170	3657109	3163953
1083	131855	102931	28924	445434	441961
47698	4794111	3642021	1152509	9716560	8278932
9835	880236	436629	443606	1901495	1698085
19946	893250	664804	236330	1517643	1276202
26907	2028939	1126176	902763	2117290	1731033
14891	887815	458514	429301	857700	711488
11491	1116828	643986	472843	1221829	988000
3764	391629	275617	116011	510332	438340
4992	494872	401073	93484	837918	646756
2012	235314	159107	76208	278336	194710
901	236609	196032	40660	572489	501777
44017	3254728	2390855	863617	8825567	8152019
37086	2591025	2018928	571841	7269001	6717895
6	108176	58752	49425	275164	265000
1684	485419	360994	124425	769493	699734
2923	103894	134589	-30695	100947	79528
6256	1846304	1385407	469722	3351439	2528577
70176	5902219	4165773	1736982	12371011	10887963
8369	838228	503417	334811	1055759	854889
2797	655104	496616	158489	1023496	951884
41	3077	3848	-771	17269	15404
11708	1144594	669729	474865	1255117	1015278
15198	975529	496168	479362	908389	754064
120	17677	14965	2712	33984	32755
32285	2828751	2145320	683258	6196264	5575683
559	30762	26662	4100	67818	59248

表 10 – 9 续表 Continued

指标	Indicators	损益与分配 税金及附加 Tax and Extra Charge	管理费用 Management Cost
零售业总计	**Total**	**64637**	**506370**
#国有控股	State – holding	6645	13051
按注册类型分	**Grouped by Registration Type**		
内资企业	Domestic Funded Enterprises	41895	426053
国有企业	State – Owned Enterprises	37	1087
集体企业	Collective – Owned Enterprises	41	469
股份合作企业	Share Cooperative Enterprises	85	3105
联营企业	Joint – owned Enterprises	27	285
有限责任公司	Limited Liability Corporations	11748	73305
股份有限公司	Share – holding Corporations Ltd.	509	-1015
私营企业	Private Enterprises	29449	348818
港、澳、台商投资企业	Hong Kong, Macao and Taiwan Funded Enterprises	12491	28149
外商投资企业	Foreign Funded Enterprises	10252	52168
按行业分	**Grouped by Sector**		
综合零售	Comprehensive Retail	19752	65186
#百货零售	General Merchandise	15415	32245
超级市场零售	Super Market	4264	30676
食品、饮料及烟草制品专门零售	Food, Beverages and Tobaccos	3362	24647
纺织、服装及日用品专门零售	Textile, Garments and Articles for Daily Use	1932	41729
文化、体育用品及器材专门零售	Culture, Sports Appliances and Equipments	1684	16119
医药及医疗器材专门零售	Medicines and Medical Appliance	1066	12712
汽车、摩托车、燃料及零配件专	Automobile, Motorcycles, Fuels and Parts	27758	187879
#汽车新车零售	New Automobiles	25007	172372
汽车旧车零售	Used Automobiles	157	1818
家用电器及电子产品专门零售	Household Appliances and Electronic Products	864	24244
五金、家具及室内装修材料专门	Hardware, Furniture and Decoration Materials	742	13969
无店铺及其他零售	Non – shop and Others	7479	119884
按经营方式分组	**Grouped by Management Method**		
#独立商店	Sole Shop	52568	349472
连锁商店总店	Chain General Shop	2531	33149
连锁直营店	Regular Chain Store	2102	9770
连锁加盟店	Franchise Chain Store	84	1411
按零售业态分组	**Grouped by Retail Sale Line**		
超市	Supermarket	4292	32529
百货店	Special Shop	15758	34251
购物中心	Shopping Mall	22	1480
专业店	Special Sale Shop	25193	166016
便利店	Convenience Shop	75	2820

单位：万元(10000 yuan)

Profit, Loss and Distribution			工资福利与税金 Wages, Welfare and Tax	
财务费用 Financial Expenses	营业利润 Business Profits	利润总额 Total Profits	本年应付职工薪酬总额 Total Employee Compensation Payable	本年应交增值税总额 Total Value-added Taxes Payable
73111	**234508**	**277364**	**671215**	**203952**
2545	52601	54338	44797	14311
60717	166672	201649	565857	165676
-51	49	49	4137	242
48	607	607	824	334
602	1205	1897	1270	679
6	2765	2762	338	227
20595	79131	86149	133856	41158
1472	-2970	-2955	5011	720
38046	85885	113139	420420	122315
2641	50211	56868	58249	17993
9754	17625	18848	47109	20283
3336	56653	59643	116537	27519
1824	42022	43191	24578	11012
1229	16553	18423	89250	16368
2920	15564	16728	31621	4369
2793	-503	2370	53266	13039
-1974	-2559	-2027	30288	5088
1943	9057	10317	34099	8592
42007	91626	110268	248091	70614
31530	58211	75899	214814	55065
1697	-11366	-11265	11361	1515
3124	-4406	-2578	28084	6695
3241	-8015	-8284	9008	1670
15722	77091	90927	120222	66365
48728	217881	245843	427868	135920
-2757	26248	25735	87914	10203
3626	-20652	-19928	30642	5032
3	-135	-125	715	302
1471	14875	17060	92780	16498
2405	52395	53541	25952	11858
313	-1522	-1506	1191	-75
24130	68081	77582	213150	58729
354	-1772	-1823	4141	187

表10-10　限额以上批发零售贸易业主要商品分类销售额（2022年）
Sales of Wholesale and Retail Trade Above Designed Size by Category of Commodities（2022）

单位：万元(10000 yuan)

类　别	Category	合　计 Total	批　发 Wholesale	零　售 Retail
粮油食品类	Food, Beverage, Tabacco and Liquor	9142702	7405592	1737110
#粮油类	Grain and Oil	3094187	2751561	342626
饮料类	Beverage	655561	528460	127101
烟酒类	Tobacco and Liquor	2655231	2371065	284166
服装鞋帽、针、纺织品类	Garments, Shoes, Hats Knitwear and Textile	14875087	11929243	2945845
#服装类	Garments	8355363	5916639	2438724
鞋帽类	Shoes and Hats	1331269	1042528	288741
针、纺织品类	Knitwear and Textile	5188455	4970076	218379
化妆品类	Cosmetics	532448	195855	336593
金银珠宝类	Jewelry	461242	210971	250271
日用品类	Articles for Daily Use	7948982	7348507	600475
五金、电料类	Hardware and Electrical Appliances	3707082	3656146	50936
体育、娱乐用品类	Recreation and Sports Articles	692938	514977	177961
书报杂志类	Books and Newspapers	177199	93398	83801
电子出版物及音像制品类	Electronic Publications and Audio－video Products	46426	45210	1215
家用电器和音像器材类	Household Appliances and Audio－video Equipments	9035436	8133096	902340
中西药品类	Medicines	2681776	2098600	583176
文化办公用品类	Culture and Office Articles	6404157	5924795	479362
家具类	Furniture	1932835	1786401	146434
通讯器材类	Telecommunication Appliances	2230889	1911869	319020
煤炭及制品类	Coal and Coal Products	33166988	33166988	
木材及制品类	Timber and Timber Products	14090621	14090621	
石油及制品类	Petroleum and Products	26679571	25176520	1503051
化工材料及制品类	Chemical Materials and Products	98887145	98883146	3999
金属材料类	Metal Materials	157813528	157800961	12567
建筑及装潢材料类	Materials for Construction and Decoration	7158683	7082619	76064
机电产品及设备类	Mechanical and Electrical Equipments	8938462	8911098	27364
汽车类	Automobile	24048089	16324855	7723234
种子饲料类	Seeds and Forage	971028	971028	
棉麻土畜类	Cotton and Flax Products	1593918	1593918	

表10-11 住宿餐饮业单位数和从业人员数(2022年)
Number of Units and Employees of Catering Trade and Hotel（2022）

指标	Indicators	法人企业数（个）Number of Corporations(unit)	从业人数（人）Number of Employees(person)
总计	**Total**	**797**	**47219**
住宿业	**Hotel**	**372**	**22826**
#国有控股	State－holding	33	3628
按登记注册类型分组	Grouped by Registration Type		
内资企业	Domestic Funded Enterprises	353	20536
国有企业	State－Owned Enterprises	2	80
集体企业	Collective－Owned Enterprises	1	
股份合作企业	Share Cooperative Enterprises	1	68
有限责任公司	Limited Liability Corporations	63	5898
股份有限公司	Share－holding Corporations Ltd.	4	265
私营企业	Private Enterprises	282	14225
港、澳、台商投资企业	Hong Kong, Macao and Taiwan Funded Enterprises	5	1085
外商投资企业	Foreign Funded Enterprises	14	1205
按行业分	Grouped by Sector		
旅游饭店	Tour Hotel	148	15605
一般旅馆	Common Hotel	211	7036
餐饮业	**Catering Trade**	**425**	**24393**
#国有控股	State－holding	5	322
按登记注册类型分组	Grouped by Registration Type		
内资企业	Domestic Funded Enterprises	415	23619
国有企业	State－Owned Enterprises		
集体企业	Collective－Owned Enterprises		
股份合作企业	Share Cooperative Enterprises	1	
有限责任公司	Limited Liability Corporations	32	2315
股份有限公司	Share－holding Corporations Ltd.	1	37
私营企业	Private Enterprises	381	21267
港、澳、台商投资企业	Hongkong, Macao and Taiwan Funded Enterprises	1	210
外商投资企业	Foreign Funded Enterprises	9	564
按行业分	Grouped by Sector		
正餐服务业	Dinner Services	367	20207
快餐服务业	Snack Services	20	1181
饮料及冷饮服务业	Beverage Services	10	852
餐饮配送及外卖送餐服务	food catering	20	1591

表10-12 星级住宿业和限额以上餐饮业经营情况(2022年)
Main Operation Indicators of Catering Trade and Star-rated Hotel（2022）

指标	Indicators	营业额 Business Revenue	其中	
			客房收入 Room Rate Revenue	餐费收入 Catering Revenue
总计	**Total**	**1339402**	**354761**	**868338**
住宿业	**Hotel**	**618927**	**318890**	**211410**
#国有控股	State – holding	90081	37588	39197
按登记注册类型分组	Grouped by Registration Type			
内资企业	Domestic Funded Enterprises	548466	290590	180252
国有企业	State – Owned Enterprises	4804	1908	617
集体企业	Collective – Owned Enterprises	1991	177	99
股份合作企业	Share Cooperative Enterprises	915	337	551
有限责任公司	Limited Liability Corporations	153959	75854	56389
股份有限公司	Share – holding Corporations Ltd.	6423	3371	1434
私营企业	Private Enterprises	380374	208943	121162
港、澳、台商投资企业	Hong Kong, Macao and Taiwan Funded Enterprises	35098	10019	19781
外商投资企业	Foreign Funded Enterprises	35363	18282	11377
按行业分	Grouped by Sector			
旅游饭店	Tour Hotel	403616	161919	173284
一般旅馆	Common Hotel	210999	154177	37104
餐饮业	**Catering Trade**	**720475**	**35871**	**656929**
#国有控股	State – holding	7367	1249	6109
按登记注册类型分组	Grouped by Registration Type			
内资企业	Domestic Funded Enterprises	697594	30657	640744
国有企业	State – Owned Enterprises			
集体企业	Collective – Owned Enterprises			
股份合作企业	Share Cooperative Enterprises			
有限责任公司	Limited Liability Corporations	69385	5239	62146
股份有限公司	Share – holding Corporations Ltd.	829	622	198
私营企业	Private Enterprises	627379	24796	578399
港、澳、台商投资企业	Hongkong, Macao and Taiwan Funded Enterprises	5449	2073	2811
外商投资企业	Foreign Funded Enterprises	17433	3141	13375
按行业分	Grouped by Sector			
正餐服务业	Dinner Services	595164	35244	545018
快餐服务业	Snack Services	30927		30195
饮料及冷饮服务业	Beverage Services	43742		41261
餐饮配送及外卖送餐服务	food catering	38947	627	30239

单位：万元(10000 yuan)

of Which			年末餐饮营业面积（平方米）Business Area of Catering in the Year-end (sq.m)	年末拥有床位数（个）Hold Beds in the Year-end (bed)	年末拥有餐位数（位）Hold Seat of Catering in the Year-end (unit)
#通过公共网络实现的餐费收入 Catering Revenue by Internet	商品销售收入 Commodity Sales Revenue	其他收入 Others			
28653	**27670**	**88633**	**2547241**	**108449**	**359928**
3532	**12232**	**76395**	**1633411**	**99269**	**131919**
450	1822	11475	268433	8352	16952
2318	10710	66915	1457449	91474	120741
	1	2278	13543	377	730
		1715	10320	158	250
2		27	2000	169	660
587	2691	19025	346455	16231	22524
1	24	1595	7305	1738	1316
1729	7994	42275	1077826	72801	95261
52	1209	4089	47189	2604	3272
1161	313	5391	128773	5191	7906
3319	10617	57796	932692	39892	71424
144	1605	18113	679553	56943	58598
25121	**15439**	**12237**	**913830**	**9180**	**228009**
		10	17659	1247	1570
25121	15242	10952	886386	8158	223092
1611	561	1438	90867	2618	17865
		10	11059	150	420
23510	14681	9504	784460	5390	204807
	50	515	19333	442	1238
	146	771	8111	580	3679
20127	6750	8152	874251	8083	216597
149	574	158	13071		3711
4407	775	1706	14118		3128
352	5966	2116	6530	1097	2390

表10-13 部分年份限额以上批发零售贸易业主要财务指标
Main Financial Indicators of Wholesale and Retail Trade Above Designed Size of Partial Years

单位：亿元（100million yuan）

指标	Indicators	2018	2019	2020	2021	2022
营业收入	Operating Revenue	18242. 90	22916. 50	26179. 40	36270. 42	41927. 76
营业成本	Operating Costs	17441. 30	21909. 00	25025. 20	34789. 40	40469. 50
营业税金及附加	Tax and Extra Charge	40. 10	41. 80	42. 40	55. 02	59. 20
其他业务利润	Profits from Other Business	32. 30	20. 10	20. 60	34. 46	33. 61
管理费用	Management Cost	154. 10	192. 20	198. 30	264. 53	287. 61
财务费用	Financial Expenses	66. 40	69. 30	73. 50	82. 00	68. 16
利润总额	Total Profits	259. 90	343. 30	407. 40	552. 78	528. 33
资产总计	Total Assets	6252. 60	7904. 10	9446. 30	12056. 37	14517. 17
#流动资产	Current Assets	5354. 40	6699. 40	8149. 40	10270. 66	12406. 84
#存货	Inventory	620. 70	732. 60	900. 20	1167. 06	1260. 01
负债合计	Total Liabilities	4941. 60	6049. 30	7537. 60	9360. 95	11581. 34
所有者权益合计	Total Owner's Equities	1310. 90	1623. 80	1897. 90	2565. 37	3003. 61
应付职工薪酬	Employee Compensation Payable	175. 50	213. 80	211. 30	271. 47	318. 33

表10-14 部分年份星级住宿业及限额以上餐饮业主要财务指标
Main Financial Indicators of Catering Trade Above Designated Size and Star-rated Hotel in Partial Years

单位：亿元（100million yuan）

指标	Indicators	2018	2019	2020	2021	2022
营业收入	Prime Operating Revenue	88. 60	99. 40	92. 40	119. 26	127. 41
营业成本	Operating Costs	36. 30	42. 60	42. 90	58. 54	64. 30
销售费用	Business Expenses	27. 60	31. 90	0. 90	35. 90	34. 74
税金及附加	Tax and Associate Charge	1. 10	1. 10	1. 20	1. 09	1. 18
管理费用	Management Cost	22. 80	25. 80	24. 50	29. 65	32. 57
财务费用	Financial Expenses	4. 20	6. 30	4. 80	5. 22	4. 99
利润总额	Total Profits	-0. 70	-7. 20	-6. 20	-9. 63	-4. 14
资产总计	Total Assets	197. 10	250. 40	261. 90	282. 60	291. 58
#流动资产	Current Assets	75. 90	93. 30	106. 80	119. 11	128. 86
负债合计	Total Liabilities	181. 50	224. 70	241. 10	264. 13	272. 64
所有者权益合计	Total Owner's Equities	15. 60	24. 40	21. 10	18. 85	18. 18
应付职工薪酬	Employee Compensation Payable	24. 60	27. 00	24. 30	32. 08	33. 54

表10-15 亿元以上商品交易市场成交情况(2022年)
Basic Statistics of Commodity Exchange Market with Total Sale Over 100 Million Yuan（2022）

单位：万元(10000 yuan)

指标	Indicators	摊位个数(个) Number of Stalls (unit)	总成交额 Transaction Volume
总计	**Total**	**39089**	**22965487**
粮油、食品类	Grain and Oil, Foodstuff	18231	6386145
#粮油类	Grain and Oil	634	357360
肉禽蛋类	Meat. Poultry and Egg	1881	893577
水产品类	Aquatic Product	7670	3029255
蔬菜类	Garden Stuff	5131	1200668
干鲜果品类	Dry Fruit and Fresh Fruit	1454	675240
饮料类	Beverage	87	61256
烟酒类	Tabacco and Liquor	327	242279
服装鞋帽、针、纺织品类	Garments, Shoes, Hats Knitwear and Textile	5858	470781
服装类	Garments	4298	392178
鞋帽类	Shoes, Hats	436	50425
针、纺织品类	Knitwear and Textile	1124	28178
化妆品类	Cosmetics	106	3355
日用品类	Articles for Daily Use	1711	219779
五金、电料类	Hardware and Electrical Appliances	1076	459389
体育、娱乐用品类	Recreation and Sports Articles	60	470
书报杂志类	Books and Newspapers	5	8
电子出版物及音像制品类	Electronic Publications and Audio－video Products		
家用电器和音像器材类	Household Appliances and Audio－video Equipments	122	20112
中西药品类	Medicines		
文化办公用品类	Culture and Office Articles	428	41615
家具类	Furniture	1276	150781
通讯器材类	Telecommunication Appliances	173	25018
煤炭及制品类	Coal and Products		
木材及制品类	Timber and Timber Products	153	30403
石油及制品类	Petroleum and Products		
化工材料及制品类	Chemical Materials and Products	4159	10085402
金属材料类	Metal Materials	1040	2323595
建筑及装潢材料类	Materials for Construction and Decoration	3062	1327059
机电产品及设备类	Mechanical and Electrical Equipments	125	17387
汽车类	Automobile	440	1047577
种子饲料类	Seed and Feedstuff		
棉麻类	Cotton and Flax Products	11	230
其他类	Others	638	52836

表10-16 规模（限额）以上服务业企业主要经济指标(2022年)
Main Economic Indicators of Service Enterprises Above Designated Size（2022）

指标	Indicators	企业数（个）Number of Enterprises (unit)	#亏损企业 Loss-making Enterpris	从业人员数（人）Number of employees (person)	资产总计 Total Asset
总 计	**Total**	**14796**	**4536**	**1872873**	**785371122**
#国有控股企业	State-holding Enterprises	777	186	175343	497374908
按注册类型分	**Grouped by Registration Type**				
内资企业	Domestic Funded Enterprises	14179	4393	1764049	478664077
国有企业	State-Owned Enterprises	78	11	16646	6179489
集体企业	Collective-Owned Enterprises	21	3	599	47003
股份合作企业	Share Cooperative Enterprises	34	8	2610	11971047
联营企业	Limited Liability Corporations	8	1	92	445284
有限责任公司	Share-holding Corporations Ltd.	1596	473	413160	111864456
股份有限公司	Private Enterprises	138	34	69295	225980343
私营企业	Private enterprises	12274	3851	1259738	122100419
其他企业	Other enterprises	30	12	1909	76036
港澳台商投资企业	Hongkong, Macao and Taiwan Funded	220	47	33869	21257521
外商投资企业	Foreign-invested enterprises	397	96	74955	285449523
按行业分	**Grouped by Sector**				
批发和零售业	Wholesale and retail trade	9714	2924	261644	145171742
交通运输、仓储和邮政业	Transport, storage and postal service	1291	307	100628	24142324
住宿和餐饮业	Accommodation and catering industry	855	451	47040	2915837
信息传输、软件和信息技术服务业	Information transmission, Software and Information technology industry	344	86	62411	5336808
金融业	Financial sector	140	27	93268	572625342
房地产业	Real Estate industry	281	100	84387	7373449
租赁和商务服务业	Rental and business services sector	1177	368	1102666	14219231
科学研究和技术服务业	Scientific research, technical services industry	455	61	56219	8283358
水利、环境和公共设施管理业	Irrigation works, environment and public facilities management	50	18	10459	2159456
居民服务、修理和其他服务业	Resident, Repairs and Other services	174	59	28850	582659
教育	Education	50	18	1962	87407
卫生和社会工作	Hygiene and Social work	88	39	13360	1046941
文化、体育和娱乐业	Civilization, sports and entertainment industry	177	78	9979	1426568
公共管理、社会保障和社会组织	Public management, The social security and Social organization				

注：房地产业不包括房地产开发经营.限上服务业企业包含了批发和零售、住宿和餐饮业。
Note:Real Estate excludes Real estate development and management. Wholesale, retail, accommodation and catering ware included above designated size.

单位：万元(10000 yuan)

负债合计 Total Liabilities	所有者权益合计 Crediters' Equity	营业收入 Business Revernue	营业成本 Business Costs	营业税金及附加 Tax and Extra Charge	增值税 Value Added Tax	三项费用 Three Costs	应付职工薪酬 Employee Compensation Payable	营业利润 Business Profits	利润总额 Total Profits
698044259	**87996933**	**510479499**	**477683896**	**970669**	**4015132**	**20398434**	**19111926**	**14041073**	**15047588**
451676888	45655609	91854141	80050822	485161	1532726	5081388	4243938	7192945	7344398
426015249	53311681	452889587	429252935	828987	3166157	15716673	16056491	9109467	10047529
3944744	2231868	4217412	3513704	248746	87590	118775	230082	380924	381700
19994	27009	82751	70113	338	728	10119	7670	3562	3691
11206763	764284	600339	381004	2297	7258	109722	83572	107988	105158
434348	10936	798257	796770	302	776	1233	1186	1252	3107
91219042	21454663	122413694	116941964	217105	1021802	3600222	4591079	2623474	2918435
218760475	7219869	25360491	20258607	88976	531975	2052273	1467053	3098219	3150381
100380976	21575890	299336615	287239088	270976	1514333	9797417	9644608	2892368	3481783
48907	27162	80028	51685	246	1695	26914	31243	1679	3276
10535743	10721772	12392701	10803102	37676	55622	894078	609741	1032507	1054850
261493266	23963479	45197211	37627858	104006	793353	3787682	2445693	3899099	3945208
115813382	30036083	419277635	404695021	592011	1769496	10640803	3183331	4708658	5283347
9081007	15061316	26178918	23957584	34529	156825	1242168	1690448	1716297	1851758
2726430	181755	1274125	642954	11832	19536	723581	335363	−51871	−41383
2335116	3001692	4643288	3268810	19196	124967	820423	887530	612710	666409
545493418	27131923	31386420	20525832	145038	1123908	4500684	2928437	6060798	6039863
5224198	2149251	1512236	1123197	37133	58746	350613	571195	56139	115471
8683393	5535838	18289659	17266618	97568	503229	906901	7774955	256441	380783
4763598	3519759	5088184	3796710	17526	171405	737684	1124774	654467	681215
1820061	339394	254882	218779	2694	9744	88789	82457	−54446	−47980
392542	190117	1422380	1275065	7605	60427	102093	205052	78844	83125
65435	21972	71226	51840	165	1921	19801	29128	−374	−494
725526	321415	620981	445583	1837	1045	145164	196486	30670	36122
920152	506416	459564	415905	3534	13883	119729	102770	−27260	−647

表10-17 按行业分企业信息化及电子商务情况（2022年）
Enterprises Informatization and E-commerce by Industry（2022）

行业	Sector	企业数（个）Number of enterprises（unit）	期末使用计算机数（台）Number of computers used (Unit)
总 计	**Total**	**25623**	**1064799**
采矿业	Mining	13	213
制造业	Manufacturing	10116	599987
电力、热力、燃气及水生产和供应业	Electricity, heat, gas and water production and supply	124	13126
建筑业	Constructions	1506	63446
批发和零售业	Retail and Wholesale Industries	8684	160368
交通运输 、仓储和邮政业	Transportation, Storage and Post	1140	47153
住宿和餐饮业	Hoteling and Catering	769	13998
信息传输、软件和信息技术服务业	Information Transmission, Software and Information Technology Service	276	46090
房地产业	Real Estate Industry	1214	21814
租赁和商务服务业	Leasehold and Business Service	959	26460
科学研究和技术服务业	Scientific Research and Technology Service	384	49742
水利 、环境和公共设施管理业	Water Conservancy, Environment and Public Facility Manage	41	1560
居民服务 、修理和其他服务业	Residential Service, Repairing & Maintenance and Other Ser	135	4835
教育	Education	26	2022
卫生和社会工作	Health Care and Social Work	75	9485
文化 、体育和娱乐业	Culture, Sports and Entertainment	161	4500

注：（1）分行业企业数根据《信息通信技术应用和数字化转型情况》年度调查结果汇总。
（2）有电子商务交易活动的企业是指通过互联网开展电子商务销售或电子商务采购的企业（下表同）。

Notes:(1)The number of enterprises by industry is summarized according to the annual Information and communication technology application and Digital transformation.
(2)Enterprises with e–commerce transactions refer to enterprises that carry out e–commerce sales or e–commerce procurement through the Internet (the same as the following table).

每百人使用计算机数(台) Number of computers used per 100 people (Unit)	企业拥有网站数(个) Number of websites (unit)	每百家企业拥有网站数(个) Number of websites owned by each hundred enterprises (unit)	有电子商务交易活动 (E-commerce transactions)		电子商务销售额(亿元) E-Commerce sales (100 million yuan)	电子商务采购额(亿元) E-Commerce procurement amount (100million yuan)
			企业数(个) Number of enterprises (unit)	比重(%) proportion(%)		
30. 0	**11811**	**46. 0**	**2627**	**10. 3**	**3926. 96**	**1376. 71**
33. 0	5	38. 0	1	7. 7	6. 66	
38. 0	6877	68. 0	1278	12. 6	919. 79	496. 35
92. 0	59	48. 0	6	4. 8	0. 02	8. 79
12. 0	460	31. 0	34	2. 3	0. 96	26. 02
74. 0	2335	27. 0	788	9. 1	2802. 81	794. 03
49. 0	463	41. 0	30	2. 6	62. 97	23. 75
30. 0	262	34. 0	338	44. 0	14. 17	0. 22
79. 0	317	115. 0	33	12. 0	26. 28	6. 88
22. 0	292	24. 0	11	0. 9	1. 03	0. 01
3. 0	303	32. 0	32	3. 3	79. 62	18. 23
90. 0	256	67. 0	13	3. 4	2. 75	0. 22
15. 0	24	59. 0	8	19. 5	0. 45	0. 13
17. 0	47	35. 0	11	8. 2	3. 75	2. 07
124. 0	13	50. 0	3	11. 5	0. 60	
72. 0	50	67. 0	5	6. 7	1. 01	
77. 0	48	30. 0	36	22. 4	4. 09	0. 02

表10-18 按地区分企业信息化和电子商务情况（2022年）
Enterprises Informatization and E-commerce by Region（2022）

地区	Region	企业数（个）Number of enterprises（unit）	期末使用计算机数（台）Number of computers used (Unit)
全市	**Total**	**25623**	**1064799**
海曙区	Haishu	2620	115334
江北区	Jiangbei	2130	72913
镇海区	Zhenhai	1979	63080
北仑区	Beilun	3010	159110
鄞州区	Yinzhou	4763	154073
奉化区	Fenghua	1291	38205
余姚市	Yuyao	2578	105410
慈溪市	Cixi	3516	209948
宁海县	Ninghai	1242	46780
象山县	Xiangshan	1403	40294
高新区	Gaoxin	1091	59652

每百人使用计算机数(台) Number of computers used per 100 people (Unit)	企业拥有网站数(个) Number of websites (unit)	每百家企业拥有网站数(个) Number of websites owned by each hundred enterprises (unit)	有电子商务交易活动 (E-commerce transactions)		电子商务销售额(亿元) E-Commerce sales (100 million yuan)	电子商务采购额(亿元) E-Commerce procurement amount (100 million yuan)
			企业数(个) Number of enterprises (unit)	比重(%) proportion(%)		
30.0	**11811**	**46.0**	**2627**	**10.3**	**3926.96**	**1376.71**
25.0	1429	55.0	323	12.3	212.84	37.48
25.0	754	35.0	224	10.5	862.16	321.74
32.0	871	44.0	171	8.6	568.13	328.12
31.0	1373	46.0	209	6.9	1001.21	282.22
28.0	2218	47.0	415	8.7	421.50	208.38
25.0	561	43.0	115	8.9	31.49	26.51
35.0	1257	49.0	333	12.9	43.82	6.84
40.0	1675	48.0	517	14.7	232.96	47.50
28.0	652	52.0	126	10.1	323.31	56.51
16.0	511	36.0	113	8.1	77.63	36.38
45.0	510	47.0	81	7.4	151.91	25.02

表10-19 批发业销售收入前20位企业（2022年）
The Top 20 Enterprises of Wholesales Trade at Sales Revenue（2022）

排名 No.	企业名称	Name of Corporation	所在区域	Location
1	浙江浙能富兴燃料有限公司	Zhejiang Zheneng Fuxing Fuel Co.,Ltd.	北仑区	Beilun
2	中基宁波集团股份有限公司	Zhongji Ningbo Group Co.,Ltd.	鄞州区	Yinzhou
3	远大能源化工有限公司	Yuanda Energy & Chemical Co.,Ltd.	北仑区	Beilun
4	浙江前程石化股份有限公司	Zhejiang Prospect Petrochemical Co.,Ltd.	高新区	Gaoxin
5	中海油（宁波）贸易有限公司	CNOOC (Ningbo) Trading Co.,Ltd	北仑区	Beilun
6	宁波美的联合物资供应有限公司	Ningbo Midea United Material Supply Co.,Ltd.	北仑区	Beilun
7	宁波丰铭金属材料有限公司	Ningbo Fengming Metal Materials Co., Ltd	北仑区	Beilun
8	中石化化工销售(宁波)有限公司	Sinopec Chemical Sales (Ningbo) Co., Ltd	镇海区	Zhenhai
9	中信金属宁波能源有限公司	CITIC Metal Ningbo Energy Co., Ltd	北仑区	Beilun
10	宁波则立贸易有限公司	Ningbo Zeli Trading Co.,Ltd	北仑区	Beilun
11	领克汽车销售有限公司	Lynk & Co Automobile Sales Co.,Ltd.	慈溪市	Cixi
12	宁波中拓供应链管理有限公司	Ningbo Zhongtuo Supply Chain Management Co.,Ltd	北仑区	Beilun
13	万华化学（宁波）能源贸易有限公司	Wanhua Chemical(Ningbo)Energy Trading Co.,Ltd	北仑区	Beilun
14	浙江美芝压缩机有限公司	Zhejiang Meizhi Compressor Co.,Ltd.	北仑区	Beilun
15	宁波邦普循环科技有限公司	Ningbo Bangpu Recycling Technology Co., Ltd	北仑区	Beilun
16	宁波敖晖贸易有限公司	Ningbo Aohui Trading Co.,Ltd.	北仑区	Beilun
17	宁波铭佑金属材料有限公司	Ningbo Mingyou Metal Materials Co.,Ltd	北仑区	Beilun
18	宁波海天同创实业有限公司	Ningbo Haitian Tongchuang Industrial Co., Ltd	北仑区	Beilun
19	淮北矿业集团大榭能源化工有限公司	Huaibei Mining Group Daxie Energy and Chemical Co., Ltd	北仑区	Beilun
20	中基石化有限公司	Zhongji Petrochemical Co., Ltd	鄞州区	Yinzhou

表10-20 零售业销售收入前20位企业（2022年）
The Top 20 Enterprises of Retail Trade at Sales Revenue（2022）

排名 No.	企业名称	Name of Corporation	所在区域	Location
1	三江购物俱乐部股份有限公司	Ningbo Sanjiang Shopping Mall Co.,Ltd.	海曙区	Haishu
2	中国石油天然气股份有限公司浙江宁波销售分公司	PetroChina Co.,Ltd. Zhejiang Ningbo Sales Branch	江北区	Jiangbei
3	特斯拉汽车销售服务(宁波)有限公司	Tesla automobile sales service (Ningbo) Co., Ltd	江北区	Jiangbei
4	锐力体育(浙江)有限公司	Ruili sports (Zhejiang) Co., Ltd	北仑区	Beilun
5	车淘淘(宁波)电子商务有限公司	Chetaotao (Ningbo) E－commerce Co., Ltd	余姚市	Yuyao
6	宁波博洋控股集团有限公司	Ningbo Boyang Holding Group Co., Ltd	海曙区	Haishu
7	宁波蔚来汽车销售服务有限公司	Ningbo Weilai Automobile Sales and Service Co., Ltd	海曙区	Haishu
8	宁波捷骏汽车销售服务有限公司	Ningbo Jiejun Automobile Sales Service Co.,Ltd.	鄞州区	Yinzhou
9	宁波利星汽车服务有限公司	Ningbo Lixing Automobile Service Co.,Ltd.	江北区	Jiangbei
10	京东五星电器集团宁波电器有限公司	JD Five Star Electrical Appliances Group Ningbo Electrical Appliances Co., Ltd	海曙区	Haishu
11	银泰百货宁波海曙有限公司	Intime Department Store Co.,Ltd. Ningbo Haishu	海曙区	Haishu
12	宁波宝恒汽车集团有限公司	Ningbo Baoheng Auto Sale & Service Co.,Ltd.	鄞州区	Yinzhou
13	宁波利之星汽车服务有限公司	Ningbo Lizhixing Automobile Service Co.,Ltd.	鄞州区	Yinzhou
14	宁波瑞星时光商业股份有限公司	Ningbo Ruixing time commerce Co., Ltd	鄞州区	Yinzhou
15	宁波太平鸟电子商务有限公司	Ningbo Peacebird E－commerce Co.,Ltd.	海曙区	Haishu
16	宁波良品互娱网络科技有限公司	Ningbo Liangpin Mutual Entertainment Network Technology Co., Ltd	北仑区	Beilun
17	杉井商业管理（宁波）有限公司	Sugii Commercial Management (Ningbo) Co.,Ltd.	海曙区	Haishu
18	宁波保税区宁兴优贝国际贸易有限公司	Ningbo Free Trade Zone Ningxing youbei International Trade Co., Ltd	北仑区	Beilun
19	宁波阪急商业有限公司	Ningbo Banji Commercial Co., Ltd	鄞州区	Yinzhou
20	宁波市康发汽车销售服务有限公司	Ningbo Kangfa Automobile Sales and Service Co., Ltd	鄞州区	Yinzhou

表10-21 星级住宿业营业收入前20位企业（2022年）
The Top 20 Enterprises of Hotel at Business Revenue（2022）

排名 No.	企业名称	Name of Corporation	所在区域	Location
1	宁波南苑投资发展有限公司	Ningbo Nanyuan Investment Development Co.,Ltd	鄞州区	Yinzhou
2	宁波南苑集团股份有限公司	Ningbo Nanyuan Group Co.,Ltd.	海曙区	Haishu
3	香格里拉大酒店（宁波）有限公司	Shangri–La Hotel (Ningbo) Co.,Ltd.	鄞州区	Yinzhou
4	宁波宁兴中基置业有限公司	Ningbo Ningxing Zhongji Real Estate Co.,Ltd	奉化区	Fenghua
5	宁波杭州湾新区世纪金源大饭店有限公司	Ningbo Hangzhou Bay New Area Century Jinyuan Hotel Co.,Ltd	慈溪市	Cixi
6	宁波华侨饭店有限公司	Ningbo Howard Johnson Hotel Co.,Ltd.	海曙区	Haishu
7	宁波太平洋大酒店有限公司	Ningbo Pacific Hotel Co.,Ltd	余姚市	Yuyao
8	天港酒店集团有限公司	Tiangang Hotel Group Co.,Ltd	海曙区	Haishu
9	宁波市钱湖国际会议中心开发有限公司	Ningbo Qianhu International Conference Center Development Co.,Ltd	鄞州区	Yinzhou
10	宁波东港波特曼大酒店有限公司	Ningbo Portman Hotel Co.,Ltd.	鄞州区	Yinzhou
11	象山半边山紫冠投资有限公司	Xiangshan Banbianshan Ziguan Investment Co.,Ltd	象山县	Xiangshan
12	宁波开元名都大酒店有限公司	Ningbo Kaiyuan Mingdu Hotel Co.,Ltd	鄞州区	Yinzhou
13	宁波影秀城酒店管理有限公司	Ningbo Yingxiucheng Hotel Management Co.,Ltd	北仑区	Beilun
14	宁波伯豪酒店管理有限公司	Ningbo Bohao Hotel Management Co., Ltd	海曙区	Haishu
15	宁波华茂教育文化投资有限公司	Ningbo Huamao education and culture Investment Co.,Ltd	鄞州区	Yinzhou
16	宁波钱湖酒店有限公司	Ningbo Qianhu Hotel Co.,Ltd	鄞州区	Yinzhou
17	慈溪市杭州湾大酒店有限公司	Cixi Hangzhou Bay Hotel Co.,Ltd.	慈溪市	Cixi
18	宁波九龙湖开元酒店有限公司	Ningbo Jiulong Lake Kaiyuan Hotel Co.,Ltd	镇海区	Zhenhai
19	宁波逸东酒店投资发展有限公司	Ningbo Yidong Hotel Investment Development Co.,Ltd.	鄞州区	Yinzhou
20	余姚辰茂河姆渡酒店有限公司	Yuyao Chenmao HemuduHotel Co.,Ltd	余姚市	Yuyao

表10-22 餐饮业营业收入前20位企业（2022年）
The Top 20 Enterprises of Catering Trade at Business Revenue（2022）

排名 No.	企业名称	Name of Corporation	所在区域	Location
1	宁波康喜乐嘉餐饮管理有限公司	Ningbo Kangxilejia Catering Management Co.,Ltd.	北仑区	Beilun
2	宁波海底捞餐饮管理有限公司	Ningbo Haidilao Restaurant Management Co.,Ltd.	海曙区	Haishu
3	慈溪白金汉爵投资有限公司	Cixi Platinum Hanjue Investment Co.,Ltd.	慈溪市	Cixi
4	瑞幸咖啡（宁波）有限公司	Ruixing coffee (Ningbo) Co.,Ltd	海曙区	Haishu
5	宁波市江徽美食餐饮有限公司	Ningbo Jianghui food and Beverage Co.,Ltd	海曙区	Haishu
6	宁波伯瑞特酒店有限公司	Ningbo Buruite Hotel Co.,Ltd	余姚市	Yuyao
7	宁波七欣天企业管理有限公司	Ningbo Qixintian Enterprise Management Co.,Ltd	海曙区	Haishu
8	宁波状元楼禧宴酒店管理有限公司	Ningbo Zhuangyuanlou Xiyan Hotel Management Co.,Ltd	鄞州区	Yinzhou
9	宁波石浦投资控股有限公司	Ningbo Shipu Investment Holding Co.,Ltd	高新区	Gaoxin
10	宁波老娘舅餐饮管理有限公司	Ningbo Laoniangjie Catering Management Co., Ltd	鄞州区	Yinzhou
11	宁波润家餐饮有限公司	Ningbo Runjia catering Co.,Ltd	镇海区	Zhenhai
12	宁波外婆家餐饮有限公司	My Grandmother's Home in Ningbo Catering Co.,Ltd.	海曙区	Haishu
13	余姚德悦盛宴大酒店有限公司	Yuyao Deyue Shengyan Hotel Co., Ltd	余姚市	Yuyao
14	宁波笑哈哈后勤服务有限公司	Ningbo Xiaohaha Logistics Service Co., Ltd	江北区	Jiangbei
15	慈溪市杭州湾环球酒店有限公司	Cixi Hangzhou Bay Global Hotel Co., Ltd	慈溪市	Cixi
16	宁海金海开元名都大酒店有限公司	Ninghai Jinhai Kaiyuan Mingdu Hotel Management Co.,Ltd.	宁海县	Ninghai
17	余姚市建标大酒店有限公司	Yuyao Jianbiao Hotel Co., Ltd	余姚市	Yuyao
18	慈溪市艾丽丝餐饮管理有限公司	Cixi Alice Catering Management Co., Ltd	慈溪市	Cixi
19	浙江竹林人家餐饮有限公司	Zhejiang Bamboo Country Food Co.,Ltd.	海曙区	Haishu
20	宁波新荣记餐饮管理有限公司	Ningbo Xinrongji Catering Management Co., Ltd	鄞州区	Yinzhou

表10-23 年成交额前20位交易市场（2022年）
The Top 20 Commodity Exchange Market with Transaction Volume（2022）

排名 No.	企业名称	Name of Corporation	所在区域	Location
1	余姚市中国塑料城	China Plastic Exchange Market (Yuyao)	余姚市	Yuyao
2	宁波镇海液体化工产品交易市场	Ningbo Zhenhai Liquid Chemical Products Market	镇海区	Zhenhai
3	宁波华东物资城	East China Material Market of Ningbo	鄞州区	Yinzhou
4	宁波市路林综合市场股份有限公司	Ningbo Lulin Comprehensive Market Co.,Ltd.	江北区	Jiangbei
5	宁波江北华东物资城浙甬市场开发有限公司	Ningbo Jiangbei East China Material City Zheyong Market Development Co., Ltd	江北区	Jiangbei
6	慈溪长三角市场群投资有限公司慈溪农贸城分公司	Cixi Yangtze River Delta market Group Investment Co., Ltd. Cixi farmer's Trade City Branch	慈溪市	Cixi
7	象山中心菜市场	Xiangshan Central Vegetable Market	象山县	Xiangshan
8	浙江象山水产城实业有限公司	Zhejiang Xiangshan Aquatic Product City Industrial Co.,Ltd.	象山县	Xiangshan
9	宁波市鄞州途众二手车交易市场	Ningbo Yinzhou Tuzhong Second－hand Car Trading Market	海曙区	Haishu
10	宁波市镇海厚恒物资城	Ningbo Zhenhai Houheng Material City	镇海区	Zhenhai
11	宁波保税区进出口葡萄酒市场	Ningbo Free Trade Zone Import & export wine market	北仑区	Beilun
12	慈溪市周巷副食品批发市场	Cixi Zhouxiang non staple food wholesale market	慈溪市	Cixi
13	宁波华东物资城王家弄市场	Wangjia Long Market of East China Material Market	鄞州区	Yinzhou
14	余姚海吉星农产品批发市场有限公司	Yuyao Haijixing agricultural products wholesale market Co., Ltd	余姚市	Yuyao
15	宁波市镇海泰来模具市场	Ningbo Zhenhai Tailai mould Market	镇海区	Zhenhai
16	宁波果品批发市场有限公司	Ningbo Fruit Wholesale Market Co., Ltd	海曙区	Haishu
17	余姚中国裘皮城	China Fur Exchange Market（Yuyao）	余姚市	Yuyao
18	宁波农副肉禽蛋批发市场有限公司	Ningbo Agricultural and sideline meat, poultry and egg wholesale market Co., Ltd	奉化区	Fenghua
19	宁波世纪轿车城	Ningbo Century Car City	鄞州区	Yinzhou
20	宁波蔬菜批发市场有限公司	Ningbo Vegetable Wholesale Market Co., Ltd	奉化区	Fenghua

主要统计指标解释

【社会消费品零售额】指各种经济类型的批发零售贸易业、餐饮业、制造业和其他行业对城乡居民和社会集团的消费品零售额。这个指标反映通过各种商品流通渠道向居民和社会集团供应的生活消费品来满足他们生活需要，是研究人民生活，社会消费品购买力、货币流通等问题的重要指标。社会消费品零售额包括：(1)售给城乡居民作为生活用的商品和修建房屋用的建筑材料；(2)售给社会集团的各种办公用品和公用消费品(3)售给 机关、团体、学校、部队、企业、事业单位的职工食堂和旅店(招待所)附设专门供本店旅客食用，不对外营业的食堂的各种食品、燃料；企业、单位和国有农场直接售给本单位职工和职工食堂的自己生产的产品；(4)售给部队干部、战士生活用的粮食、副食品、衣着品、日用品、燃料；(5)售给来华的外国人、华侨、港澳(台)同胞的消费品；(6)居民自费购买的中、西药品、中药材及医疗用品；(7)报社、 出版社直接售给居民和社会集团的报纸、图书、杂志、集邮公司出售的新、旧纪念邮票、特种邮票、首日封、集邮册、集邮工具等；(8)旧货寄售商店自购、自销部分的商品；(9)煤气公司、液化石油气站售给居民和社会集团的煤气灶具和罐装液化石油气；(10)农民售给非农业居民和社会集团的商品。不包括售给国民经济各部门企业、事业单位(包括国有经济的农场) 生产经营用的各种原材料、燃料、设备、工具等和售给批发零售贸易业、餐饮业作为转卖用的商品、旧货寄售商店受托寄售卖出的商品、服务业的营业收入、邮局出售邮票的收入、自来水、电力、煤气生产(供应)单位的产品供应收入，也不包括农民之间的商品销售。

【限额以上批发企业】指年销售额在2000万元及以上，并且年末从业人员在20人及以上的批发贸易企业。

【限额以上零售企业】指年销售额在500万元及以上，并且年末从业人员在60人及以上的零售企业。

【限额以上餐饮企业】指年销售额在200万元及以上，并且年末从业人员在40人及以上的餐饮企业。

【批发零售贸易业商品购、销、存总额】指以各种经济类型的批发、零售贸易业(不包括个体)为总体的商品购、销、存。

【商品购进总额】指从本企业(单位)以外的单位和个人购进(包括从国外直接进口)作为转卖或加工后转卖的商品。这个指标反映批发零售贸易业从国内、国外市场上购进商品的总量。商品购进总额包括：(1)从工农业生产者购进的商品；(2)从出版社、报社的出版发行部门购进的图书、杂志和报纸；(3)从各种经济类型的批发零售贸易企业（单位）购进的商品；(4)从其他单位购进的商品，如从机关、团体、企业单位购进的剩余物资，从餐饮业、服务业购进的商品，从海关、市场管理部门购进的缉私和没收的商品，从居民收购的废旧商品等；(5)从国(境)外直接进口的商品。不包括企业(单位)为自身经营用，和未通过买卖行为而收入的商品以及销售退回、商品升溢等。

【商品销售总额】指对本企业(单位)以外的单位和个人出售(包括对国(境)外直接出口)的商品。这个指标反映批发零售贸易业在国内市场上销售商品以及出口商品的总量。商品销售总额包括：(1)售给城乡居民和社会集团消费用的商品；(2)售给工业、农业、建筑业、运输邮电业、批发零售贸易业、餐饮业、服务业等作为生产、经营使用的商品；(3)售给批发零售贸易业作为转卖或加工后转卖的商品；(4)对国(境)外直接出口的商品。不包括：出售本企业(单位)自用的废旧包装用品，未通过买卖行为付出的商品，经本单位介绍，由买卖双方直接结算，本单位只收取手续费的业务，购货退出的商品以及商品损耗和损失等。

Explanatory Notes on Main Statistical Indicators

【Total Retail Sales of Consumer Goods】 refer to the sum of retail sales of consumer goods by the establishments in wholesale trade, retail sale trade, catering trade, manufacturing industry and other industries of different types of ownership, to urban and rural residents and social groups. This indicator is used to show the supply of consumer goods through various channels to households and institutions to meet their demands, and is therefore very important for the study of the issues on people's livelihood, on the purchasing power of consumer goods and on the circulation of money. The retail sales of consumer goods include: (1)commodities sold to urban and rural residents for residential use and building materials sold to them for the construction or repair of houses;(2)food and fuels sold to canteens of institutions, enterprises, schools, military units and to canteens of hotels and hostels that only serve their guests, and commodities produced by enterprises, institutions or state farms and sold directly to their employees or their canteens; (3)grain and non–staple food, clothing, daily articles and fuels sold to military personnel; (4)consumer goods sold to foreigners, overseas Chinese, and Chinese compatriots from Taiwan, Hong Kong and Macao during their stay in the mainland of China; (5)Chinese an d western medicines, herbs and medical facilities purchased by residents; (6)newspapers, books and magazines directly sold to residents and social groups by publishers, new and old commemorative stamps, special stamps, first day covers, stamp albums and other stamp collection articles sold by stamp companies; (7)consumer goods purchased and then sold by second–hand shops; (8)stoves and other heating facilities and liquified gas sold by gas companies to households and institutions; (9)commodities sold by farmers to non–agricultural residents and social groups. Excluded under this heading are: raw materials, fuels, equipment, tools sold to enterprises, institutions and state farms for production purpose; commodities sold to trade establishments for re–selling; commissioned sales at second–hand shops; operational income of urban public utilities; stamps sold at post offices; income of water, power, gas production and supply establishments from the supply of their products; and sales of commodities among farmers.

【Enterprises of Over–norm Wholesale Volume】 refers to wholesale trade enterprises that register an annual sales volume of over 20 million yuan RMB and a total year end staff of more than 20.

【Enterprises of Over–norm Retail Sales Volume】 refers to those that register an annual sales volume of over 5 million yuan RMB and a total year–end staff of more than 60.

【Catering Enterprises of Over–norm Sales Volume】 refers to those that register an annual sales volume of over 2 million yuan RMB and a total year–end staff of more than 40.

【Purchase, Sales and Stock of Commodities by Wholesale and Retail Trade】 refer to the purchase, sales and stock of commodities by wholesale and retail establishments of different ownership(excluding individual sellers).

【Total Purchases of Commodities】 refer to the purchases of commodities by the establishments from other establishments or individuals (including direct import from abroad) for the purpose of re–selling, either with or without further processing of the commodities purchased. This indicator is used to show the total value of purchases of commodities by wholesale and retail establishments from domestic and overseas markets. The total purchases include:(1)agricultural and industrial products purchased from producers; (2)books, magazines and newspapers purchased from distribution departments of the publishers; (3) commodities purchased from wholesale and retail establishments; (4)commodities purchased from other units, such as surplus materials purchased from government agencies, enterprises or institutions, commodities purchased from catering and service establishments, confiscated goods purchased from customs authorities or market management agencies, second–hand goods and wastes purchased from residents; and (5)commodities directly imported from abroad. Excluded are commodities purchased by establishments(units)for use in their own business operation, commodities obtained without buying or selling procedures, rejected commodities, etc.

【Total Sales of Commodities】 refer to selling of commodities by the establishments to other establishments and individuals(including direct export) . This indicator is used to show the total value of sales of commodities at domestic markets and export. The total sales include: (1)commodities sold to urban and rural residents and social groups for their consumption; (2)commodities so ld to establishments in industry, agriculture, construction, transportation, post and telecommunications, wholesale and retail trades, catering trade and public utility for their production and operation; (3)commodities sold to wholesale an d retail establishments for re–selling, with or without further processing; and (4)commodities for direct export to other countries. Excluded are selling of waste packaging materials used by the establishments(units) themselves, commodities transferred without buying or selling procedures, commission income from brokerage in transactions whose settlement is directly handled by buyers and sellers , rejected commodities in the purchase, loss in commodities, etc.

NINGBO 2023 Statistical Yearbook

11 CHAPTER

第十一篇

对外经济、旅游

FOREIGN TRADE AND TOURISM

对外经济、旅游
Foreign Trade and Tourism

主要统计指标
Major Statistics Indicators

2022年自营进出口总额	Total Direct Import and Export	519049837	万美元	USD 10000
比上年增长	Increase Over Last Year	3.3	%	
2022年自营出口总额	Total Exports	12373855	万美元	USD 10000
比上年增长	Increase Over Last Year	4.9	%	
2022自营进口总额	Total Imports	6675982	万美元	USD 10000
比上年增长	Increase Over Last Year	0.5	%	
2022年新签合同数	Number of Projects of Signed Contracts	410	个	unit
比上年增长	Increase Over Last Year	-27.3	%	
2022年实际利用外资金额	Value of Foreign Captial Actually Used	372658	万美元	USD 10000
比上年增长	Increase Over Last Year	13.8	%	
2022年接待过夜境外旅游者人数	Number of Received Oversea Tourists	32467	人	person
2022年旅游创汇收入	Foreign Exchange Earnings	990	万美元	USD 10000
2022年国内旅游总收入	Earning From Domestic Tourism	775.6	亿元	100 million yuan
比上年增长	Increase Over Last Year	-5.3	%	

表11-1 历年对外经济贸易基本情况
Basic Statistics on Foreign Economy and Trade Over the Years

单位：万美元(USD 10000)

年份 Year	外商直接投资情况 Foreign Direct Investments			自营进出口 Self-supporting Import and Export		口岸进出口 Import and Export of Port	
	新批项目数(个) Number of Newly Approved Projects(unit)	合同利用外资 Contractual Utilization of Foreign Capital	实际利用外资 Foreign Capital Actually Used	进出口 Total	出口 Exports	进出口 Total	出口 Exports
1980	1	5	5				
1981							
1982						14917	10963
1983						17683	12173
1984	8	850	21			26336	16102
1985	11	682	359	1029	389	45474	23521
1986	7	447	500	2079	540	54690	34432
1987	13	4341	429	2061	791	52493	29999
1988	62	4002	689	14766	11458	78717	39155
1989	64	6295	1758	22024	18005	110175	53615
1990	89	5624	2197	29840	27962	125527	63253
1991	184	17460	2680	57339	47532	219638	87101
1992	636	156725	11497	99072	78389	260387	101699
1993	1015	107152	34455	169434	110824	328871	120138
1994	680	77149	35812	251462	174992	375919	168340
1995	496	114630	39909	385335	226825	521501	232789
1996	322	87838	50162	418573	233003	586140	252248
1997	260	45849	55408	460896	293332	663807	311848
1998	281	51198	50329	421237	296386	610109	339904
1999	364	65660	52035	500898	347721	774194	411200
2000	550	95151	62186	754065	516781	1372547	703357
2001	806	195519	87446	889202	624500	1613794	869768
2002	1017	320024	124696	1227343	816304	2145755	1232723
2003	1209	344382	172727	1880962	1207398	3394193	1888206
2004	1081	413633	210322	2611222	1668967	5157576	2664100
2005	873	421015	231079	3349427	2223256	6749471	3614462
2006	1034	442746	243018	4221188	2877052	8649306	4958297
2007	854	450107	250518	5649909	3825509	11176033	6744103
2008	528	412339	253789	6784036	4632638	14018503	8371436
2009	403	342362	220541	6081252	3865068	11692277	7317493
2010	495	404608	232336	8290424	5196745	16134445	10052342
2011	411	501463	280929	9818682	6083159	20044269	12375307
2012	437	531276	285252	9657269	6144526	19757789	12419370
2013	442	582029	327483	10032895	6571020	21190173	13397419
2014	468	702083	402514	10470406	7310904	21860834	14495673
2015	444	765369	423375	10046583	7142948	19363826	14152661
2016	458	799048	451333	9492322	6609658	17679749	13332738
2017	555	621090	402995	11219657	7353388	20422502	14596347
2018	623	734633	432017	13010408	8416752	24278973	16756472
2019	737	774215	236341	13307639	8660343	24793426	17550867
2020	486	469961	246784	14127714	9244553	23939852	17547434
2021	564	864060	327427	18452755	11797134	31770854	22641094
2022	410	574618	372658	19049837	12373855	37561142	26986732

注：2019年起，实际利用外资采用商务部口径。表11-5至表11-8同。
Note: From 2019, using foreign capital adopts the standard of Ministry of Commerce, the same as Table 11-5 to Table 11-8.

表11-2 按企业性质分的进出口总值(2022年)
Total Value of Imports and Exports by Registered Type of Enterprises（2022）

单位：万元(10000 yuan)

企业性质	Grouped by Registered Type	进出口 Imports and Exports		其中 of Which 出口 Exports		其中 of Which 进口 Imports	
		贸易额 Value	增长率(%) Rate of Increase	贸易额 Value	增长率(%) Rate of Increase	贸易额 Value	增长率(%) Rate of Increase
合计	**Total**	**126702648**	**6.3**	**82280935**	**7.9**	**44421713**	**3.4**
国有企业	State-Owned Enterprises	8970833	2.8	3611624	-3.6	5359210	7.5
外商投资企业	Foreign Funded Enterprises	25273816	-4.5	13904360	-5.4	11369456	-3.3
民营企业	Private Enterprises	92392165	10.1	64736639	12.1	27655526	5.6

注：本表至11-4表数据来自宁波海关。
Note: Data from Tables 11-2 to 11-4 are obtained from Ningbo Customs.

表11-3 按贸易方式分的进出口总值（2022年）
Total Value of Imports and Exports by Trade Property（2022）

单位：万元(10000 yuan)

贸易方式	Trade Property	进出口 Imports and Exports		其中 of Which 出口 Exports		其中 of Which 进口 Imports	
		贸易额 Value	增长率(%) Rate of Increase	贸易额 Value	增长率(%) Rate of Increase	贸易额 Value	增长率(%) Rate of Increase
总额	**Total**	**126536714**	**6.2**	**82115365**	**7.7**	**44421348**	**3.5**
一般贸易	General Trade	113745766	7.3	75572863	10.2	38172903	2.0
加工贸易	Processing by Supplied Material	7450656	-18.7	5450846	-13.8	1999810	-29.7
其中：来料加工贸易	Processing by Import Material	891174	-2.3	540642	-3.3	350532	-0.7
外商投资企业作为投资进口的设备、物品	Imports of Foreign-invested Enterprises As Investment in Equipment&Goods	9725	173.9			9725	173.9
保税监管场所进出境货物	Import&Export in Supervision Areas of Protective Tariff Zone	2191341	74.2	127422	8.0	2063919	81.0
海关特殊监管区域物流货物	Goods of Special Customs Supervision Logistics	2957026	17.5	898684	-17.1	2058342	43.8
海关特殊监管区域进口设备	Imported Equipment of Special Customs Supervision Zones	49761	85.2			49761	85.2

表11-4 主要国家（地区）的进出口总值(2022年)
Total Value of Exports and Imports by Continent and Country（2022）

单位：万元(10000 yuan)

国家（地区）	Country(Region)	进出口 Imports and Exports		其中 of Which			
				出口 Exports		进口 Imports	
		贸易额 Value	增长率(%) Rate of Increase	贸易额 Value	增长率(%) Rate of Increase	贸易额 Value	增长率(%) Rate of Increase
东盟	The Association of Southeast Asian Nations	14958350	19. 7	7935789	24. 6	7022561	14. 6
日本	Japan	5832743	-0. 5	2744602	5. 5	3088141	-5. 3
韩国	South Korea	5343079	-7. 9	1992640	7. 5	3350439	-15. 1
中国台湾	Taiwan, China	4925099	-7. 3	1195248	7. 4	3729851	-11. 1
欧盟	European Free Trade Association	22935591	7. 8	18981141	7. 3	3954450	10. 6
俄罗斯	Russia	4039901	4. 9	2541153	3. 4	1498748	7. 6
英国	Britain	3243834	-5. 2	2848442	-7. 9	395392	20. 3
美国	USA	21628398	3. 8	17948460	0. 6	3679937	22. 6
巴西	Brazil	3518138	3. 4	1975451	11. 4	1542688	-5. 3
澳大利亚	Australia	5949953	-7. 1	2410796	6. 0	3539157	-14. 4

表11-5 按投资方式分的利用外资基本情况(2022年)
Utilization of Foreign Capital by Investment Ways（2022）

单位：万美元(USD 10000)

指标	Indicators	项目数（个）Projects(unit)	合同利用外资 Foreign Capital Contracted	实际利用外资 Foreign Capital Actually Used
总计	**Total**	**410**	**574618**	**372658**
对外借款	**Foreign Loans**			
外国政府贷款	Foreign Government Loans			
国际金融组织贷款	Loans from International Financial Organization			
外国银行商业贷款	Commercial Loans from Foreign Banks			
其他	Others			43
外商直接投资	**Foreign Direct Investment**	**410**	**574618**	**372658**
合资经营	Joint Venture Enterprises	184	127410	128727
合作经营	Cooperative Operation Enterprises			
独资企业	Foreign－funded Sole Enterprises	168	433307	235456
外商投资股份制	Share－system Enterprises	1	5713	4820
合伙企业	Partnership Enterprises	57	8188	3612

注：本表至11-8表数据来自宁波市商务局。
Note:Data from Tables 11-5 to 11-8 are obtained from Ningbo Commerce Bureau.

表11-6 部分年份按投资方式分的利用外资基本情况
Utilization of Foreign Capital by Investment Ways in Partial Years

单位：万美元(USD 10000)

指标	Indicators	2018	2019	2020	2021	2022
合同利用外资	**Foreign Capital Contracted**	**734633**	**774215**	**469961**	**864060**	**574618**
对外借款	Foreign Loans					
外商直接投资	Foreign Direct Investment	734633	774215	469961	864060	574618
合资经营	Joint Venture Enterprises	109833	149392	187363	262286	127410
合作经营	Cooperative Operation Enterprises	4	7	118	225	
独资企业	Foreign－funded Sole Enterprises	620591	620455	266763	515545	433307
外商投资股份制	Foreign Invested Enterprises Limited by Shares	3858	4361	1492	28823	5713
合伙企业	Partnership Enterprises	347		12189	57181	8188
实际利用外资	**Actual Used Foreign Capital**	**432017**	**236341**	**246784**	**327427**	**372658**
对外借款	Foreign Loans					
外商直接投资	Foreign Direct Investment	432017	236341	246784	327427	372658
合资经营	Joint Venture Enterprises	121831	46721	53342	127818	128727
合作经营	Cooperative Operation Enterprises					
独资企业	Foreign－funded Sole Enterprises	297195	189475	192804	164700	235456
外商投资股份制	Foreign Invested Enterprises Limited by Shares	12991	145	638	30668	4820
合伙企业	Partnership Enterprises				4241	3612

表11-7 部分年份按行业分外商直接投资情况
Foreign Direct Investments by Sectors in Partial Years

指标	Indicators
总计	**Total**
农、林、牧、渔业	Farming, Forestry, Animal Housbandry and Fishery
#农业	Farming
制造业	Manufacturing
#纺织业	Textile Industry
纺织服装、鞋、帽制造业	Textile Clothing, Shoes and Cap Manufacturing
文教体育用品制造业	Cultural, Educational and Sports Goods Manufacturing
化学原料及化学制品制造业	Raw Chemical Materials and Chemical Products
塑料制品业	Plastic Products
金属制品业	Metal Products
通用设备制造业	General Equipment Manufacturing
专用设备制造业	Special Equipment Manufacturing
交通运输设备制造业	Transport Equipment Manufacturing
电气机械及器材制造业	Electric Equipment and Machinery Manufacturing
通信设备、计算机及其他电子设备制造业	Communication Equipment, Computer and Other Electronic
仪器仪表及文化、办公用机械制造业	Instruments, Meters, Cultural and Office Machinery
电力、燃气及水的生产和供应业	Electricity, Gas and Water Production and Supply
建筑业	Construction
交通运输、仓储和邮政业	Transport, Storage and Post
批发和零售贸易业	Wholesale and Retail Sale Trade
餐饮业	Catering Service
房地产业	Real Estate Management
居民服务和其他服务业	Resident Services and Other Services Industries

单位：万美元(USD 1000)

新批项目数（个） Number of Newly Approved Projects(unit)			合同利用外资 Contractual Utilization of Foreign Capital			实际利用外资 Foreign Investment Actually Used		
2020	2021	2022	2020	2021	2022	2020	2021	2022
486	**564**	**410**	**469961**	**864060**	**574618**	**246784**	**327427**	**372658**
2	2		617	1786	100	489	300	
2	2		617	1786	100	489	300	
65	63	45	102817	105350	41543	109204	78735	75097
3	1		16584	1	3712	2703	15565	4200
1	1		258	1105	3843	6047	428	1672
1	1	1	1259	1325	530	200	570	526
3	2	3	526	14306	229	26665	19313	3710
2	2	1	4140	−2046	758	1419	499	1570
7	13	3	4333	9494	342	3262	3147	3128
4	5	7	6154	13016	333	2449	3913	6427
9	10	7	2137	24282	9149	1655	5898	9086
3	1	8	12	1544	3558	3655	585	1576
6	4	4	3812	5868	7561	3970	2751	8920
4	8	6	4357	11343	6118	1957	1593	11266
	3		371	−1149	2000	145	100	2000
3	2	4	20384	1464	16929	2223	198	2896
4	5	5	22000	51491	45377	12	24341	32625
5	9	8	2876	−2418	3558	693	1841	1576
170	194	116	135252	214214	123894	42456	66479	59340
7	4	3	859	102	23	290		
11	14	5	−15556	27443	8491	8241	8484	19025
1	4	5	312	1026	15035	100		705

表11-8 部分年份按国别（地区）分的外商直接投资情况
Foreign Direct Investment by Country and Territory in Partial Years

国别、地区	Country,Region	新批项目数（个）Number of Newly Approved Projects(unit)		
		2020	2021	2022
总计	**Total**	**486**	**564**	**410**
中国香港	Hong Kong, China	130	196	144
中国台湾	Taiwan,China	66	61	49
日本	Japan	6	2	8
韩国	South Korea	10	16	13
印度尼西亚	Indonesia		2	5
新加坡	Singapore	22	24	29
文莱	Brunei	1		
马来西亚	Malaysia	3	1	2
泰国	Thailand		5	
阿拉伯联合酋长国	United Arab Emirates		2	
毛里求斯	Mauritius	2		
英国	the United Kingdom	9	8	7
德国	Germany	12	10	5
法国	France	4	10	4
意大利	Italy	9	4	8
荷兰	Netherlands	1	5	5
比利时	Belgium	3		
西班牙	Spain	1	1	
瑞典	Sweden	6	1	
瑞士	Switzerland	2	2	2
俄罗斯	Russia	6	10	6
巴哈马	The Bahamas			
巴西	Brazil		1	1
开曼群岛	Cayman Islands		2	3
乌拉圭	Uruguay			
英属维尔京群岛	British Virgin Islands	8	6	3
加拿大	Canada	12	10	14
美国	the United States	47	33	35
澳大利亚	Australia	4	6	7
库克群岛	The Cook Islands			
新西兰	New Zealand	4	4	1
萨摩亚	Samoa	1	2	1

单位：万美元(USD 1000)

合同利用外资 Contractual Utilization of Foreign Capital			实际利用外资 Foreign Investment Actually Used		
2020	2021	2022	2020	2021	2022
469961	**864060**	**574618**	**246784**	**327427**	**372658**
255916	604529	461656	176057	239410	260053
34229	6950	16909	776	563	1260
1148	5451	4480	4413	285	1725
1694	15411	1929	1241	3517	2483
	5034	24995			200
8441	33249	41496	11245		31840
279		-498			
606	17	61			
	1113			1083	
	1139			450	
15	-223		1150		
3553	54393	2415	585	4303	173
41270	10537	42	5732	14014	1582
18774	2064	-3359	719	962	525
1803	2064	1148	1103	460	969
7654	48	2846	5850	1924	3087
100					5
56	-34	-94	131	21	
4394	227	2791	2844		210
164	47	323			38
76	96	2183			
	4	1		5	
5567	11632	127	550	10702	1767
-10					
23699	47298	4407	13392	17874	45740
1363	1873	1604	100	50	2
31588	33737	1728	15568	4963	6055
476	1640	105	260	78	
-1349	369	87		10	23
7827	13104	2027	994	2545	11310

表11-9 部分年份旅游业简况
Basic Statistic on Tourism in Partial Years

指标	单位	Indicators	Unit	2020	2021	2022
旅行社合计	(家)	International Travel Agencies	(unit)	354	381	390
#出境旅行社	(家)	Outbound Travel Agencies	(unit)	26	28	29
国内入境旅行社	(家)	Domestic Inbound Travel Agencies	(unit)	328	353	361
旅游星级饭店	(家)	Star－rated Hotel	(unit)	102	80	75
国内旅游总人数	(万人次)	Number of Domestic Tourists	(10000 person－times)	12524	5151	5084
旅游总收入	(亿元)	Income of Tourism	(100 million yuan)	1999. 5	838. 8	776. 3
#旅游创汇	(万美元)	Foreign Exchange Earnings	(USD 10000)	1596	1446	990
国内旅游总收入	(亿元)	Domestic Tourism Receipts	(100 million yuan)	1998. 4	837. 8	775. 6

注：（1）本表至11-11表数据来自宁波市文化广电旅游局。
（2）据上级文旅部门统一部署，自2021年起旅游业的统计方法和口径有调整。

Notes: (1) Data from Tables 11-9 to 11-11 are obtained from Ningbo Municipal Bureau of Culture, Radio, Television and Tourism.
(2) According to the unified deployment of the superior cultural and tourism department, the statistical method and caliber of tourism industry have been adjusted since 2021.

表11-10 部分年份国际旅游情况
Basic Statistic on International Tourism in Partial Years

指标	单位	Indicators	Unit	2020	2021	2022
接待过夜境外旅游者人数	(人)	**Number of Oversea Tourists Staying Overnight**	**(person)**	**56007**	**48217**	**32467**
外国人		Foreigner		41473	34887	21490
中国台湾同胞		Compatriots from Taiwan, China		7172	6744	6794
中国香港同胞		Compatriots from Hong Kong, China		6935	6139	3958
中国澳门同胞		Compatriots from Macao, China		427	448	225
接待过夜境外旅游者人天数	(人天)	**Person-days of Oversea Tourists Staying Overnight**	**(person－day)**	**91816**	**83847**	**57387**
外国人		Foreigner		67072	61123	39545
中国台湾同胞		Compatriots from Taiwan, China		12700	10571	9466
中国香港同胞		Compatriots from Hong Kong, China		11400	11509	8002
中国澳门同胞		Compatriots from Macao, China		644	644	375

表11-11 部分年份接待外国旅游者人数(按国别分)
Number of Foreign Tourists by Country in Partial Years

单位：人（person）

国家（地区）	Country	2018	2019	2020	2021	2022
总计	**Total**	**550101**	**601670**	**41432**	**34887**	**21490**
亚洲	Asia	161857	207198	14287	12901	7026
#日本	Japan	54834	58208	4371	4708	2045
韩国	South Korea	58956	50102	4095	3354	2234
印度尼西亚	Indonesia	5430	4997	115	135	54
马来西亚	Malaysia	10334	10433	688	529	328
新加坡	Singapore	12009	10853	1325	979	478
泰国	Thailand	5524	6639	580	715	646
印度	India	14770	15727	469	337	310
欧洲	Europe	108252	184274	11840	11140	7607
#英国	the United Kingdom	27945	21140	1204	794	621
法国	France	17819	19587	1115	690	701
德国	Germany	38298	35291	2816	4626	3004
意大利	Italy	16022	15585	962	773	444
俄罗斯	Russia	8168	10182	1108	693	343
美洲	America	170442	98428	8249	7398	5519
#美国	the United States	68645	63087	5957	5608	3654
加拿大	Canada	101797	12241	1091	941	1420
大洋洲	Oceania	16457	30018	1458	1087	760
#澳大利亚	Australia	16457	18338	729	844	633
非洲	Africa	18772	18830	1251	526	578
其他	Others	74321	62922	4335	1834	

注：自2018年开始，入境游客统计口径调整为“住宿单位接待入境过夜游客”。
Note：From 2018，the standard of “Oversea Tourists” adjusted to “Oversea Tourists Staying Overnight received by hotels”.

主要统计指标解释

【进出口总额】海关进出口总额是指实际进出我国国境的货物总金额。包括对外贸易实际进出口货物，来料加工装配进出口货物，国家间、联合国及国际组织无偿援助物资和赠送品，华侨、港澳台同胞和外籍华人捐赠品，租赁期满归承租人所有的租赁货物，进料加工进出口货物，边境地方贸易及边境地区小额贸易进出口货物(边民互市贸易除外)，中外合资经营企业、中外合作经营企业、外商独资经营企业进出口货物和公用物品，到、离岸价格在规定限额以上的进出口货样和广告品（无商业价值、无使用价值和免费提供出口的除外），从保税仓库提取在中国境内销售的进口货物以及其他进出口货物。进出口总额用以观察一个国家在对外贸易方面的总规模。我国规定出口货物按离岸价格计算，进口货物按到岸价格计算。

【利用外资】指我国各级政府、部门、企业和其他经济组织通过对外借款、 吸收外商直接投资以及用其他方式筹措的境外现汇、设备、技术等。

【对外借款】是我国利用外资的主要部分。包括我国通过外国政府贷款，国际金融组织贷款，外国银行商业贷款，出口信贷以及对外发行债券，股票等方式，从境外筹措的资金。

【外商直接投资】是指外国企业和经济组织或个人（包括华侨、港澳台胞以及 我国在境外注册的企业）按我国有关政策、法规，用现汇、实物、技术等在我国境内开办外 商独资企业、与我国境内的企业或经济组织共同举办中外合资经营企业、合作经营企业或作 合作开发资源的投资（包括外商投资收益的再投资）以及经政府有关部门批准的项目投资总 额内，企业从境外借入的资金。

【外商其他投资】指除对外借款和外商直接投资以外的各种利用外资的形式。包括企业在境内外股票市场公开发行的以外币计价的股票（目前主要是在香港证券市场发行的H股和在境内证券市场发行的B股）发行价总额，国际租赁进口设备的应付款，补充贸易中外商提供的进口设备、技术、物料的价款，加工装配贸易中外商提供的进口设备、物料的价款。

【旅游人数】包括入境国际旅游者人数、出境居民人数和国内旅游者人数。

⑴入境国际旅游者人数：指来中国参观、访问、旅行、探亲、访友、休养、考察、参加会议和从事经济、科技、文化、教育、宗教等活动的外国人、港澳和台湾同胞的人数。不包括外国在我国的常驻机构，如使领馆、通讯社、企业办事处的工作人员；来我国常住的外国专家、留学生以及在岸逗留不过夜人员。

⑵出境居民人数：指大陆居民因公务活动或私人事务短期出境的人数。公务活动出境居民人数包括在国际交通工具上的中国服务员工，因私出境居民人数不包括在国际交通工具上的中国服务员工。 ⑶国内旅游者人数：指我国大陆居民和在我国常住1年以上的外国人、港澳台同胞离开常住地在境内其他地方的旅游设施内至少停留一夜，最长不超过6个月的人数。

【国际旅游（外汇）收入】指入境旅游的外国人、华侨、港澳台同胞在中国大陆旅游过程中发生的一切旅游支出，对国家来说就是国际旅游（外汇）收入。

Explanatory Notes on Main Statistical Indicators

【Total Imports and Exports】 The total amount of customs import and export is the total amount of goods actually entering and leaving our country, including actual import and export goods for foreign trade, imported and exported goods for processing and assembly, free aid and gifts between countries, the United Nations and international organizations, donations from overseas Chinese, compatriots from Hong Kong, Macao, and Taiwan and foreign Chinese, Leasing goods owned by the lessee at the end of the lease period, import and export goods processed with incoming materials, import and export goods (except frontier local trade and small trade in border areas), Sino–foreign equity joint ventures and Chinese–foreign contractual joint ventures, Import and export of goods and public goods by a wholly foreign–owned enterprise, and import and export samples and advertising goods (without commercial value) with FOB prices above the prescribed limit, Except for non–use value and free export), import goods sold in China and other import and export goods shall be drawn from bonded warehouses. The total volume of imports and exports is used to observe the total scale of a country's foreign trade. Our country stipulates that export goods shall be calculated at FOB prices and imported goods at CIF prices.

FOB refer to Free on Board. CIF refer to Cost Insurance and Freight.

【Utilization of Foreign Capital】 Utilization of Foreign Capital refers to the governments, departments, enterprises and other economic organizations at all levels of our country through foreign loans, foreign direct investment and other ways to raise foreign exchange, equipment, technology, etc.

【Foreign Loans】 It is a major part of China' s utilization of foreign capital, including loans of foreign governments, loans of international financial institutions, commercial loans of foreign banks, export credit, and funds raised by Chinese bonds and shares issued abroad.

【Direct Investment by Foreign Entrepreneurs】 refers to the investments inside China by foreign enterprises and economic organizations or individuals (including overseas Chinese, compatriots from Hong Kong and Macao, and Chinese enterprises registered abroad),following the relevant policies and laws of China, for the establishment of ventures exclusively with foreign own investment, Sino–foreign joint ventures and cooperative enterprises or for cooperative exploration of resources with enterprises or economic organizations in China. It includes the re–investment of the foreign entrepreneurs with the profits gained from the investment and the funds that enterprises borrow from abroad in the total investment of projects which are approved by the relevant department of the government.

【Other Overseas Investments】 refer to all kinds of investments except the foreign loan and the FDI. They include: the total value(in foreign currency) of the stocks of one enterprises distributed publicly both at home and abroad(now mainly refer to H.shares at HK bond market, and B.shares at China mainland bond market); the rent charges of the foreign equipments; the total value of Technology, raw material and foreign equipment provided by foreign investors in supplemental trades, and value of foreign raw material, equipment in the trade of assemble machining.

【tourists number】 is a sum of overseas tourists, local residents going abroad and domestic tourists.

overseas tourists number. Which refers to the number of foreigners and residents from Hongkong, Macao and Taiwan who come to China to go sightseeing, travel, visit relatives and friends, spend holidays, inspect, attend conferences and to do activities in economics, science, education, religious etc. Personnel as below are not taken into calculation, office workers in Chinese standing bodies at abroad, such as in embassies, news agencies, oversea offices of companies. Foreign experts and students living in China and foreigners who enter China only for voyage transferring are also not calculated.

number of local residents going abroad. Which refers to the number of mainland China residents who go abroad either for official business or for private affairs. Number of Chinese workers who serve in the international transportation vehicles are included in those who exit for official business, but not in those for private affairs.

domestic tourists. Which refers to the number of people who leave their living places to stay in the tourism facilities for at least one night but no more than 6 months, including mainland China residents, foreigners, residents from HK, Macao and TW who lived in China for more than one year.

【Foreign Exchange Earnings from International Tourism】 refer to the total expenditures of the foreigners, overseas Chinese, compatriots from Hong Kong, Macao and Taiwan in the process of their tourism in the mainland of China. Their expenditures mentioned above are foreign exchange earnings to China.

NINGBO 2023 Statistical Yearbook

12 CHAPTER

第十二篇

文化、教育、卫生、体育、科学技术

CULTURE,EDUCATION, PUBLIC HEALTH AND SPORTS,SCIENCE & TECHNOLOGY

文化、教育、卫生、体育、科学技术
Culture, Education, Public Health, Sports and Science & Technology

主要统计指标
Major Statistics Indicators

2022年群艺馆、文化馆	Number of Mass Art Center and Cultural Center	11	个	unit
2022年公共图书馆	Number of Public Libraries	12	个	unit
2022年电影观众人次	Number of Spectator	1051.13	万人次	10000 person – times
2022年各类学校数	Number of Various School	2129	所	unit
2022年各类学校招生人数	Number of New Students Enrollment of Various Schools	323525	人	person
2022年各类学校在校学生数	Number of Students Enrollment of Various Schools	1481674	人	person
2022年各类学校毕业人数	Number of Graduates by Various Schools	281424	人	person
2022年专任教师数	Number of Full – time Teacher	97451	人	person
2022年高等学校在校生人数	Number of Service Enrollment in Institutions of Higher Education	191051	人	person
2022年卫生事业床位数	Number of Beds in Health Institutions	46804	张	bed
2022年卫生技术人员数	Number of Medical Technical Personnel	87485	人	person
2022年医生数	Number of Doctors	35939	人	person
2022年参赛获奖数	Number of Obtain Awards by Athletic Competition	809	枚	unit
2022年有线电视用户数	Number of User Terminal for Cable TV Station	228.05	万户	10000 users

表12-1 部分年份文化事业单位、机构、人员及活动情况
Basic Statistics on Cultural Institutions and Personnel in Partial Years

指标	单位	Indicators	Unit	2019	2020	2021	2022
艺术表演团体	个	**Art Performance Troupes**	**unit**	**300**	**209**	**187**	**191**
机构人员数	人	Persons of Institutions	persons	7398	8163	7020	16034
国内演出场次	场次	Internal Performances	times	31585	20192	16014	31499
国内观众人次	千人	Internal Spectator	1000 persons times	18799	13909	10449	13968
艺术表演场所	所	**Art Performance Places**	**unit**	**98**	**55**	**47**	**47**
机构人员数	人	Persons of Institutions	persons	2095	1446	1380	3479
演出场次	场次	Performances	times	8854	1710	1431	5357
观众人次	千人	Spectator	1000 persons times	4235	2266	2222	4347
公共图书馆	个	**Public Libraries**	**unit**	**12**	**12**	**12**	**12**
机构人员数	人	Persons of Institutions	persons	847	487	496	491
总藏量	万册	Total Collections	10000 volumes	1243	1164	1241	1401
古籍	千册	Ancient Books	1000 volumes	142	125	125	125
图书	万册	Books	10000 volumes	1148	1070	1120	1281
群艺馆. 文化馆	个	**Mass Art Center and Cultural Center**	**unit**	**11**	**11**	**11**	**11**
机构人员数	人	Persons of Institutions	persons	303	297	301	289
文化站	个	**Cultural Center**	**unit**	**150**	**150**	**150**	**150**
机构人员数	人	Persons of Institutions	persons	670	670	1002	1030
文物单位		**Historical Relic Protection Units**					
文物保护管理机构	个	Historical Relic Protection Institutions	unit	12	12	12	11
国家级文保单位	个	Historical Relic Protection Units of State Level	unit	33	33	33	33
博物馆. 纪念馆	个	Museums, Memorial Hall	unit	71	73	79	78
文物商店	个	Historical Relic	unit	1	1		
电影放映单位		**Film Projecting Units**					
放映管理机构	个	Projecting Management Institutions	unit	8	16	11	11
电影院	个	Movie House	unit	111	91	111	109
放映队	个	Projecting Teams	unit	111	95	110	110
电影放映场次	万场	Projecting Performance	10000 times	143. 44	51. 36	132. 28	125. 30
电影观众人次	万人次	Spectator	10000 persons times	2232. 25	693. 99	1525. 81	1051. 13

注：（1）本表至12-4表数据来自宁波市文化广电旅游局。
（2）艺术表演团体（场所）指标口径包含市直属、部门所属和社会自办的所有表演团体（场所）。

Notes:（1）Data from Tables 12-1 to 12-4 are obtained from Ningbo Municipal Bureau of culture, radio, television and Tourism.
（2）The indicators of art performance groups (places) include all the performing groups (places) directly under the city, departments and society

表12-2 各区（县、市）文化事业单位、机构、人员及活动情况(2022年)
Basic Statistics of Cultural Institutions and Personnel by Region（2022）

指标	单位	Indicators	Unit	全市 Total	市区 Urban District	海曙区 Haishu
艺术表演团体	个	**Art Performance Troupes**	**unit**	**191**	**113**	**29**
机构人员数	人	Persons of Institutions	persons	16034	4515	435
国内演出场次	场次	Internal Performances	times	31499	10666	6380
国内观众人次	千人	Internal Spectator	1000 persons times	13968	2942	1148
艺术表演场所	所	**Art Performance Places**	**unit**	**47**	**38**	**12**
机构人员数	人	Persons of Institutions	persons	3479	2320	1296
演出场次	场次	Performances	times	5357	5357	4808
观众人次	千人	Spectator	1000 persons times	4347	2367	865
公共图书馆	个	**Public Libraries**	**unit**	**12**	**8**	**1**
机构人员数	人	Persons of Institutions	persons	491	356	19
总藏量	万册	Total Collections	10000 volumes	1400. 97	1086. 79	124. 42
古籍	千册	Ancient Books	1000 volumes	125. 34	62. 05	
图书	万册	Books	10000 volumes	1280. 56	1015. 87	124. 13
群艺馆. 文化馆	个	**Mass Art Center and Cultural Center**	**unit**	**11**	**7**	**1**
机构人员数	人	Persons of Institutions	persons	289	174	18
文化站	个	**Cultural Center**	**unit**	**150**	**74**	**17**
机构人员数	人	Persons of Institutions	persons	1030	675	376
文物单位		**Historical Relic Protection Units**				
文物保护管理机构	个	Historical Relic Protection Institutions	unit	12	8	1
国家级文保单位	个	Historical Relic Protection Units of State Level	unit	33	17	8
博物馆. 纪念馆	个	Museums, Memorial Hall	unit	78	43	10
文物商店	个	Historical Relic	unit			
电影放映单位		**Film Projecting Units**				
放映管理机构	个	Projecting Management Institutions	unit	11	7	1
电影院	个	Movie House	unit	109	71	18
放映队	个	Projecting Teams	unit	110	51	8
电影放映场次	万场	Projecting Performance	10000 times	125. 30	123. 10	
电影观众人次	万人次	Spectator	10000 persons times	1051. 13	871. 01	

江北区 Jiangbei	镇海区 Zhenhai	北仑区 Beilun	鄞州区 Yinzhou	奉化区 Fenghua	余姚市 Yuyao	慈溪市 Cixi	宁海县 Ninghai	象山县 Xiangshan
7	**6**	**6**	**39**	**26**	**19**	**21**	**16**	**22**
263	160	212	1370	2075	4994	3120	812	2593
516	50	123	1567	2030	7201	5055	4110	4467
242	14	65	571	902	4117	2432	4101	376
2	**7**	**4**	**6**	**7**	**3**	**2**	**4**	**1**
157	108	30	513	216	285	814	60	12
	502	47						
162	91	31	893	326	380	1430	170	
1	**1**	**2**	**1**	**1**	**1**	**1**	**1**	**1**
9	33	58	37	24	27	51	31	26
51.77	67.78	101.33	301.67	77.49	83.39	102.27	57.45	71.08
		0.05	1.09	0.03	35.65	7.53	20.10	
28.69	58.54	96.51	294.23	77.41	74.20	74.74	50.70	65.05
1	**1**	**1**	**1**	**1**	**1**	**1**	**1**	**1**
10	18	17	29	19	34	28	31	22
8	**6**	**10**	**21**	**12**	**21**	**19**	**18**	**18**
46	30	67	116	40	112	112	77	54
1	1	1	1	2	1	1	1	1
4	2	1	5	3	8	4	1	3
1	1	1	19	5	11	12	7	5
1	1	1	1	1	1	1	1	1
9	7	6	24	7	9	17	6	6
4	4	6	17	12	17	18	16	8

表12-3 各区（县、市）广播电视基本情况(2022年）
Basic Statistics on Broadcasting and Television by Region（2022）

指标	单位	Indicators	Unit	全市 Total	市区 Urban District	海曙区 Haishu
广播电视机构		**Broadcasting and Television Institutions**				
电台	座	Broadcasting Station	set	9	1	
电视台	座	Broadcasting and Relaying Stations	set	9	1	
广播电视站	个	TV and Transfer Stations	set	104		
全年播出公共节目时间		**Full－year Broadcasting & TV Hours**				
广播播音时间	小时	Broadcasting Hours	hour	93957	34236	
#制作节目播出时间	小时	Time of Self－Producting Programs	hour	66136	30347	
电视播出时间	小时	Hours Through TV Broadcasting	hour	82258	26483	
#制作节目播出时间	小时	Time of Self－Producting Programs	hour	10661	1685	
公共电视套数	**套**	**TV Channel**	**set**	**13**	**5**	
公共广播套数	**套**	**Public Broadcasting Band**	**set**	**13**	**5**	
发送功率		**Transfer Power**				
中波功率	千瓦	Middle－Wave Power	kW	30. 00	30. 00	
调频功率	千瓦	Frequency Modulation Power	kW	37. 80	28. 00	
电视功率	千瓦	TV Power	kW	19. 85	6. 50	
有线电视用户数	**万户**	**Number of User Terminal of Cable TV Station**	**10000users**	**228. 05**	**23. 65**	**23. 54**

表12-4 部分年份广播电视基本情况
Basic Statistics on Broadcasting and Television in Partial Years

指标	单位	Indicators	Unit	2020	2021	2022
广播电视机构		**Broadcasting and Television Institutions**				
电台	座	Broadcasting Station	set	9	9	9
电视台	座	Broadcasting and Relaying Stations	set	9	9	9
广播电视站	个	TV and Transfer Stations	set	104	104	104
全年播出公共节目时间		**Full－year Broadcasting & TV Hours**				
广播播音时间	小时	Broadcasting Hours	hour	98754	94291	93957
#制作节目播出时间	小时	Time of Self－Producting Programs	hour	80538	70285	66136
电视播出时间	小时	Hours Through TV Broadcasting	hour	79723	82998	82258
#制作节目播出时间	小时	Time of Self－Producting Programs	hour	31665	9997	10662
公共电视套数	**套**	**TV Channel**	**set**	**13**	**13**	**13**
公共广播套数	**套**	**Public Broadcasting Band**	**set**	**13**	**13**	**13**
有线电视用户数	**万户**	**Number of User Terminal of Cable TV Station**	**10000 users**	**210. 78**	**212. 11**	**228. 05**

江北区 Jiangbei	镇海区 Zhenhai	北仑区 Beilun	鄞州区 Yinzhou	奉化区 Fenghua	余姚市 Yuyao	慈溪市 Cixi	宁海县 Ninghai	象山县 Xiangshan
	1	1	1	1	1	1	1	1
	1	1	1	1	1	1	1	1
1	7	8	20	9	19	19	8	13
	8590	8552	8640	7872	5960	6387	8610	5110
	2331	7308	8640	4826	1441	4647	4893	1703
	5746	8451	7457	6200	5860	8614	7400	6047
	107	1266	360	680	364	2184	1854	1482
	1	**1**	**1**	**1**	**1**	**1**	**1**	**1**
	1	**1**	**1**	**1**	**1**	**1**	**1**	**1**
	0.80	0.60	0.60	1.00	3.00	0.20	3.00	0.60
			2.00	0.05	2.40	3.20	2.30	3.40
7.77	**6.42**	**10.93**	**29.09**	**14.34**	**32.00**	**38.37**	**21.95**	**20.00**

表12-5 部分年份学生入、升学率
Percentage for Enrollment and Graduation of Students

单位：%

指标	Indicators	2018	2019	2020	2021	2022
小学学龄儿童入学率	Enrollment Rate for Children of School Age	100.00	100.00	100.00	100.00	100.00
小学毕业升学率	Graduation Rate for Pupils	100.00	100.00	100.00	100.00	100.00
初中毕业升学率	Graduation Rate for Students of Secondary School	99.30	99.61	99.75	99.88	99.90
升入普通高中	Rate of Enrolling Senior School	48.89	51.02	51.04	52.55	56.24
升入职业高中	Rate of Enrolling Vacational Senior School	50.41	48.59	48.71	47.33	43.66

表12-6 各区（县、市）各类学校数（2022年）
Number of Various Schools by Region（2022）

指标	Indicators	全市 Total	市区 Urban District	海曙区 Haishu
各类学校数	**Number of Various School**			
（一）全日制学校	**Number of Full－time School**	**2128**	**1095**	**224**
高等学校	Regular Institutions of Higher Education	14	14	
#大专	Junior Colleges	6	6	
初中	Regular Secondary Schools	243	14	25
高中	Senior Secondary Schools	85	15	
职业中学	Vocational Secondary Schools	32	16	
普通小学	Primary Schools	388	17	39
特殊教育学校	Special Education Schools	10	18	1
幼儿园	Kindergarten	1028	19	134
（二）成人学校数	**Number of School for Adult Education**			
成人高校数	Number of Higher Education for Adult	1	1	

注：本表至12-8表数据来自宁波市教育局。高等学校中包括省属学校。
Note: Data from Tables 12-6 to 12-8 are obtained from Ningbo Municipal Bureau of Education.Regular institutions of higher education include the provincial school.

单位: 个(unit)

江北区 Jiangbei	镇海区 Zhenhai	北仑区 Beilun	鄞州区 Yinzhou	奉化区 Fenghua	余姚市 Yuyao	慈溪市 Cixi	宁海县 Ninghai	象山县 Xiangshan
119	**106**	**158**	**261**	**147**	**310**	**380**	**198**	**145**
18	9	23	26	16	28	44	22	24
1	5	6	2	7	10	14	8	5
	1	1		2	6	4	4	3
14	19	22	52	25	65	65	50	24
0	1	1	1	1	1	1	1	1
67	57	76	136	73	162	149	83	59

表12-7 各区（县、市）各类学校学生情况(2022年)
Basic Statistics on Student of Various Schools by Region（2022）

指标	Indicators	全市 Total	市区 Urban District	海曙区 Haishu
各类学校招生人数	**New Students Enrollment of Various Schools**	**323525**	**217492**	**18644**
研究生	Postgraduates	4074	4074	
普通高校	Institutions of Higher Education	59428	59428	
#大专	Junior Colleges	25301	25301	
初中	Regular Secondary Schools	78337	41859	8190
高中	Senior Secondary Schools	36129	19119	
职业中学	Secondary Vacational Schools	20760	10804	
普通小学	Primary Schools	95666	53187	10430
特殊教育学校	Special Education Schools	199	89	24
成人高校	Higher Education for Adult	28932	28932	
各类学校在校学生数	**Students Enrollment of Various Schools**	**1481674**	**934920**	**116646**
研究生	Postgraduates	11738	11738	
普通高校	Institutions of Higher Education	179313	179313	
#大专	Junior Colleges	69805	69805	
初中	Regular Secondary Schools	228434	126044	24108
高中	Senior Secondary Schools	103134	55097	
职业中学	Secondary Vacational Schools	60930	32819	
普通小学	Primary Schools	555101	310578	60599
特殊教育学校	Special Education Schools	1347	677	149
成人高校	Higher Education for Adult	56213	56213	
幼儿园在园人数	Persons of Kindergarten	285464	162441	31790
各类学校毕业人数	**Graduates by Various Schools**	**281424**	**186251**	**16320**
研究生	Postgraduates	2246	2246	
普通高校	Institutions of Higher Education	52285	52285	
#大专	Junior Colleges	25751	25751	
初中	Regular Secondary Schools	69388	36413	7360
高中	Senior Secondary Schools	31269	16179	
职业中学	Secondary Vacational Schools	19538	10171	
普通小学	Primary Schools	79458	41807	8943
特殊教育学校	Special Education Schools	161	71	17
成人高校	Higher Education for Adult	27079	27079	

单位：人(person)

江北区 Jiangbei	镇海区 Zhenhai	北仑区 Beilun	鄞州区 Yinzhou	奉化区 Fenghua	余姚市 Yuyao	慈溪市 Cixi	宁海县 Ninghai	象山县 Xiangshan
10335	**13780**	**18037**	**31434**	**13513**	**29917**	**40736**	**20380**	**15000**
4107	4608	6141	13200	4731	10460	12912	7343	5763
469	2210	2812	230	2304	4243	6199	3780	2788
	1044	1168		1342	2710	3497	2423	1326
5759	5910	7875	17997	5134	12486	18101	6818	5074
	8	41	7	2	18	27	16	49
59832	**70551**	**99053**	**175086**	**69976**	**162480**	**197122**	**107879**	**79273**
12403	13049	17584	35994	13845	30484	32636	22413	16857
1025	6023	7780	551	6623	12122	17453	10763	7699
	2886	3760		4039	6928	10107	6922	4154
29815	31436	45005	92149	30949	75210	90727	44104	34482
	66	155	142	72	163	175	145	187
16589	17091	24769	46250	14448	37573	46024	23532	15894
7880	**10927**	**14514**	**24135**	**12416**	**26872**	**33346**	**19982**	**14973**
3653	3803	5165	10835	4353	9177	11576	7017	5205
160	1751	2214	161	1937	3813	5797	3062	2418
	898	1152		1251	2578	3178	2278	1333
4067	4472	5975	13119	4864	11288	12767	7621	5975
	3	8	20	11	16	28	4	42

表12-8 各区（县、市）各类学校教职工情况（2022年）
Basic Statistics on Teachers and Staff of Various Schools by Region（2022）

指标	Indicators	全市 Total	市区 Urban District	海曙区 Haishu
各类学校教职工人数	**Number of Teachers and Staff of Various Schools**	**127176**	**75633**	**10507**
高等学校	Regular Institutions of Higher Education	13525	13525	
#大专	Junior Colleges	3374	3374	
普通中学	Regular Secondary Schools	36074	19875	2749
职业中学	Secondary Vacational Schools	5337	2946	
普通小学	Primary Schools	27079	14253	2550
特殊教育学校	Special Education Schools	480	281	59
成人高校	Higher Education for Adult	179	179	
幼儿园	Kindergarten	44502	24574	5149
各类学校专任教师人数	**Number of Full-time Teachers of Various Schools**	**97541**	**57293**	**7715**
普通高校	Institutions of Higher Education	9826	9826	
#大专	Junior Colleges	2514	2514	
初中	Regular Secondary Schools	17881	9537	1846
高中	Senior Secondary Schools	9641	5182	
职业中学	Secondary Vacational Schools	5037	2735	
普通小学	Primary Schools	31356	16833	3199
特殊教育学校	Special Education Schools	385	231	33
成人高校	Higher Education for Adult	107	107	
#电大	Radio and TV Universities	107	107	
幼儿园	Kindergarten	23308	12842	2637
各类学校兼任教师人数	**Number of Part-time Teachers of Various Schools**	**473**	**302**	**185**
普通中学	Regular Secondary Schools	112	112	94
职业中学	Secondary Vacational Schools	221	62	
普通小学	Primary Schools	140	128	91
成人高校	Higher Education for Adult			

单位：人(person)

江北区 Jiangbei	镇海区 Zhenhai	北仑区 Beilun	鄞州区 Yinzhou	奉化区 Fenghua	余姚市 Yuyao	慈溪市 Cixi	宁海县 Ninghai	象山县 Xiangshan
5771	**6069**	**8949**	**18261**	**6178**	**14547**	**20485**	**9464**	**7047**
2273	1684	3088	4020	2011	4097	6453	2711	2938
	223	319		341	734	814	421	422
904	1545	1680	5957	1617	3978	4743	2803	1302
	18	35	64	24	38	56	68	37
2594	2599	3827	8220	2185	5700	8419	3461	2348
4336	**4702**	**7018**	**13126**	**5002**	**11439**	**15556**	**7607**	**5646**
1058	955	1388	2908	1091	2379	3034	1600	1331
99	514	766	44	669	1161	1659	977	662
	217	301		325	704	790	410	398
1831	1669	2489	5816	1717	4192	5637	2760	1934
	16	34	48	24	38	51	29	36
1348	1331	2040	4310	1176	2965	4385	1831	1285
	7		**33**	**8**	**71**		**79**	**21**
				4				
	7				59		79	21
			33	4	12			

表12-9 历年教职工数和在校学生数

Number of Teachers and Staff and Students Enrollment Over the Years

单位：万人(10000 persons)

年份 Year	在校教职工 Teachers and Staff	#教师 Teachers	在校学生 Students Enrollment 大学生 Higher Education	中学生 Secondary Schools	小学生 Primary Schools
1978	4. 15	3. 55	0. 10	27. 16	59. 11
1979	4. 01	3. 53	0. 21	23. 04	57. 85
1980	4. 28	3. 48	0. 25	20. 99	56. 39
1981	4. 13	3. 23	0. 20	19. 36	52. 02
1982	3. 31	2. 75	0. 15	18. 77	46. 67
1983	3. 72	3. 06	0. 16	19. 48	41. 71
1984	3. 73	3. 00	0. 21	21. 42	38. 50
1985	3. 94	3. 16	0. 27	23. 47	36. 43
1986	4. 09	3. 28	0. 34	24. 35	36. 90
1987	4. 21	3. 34	0. 39	23. 48	36. 41
1988	4. 32	3. 47	0. 45	20. 34	38. 69
1989	4. 45	3. 56	0. 49	18. 75	41. 84
1990	4. 24	3. 34	0. 49	19. 65	42. 70
1991	4. 34	3. 39	0. 48	22. 01	41. 62
1992	4. 37	3. 47	0. 53	24. 39	40. 16
1993	4. 59	3. 61	0. 66	25. 03	40. 40
1994	4. 75	3. 76	0. 83	26. 76	41. 92
1995	5. 00	4. 01	0. 98	28. 93	41. 29
1996	5. 12	4. 17	1. 04	30. 07	41. 80
1997	5. 27	4. 32	1. 15	29. 93	43. 14
1998	5. 44	4. 40	1. 25	29. 00	43. 91
1999	6. 16	4. 81	1. 68	25. 12	43. 36
2000	6. 59	5. 17	2. 59	27. 98	42. 40
2001	6. 86	5. 12	4. 34	29. 60	42. 24
2002	7. 05	5. 27	6. 21	30. 86	44. 55
2003	7. 46	5. 61	7. 99	30. 99	45. 26
2004	7. 85	5. 92	9. 60	32. 09	47. 61
2005	8. 59	6. 46	11. 12	40. 25	47. 60
2006	8. 68	6. 55	12. 13	40. 95	47. 38
2007	9. 09	6. 84	12. 76	41. 12	47. 15
2008	9. 27	7. 04	13. 04	41. 70	46. 80
2009	9. 13	7. 42	13. 75	41. 42	45. 03
2010	9. 61	7. 29	14. 08	40. 61	46. 19
2011	9. 82	7. 70	14. 14	39. 13	47. 61
2012	9. 95	7. 63	14. 54	37. 55	47. 88
2013	10. 37	7. 82	14. 90	36. 43	48. 70
2014	10. 57	7. 92	15. 09	34. 94	48. 26
2015	10. 83	8. 20	15. 58	34. 29	48. 02
2016	10. 91	8. 41	15. 51	34. 39	47. 70
2017	11. 13	8. 66	15. 61	35. 43	47. 76
2018	11. 33	8. 70	15. 60	36. 12	49. 03
2019	11. 65	8. 94	16. 34	36. 93	50. 45
2020	12. 00	9. 22	17. 67	37. 92	51. 73
2021	12. 40	9. 51	18. 41	38. 21	53. 79
2022	12. 72	9. 75	19. 11	39. 25	55. 51

注：在校教职工包括幼儿园。
Note: The number of teachers and staff include kinder-gardens

表12-10 部分年份教育事业基本情况
Basic Statistics on Education in Partial Years

单位：人(person)

指标	Indicators	2017	2018	2019	2020	2021	2022
学校数(所)	**Number of Schools(unit)**						
高等学校	Institutions of Higher Education	14	13	14	14	14	14
普通中学	Regular Secondary Schools	299	304	309	316	322	329
职业中学	Vocational Secondary Schools	39	38	36	35	33	32
小学	Primary Schools	440	433	427	427	418	388
专任教师	**Number of Full－time Teachers**						
高等学校	Institutions of Higher Education	8432	8409	8868	9271	9743	9826
普通中学	Regular Secondary Schools	24119	24603	25104	25721	26785	27522
职业中学	Vocational Secondary Schools	5307	5283	5308	5398	4980	5037
小学	Primary Schools	27037	27880	28461	29294	30518	31356
招生数	**New Student Enrollment**						
高等学校	Institutions of Higher Education	45625	46326	52874	57198	55125	63502
普通中学	Regular Secondary Schools	100406	100426	105400	107379	111066	114466
职业中学	Vocational Secondary Schools	23710	22166	23339	24410	20482	20760
小学	Primary Schools	83868	92729	92084	91403	96303	95666
在校学生数	**Student Enrollment**						
高等学校	Institutions of Higher Education	156110	155990	163438	176734	184114	191051
普通中学	Regular Secondary Schools	286402	295214	302759	310088	321592	331568
职业中学	Vocational Secondary Schools	67880	66000	66510	69158	60540	60930
小学	Primary Schools	477640	490328	504476	517347	537935	555101
毕业生数	**Number of Graduates**						
高等学校	Institutions of Higher Education	42416	43205	43408	43651	45466	54531
普通中学	Regular Secondary Schools	86442	87214	92626	95895	95762	100657
职业中学	Vocational Secondary Schools	20120	22330	19618	21762	17720	19538
小学	Primary Schools	77826	78134	77631	77388	77965	79458

表12-11 部分年份平均每一专任教师负担的学生数
The Average Number of Registered Students Allocated to Each Full-time Teacher in Partial Years

单位：人(person)

年份 Year	高等学校 Institutions of Higher Education	中等专业学校 Specialized Scendary Schools	普通中学 Regular Secondary Schools	职业中学 Vocational Secondary Schools	小学 Primary Schools
2000	11. 3	24. 1	17. 7	16. 2	23. 9
2001	15. 7	30. 5	17. 8	16. 5	23. 7
2002	17. 6	26. 1	17. 8	17. 5	24. 4
2003	18. 9	24. 1	17. 0	27. 9	24. 5
2004	17. 0	20. 4	16. 6	26. 5	24. 7
2005	18. 5	15. 9	16. 0	29. 6	23. 9
2006	18. 7	9. 4	16. 0	28. 0	23. 5
2007	19. 2	7. 0	15. 6	27. 1	22. 9
2008	19. 1	6. 2	15. 4	23. 4	22. 4
2009	19. 8		14. 7	17. 2	21. 3
2010	19. 7		14. 2	16. 3	21. 4
2011	15. 6		13. 5	15. 7	21. 4
2012	19. 7		12. 8	14. 6	20. 7
2013	19. 8		12. 3	13. 7	20. 3
2014	19. 3		12. 0	12. 3	19. 4
2015	18. 5		11. 7	12. 2	18. 9
2016	19. 3		11. 8	11. 9	18. 2
2017	18. 5		11. 9	12. 8	17. 7
2018	18. 6		12. 0	12. 5	17. 6
2019	18. 4		12. 1	12. 5	17. 7
2020	19. 1		12. 1	12. 8	17. 7
2021	18. 9		12. 0	12. 2	17. 6
2022	19. 4		12. 0	12. 1	17. 7

表12-12 部分年份平均每万人口在校学生数
The Enrollment of Students Per 10000 Populations in Partial Years

单位：人(person)

年份 Year	大学生 University and College Students	中专学生 Specialized Scendary Schools Students	中学学生 Regular Secondary Schools Students	职业中学生 Vocational Secondary Schools Students	小学生 Primary Schools Schools
2000	48. 0	46. 5	518. 4	81. 6	785. 6
2001	80. 1	41. 8	545. 9	83. 3	779. 1
2002	113. 9	35. 3	566. 5	93. 5	817. 8
2003	145. 9	34. 4	565. 8	119. 0	826. 4
2004	174. 3	32. 3	582. 5	134. 6	864. 2
2005	199. 3	26. 1	582. 3	143. 4	858. 2
2006	215. 2	17. 8	595. 6	137. 6	848. 1
2007	226. 0	13. 4	594. 2	134. 2	835. 2
2008	229. 6	11. 1	604. 6	129. 4	823. 8
2009	240. 8		583. 1	142. 4	788. 6
2010	245. 3		566. 8	140. 6	804. 6
2011	245. 7		536. 4	143. 9	827. 6
2012	251. 9		650. 7	139. 1	829. 8
2013	257. 3		493. 9	135. 3	841. 2
2014	259. 3		481. 4	119. 0	829. 3
2015	266. 2		468. 0	118. 0	820. 6
2016	263. 5		472. 5	109. 1	810. 1
2017	262. 8		482. 2	114. 3	804. 2
2018	260. 0		492. 1	110. 0	817. 3
2019	269. 8		499. 8	109. 8	832. 9
2020	289. 2		507. 5	113. 2	846. 6
2021	298. 9		522. 1	98. 3	873. 3
2022	307. 6		533. 9	98. 1	893. 8

表12-13 历年卫生事业主要指标
Basic Statistics on Health Care Over the Years

年份 Year	卫生机构数（个）Number of Health Institutions (unit)	#医院 Hospitals	卫生事业床位数（张）Number of Beds in Health Service (bed)	#医院 Hospitals	卫生技术人员（万人）Number of Medical technical (10000 persons)	#医生 Doctors
1978	949	400	5989	5549	0.93	0.36
1979	1013	398	6618	5871	0.99	0.36
1980	1032	397	6948	6368	1.06	0.38
1981	1077	394	7537	7015	1.13	0.44
1982	1100	400	8130	7230	1.19	0.48
1983	1107	396	8372	7525	1.24	0.50
1984	1117	396	8823	7954	1.28	0.53
1985	1123	311	9067	8250	1.30	0.54
1986	1181	320	9436	8605	1.34	0.56
1987	1199	327	9922	9057	1.41	0.60
1988	1259	330	10447	9629	1.46	0.73
1989	1293	331	11073	10067	1.53	0.74
1990	1301	344	11449	10522	1.58	0.75
1991	1313	345	11731	10816	1.66	0.76
1992	1270	303	12175	11259	1.69	0.78
1993	1262	300	12529	11633	1.70	0.80
1994	1257	345	12976	12090	1.76	0.84
1995	1257	345	13193	12316	1.74	0.87
1996	1123	297	13012	12299	1.78	0.88
1997	1678	296	13654	8849	1.83	0.92
1998	1407	296	13689	9481	1.86	0.91
1999	961	54	13795	9364	1.89	0.93
2000	929	56	14535	9968	1.92	0.95
2001	921	57	14393	10246	1.96	0.97
2002	1263	58	14653	10292	2.01	0.99
2003	1297	55	15279	10654	2.15	1.06
2004	1555	58	17053	12119	2.51	1.14
2005	1667	265	18458	17856	2.91	1.32
2006	1854	268	19711	19339	3.25	1.46
2007	2270	255	21000	20306	3.53	1.54
2008	2276	257	22155	21523	3.69	1.51
2009	2359	243	23475	22299	4.00	1.62
2010	2377	230	26097	24762	4.31	1.72
2011	4221	106	27127	23046	4.67	1.84
2012	4035	108	28290	24296	4.92	1.91
2013	4032	109	29356	25753	5.15	1.99
2014	4077	123	30852	27538	5.41	2.10
2015	4069	132	32871	29607	5.66	2.19
2016	4115	143	34577	31451	5.94	2.30
2017	4157	154	37315	34135	6.24	2.43
2018	4252	170	38718	35591	6.63	2.59
2019	4530	180	43373	37354	8.81	2.96
2020	4707	195	44447	38420	7.95	3.19
2021	4787	198	45181	39686	8.32	3.43
2022	4916	204	46804	41423	8.75	3.59

表12-14 各区(县、市)卫生事业单位机构情况(2022年)
Basic Statistics on Health Care Institutions by Region (2022)

指标	Indicators	全市 Total	市区 Urban District	海曙区 Haishu
卫生事业机构数	**Number of Health Care Institutions**	**4916**	**2637**	**532**
1. 医院合计	Total Hospitals	204	137	35
综合医院	Comprehensive Hospitals	72	47	11
中医医院	Hospitals of Chinese Medicine	26	15	4
中西医结合医院	Combined Chinese and Western Medicine Hospital	2	2	
专科医院	Specialized Hospitals	98	69	20
口腔医院	Oral and Dental Hospitals	33	24	5
眼科医院	Ophthalmology Hospitals	14	7	2
心血管病医院	Cardiovascular Hospital	1	1	
妇产(科)医院	Obstetrics and Gynecology Hospitals	8	5	3
儿童医院	The Children's Hospital	1	1	
精神病医院	Mental Hospitals	8	4	
皮肤病医院	Dermatology Hospital	1	1	1
骨科医院	Orthopedist Hospitals	6	5	1
康复医院	Healing Hospitals	13	10	2
整形外科医院	Plastic surgery hospitals	1	1	1
美容医院	Cosmetic Surgery Clinic	5	4	
其他专科医院	Others Specialized Hospitals	6	5	4
护理院	Nursing Home	6	4	
2. 社区卫生服务中心(站)	Community Sanitation Service Sites	560	408	49
社区卫生服务中心	Community Health Center	71	52	8
社区卫生服务站	Community Health Service Station	489	356	41
3. 卫生院	Local Hospitals	86	23	7
乡镇卫生院	Town and Township Local Hospitals	86	23	7
中心卫生院	Center Locale Hospitals	26	6	1
乡卫生院	Township Locale Hospitals	60	17	6
4. 村卫生室	Village Health Room	1809	695	121
5. 门诊部	Clinics	501	382	89
6. 诊所、卫生所、医务室	Special Clinics	1675	942	216
7. 急救中心(站)	First-aid Centre(Stations)	10	6	1
8. 采供血机构	Blood Collecting and Supplying Organization	2	1	1
9. 妇幼保健院(所、站)	Maternity and Child Care Centers or Stations	12	8	2
10. 专科疾病防治院(所、站)	Specialized Prevention and Treatment Centers or Stations	2	1	
11. 疾病预防控制中心	Center for Disease Control and Prevention	11	7	2
12. 卫生监督所(中心)	Health Supervision Centers(Center)	11	7	2
13. 计划生育技术服务机构	Family Planning Technical Service Institutions	1		
14. 医学科学研究机构	Research Institution of Medicine	1	1	
15. 医学在职培训机构	Medical Institution of On-the-job Training	5	1	
16. 临床检验中心(所、站)	Clinical Laboratory (Station)	11	9	3
17. 统计信息中心	Statistical Information Center	1	1	1
18. 其他卫生机构	Others Health Care Institutions	10	5	3

注：本表至12-17表数据来自宁波市卫生健康委。
Note: Data from Tables 12-14 to 12-17 are obtained from Ningbo Municipal Health Commission.

单位：个(unit)

江北区 Jiangbei	镇海区 Zhenhai	北仑区 Beilun	鄞州区 Yinzhou	奉化区 Fenghua	余姚市 Yuyao	慈溪市 Cixi	宁海县 Ninghai	象山县 Xiangshan
228	**269**	**364**	**781**	**463**	**646**	**827**	**490**	**316**
17	11	18	43	13	14	27	11	15
5	5	10	13	3	5	13	2	5
1	2	1	6	1	1	5	3	2
			1	1				
8	4	7	23	7	6	9	6	8
2	2	4	9	2	2	1	3	3
1		1	2	1		4	1	2
				1				
1			1		1	1		1
1								
1	1			2	1	1	1	1
		1	2	1	1			
2	1	1	4		1		1	1
			4			1		
			1			1		
3				1	2			
55	64	73	109	58	65	42	36	9
7	5	11	13	8	6	7	3	3
48	59	62	96	50	59	35	33	6
1	2		9	4	15	13	20	15
1	2		9	4	15	13	20	15
1			3	1	6	4	5	5
	2		6	3	9	9	15	10
9	71	101	145	248	288	432	222	172
37	22	53	166	15	20	76	23	
99	95	112	301	119	234	229	171	99
1	1	1	1	1	1	1	1	1
					1			
2	1	1	1	1	1	1	1	1
			1			1		
1	1	1	1	1	1	1	1	1
1	1	1	1	1	1	1	1	1
						1		
1								
		1			1	1	1	1
1		2	2	1	1		1	
1				1	2	1	1	1

表12-15 各区(县、市)卫生事业人员、床位情况(2022年)

Number of Health Care Personnel and Beds by Region（2022）

指标	Indicators	全市 Total	市区 Urban District	海曙区 Haishu
从业人员总计(人)	**Total Employment(person)**	**102394**	**65803**	**19593**
卫生技术人员	Medical Technical Personnel	87485	55623	16706
医生数	Number of Doctors	35939	22231	6438
执业医师	Medical Practitioner	32631	20748	6156
执业助理医师	Assistant Medical Practitioner	3308	1483	282
注册护士	Register Nurse	37657	24378	7367
药师（士）	Pharmacists	4874	3051	941
技师（士）	Laboratory Technicians	5107	3345	1109
检验师	Laboratory Examiner	3240	2049	652
影像师	Imagists	1239	836	270
康复师	Rehabilitation therapist	533	389	177
卫生监督员	Health Supervisor	340	193	81
其他	Others	3568	2425	770
见习医师	Trainee Doctors	1275	739	212
其他技术人员	Other Technical Personnel	2907	1972	570
管理人员	Manager	10407	7251	2398
#仅从事管理的人员	Personnel engaged only in management	3577	2729	897
工勤技能人员	Logistics Workers	7121	5064	1401
每千人拥有卫生技术人员	Number of Medical Technical Personnel Per 1000 Persons	9. 10	10. 69	15. 79
每千人拥有医生	Number of Doctors Per 1000 Persons	3. 74	4. 27	6. 09
每千人拥有注册护士	Number of R.N. Per 1000 Persons	3. 92	4. 68	6. 96
卫生事业床位数(张)	**Number of Beds (bed)**	**46804**	**30424**	**9049**
医院床位	Beds of Hospitals	41423	28327	7510
社区卫生服务中心床位	Beds of Health Service Center of Communities	685	266	50
卫生院床位	Beds of Local Hospitals	2155	320	48
妇幼保健院(所、站)床位	Beds of Maternity and Child Care Centers	2481	1511	1441
专科疾病防治院(所、站)床位	Beds of Specialized Prevention Stations	60		
每千人拥有总床位	Total Beds of Per 1000 Persons	4. 87	5. 85	8. 55
每千人拥有医院卫生院床位	Beds of Hospitals and Local Hospitals Per 1000 Persons	4. 53	5. 50	7. 14

江北区 Jiangbei	镇海区 Zhenhai	北仑区 Beilun	鄞州区 Yinzhou	奉化区 Fenghua	余姚市 Yuyao	慈溪市 Cixi	宁海县 Ninghai	象山县 Xiangshan
6834	**5496**	**6712**	**21397**	**5771**	**10012**	**14493**	**6992**	**5094**
5621	4580	5793	18077	4846	8703	12400	6157	4602
2191	1908	2421	7251	2022	3815	5318	2580	1995
2058	1735	2238	6829	1732	3287	4701	2194	1701
133	173	183	422	290	528	617	386	294
2534	1906	2332	8140	2099	3625	5076	2755	1823
283	287	350	936	254	483	781	271	288
276	258	437	1056	209	481	748	287	246
160	160	300	628	149	319	491	200	181
76	63	105	277	45	109	176	63	55
33	26	23	123	7	44	75	21	4
24	22	27	19	20	38	61	26	22
313	199	226	675	242	261	416	238	228
60	43	121	178	125	117	195	85	139
202	139	185	676	200	237	345	186	167
708	566	664	2309	606	1078	1343	410	325
330	228	186	959	129	246	434	86	82
672	482	455	1658	396	580	982	404	91
11.17	8.88	6.59	10.88	8.27	6.89	6.65	8.68	7.99
4.36	3.70	2.75	4.36	3.45	3.02	2.85	3.64	3.46
5.04	3.69	2.65	4.90	3.58	2.87	2.72	3.89	3.16
3581	**2541**	**2877**	**9650**	**2726**	**3842**	**7098**	**3038**	**2402**
3561	2501	2821	9393	2541	2971	5862	2147	2116
20	30	50	62	54	47	190	62	120
	10		195	67	384	730	556	165
		6		64	440	256	273	1
						60		
7.12	4.92	3.27	5.81	4.65	3.04	3.81	4.28	4.17
7.08	4.87	3.21	5.77	4.45	2.65	3.53	3.81	3.96

表12-16 各级医院工作情况(2022年)
Medical Treatment of Various Hospitals（2022）

指标	Indicators	门诊人次合计 (万人次) Out-Patients (10000 person-times)
全市总计	**Total**	**10264**
1. 医院合计	Total Hospitals	4561
综合医院	Comprehensive Hospitals	3304
省辖市属医院	Urban Hospitals Administered by Province	782
#市第一医院	The No.1 Hospital of Ningbo	262
国科大华美医院	Hua Mei Hospital, University of Chinese Academy of Sciences	173
宁大附院	The No.3 Hospital of Ningbo	108
市李惠利医院	Li Huili Hospital of Ningbo	222
市华慈医院	Hua Ci Hospital of Ningbo	16
中医医院	Hospitals of Chinese Medicine	680
#市中医院	Hospital of Chinese Medicine of Ningbo	144
中西医结合医院	Combined Chinese and Western Medicine Hospital	20
专科医院	Specialized Hospitals	553
口腔医院	Oral and Dental Hospitals	139
眼科医院	Ophthalmology Hospitals	89
心血管病医院	Cardiovascular Hospital	16
妇产（科）医院	Obstetrics and Gynecology Hospitals	23
儿童医院	The Children's Hospital	8
精神病医院	Mental Hospitals	92
#市康宁医院	Kangning Hospital of Ningbo	29
皮肤病医院	Dermatology Hospital	5
骨科医院	Orthopedist Hospitals	102
康复医院	Healing Hospitals	49
整形外科医院	Plastic surgery hospital	1
美容医院	Cosmetic Surgery Clinic	12
其他专科医院	Others Specialized Hospitals	18
护理院	Nursing Home	4
2. 社区卫生服务中心（站）	Health Service Center of Communities	1599
3. 卫生院	Local Hospitals	1742
4. 村卫生室	Policlinic	841
5. 门诊部	Village Health Room	345
6. 诊所、卫生所、医务室	Clinic	573
7. 妇幼保健院（所、站）	Maternity and Child Care Centers or Stations	563
#市妇儿医院	Hospital for Maternity and Child of Ningbo	244
8. 专科疾病防治院（所、站）	Specialized Prevention and Treatment Centers or Stations	25

本年入院人数 (万人) Inpatients in this Year (10000 persons)	平均住院日 (天) Average Day In – patients (day)	本年出院人数 (万人) Discharged Patient in this Year (10000 persons)	期末实有病床数 (张) Factual Beds at the Year– end (bed)	平均开放病床数 (张) Average Openning Bed (bed)	病床使用率 (%) Occupancy of Hospital Beds (%)
144.52	**7.70**	**143.87**	**46804**	**42755**	**72.10**
129.77	7.90	129.12	41423	38157	74.80
100.47	6.60	100.29	26175	24131	76.22
39.13	6.20	39.15	7777	7287	91.93
11.84	5.60	11.81	2507	1980	91.90
10.29	6.60	10.33	1925	1982	93.53
5.47	6.40	5.46	1115	1112	86.87
11.53	6.50	11.56	2230	2213	93.07
11.85	8.40	11.72	4630	4278	64.37
2.56	9.40	2.53	850	761	85.33
0.21	5.10	0.21	76	76	36.40
16.80	14.70	16.69	10175	9306	76.15
0.02	1.00	0.02	620	357	0.37
2.96	2.30	2.96	589	587	31.45
1.09	8.50	1.07	300	300	82.94
0.72	8.40	0.68	416	367	43.55
0.23	5.80	0.23	45	45	82.17
2.60	37.00	2.59	3003	2835	94.07
0.82	32.30	0.82	768	766	95.73
			20	20	
6.56	7.40	6.59	1728	1627	84.50
1.73	40.20	1.66	2765	2588	81.12
	2.30		72	72	0.24
0.16	2.60	0.16	101	103	11.28
0.73	14.10	0.73	446	377	80.36
0.44	42.10	0.22	367	367	76.85
0.29	11.10	0.29	685	505	20.71
1.75	10.10	1.76	2155	1677	30.16
12.70	4.80	12.70	2481	2366	70.76
8.61	4.80	8.62	1441	1437	78.08
			60	50	

表12-17 居民病伤死亡原因(2022年)
Main 10 Diseases of Death in Urban Residents（2022）

指标	Indicators	死亡人数（人） 合计 Total
宁波市总计	**Total in Ningbo**	**47160**
十种死因合计	Main 10 Causes of Death	44411
1. 恶性肿瘤	Malignant Tumour	13710
2. 脑血管病	Cerebral Vascular Disease	7750
3. 心脏病	Cardiopathy	7171
4. 呼吸系统疾病	Respiratory Disease	5015
5. 损伤和中毒	Trauma and Toxicosis	4861
6. 神经系统疾病	Internal System Disease	1668
7. 内分泌等疾病	Digestive Disease	1653
8. 消化系统疾病	Nervous system diseases	1388
9. 泌尿系疾病	Urologic Diseases	799
10. 肌肉骨骼和结缔组织疾病	Mental Disorder	396
市区总计	**Total in Urban Area**	**21482**
十种死因合计	Main 10 Causes of Death	20290
1. 恶性肿瘤	Malignant Tumour	6668
2. 脑血管病	Cerebral Vascular Disease	3379
3. 心脏病	Heart Disease	3304
4. 呼吸系统疾病	Respiratory Disease	2197
5. 损伤和中毒	Injury and Poisoning	2014
6. 神经系统疾病	Internal System Disease	840
7. 内分泌等疾病	Nervous system diseases	811
8. 消化系统疾病	Digestive Disease	529
9. 泌尿系疾病	Urologic Diseases	354
10. 肌肉骨骼和结缔组织疾病	Mental Disorder	194

Number of Death (person)		死因构成 (%) Composition of Death (%)	死亡专率(/10万) Death Rate (per 0.1 million persons)		
男 Male	女 Female		合计 Total	男 Male	女 Female
26707	**20453**	**100.00**	**761.01**	**876.08**	**649.60**
25323	19088	94.17	716.65	830.68	606.24
9225	4485	29.07	221.24	302.61	142.45
4204	3546	16.43	125.06	137.91	112.62
3504	3667	15.21	115.72	114.94	116.47
3086	1929	10.63	80.93	101.23	61.27
2263	2598	10.31	78.44	74.23	82.51
848	820	3.54	26.92	27.82	26.04
800	853	3.51	26.67	26.24	27.09
727	661	2.94	22.40	23.85	20.99
500	299	1.69	12.89	16.40	9.50
166	230	0.84	6.39	5.45	7.30
12349	**9133**	**100.00**	**686.92**	**811.43**	**568.89**
11730	8560	94.45	648.80	770.75	533.20
4508	2160	31.04	213.22	296.21	134.55
1835	1544	15.73	108.05	120.57	96.17
1648	1656	15.38	105.65	108.29	103.15
1386	811	10.23	70.25	91.07	50.52
968	1046	9.38	64.40	63.61	65.15
420	420	3.91	26.86	27.60	26.16
394	417	3.78	25.93	25.89	25.97
274	255	2.46	16.92	18.00	15.88
216	138	1.65	11.32	14.19	8.60
81	113	0.90	6.20	5.32	7.04

表12-18 部分年份全市体育工作情况
Basic Statistics on Physical Culture Schools and Sports in Partial Years

指标	单位	Indicators	Unit	2019	2020	2021	2022
各类体校情况		**Various Physical Culture and Sports School**					
体育运动学校数	个	Physical Education and Sports School	unit	1	1	1	1
在校学生数	人	Student Enrollment	person	668	990	755	833
专职教练员	人	Full-time Coaches	person	47	75	74	77
业余体校个数	个	Sparetime Sports Schools	unit	14	14	13	13
#重点业余体校	个	Emphatic Sparetime Sports School	unit	5	4	3	3
业余体校在校学生数	人	Student Enrollment in Sparetime Sports Schools	person	2230	2350	2461	2376
业余体校送入优秀运动队	人	Number of Persons from Sparetime Sports School Enrolling Excelent Sports Team	person	56	25	40	38
业余体校考入高等院校	人	Number of Persons Admitted to Institutions Higher Education from Sparetime Sports School	person	78	66	86	72
传统项目布局情况		**Distribution on Traditional Events**					
分布学校数	个	Number of Distributing Schools	unit	177	177	183	183
#中学	个	Secondary Schools	unit	54	54	53	53
小学	个	Primary Schools	unit	123	123	130	130
市区新增健身设施	套	New built Health-care Facilities in Urban Districts	set			112	
参加活动学生人数	人	Number of Participants in Student	person	21500	21500	27839	23341
参加田径学生	人	Track and Field	person	10100	10100	3402	5613
参加游泳学生	人	Swimming	person	2100	1486	1933	2993
参加射击学生	人	Shoot	person	360	368	562	805
参加篮球学生	人	Basketball	person	2300	956	2520	3920
参加排球学生	人	Volleyball	person	700	630	894	1191
参加足球学生	人	Football	person	3100	2003	2768	4035
参加乒乓排球学生	人	Pingpong	person	1100	1148	1823	2410
参加羽毛球学生	人	Badminton	person	1600	925	1707	2374
游泳池情况(体育系统)		**Swimming Pool Managed by Physical Department**					
游泳池个数	个	Number of Swimming Pools	unit	35	11	17	18
#室内游泳池	个	Indoor	unit	22	10	15	16
游泳池活动场次	场次	Number of Running Swimming Pool	times	195000	450	700	500
#室内游泳池	场次	Indoor	times	142000	360	550	360
参赛获奖数	**枚**	**Number of Obtain Awards by Athletic Competition**	**unit**	**467**	**594**	**775**	**809**
#省级及以上金牌	枚	Gold Medals Won in Province Level Competitions	unit	163	229	299	301
#省级及以上银牌	枚	Silver Medals Won in Province Level Competitions	unit	111	163	228	240
#省级及以上铜牌	枚	Bronze Medals Won in Province Level Competitions	unit	193	202	249	269

表12-19 部分年份科技活动情况
Scientific and Technological Activities in Partial Years

指标	Indicators	2018	2019	2020	2021	2022
研究与试验发展经费支出（亿元）	Expenditure on R&D(100 million yuan)	276.17	323.94	354.84	402.73	460.96
#规上工业（亿元）	Industrial Enterprises above Designated Size(100 million yuan)	239.62	263.10	289.01	328.56	364.73
研究与试验发展经费支出占地区生产总值的比重（%）	of GDP（%）	2.57	2.70	2.86	2.76	2.94

表12-20 部分年份规模以上工业企业科技活动情况
Scientific and Technological Activities of Industrial Enterprises in Partial Years

指标	Indicators	2019	2020	2021	2022
企业数（个）	Number of Enterprises (unit)	8240	8567	9834	10340
#有R&D活动(个）	Number of Enterprises Having R&D Activities(unit)	3832	4053	4409	4206
#有科技机构（个）	Number of R&D Institutions(unit)	3146	3810	3877	4751
年末从业人员（人）	Number of Employees at the End of the Year (person)	1477751	1532922	1644634	
R&D经费外部支出(万元）	External Expenditure on R&D Projects (10000 yuan)	146863	205615	181370	378028
专利申请数（件）	Patent Applications(piece)	26392	28579	31636	34390
#发明专利（件）	Inventions (piece)	7937	7820	8348	8987
有效发明专利数（件）	Inventions In Force(piece)	16032	18235	23675	27975
引进技术经费支出（万元）	Expenditure for Acquisition of Technology(10000 yuan)	19267	34452	44940	49843
消化吸收经费支出（万元）	Expenditure for Assimilation of Technology(10000 yuan)	2332	1822	711	819
购买国内技术经费支出（万元）	Expenditure for Purchase of Domestic Technology (10000 yuan)	108398	65177	77407	110647
技术改造经费支出（万元）	Expenditure for Technical Renovation (10000 yuan)	576694	544287	593753	845178

表12-21 2010年以来规模以上工业企业科技活动情况
Scientific and Technological Activities of Industrial Enterprises Above Designated Size since 2010

年份 Year	R&D经费内部支出（万元） Internal expenditure of R&D funds (10000 yuan)	基础研究支出 Basic research	应用研究支出 Application research	试验发展支出 Test development	R&D人员合计（人） Total R&D personnel (person)
2010	782537			782537	52569
2011	975034			975034	57026
2012	1222028	149	2059	1219820	69815
2013	1419568		604	1418964	79807
2014	1600005		4239	1595766	83473
2015	1778514		3105	1775409	91287
2016	1848716		445	1848272	90009
2017	2166461		7392	2159069	99714
2018	2396158		14401	2381756	112311
2019	2631024	64	7790	2623170	115649
2020	2890050		488	2889563	117522
2021	3285632	1543	2263	3281826	129571
2022	3647254				134225

参加项目人员 Project participants	管理和服务人员 Management and service personnel	R&D人员折合全时当量（人年） Full – time equivalent of R&D personnel (person year)	新产品开发项目数（个） Number of new products(unit)	新产品开发经费支出（万元） New product development expenditure (10000 yuan)	新产品销售收入（万元） Sales revenue of new products (10000 yuan)	出口 Export
48988	3581	44480	9235	1017296	15286651	5491557
53757	3269	47555	9904	1213976	18336441	6187070
66465	3350	54934	12359	1493212	22534629	6868378
76711	3096	63972	13648	1671386	27267747	6996232
80315	3158	67070	14473	1770151	29093609	7851461
89330	1957	72138	14949	1804910	36426329	8301777
88892	1117	70079	16250	2034169	41302874	8896090
98424	1290	75304	18321	2418551	48325905	9777067
105602	6709	86893	21485	2690291	51604367	11107740
109878	5771	92265	24759	3144030	58515484	12608477
113673	3849	93383	27804	3441901	58548178	12877161
124678	4893	101170	33533	4476876	72119783	15696479
130924	3301	108380	38716	5213349	76208098	16238112

表12-22 规模以上工业企业科技活动情况(2022年)
Scientific and Technological Activities of Industrial Enterprises Above Designated Size（2022）

指标	Indicators	企业个数（个）Number of Enterprises (unit)	有R&D的企业数（个）Number of Enterprises Having R&D Activities(unit)
总计	**Total**	**10340**	**4206**
按企业规模分	**Grouped by Enterprises Size**		
大型企业	Large-Sized	149	124
中型企业	Medium-Sized	861	681
按登记注册类型分	**Grouped by Registered Type**		
内资企业	Domestic Funded Enterprises	9036	3572
国有企业	State-owned Enterprises	7	1
集体企业	Collective-owned Enterprises	5	
股份合作企业	Share Cooperative Enterprises	30	13
有限责任公司	Limited Liability Corporations	433	191
股份有限公司	Share-holding Corporations Ltd.	94	77
私营企业	Private Enterprises	8467	3290
其他企业	Other Enterprises		
港、澳、台商投资企业	Hong Kong, Macao & Taiwan Funded	616	325
合资经营企业	Joint venture Enterprises	262	138
合作经营企业	Cooperative Enterprises	5	3
港、澳、台商独资经营企业	Hong Kong, Macao and Taiwan-funded Enterprises	314	154
港、澳、台商投资股份有限公司	Hong Kong, Macao and Taiwan Investment Ltd.	32	29
其他港澳台投资企业	Other Hong Kong, Macao and Taiwan Funded Enterprises	3	1
外商投资企业	Foreign Funded Enterprises	688	309
中外合资经营企业	Sino-foreign Joint Venture Enterprises	280	137
中外合作经营企业	Sino-foreign Contractual Joint Ventures	6	3
外资企业	Foreign-funded Enterprises	386	160
外商投资股份有限公司	Foreign Investment Joint Stock company	14	8
其他外商投资企业	Other Foreign Funded Enterprises	2	1

企业办科技机构（个）Number of R&D Institutions (unit)	企业办机构仪器设备原价（万元）Original Value of Machine and Equipment for Operated (10000 yuan)	R&D人员（人）R&D Personnel (person)	R&D人员折合全时当量合计（人年）Full-time Equivalent of R&D Personnel (man-years)	R&D经费内部支出（万元）Intramural Expenditure R&D Projects (10000 yuan)	新产品开发经费支出（万元）Expenditure on New Products Development (10000 yuan)	发明专利申请数（项）Invention Patent Number of Applications	有效发明专利数（项）Effective Invention Number of patents
4781	**3428457**	**134225**	**108380**	**3647254**	**5213349**	**34390**	**27975**
134	1148514	36353	28950	1197795	1577282	10492	8792
705	1084175	43528	35523	1217395	1688762	7091	7771
4083	2288275	98165	78940	2558589	3685942	28234	22642
1	405	86	68	3583	2730	2	24
1	7				18		
15	7948	245	200	6224	8914	64	56
204	243468	8287	6307	321593	477149	1626	2197
83	169576	7807	6066	280840	371032	3456	4041
3779	1866872	81740	66298	1946349	2826098	23086	16324
360	869847	22100	18245	623402	896547	3807	2962
154	309520	5385	4477	156746	301247	1056	925
3	511	102	88	2243	3027	8	25
171	277042	10397	8742	287704	383895	1893	1004
30	277730	6041	4824	169755	199849	814	929
2	5044	175	113	6955	8528	36	79
338	270335	13960	11195	465264	630861	2349	2371
147	137824	6500	5235	228769	311974	1016	1244
4	993	55	50	1588	2025	13	8
177	114593	5978	4796	190272	266331	963	917
9	16923	1416	1106	44512	50359	355	200
1	2	11	9	123	172	2	2

表12-23 规模以上工业企业R&D人员情况(2022年)
R&D Personnel of Industrial Enterprises Above Designated Size（2022）

指标	Indicators
总计	**Total**
按企业规模分	**Grouped by Enterprises Size**
大型	Large-Sized
中型	Medium-Sized
小型	Small-Sized
微型	Micro-Sized
按登记注册类型分	**Grouped by Registered Type**
国有企业	State-owned Enterprises
集体企业	Collective-owned Enterprises
股份合作企业	Share Cooperative Enterprises
有限责任公司	Limited Liability Corporations
股份有限公司	Share-holding Corporations Ltd.
私营企业	Private Enterprises
其他企业	Other Enterprises
港、澳、台商投资企业	Hong Kong, Macao & Taiwan Funded
外商投资企业	Foreign Funded Enterprises
按国民经济行业大类分	**Grouped by Sector**
非金属矿采选业	Non-metallic Mining Industry
农副食品加工业	Farm and Sideline Products Processing
食品制造业	Food Manufacturing
酒、饮料和精制茶制造业	Wine, Beverages and Refined Tea Manufacturing
纺织业	Textile Industry
纺织服装、服饰业	Clothing, Apparel Industry
皮革、毛皮、羽毛及其制品和制鞋业	Leather, Fur, Feather and Its Products and Footwear Industry
木材加工和木、竹、藤、棕、草制品业	Timber Processing, Bamboo, Rattan, Cane Palm, and Straw Products
家具制造业	Furniture Manufacturing
造纸和纸制品业	Paper-making and Paper Products Manufacturing
印刷和记录媒介复制业	Printing and Record Duplicating
文教、工美、体育和娱乐用品制造业	Culture, Art, Sports and Recreation Supplies Manufacturing
石油加工、炼焦和核燃料加工业	Petroleum Processing, Coking & Nuclear Fuel Processing
化学原料和化学制品制造业	Raw Chemical Materials and Chemical Products
医药制造业	Medicines Manufacturing

单位：人（person ）

R&D 人员合计 Total	#女性 Female	#研究人员 Researchers	#1. 全时人员 Full - time	2. 非全时人员 Part - time	R&D 人员折合全时当量合计（人年） Full-time Equivalent
134225	**27472**	**28865**	**94117**	**40108**	**108380**
36353	7332	11045	25762	10591	28950
43528	9015	9137	30988	12540	35523
54078	11085	8631	37244	16834	43680
266	40	52	123	143	228
86	25	22	62	24	68
245	42	59	182	63	200
8287	1889	2259	5298	2989	6307
7807	1444	2478	5717	2090	6066
81740	16543	14053	56932	24808	66298
22100	4721	5907	15891	6209	18245
13960	2808	4087	10035	3925	11195
15	1	7	10	5	10
140	47	44	102	38	115
268	99	75	193	75	196
57	14	13	40	17	41
2250	1083	381	1547	703	1866
2288	1431	380	1853	435	1945
162	69	9	68	94	134
81	22	9	57	24	64
1465	366	212	828	637	1105
405	78	50	232	173	334
920	341	145	572	348	783
3486	1036	510	2303	1183	2873
138	13	54	27	111	94
3321	681	889	2379	942	2706
1519	679	514	1028	491	1196

表 12 –23 续表 Continued

指标	Indicators
化学纤维制造业	Chemical Fiber Manufacturing
橡胶和塑料制品业	Rubber and Plastic Products Industry
非金属矿物制品业	Nonmetal Mineral Products
黑色金属冶炼和压延加工业	Smelting and Pressing of Ferrous Metals
有色金属冶炼和压延加工业	Smelting and Pressing of Nonferrous Metals
金属制品业	Metal Products Manufacturing
通用设备制造业	General Purpose Equipment Manufacturing
专用设备制造业	Special Purpose Equipment Manufacturing
汽车制造业	Automobile Manufacturing
铁路、船舶、航空航天和其他运输设备制造	Railroad, Marine, Aviation and Other Transport Equipment Manufacturing
电气机械和器材制造业	Electric Equipment and Machinery Manufacturing
计算机、通信和其他电子设备制造业	Computer, Communications and Other Electronic Equipment Manufacturing
仪器仪表制造业	Instrument Manufacturing
其他制造业	Other Manufacturing
废弃资源综合利用业	Waste Comprehensive Utilization of Resources Industry
金属制品、机械和设备修理业	Metal Products, Machinery and Equipment Repair Industry
电力、热力生产和供应业	Production and Supply Electric Power and Thermal Power
燃气生产和供应业	Production and Supply Gas
水的生产和供应业	Production and Supply Tap Water
按地区分	**Grouped by Districts**
海曙区	Haishu
江北区	Jiangbei
北仑区	Beilun
镇海区	Zhenhai
鄞州区	Yinzhou
奉化区	Fenghua
象山县	Xiangshan
宁海县	Ninghai
高新区	Gaoxin
余姚市	Yuyao
慈溪市	Cixi

单位：人（person ）

R&D 人员合计 Total	#女性 Female	#研究人员 Researchers	#1. 全时人员 Full - time	2. 非全时人员 Part - time	R&D 人员折合全时当量合计（人年）Full-time Equivalent
287	62	27	162	125	202
5860	1323	774	4053	1807	4762
1566	216	282	945	621	1184
766	86	183	555	211	603
1378	161	194	861	517	1141
7109	1201	1043	5107	2002	5739
16077	2768	2936	11736	4341	13201
9100	1052	2151	6815	2285	7551
20216	3176	4798	14325	5891	16282
1447	242	236	1000	447	1163
25672	5603	4328	17773	7899	20614
19744	4112	5843	14395	5349	16117
7432	1328	2628	4527	2905	5538
626	140	42	405	221	492
119	29	24	88	31	96
53	2	12	41	12	43
248	11	67	90	158	185
10		5			6
8183	2247	1585	6156	2027	6780
7576	1351	1789	4208	3368	5725
18133	3438	4931	14140	3993	14852
8442	1730	1623	5772	2670	6664
14941	2980	3442	11347	3594	12844
7924	1588	1115	5360	2564	6343
4409	761	1036	2946	1463	3496
9124	2076	1418	5934	3190	7246
3920	727	1457	2900	1020	2878
19468	4029	4237	13153	6315	15637
32105	6545	6232	22201	9904	25917

表12-24 规模以上工业企业R&D经费情况(2022年)
R&D Fund of Industrial Enterprises Above Designated Size (2022)

指标	Indicators
总计	**Total**
按企业规模分	**Grouped by Enterprises Size**
大型	Large-Sized
中型	Medium-Sized
小型	Small-Sized
微型	Micro-Sized
按登记注册类型分	**Grouped by Registered Type**
国有企业	State-owned Enterprises
集体企业	Collective-owned Enterprises
股份合作企业	Share Cooperative Enterprises
有限责任公司	Limited Liability Corporations
股份有限公司	Share-holding Corporations Ltd.
私营企业	Private Enterprises
其他企业	Other Enterprises
港、澳、台商投资企业	Hong Kong, Macao & Taiwan Funded
外商投资企业	Foreign Funded Enterprises
按国民经济行业大类分	**Grouped by Sector**
非金属矿采选业	Non-metallic Mining Industry
农副食品加工业	Farm and Sideline Products Processing
食品制造业	Food Manufacturing
酒、饮料和精制茶制造业	Wine, Beverages and Refined Tea Manufacturing
纺织业	Textile Industry
纺织服装、服饰业	Clothing, Apparel Industry
皮革、毛皮、羽毛及其制品和制鞋业	Leather, Fur, Feather and Its Products and Footwear Industry
木材加工和木、竹、藤、棕、草制品业	Timber Processing, Bamboo, Rattan, Cane Palm, and Straw Products
家具制造业	Furniture Manufacturing
造纸和纸制品业	Paper-making and Paper Products Manufacturing
印刷和记录媒介复制业	Printing and Record Duplicating
文教、工美、体育和娱乐用品制造业	Culture, Art, Sports and Recreation Supplies Manufacturing
石油加工、炼焦和核燃料加工业	Petroleum Processing, Coking & Nuclear Fuel Processing
化学原料和化学制品制造业	Raw Chemical Materials and Chemical Products
医药制造业	Medicines Manufacturing

单位：万元(10000 yuan)

R&D经费内部支出合计 Internal Expenditures	（一）按支出用途分组(Grouped by Objects of Expenditure)				（二）按资金来源分组	
	1.日常性支出 Regular fee Expenditure	#人员劳务费 Staff Labour Costs	2.资产性支出 Asset Expenditures	#仪器设备 Instruments and Equipment	1.政府资金 Government Funds	2.企业资金 Enterprise Funds
3647254	**3398905**	**1382298**	**248349**	**243364**	**26888**	**3619758**
1197795	1109267	482512	88529	87564	5025	1192770
1217395	1136526	442034	80869	78937	11661	1205679
1224217	1145960	455853	78257	76184	9718	1213946
7847	7153	1898	694	679	484	7363
3583	3583	1321				3583
6224	5846	2470	378	369	200	6024
321593	296383	91503	25209	23984	2447	319145
280840	270120	94538	10721	10410	3877	276964
1946349	1814247	740303	132102	130084	11547	1934282
623402	561116	256268	62285	61702	6406	616907
465264	447610	195895	17654	16816	2411	462853
272	272	96				272
3064	2765	995	299	299	394	2670
4880	4513	2144	366	363	233	4646
1105	990	672	115	115		1105
52385	47750	21886	4635	4621	135	52251
41965	41350	21048	615	590	270	41695
1761	1759	937	2	2		1761
2556	2217	970	339	339	68	2488
23827	22835	11079	992	937	70	23757
6934	6933	3174	1		27	6907
13474	13201	6156	273	265		13474
52531	51872	30283	659	651	30	52501
5552	5442	3151	110	110		5552
158087	146053	53837	12034	10481	1616	156472
61679	56716	16318	4963	4939	440	61101

表 12 –24 续表 1 Continued 1

指标	Indicators
化学纤维制造业	Chemical Fiber Manufacturing
橡胶和塑料制品业	Rubber and Plastic Products Industry
非金属矿物制品业	Nonmetal Mineral Products
黑色金属冶炼和压延加工业	Smelting and Pressing of Ferrous Metals
有色金属冶炼和压延加工业	Smelting and Pressing of Nonferrous Metals
金属制品业	Metal Products Manufacturing
通用设备制造业	General Purpose Equipment Manufacturing
专用设备制造业	Special Purpose Equipment Manufacturing
汽车制造业	Automobile Manufacturing
铁路、船舶、航空航天和其他运输设备	Railroad, Marine, Aviation and Other Transport Equipment Manufacturing
电气机械和器材制造业	Electric Equipment and Machinery Manufacturing
计算机、通信和其他电子设备制造业	Computer, Communications and Other Electronic Equipment Manufacturing
仪器仪表制造业	Instrument Manufacturing
其他制造业	Other Manufacturing
废弃资源综合利用业	Waste Comprehensive Utilization of Resources Industry
金属制品、机械和设备修理业	Metal Products, Machinery and Equipment Repair Industry
电力、热力生产和供应业	Production and Supply Electric Power and Thermal Power
燃气生产和供应业	Production and Supply Gas
水的生产和供应业	Production and Supply Tap Water
按地区分	**Grouped by Districts**
海曙区	Haishu
江北区	Jiangbei
北仑区	Beilun
镇海区	Zhenhai
鄞州区	Yinzhou
奉化区	Fenghua
象山县	Xiangshan
宁海县	Ninghai
高新区	Gaoxin
余姚市	Yuyao
慈溪市	Cixi

单位：万元(10000 yuan)

R&D经费内部支出合计 Internal Expenditures	（一）按支出用途分组(Grouped by Objects of Expenditure)				（二）按资金来源分组	
	1.日常性支出 Regular fee Expenditure	#人员劳务费 Staff Labour Costs	2.资产性支出 Asset Expenditures	#仪器设备 Instruments and Equipment	1.政府资金 Government Funds	2.企业资金 Enterprise Funds
11539	11311	1691	227	120	120	11419
133172	117399	48700	15774	15571	2164	130807
39249	37217	12212	2032	2011	1142	38106
50344	49313	13017	1031	997	640	49704
46841	39484	12416	7357	7350	1763	45078
168161	140319	55678	27842	27783	801	167347
385329	364202	155303	21127	20882	3153	382096
247760	234480	111004	13281	12991	480	247219
583378	543388	243657	39989	39563	2498	580880
44699	42852	12539	1847	1829	58	44641
629055	602724	218055	26331	25917	1869	627128
651542	612999	238106	38543	37565	6498	645044
194224	168215	77890	26009	25659	2420	191804
8179	8054	3773	125	122		8124
2463	2404	987	60	47		2463
763	763	567				763
19662	18291	3781	1372	1247		19662
823	823	178				823
217720	203707	75541	14013	13773	837	216883
199790	187655	75963	12134	11935	5484	194305
582381	528192	227960	54189	53741	2346	580035
227882	215567	95178	12315	11138	551	227264
392542	371179	155414	21363	21056	3355	389084
172676	160523	66388	12153	11697	3163	169513
159837	149528	47749	10309	10219	121	159709
265728	244497	78055	21231	20968	1879	263849
154003	141449	54125	12553	11772	3156	150846
529836	487497	180154	42339	41898	3343	526075
744861	709112	325771	35750	35168	2652	742196

表 12 -24 续表 2 Continued 2

指标	Indicators
总计	**Total**
按企业规模分	**Grouped by Enterprises Size**
大型	Large-Sized
中型	Medium-Sized
小型	Small-Sized
微型	Micro-Sized
按登记注册类型分	**Grouped by Registered Type**
国有企业	State-owned Enterprises
集体企业	Collective-owned Enterprises
股份合作企业	Share Cooperative Enterprises
有限责任公司	Limited Liability Corporations
股份有限公司	Share-holding Corporations Ltd.
私营企业	Private Enterprises
其他企业	Other Enterprises
港、澳、台商投资企业	Hong Kong, Macao & Taiwan Funded
外商投资企业	Foreign Funded Enterprises
按国民经济行业大类分	**Grouped by Sector**
非金属矿采选业	Non-metallic Mining Industry
农副食品加工业	Farm and Sideline Products Processing
食品制造业	Food Manufacturing
酒、饮料和精制茶制造业	Wine, Beverages and Refined Tea Manufacturing
纺织业	Textile Industry
纺织服装、服饰业	Clothing, Apparel Industry
皮革、毛皮、羽毛及其制品和制鞋业	Leather, Fur, Feather and Its Products and Footwear Industry
木材加工和木、竹、藤、棕、草制品业	Timber Processing, Bamboo, Rattan, Cane Palm, and Straw Products
家具制造业	Furniture Manufacturing
造纸和纸制品业	Paper-making and Paper Products Manufacturing
印刷和记录媒介复制业	Printing and Record Duplicating
文教、工美、体育和娱乐用品制造业	Culture, Art, Sports and Recreation Supplies Manufacturing
石油加工、炼焦和核燃料加工业	Petroleum Processing, Coking & Nuclear Fuel Processing
化学原料和化学制品制造业	Raw Chemical Materials and Chemical Products
医药制造业	Medicines Manufacturing

单位：万元(10000 yuan)

(Grouped by Sources of Fund)						
3.境外资金 Offshore Funds	4.其他资金 Other Funds	R&D经费外部支出 External Expenditures	对境内研究机构支出 Research Institutions in Spending	对境内高等学校支出 Within the College Expenses	对境内企业支出 On Domestic enterprise	对境外支出 On Foreign Spending
71	**537**	**378028**	**30008**	**21337**	**286314**	**40369**
		286160	23299	9788	230782	22291
	55	51496	2649	4879	32289	11678
71	482	39558	4050	6500	22958	6051
		815	9	170	286	350
		1898		137	1761	
		39376	21423	6971	10962	20
		15972	2452	1492	7333	4695
25	495	61627	3653	9620	42807	5548
46	42	29083	1694	1955	17282	8151
		230073	787	1163	206169	21954
		46		46		
		373	348	20	5	
		5152		26	5126	
		427	127	70	230	
		81		81		
		653	7	30	617	
		1235	1178	53	5	
		1126		18		1108
		3705		122	3234	350
		1989	232	470		1287
		16644	220	7079	9346	
	139	3680	127	340	2416	797

表 12 –24 续表 3 Continued 3

指标	Indicators
化学纤维制造业	Chemical Fiber Manufacturing
橡胶和塑料制品业	Rubber and Plastic Products Industry
非金属矿物制品业	Nonmetal Mineral Products
黑色金属冶炼和压延加工业	Smelting and Pressing of Ferrous Metals
有色金属冶炼和压延加工业	Smelting and Pressing of Nonferrous Metals
金属制品业	Metal Products Manufacturing
通用设备制造业	General Purpose Equipment Manufacturing
专用设备制造业	Special Purpose Equipment Manufacturing
汽车制造业	Automobile Manufacturing
铁路、船舶、航空航天和其他运输设备	Railroad, Marine, Aviation and Other Transport Equipment Manufacturing
电气机械和器材制造业	Electric Equipment and Machinery Manufacturing
计算机、通信和其他电子设备制造业	Computer, Communications and Other Electronic Equipment Manufacturing
仪器仪表制造业	Instrument Manufacturing
其他制造业	Other Manufacturing
废弃资源综合利用业	Waste Comprehensive Utilization of Resources Industry
金属制品、机械和设备修理业	Metal Products, Machinery and Equipment Repair Industry
电力、热力生产和供应业	Production and Supply Electric Power and Thermal Power
燃气生产和供应业	Production and Supply Gas
水的生产和供应业	Production and Supply Tap Water
按地区分	**Grouped by Districts**
海曙区	Haishu
江北区	Jiangbei
北仑区	Beilun
镇海区	Zhenhai
鄞州区	Yinzhou
奉化区	Fenghua
象山县	Xiangshan
宁海县	Ninghai
高新区	Gaoxin
余姚市	Yuyao
慈溪市	Cixi

单位：万元(10000 yuan)

(Grouped by Sources of Fund)						
3.境外资金 Offshore Funds	4.其他资金 Other Funds	R&D经费外部支出 External Expenditures	对境内研究机构支出 Research Institutions in Spending	对境内高等学校支出 Within the College Expenses	对境内企业支出 On Domestic enterprise	对境外支出 On Foreign Spending
		43		43		
	201	1426	214	554	645	13
		1789	210	595	984	
		1473	582	100	790	
		367	164	203		
	13	1907	243	356	1026	282
	80	9306	385	2982	5589	351
	62	4861	1362	1709	1350	439
		218068	20770	1122	186241	9935
		3738	3	53	3682	
25	33	29614	1719	1897	24781	1217
		66383	1855	2102	37882	24545
		3856	262	1246	2303	46
46	10					
		69		7	62	
		16		16		
		2805	742	1235	828	
		7887	1887	855	5145	
		64858	2444	8551	51213	2650
	67	10970	1423	1540	6682	1324
		16898	958	1507	6189	8245
		2043	164	1033	845	
	7	1209	358	648	203	
		8431	425	1536	4776	1695
		43591	370	924	20721	21577
71	347	76440	380	1743	72796	1521
	14	142898	20859	1766	116917	3357

表12-25 部分年份科协系统活动情况
Basic Statistics on Science and Technology Associations in Partial Years

指标	Indicators	2019	2020	2021	2022
基本情况	**Basic Situation**				
科协机构数(个)	Institutions of Science and Technology(unit)	11	11	11	11
直属单位	Organizations Attached to the Institutions	9	8	9	17
实体科技馆	S&T Museum	9	8	16	16
活动情况	**Activity Situation**				
举办国内学术会议(场次)	Hold domestic academic conferences	63	59	56	61
科普宣讲活动(次)	Popular science propaganda activities	1862	1459	1599	2581
宣讲活动受众人数(人)	Propaganda Lecture the Audience	441476	868435	931728	1448488
播放科技广播、影视节目(分钟)	Radio and Television Programs about S&T	32835	28290	23740	50554
编著科技图书(种)	Number of Editor S&T Books				
举办青少年科技竞赛(次)	Number of Teenagers' S&T Competition	51	56	128	125
开展“讲、比”活动企业数(个)	Enterprise Number of S&T Competition Activities				

注:(1)本表和12-27表数据来自宁波市科协。
(2)2019年起，所列指标不包括市级学(协)会数据。原科技馆指标调整为实体科技馆，原举办学术交流活动指标调整为举办国内学术会议（场次），原科普讲座次数指标调整为科普宣讲活动。

Notes:(1) Data in Tables 12-25 and 12-27 are obtained from Ningbo Associations for Science and Technology.
(2) From 2019, the listed indicators do not include the data of Municipal Association. The original indicators of science and Technology Museum, academic exchange activities and popular science lectures are adjusted to physical science and Technology Museum, domestic academic conferences (sessions) and popular science propaganda activities

表12-26 部分年份市级以上科技成果鉴定、获奖、专利权情况
Basic Statistics on Verification, Award-winning and Patent Right of Above Municipal Level in Partial Years

单位:个(Unit)

指标	Indicators	2018	2019	2020	2021	2022
科技成果登记	Scientific and Technological Enrollment of Results	669	717	865	1036	900
科学技术奖	Science and Technology Awards	119	136	140	92	107
国家级	State Level	6	5			
省级	Province Level	21	39	47		28
市级	Municipal Level	92	92	93	92	79
授权专利数	Number of Patent Applications Approved	44777	47220	60520	72390	76127
发明	Inventions	5302	5075	5331	7819	9611
实用新型	Utility Models	23428	24733	32098	42010	44120
外观设计	Designs	16047	17412	23091	22561	22396

注：本表和12-29表数据来自宁波市科技局和宁波市知识产权局。
Note: Data in Tables 12-26 and 12-29 are obtained from Ningbo Municipal Bureau of Science and Technology, Ningbo Intellectual Property Office.

表12-27 科协系统情况(2022年)
Basic Statistics on Science and Technology Associations（2022）

指标	单位	Indicators	Unit	市科协 S&T Associations of Ningbo Municipal	县（市）区科协 S&T Associations by Region
科协组织和机构		**Basic Situation**			
科协机构数	个	Institutions of Science and Technology	unit	1	10
直属单位	个	Organizations Attached to the Institutions	unit	2	15
团体会员（学会、协会、研究会）	个	Group members (Academy, the Association, the Research Council)	unit	94	242
企事业科协	个	Enterprise and Non－profit Organizations Institutions of S&T	unit	6	391
为科技工作者服务		**S&T Activities and Social services**			
举办干部教育培训	场次	Organizing cadre education and training	unit	2	87
表彰奖励科技工作者	人	Award of Scientific and Technical Workers	person	35	198
通过媒体宣传科技工作者	人次	Publicizing S&T workers through the media	person－time	53	327
科技志愿者人数	人	Number of S&T volunteers	person	9684	13743
科普基础设施建设		**Infrastructure of Popular Science**			
实体科技馆	个	S&T Museum (Activity Center of Popular Science)	unit	1	15
科普画廊（活动站、中心室）	个	Gallery of Popular Science	unit		1479
科普画廊建筑面积	平方米	Construction area of popular science Gallery	square		25765
科学普及活动		**Activity for Popular Science**			
举办科普讲座	次	Number of S&T Popularization Lectures	times	237	2344
宣讲活动受众人数	人	Propaganda Lecture the Audience	person	96786	1351702
参加活动的科技人员、专家人数	人	The number of S&T personnel and experts participating in the activities	person	10000	52436
播放科技广播、影视节目	分钟	Radio and Television Programs about S&T	minute	2400	48154
青少年科技教育		**Teenagers S&T Education**			
举办青少年科技竞赛	次	Number of Teenagers' S&T Competition	times	8	117
举办青少年高校科学营	次	Number of Teenagers' S&T Camp	times		9
举办青少年科技教育活动和培训	人次	Number of Teenagers' S&T Training	person－time	3	302
学术交流		**Academic Activities**			
举办国内学术会议	次	Hold domestic academic conferences	unit	14	47
专家服务工作站（中心）	个	Expert service workstation	unit	245	89
参加大陆境外科技活动人数	人次	Number of participants in overseas S&T activities	person－time	2	16
接待大陆境外专家学者人数	人次	Number of foreign experts and scholars received	person－time	5	39

表12-28 各区（县、市）计量标准质监情况（2022年）
Basic Statistics on Standard Measuring and Quality Supervising by Region（2022）

指标	单位	Indicators	Unit	全市 Total	市区 Urban District	海曙区 Haishu
计量验收情况		**Measuring Implements Test**				
已开展强制检定数	项	Measurement Implement Tested Compulsively	kind	23	23	23
开展强制检定种数	种	The Kind of Measurement Implement Tested Compulsively	kind	29	29	23
强制检定实际检出数	件	Actual Quantity Checked by Compulsively Examined Out	piece	1741031	1065440	280855
计量仪器实际检出数	件	Actual Quantity Checked by Messurement Implement Tested	piece	2071911	1330241	309634
质监情况		**Quality Supervision**				
国家监督抽查批次	批次	Batch of supervises and Check by Country	batch.time	686		
#合格批次	批次	Regular Batch	batch.time	626		
批次合格率	%	Ratio of Regular by Batch	%	91.3		
省定期监督抽查企业数	个	Number of Enterprises Subject to regular Provincal Supervision and Check by Province	unit			
省定期监督抽查批次	批次	Batch of Periodic supervises and Check by Province	batch.time	4894	2436	473
#合格批次	批次	Regular Batch	batch.time	4098	2058	396
批次合格率	%	Ratio of Regular by Batch	%	83.7	84.5	83.7
宁波市质量指数		Index of Product Quality about NingBo				

注：本表数据来自宁波市市场监督管理局。
Note: Data in this table are obtained from Ningbo Administration for Market Regulation.

江北区 Jiangbei	镇海区 Zhenhai	北仑区 Beilun	鄞州区 Yinzhou	奉化区 Fenghua	余姚市 Yuyao	慈溪市 Cixi	宁海县 Ninghai	象山县 Xiangshan
23	23	23	12	11	8	10	10	9
23	23	23	15	13	9	12	12	10
137561	132657	151727	216667	145973	166821	187323	156253	165194
163248	202329	226230	275865	152935	191967	214899	162628	172176
244	376	406	727	210	447	1043	341	243
209	313	347	610	183	387	824	284	210
85.7	83.2	85.5	83.9	87.1	86.6	79.0	83.3	86.4

表12-29 各区（县、市）市级以上科技成果鉴定、获奖、专利情况(2022年)
Basic Statistics on Verification, Award-winning and Patent Right of Above Municipal Level by Region（2022）

指标	Indicators	全市 Total	市区 Urban District	海曙区 Haishu
科技成果登记	Scientific and Technological Enrollment of Results	900	555	19
科学技术奖	Science and Technology Awards	107	55	4
国家级	State Level			
省级	Province Level	28	11	2
市级	Municipal Level	79	44	2
授权专利数	Number of Patent Applications Approved	76127	38401	5561
发明	Inventions	9611	5968	589
实用新型	Utility Models	44120	23643	3598
外观设计	Designs	22396	8790	1374

单位：个(unit)

江北区 Jiangbei	镇海区 Zhenhai	北仑区 Beilun	鄞州区 Yinzhou	奉化区 Fenghua	余姚市 Yuyao	慈溪市 Cixi	宁海县 Ninghai	象山县 Xiangshan
21	14	67	98	12	37	47	13	17
6	3	6	15	1	7	2	2	6
2	2	2	3		2	1	1	2
4	1	4	12	1	5	1	1	4
4434	3923	6664	14487	3332	11093	18969	5717	1888
1016	847	761	2409	346	1147	1992	262	236
2439	2423	4501	8309	2373	6037	10057	2945	1408
979	653	1402	3769	613	3909	6920	2510	244

主要统计指标解释

【艺术表演团体】指从事戏曲、音乐、舞蹈、杂技等专业艺术表演，有独立账户，实行单独核算的团体。不包括半工半艺、半农半艺和民间职业剧团。

【艺术表演观众人数（人次）】指售票、包场演出或民族地区免费演出的艺术表演观众人次数。不包括彩排审查和内部观摩演出的观众人次数。

【电影放映单位】指具有放映机器设备、固定或不固定的放映场所与专职或兼职的放映技术人员，经有关部门登记批准，经常为一定的观众对象放映电影的机构。包括经批准对外开放进行营业，并与电影发行放映管理机构分账的专用放映单位和军委系统租片单位。

【普通高等学校】指按照国家规定的设置标准和审批程序批准举办,通过国家统一招生考试,招收高中毕业生为主要培养对象,实施高等教育的全日制大学、独立设置的学院和高等专科学校、短期职业大学。

【成人高等学校】指按照国家有关规定审批，招收通过全国成人高教统一招生 考试的具有高中毕业或同等学历的在职从业人员利用脱产、半脱产、业余或函授等多种形式 对其实施高等学历教育，培养高等教育专科或本科毕业水平的专门人才，修业年限、课程设 置和总学时数均按高等学历教育要求付诸实施的学校。包括广播电视大学、职工高等学校、农民高等学校、管理干部学院、教育学院、独立设置的函授学院等。

【小学学龄儿童入学率】指调查范围内已入小学学习的学龄儿童占校内外学龄儿童总数（包括智障儿童在内，但不包括盲聋哑儿童）的比重。计算公式为：

$$\text{小学学龄儿童入学率}=\frac{\text{已入学的小学学龄儿童数}}{\text{校内外小学学龄儿童总数}}\times 100\%$$

【医院】指名称为医院，设有固定床位能收容病人住院并能为病人提供医疗、 护理服务的医疗机构。包括县及县以上医院、农村乡卫生院、其他医院三部分。按所属性质分为卫生部门、工业及其他部门，集体经济单位三类。其中县及县以上医院按业务性质分为 综合医院和专科医院。

【卫生技术人员】指卫生事业机构支付工资的全部固定职工和合同制职工中现任职务为卫生技术工作的专业人员。包括中医师、西医师、中西医结合高级医师、护师、中 药师、西药师、检验师、其他技师、中医士、西医士、护士、助产士、中药剂士、西药剂士 、检验士、其他技士、其他中医、护理员、中药剂员、西药剂员、检验员，其他初级卫生技术人员。

【医生】指经卫生部门审查合格，从事医疗工作的专业人员。分为中医医生和西医医生。包括卫生技术人员中的中医师、西医师、中西结合高级医师、中医士、西医士和其他中医。

Explanatory Notes on Main Statistical Indicators

【**Art Troupe**】refers to the troupe which is engaged in drama, opera, music, dance, acrobatics or other art performance, opens independent accounts with banks and has self–supporting accounting system; excluding the troupes which h are engaged partly in industrial or agricultural activities, partly in art performance and the professional troupes organized by the people.

【**Number of Sectors at Art Performance**】refers to the number of attendants at commercial shows completely booked shows or free shows given in minority national areas, and does not include the number of spectators at rehearsals for examination and initial shows for study.

【**Film Projection Units**】refer to units with film projection equipment, full or part time projectionists, permanent or nonpermanent places, approved by related administrative departments to show films regularly for certain groups of audience, including those film projection units which have been approved to give commercial shows and run business with independent accounting system as well as those film renting units of the military system.

【**Regular Institutions of Higher Learning**】refer to educational establishments set up according to the government evaluation and approval procedures, enrolling graduates from senior secondary schools and providing higher education courses and training for senior professionals. They include full–time universities, colleges, high professional schools and short–term professional universities.

【**Institutions of Higher Learning for Adults**】refer to educational establishments, set up in line with relevant rules approved by the government, enrolling staff and workers with senior secondary school or equivalent education, and providing higher education courses in many forms of full–time, part–time, spare–time, or correspondence for adults. Professionals thus trained receive a qualification equivalent to graduates studying regular courses at regular universities, colleges and professional colleges. Institutions of higher learning for adults include Radio and TV universities, schools of high education for staff and workers and peasants, colleges for management cadres, pedagogical colleges, independent correspondence colleges.

【**Enrollment Rate of Primary School–age Children**】refers to the proportion of school–age children enrolled at schools to the total number of school–age both in and outside schools (including retarded children, but excluding blind, deaf and mute children). The formula is:

$$\text{Enrollment Rate of Primary School–age Children} = \frac{\text{Total Primary School–age Children at Schools}}{\text{Total Primary School–age Children at and Outside Schools}} \times 100\%$$

【**Hospitals**】refer to medical institutions named as "hospital" with permanent hospital beds, which are able to take in patients and provide them with medical and nursing services. Hospitals are classified into three categories : hospitals at or above the county–level, hospitals of rural townships, and other hospitals. According to their ownership, hospitals can be classified into three categories: hospitals under the public health departments, hospitals under industrial and other departments and collective–owned hospitals. Hospitals at or above county level are divided into comprehensive and specialized hospitals.

【**Medical Technical Personnel**】refers to all permanent medical staff and workers employed by medical institutions, including doctors of Chinese and Western medicine, senior doctors who integrate traditional Chinese therapeutics with Western therapeutics in practice, senior nurses, pharmacists of Chinese and Western medicine, laboratory specialists, other specialists, paramedics of Chinese and Western medicine, nurses, midwives, druggists in Chinese and Western medicine, laboratory technicians, other technicians, other practitioners of Chinese medicine, nursing attendants, pharmacological workers of Chinese and Western medicine, laboratory workers, and other primary medical personnel.

【**Doctors**】refer to qualified professional medical workers approved to practice by public health departments. They are classified into doctors of Chinese medicine, doctors of Western medicine, senior doctors who integrate traditional Chinese therapeutics with Western therapeutics in practice, paramedics of Chinese medicine and Western medicine, and other specialists of Chinese medicine.

NINGBO 2023 Statistical Yearbook

13 CHAPTER

第十三篇

市政、环保、民政、政法及其他

CIVIL FACILITIES, ENVIRONMENT, CIVIL AFFAIRS, JUDICATURE AND OTHERS

市政、环保、民政、政法及其他
Civil Facilities, Environment, Social Welfare, Judicature and Others

主要统计指标
Major Statistics Indicators

2022年人均日生活用水量	Per Capita Daily Consuption of Tap water for Resiential Use	237.91	升	liter
2022年人均拥有道路面积	Per Capita Area of Paved Roads	21.76	平方米	sq. m
2022年人均公园绿地面积	Per Capita Public Green Areas	14.60	平方米	sq. m
2022年建成区绿化覆盖率	Coverage Rate of Green Area in Developed Area	43.49	%	
2022年废水排放总量	Total Volume of Waste Water Discharged	59227.36	万吨	10000 tons
2022年工业废气排放量	Volume of Industrial Waste Gas Emission	9347.02	亿标立米	100 million cu. m
2022年社会救济总人数	Number of Persons Receiving Relief	57502	人	person
2022年末实有社团机构数	Factual Number of Social Organizations at The Year –	2621	个	unit
2022年基层工会数	Number of Trade Unions at Basic – Level	24771	个	unit
2022年律师人数	Number of Lawyers	5097	人	person
2022年办理公证事项	Number of Notarized Documents	75814	件	case
2022年调解纠纷总件数	Number of Mediating Disputes	115189	件	case
2022年交通事故数	Number of Traffic Accident	1550	件	case
2022年档案馆数	Number of Archives	11	个	unit

表13-1 部分年份市政公用事业基本情况
Basic Statistics on Municipal Public Utilities in Partial Years

指标	单位	Indicators	Unit	2019	2020	2021	2022
供水及供气		**Water Supply and Gas Supply**					
年供水总量	万吨	Annual Volume of Tap Water Supply	10000 tons	80820	87745	94533	96626
#居民家庭用水量	万吨	Water Consumption for Residents Use	10000 tons	32522	33067	35627	35896
人均日生活用水量	升	Per Capita Daily Consumption of Tap Water	liter	249.21	227.22	230.31	237.91
供水普及率	%	Water supply penetration rate	%	100.00	100.00	100.00	100.00
液化石油气供气总量	万吨	Total Volume of Liquefied Petroleum Gas	10000 tons	19.65	23.33	27.75	20.19
#家庭用量	万吨	For Residents Use	10000 tons	13.33	16.06	17.39	15.99
用液化气人口	万人	Population with Access Liquefied Petroleum Gas	10000 persons	181.10	171.69	178.02	156.87
燃气普及率	%	Percentage of Population with Access to Gas	%	100.00	100.00	100.00	100.00
市政设施		**Municipal Facilities**					
年末城市实有道路面积	万平方米	Area of Paved Roads(Year－end)	10000 sq.m	8300.17	10526.53	10692.73	11263.79
人均拥有道路面积	平方米	Per Capita Area of Paved Roads	sq.m	17.61	21.68	20.77	21.76
排水管道长度	公里	Length of Sewage Pipes	km	10089.00	7933.89	12736.59	10938.10
建成区排水管道密度	公里/平方公里	Density of drainage pipelines in built－up areas	km/sq.km	15.80	12.95	15.10	15.91
公共交通		**Public Traffic**					
年末实有公交营运车辆	标台	Number of Public Transportations Vehicles	unit	10081.60	10023.10	9981.40	9895.10
每万人拥有公共交通车辆	标台	Number of Public Transportations Vehicles	unit	11.80	10.64	10.46	10.29
年末实有出租汽车数	辆	Operating Taxes at Year－end	unit	6267	6281	6111	6135
城市绿化		**Afforestation in Cities**					
绿地面积	公顷	Green Areas in Parks and Gardens	hectare	35783	36663	38388	38963
#公园绿地面积	公顷	Public Green Areas	hectare	6484	6732	7483	7557
人均公园绿地面积	平方米	Per Capita Public Green Areas	sq.m	13.76	13.86	14.54	14.60
建成区绿地率	%	Rate of Green Area in Developed Area	%	37.87	38.52	39.71	39.90
建成区绿化覆盖率	%	Coverage Rate of Green Area in Developed Area	%	41.63	42.08	43.29	43.49
环境卫生		**Environmental Sanitation**					
污水处理率	%	Percentage of Sewage Disposed	%	98.27	99.15	99.36	99.60
城市生活垃圾无害化处理率	%	Innocuous Disposal Rate of Living Garbage	%	100.00	100.00	100.00	100.00

注：（1）2009年开始，排水管道密度为建成区排水管道密度。
（2）2019年起，用水普及率调整为供水普及率。

Notes：（1）Density of sewage pipes from 2009 refered to builting area.
（2）From 2019，water utilization rate adjusted to Water supply penetration rate.

表13-2 各区（县、市）城市市政、公用事业情况(2022年)
Basic Statistics on Civil Facilities and Public Utilities by Region（2022）

指标	单位	Indicators	Unit
城市面积		**City Areas**	
建成区面积	平方公里	Developed Areas	sq.km
城市建设用地面积	平方公里	land Areas of the Urban Construction	sq.km
居住用地面积	平方公里	For Residential Building Uses	sq.km
公共管理与公共服务用地面积	平方公里	For Public Management and Public Service Uses	sq.km
工业用地面积	平方公里	For Industry Uses	sq.km
供水及供气		**Water Supply and Gas Supply**	
年供水总量	万吨	Annuall Volume of Tap Water Supply	10000 tons
#居民家庭用水量	万吨	Water Consumption for Residents Use	10000 tons
人均日生活用水量	升	Per Capita Daily Consumption of Tap Water for Resi	liter
供水普及率	%	Water supply penetration rate	%
液化石油气供气总量	吨	Total Volume of Liquefied Petroleum Gas	ton
#家庭用量	吨	For Residents Use	ton
用液化气人口	万人	Population with Access Liquefied Petroleum Gas	10000persons
燃气普及率	%	Percentage of Population with Access to Gas	%
市政设施		**Municipal Infra－strucutre**	
年末城市实有道路面积	万平方米	Area of Paved Roads(Year－end)	10000sq.m
人均拥有道路面积	平方米	Per Capita Area of Paved Roads	sq.m
排水管道长度	公里	Length of Sewage Pipes	km
建成区排水管道密度	公里/平方公里	Density of Drainpipes	km/sq.km
城市绿化		**Afforestation in Cities**	
绿地面积	公顷	Green Areas in Parks and Gardens	hectare
#公园绿地面积	公顷	Public Green Areas	hectare
人均公园绿地面积	平方米	Per Capita Public Green Areas	sq.m
建成区绿化覆盖面积	公顷	Coverage Area of Green Area in Developed Area	hectare
建成区绿地率	%	Rate of Green Area in Developed Area	%
建成区绿化覆盖率	%	Coverage Rate of Green Area in Developed Area	%
环境卫生		**Environmental Sanitation**	
污水处理率	%	Percentage of Sewage Disposed	%
城市生活垃圾无害化处理率	%	Innocuous Disposal Rate of Living Garbage	%

注：本表数据来自宁波市住房和城乡建设局。
Note：Data in this table are obtained from Ningbo Housing and Urban–rural Development Bureau .

表 13－2 续表 Continued

指标	单位	Indicators	Unit	全市 Total	市区 Urban District
公共交通		**Public Traffic**			
年末实有公交营运车辆	标台	Number of Public Transportations Vehicles under Operation	unit	9895.10	7069.30
每万人拥有公共交通车辆	标台	Number of Public Transportations Vehicles Per 10000 Persons	unit	10.29	13.58
年末实有出租汽车数	辆	Operating Taxes at Year－end	unit	6135	4755

全市 Total	市区 Urban District	余姚市 Yuyao	慈溪市 Cixi	宁海县 Ninghai	象山县 Xiangshan
581.89	397.40	54.22	50.80	44.11	35.36
638.80	436.54	55.36	50.61	48.56	47.73
174.54	98.81	23.40	22.26	16.43	13.64
49.87	33.46	3.50	3.55	4.13	5.23
188.29	137.00	15.98	11.63	12.37	11.31
96625.93	77657.11	6558.80	4570.24	3959.31	3880.47
35896.42	26997.01	2802.43	2478.04	2110.49	1508.45
237.91	254.48	187.84	172.58	241.58	227.33
100.00	100.00	100.00	100.00	100.00	100.00
201878.78	116512.87	6027.56	52842.75	18048.60	8447.00
159867.02	84884.84	4691.10	51850.68	13490.40	4950.00
156.87	108.33	16.99	9.29	12.80	9.46
100.00	100.00	100.00	100.00	100.00	100.00
11263.79	6619.96	1185.01	1736.53	793.19	929.10
21.76	18.00	25.25	31.50	31.17	41.46
10938.10	7951.90	881.80	538.90	1056.80	508.70
15.91	17.06	8.69	9.37	23.34	14.18
38963.00	18151.00	14967.00	2384.00	1771.00	1690.00
7557.00	5457.00	604.00	766.00	370.00	362.00
14.60	14.84	12.81	13.90	14.54	16.16
25306.00	17259.00	2418.00	2279.00	1894.00	1457.00
39.90	40.04	40.04	40.07	39.91	37.78
43.49	43.43	44.59	44.86	42.93	41.20
99.60	99.89	98.50	97.99	99.01	98.19
100.00	100.00	100.00	100.00	100.00	100.00

海曙区 Haishu	江北区 Jiangbei	镇海区 Zhenhai	北仑区 Beilun	鄞州区 Yinzhou	奉化区 Fenghua	余姚市 Yuyao	慈溪市 Cixi	宁海县 Ninghai	象山县 Xiangshan
			825.60		771.20	692.20	944.90	632.70	556.00
			9.39		13.16	5.48	5.07	8.92	9.65
1771	623	60	161	2000	140	286	605	278	211

表13-3 各区（县、市）环境保护基本情况（2022年）
Basic Statistics on Environment Protection, Enviroment Sanitation by Region（2022）

指标	单位	Indicators	Unit	全市 Total	市区 Urban District
废水排放总量	**万吨**	**Volume of Waste Water Discharged**	**10000 tons**	**59227.36**	**10864.15**
工业废水排放总量	万吨	Industrial Waste Water Discharged	10000 tons	14331.84	10749.35
工业废水中氨氮排放量	吨	Ammonianitrogen in Industrial Waste Water	tons	110.20	81.61
生活污水排放量	万吨	Discharged Amount of Living Sewage	10000 tons	44715.93	
化学需氧量(COD)排放量	**吨**	**Discharged Amount of Chemical oxygen demand (COD)**	**tons**	**48199.03**	**3709.22**
工业废水中化学需氧排放量	吨	Discharged Amount of COD in Industrial Waste Water	tons	5359	3670
废水治理设施数	**套**	**Number of Administration Facility of Waste Water**	**unit**	**1003**	**568**
工业废气排放量	**亿标立米**	**Industrial Waste Gas Emission**	**100million cu.m**	**9347.02**	**6503.66**
工业二氧化硫排放量	吨	Industrial Sulphur Dioxide Emission	ton	8016.32	4321.78
工业氮氧化物(NOx)排放量	吨	Industrial Nitrogen Oxide (NOx) Emissions	ton	21442.33	15298.92
工业烟尘排放量	吨	Soot Emission	ton	11524.31	8375.88
一般工业固体废物产生量	**万吨**	**Volume of Industrial Solid Wastes Produced**	**10000 tons**	**1403.94**	**973.18**
一般工业固体废物综合利用量	万吨	Volume of General Industrial Solid Waste Utilized	10000 tons	1399.89	970.60
一般工业固体废物处理量	万吨	Volume of General Industrial Solid Waste Treated	10000 tons	4.02	2.61
一般工业固体废物倾倒丢弃量	吨	Volume of General Industrial Solid Wastes Dumped Discarded	ton		
工业固体废物综合利用率	%	Rate of Industrial Solid Waste Utilized	%	99.71	99.73
工业固体废物处置利用率	%	Rate of Industrial Solid Waste Treated and Utilized	%	99.95	99.94
工业污染处理本年施工项目数	个	Number of Projects Treating Industrial Pollution	unit	36	33
建设项目“三同时”环保投资额	万元	Investment Amount of Construction Project "Three Simultaneous" of Environment Protection	10000yuan	365966.21	234975.23

注：本表数据来自宁波市生态环境局。工业“三废”统计范围为重点调查工业企业与非重点调查单位测算之和。
Note: Data in this table are obtained from Ningbo Municipal Bureau of Ecology and Environment. Statistical Information of Waste Water, Waste Gas and Waste Residue Collected is calculated data that investigate industrial enterprise especially and non-investigate unit especially.

海曙区 Haishu	江北区 Jiangbei	镇海区 Zhenhai	北仑区 Beilun	鄞州区 Yinzhou	奉化区 Fenghua	余姚市 Yuyao	慈溪市 Cixi	宁海县 Ninghai	象山县 Xiangshan
226.20	**122.60**	**3524.38**	**6184.78**	**394.92**	**411.27**	**1148.98**	**1091.36**	**445.09**	**961.86**
171.60	122.60	3493.29	6180.06	394.92	386.88	1117.57	1082.39	428.31	954.22
0.45	0.07	27.48	49.47	1.73	2.42	5.34	4.82	0.59	10.33
42.89	**17.72**	**1396.93**	**2070.85**	**96.77**	**84.06**	**381.22**	**328.57**	**69.06**	**332.12**
30	18	1374	2071	97	80	381	329	63	330
53	**29**	**102**	**194**	**90**	**100**	**66**	**228**	**85**	**56**
66.67	**54.81**	**2272.90**	**3792.54**	**154.94**	**161.80**	**286.82**	**584.43**	**946.86**	**1025.26**
12.93	4.78	1107.50	2999.14	130.02	67.41	576.86	575.50	1313.78	1228.40
239.83	19.88	5038.70	9544.72	331.56	124.23	937.72	683.79	2825.23	1696.67
11.71	62.53	496.46	7400.17	186.24	218.78	825.40	544.27	768.43	1010.34
18.75	**2.44**	**245.42**	**689.77**	**8.53**	**8.26**	**21.11**	**38.73**	**200.83**	**170.08**
18.71	2.44	243.97	688.69	8.53	8.26	21.11	38.73	200.72	168.72
0.04		1.46	1.10	0.01				0.11	1.30
99.81	100.00	99.39	99.84	99.91	99.99	100.00	100.00	99.95	99.20
99.98	99.88	99.83	99.99	99.91	99.92	99.84	99.93	100.00	99.95
	2	4	18		9		1		2
11457.55	99415.15	55586.00	42793.67	15229.86	10493.00	41507.60	20455.06	34133.61	34894.71

表13-4 各区（县、市）社会团体机构情况(2022年)
Basic Statistics on Social Organizations and Unions by Region（2022）

指标	Indicators	全市 Total	市区 Urban District	海曙区 Haishu
上年准予登记社团机构数	Number of Social Organizations Authorized in Last Year	2610	1620	155
年末实有社团机构数	Factual Number of Social Organizations at the Year-end	2621	1640	155
年末实有民办非企业数	Factual Number of Civilian-run Non-enterprises at the Year-end	7555	4168	766

注：本表至13-8表数据来自宁波市民政局。
Note: Data from Tables 13-4 to 13-8 are obtained from Ningbo Municipal Bureau of Civil Affairs.

表13-5 各区（县、市）社会福利、优抚、救济工作情况(2022年)
Basic Statistics on Social Welfare,Subsidy and Commiseration by Region（2022）

指标	单位	Indicators	Unit	全市 Total	市区 Urban District
优待情况		**Favoured Treatment**			
安置军转干部、士兵	人	Setting Military Cadres or Soldiers Transferred to Civilian Work	person	235	48
优待军属户数	户	Service men's Families	household	3057	1397
优待总金额	万元	Total Amount of Give Special Treatment	10000 yuan	18020	9074
抚恤、补助情况		**Special Pensions, Allowances and Relief**			
年末享受定补人数	人	Number of Persons Receiving Periodical Subsidies at the Year-end	person	57428	25611
#在乡复员军人	人	Rural Demobilized Soldiers	person	716	329
伤残人员	人	Number of Wounded or Disabled Health	person	2443	1230
年末定期抚恤人数	人	Number of Persons Receiving Periodical Commiseration	person	522	239
#烈士家属	人	Members of Revolutionary Martyr's Family	person	255	107

单位: 个(unit)

江北区 Jiangbei	镇海区 Zhenhai	北仑区 Beilun	鄞州区 Yinzhou	奉化区 Fenghua	余姚市 Yuyao	慈溪市 Cixi	宁海县 Ninghai	象山县 Xiangshan
99	131	135	229	213	257	316	211	206
101	133	138	242	217	259	301	213	208
482	294	532	940	630	863	1030	804	690

海曙区 Haishu	江北区 Jiangbei	镇海区 Zhenhai	北仑区 Beilun	鄞州区 Yinzhou	奉化区 Fenghua	余姚市 Yuyao	慈溪市 Cixi	宁海县 Ninghai	象山县 Xiangshan
29	19	14	23	34	12	15	18	16	7
296	133	122	186	417	243	445	553	378	284
1943	841	795	1247	2847	1401	2889	2474	2188	1395
4776	2517	1902	3931	7139	5582	9455	10592	5293	5545
55	25	31	56	111	56	79	186	45	60
267	132	96	121	404	222	330	440	226	180
60	10	32	36	51	50	75	84	46	64
35	6	10	16	19	21	42	29	32	41

表13-6 民政部门收养性福利优抚事业情况(2022年)
Basic Statistics on Adopting,Welfare and Special Pensions by Civil Administration Department（2022）

指标	单位	Indicators	Unit	全市 Total	其中 of Which #市区 Urban District	社会福利院 Social Welfare Homes
收养性福利单位数	个	Number of Adoptive Welfare Units	unit	14	8	10
全部职工人数	人	Total Number Staff and Workers	person	452	333	347
#女性	人	Female	person	317	245	251
年末固定资产原值	万元	Original Value of Fixed Assets at the Year－end	10000 yuan	44674	29820	35949
各院病床数	张	Number of Beds in Each Hospital	bed	3545	2666	2645
年末在院人数	人	In–patients at the Year－end	person	2183	1756	1478
特困对象人员	人	Extremely impoverished people	person	439	367	325
自费人员	人	Persons on Self－expense	person	797	537	448
#老年人	人	Old People	person	1491	1108	1126
青壮年人员	人	Young People	person	583	578	348
少年儿童	人	Juvenile and Child	person	4		4

表13-6 续表 Continued

指标	单位	Indicators	Unit	其中 of Which 儿童福利院 Welfare Homes for Children	精神病福利院 Welfare Homes for Mental Patients
收养性福利单位数	个	Number of Adoptive Welfare Units	unit	3	1
全部职工人数	人	Total Number Staff and Workers	person	54	51
#女性	人	Female	person	41	25
年末固定资产原值	万元	Original Value of Fixed Assets at the Year－end	10000 yuan	1480	7244
各院病床数	张	Number of Beds in Each Hospital	bed	400	500
年末在院人数	人	In–patients at the Year－end	person	205	500
特困对象人员	人	Extremely impoverished people	person		114
自费人员	人	Persons on Self－expense	person		349
#老年人	人	Old People	person		365
青壮年人员	人	Young People	person		235
少年儿童	人	Juvenile and Child	person		

表13-7 城乡居民最低生活保障情况（2022年）
Basic Statistics on Receiving Lowest Cost-of-living in Urban and Rural Area（2022）

地区	Region	社会救济总人数（人）Number of Persons Receiving Relief (person)	城镇低保人数（人）Number of RLCU ① (person)	城镇低保家庭数（户）Households of RLCU ① (household)	城镇低保资金支出（万元）Expenditure for RLCU (10000 yuan)	农村低保人数（人）Number of RLCR ② and Receiving Relief (person)	农村低保家庭数（户）Households of RLCR ② (household)	农村救济资金支出（万元）Expenditure for RLCR② (10000 yuan)
宁波市	**Total**	**57502**	**7477**	**5838**	**10030.1**	**49989**	**36699**	**65009.5**
市区	Urban District	19653	5698	4424	7524.3	13919	10419	17898.8
#海曙区	Haishu	3420	1609	1263	2134.6	1811	1384	2755.5
#江北区	Jiangbei	1498	858	632	1136.2	640	483	825.7
#镇海区	Zhenhai	937	488	426	690.0	449	373	690.0
#北仑区	Beilun	2481	837	697	1002.4	1608	1186	1836.4
#鄞州区	Yinzhou	3317	1347	1025	1794.3	1970	1452	2777.4
#奉化区	Fenghua	8000	559	381	766.8	7441	5541	9013.8
余姚市	Yuyao	8267	523	449	772.6	7744	6113	10947.0
慈溪市	Cixi	11200	568	456	737.8	10632	8151	13014.9
宁海县	Ninghai	8960	268	184	407.6	8692	5790	10548.3
象山县	Xiangshan	9422	420	325	587.8	9002	6226	12600.5

注：（1）RLCU是城镇低保的缩写。
（2）RLCR是农村低保的缩写。
Notes:（1）RLCU is the short form that means Receiving Lowest Cost–of–living in Urban Area.
（2）RLCR is the short form that means Receiving Lowest Cost–of–living in Rural Area.

表13-8 社会收容遣送情况（2022年）
Basic Statistics on Accepted and Relief（2022）

地区 Region	遣送站情况 Repatriated Units			本年救助（人次）Relief Person in this Year (person – times)
	站数（个）Number of Units (unit)	年末职工人数（人）Number of Staff and Workers (person)	年末固定资产原值（万元）Original Value of Fixed Assets (10000 yuan)	
全市总计 Total	8	70	1431.50	842

表13-9 各区（县、市）妇联工会组织及活动情况（2022年）

Basic Statistics on Women Federation and Trade Unions by Region（2022）

指标	单位	Indicators	Unit	全市 Total	市区 Urban District
妇联组织机构		**Women's Federation**			
市、县(市)区妇联	个	Women's Federation in Municipal, County and Urban District	unit	11	7
镇、乡(街道)妇联	个	Women's Federation in Township, Town (Subdistrict)	unit	151	76
基层妇代会	个	Basic－Level Women Congress	unit	2804	1409
机关事业单位妇委会	个	Women Commission of Agencies and Institutions	unit	477	248
团体会员	个	Group Member	unit	64	22
人员状况		**Cadre of Women's Federation**			
市、县(市)区级干部	人	Level of Municipal, County and Urban District	person	126	86
镇、乡(街道)级干部	人	Cadre in Township, Town(Subdistrict)	person	558	317
妇联工作情况		**Works of Women's Federation**			
城乡女性创业就业		Urban and Rural Women's Entrepreneurship and Employment			
培育扶持的县级以上巾帼创业创新基地	个	Cultivate and Support Women's Entrepreneurship and Innovation Bases above the County Level	unit	60	24
县级以上妇联组织的城乡妇女创业就业培训班	期	Training Courses on Entrepreneurship and Employment for Women Organized by Women's Federations at or above the County Level	phase	185	83
参加县级各类创业就业培训的城乡妇女人数	人次	Number of Women Participating in Various Entrepreneurship and Employment Training at the County Level	Person－time	10333	4094
巾帼建功		Women's meritorious service			
获市级及以上“巾帼建功”标兵数	名	Number of "Women's Meritorious Service" Pacesetters at Municipal Level and above	unit	553	399
被认定为市级及以上“巾帼文明岗数	个	Number of "Women's Civilized Posts" Recognized as Municipal Level and above	unit	3179	2638

注：本表数据来自宁波市总工会和宁波市妇联。
Note: Date in this table are obtained from Ningbo Federation of Trade Unions and Ningbo Women's Federation .

海曙区 Haishu	江北区 Jiangbei	镇海区 Zhenhai	北仑区 Beilun	鄞州区 Yinzhou	奉化区 Fenghua	余姚市 Yuyao	慈溪市 Cixi	宁海县 Ninghai	象山县 Xiangshan
1	1	1	1	1	1	1	1	1	1
17	8	6	11	22	12	21	18	18	18
268	135	86	222	381	317	304	337	369	385
9	6	28	51	54	40	59	73	24	73
2	1	3	4	1	1	13	22	2	5
11	4	9	12	12	13	13	9	9	9
91	45	28	48	91	14	97	93	36	15
3		3	2		5	1	3	11	21
60	1	12	4	1	4	4	41	45	12
2780	50	620	180	50	350	1300	89	4350	500
34	20	50	24	39	32	35	65	21	33
143	74	137	108	194	95	185	228	71	57

表13－9续表 Continued

指标	单位	Indicators	Unit	全市 Total	市区 Urban District
美丽乡村		**Beautiful Countryside**			
美丽庭院创建数	户	Number of Beautiful Courtyards Created	household	79493	37493
家庭建设		**Family construction**			
文明家庭数	户	Number of civilized families	household	3556	2256
最美家庭数（全国级）	户	Number of most Beautiful Families(National Level)	household	11	8
最美家庭数（省级）	户	Number of most Beautiful Families(Provincial)	household	42	31
最美家庭数（市级）	户	Number of most Beautiful Families(Municipal Level)	household	168	129
最美家庭数（市级以下）	户	Number of most Beautiful Families(below Municipal Level)	household	9870	4730
工会基本情况		**Trade Unions**			
1. 基层工会数	个	Number of Trade Unions at Basic－Level	unit	24771	14433
2. 工会专职干部人数	人	Number of Full－Time Cadres of Trade Unions	person	2786	1580
3. 建立工会单位全部职工	人	Total Staff And Workers of Establishing Trade Unions	person	3537090	2117942
#女职工	人	Female Staff And Workers	person	1611181	955102
工会会员	人	Member of Trade Unions	person	3447450	2059138
#女会员	人	Female Member	person	1582632	933808
4. 本年度职工提出合理化建议	件	Advanced Rationalization Proposals	case	5388	3373
本年度已实施合理化建议	件	Implement Rationalization Proposals	case	4358	2635

海曙区 Haishu	江北区 Jiangbei	镇海区 Zhenhai	北仑区 Beilun	鄞州区 Yinzhou	奉化区 Fenghua	余姚市 Yuyao	慈溪市 Cixi	宁海县 Ninghai	象山县 Xiangshan
6000	2200	2500	3600	12093	11000	11000	13000	8000	10000
100	58		100	1899		76	500	615	109
				2		1	2		
4				3		3	3	2	3
22				11		11	10	9	9
200	180		100	4250		77	4900	40	123
2365	1461	1545	3358	3349	1708	3351	3314	1470	2203
132	118	116	241	264	148	499	308	331	68
373824	127562	209611	527619	410414	218596	468565	561725	216644	172214
182327	56266	86657	236368	191880	91447	237156	245741	98893	74289
364589	125602	205323	521187	399076	211739	452962	557268	212490	165592
178482	55411	85115	235337	187698	90143	233104	244549	97801	73370
126	96	399	899	742	220	412	998	418	187
80	91	225	626	592	191	341	897	306	179

表13-10 部分年份基层司法工作及人民调解情况
Basic Statistics on Basic-level Judicial Work and People Mediation in Partial Years

指标	Indicators	2019	2020	2021	2022
基层法律服务	**Basic – Level Service for Legal Advice**				
司法所工作人员总数(人)	Total staff of the Judicial Office (person)	760	440	789	798
司法所专职人员数(人)	Full – time personnel of the Judicial Office (person)	372	396	424	
司法所辅助人员数(人)	Auxiliary personnel of the Judicial Office (person)	41	44	365	
基层法律服务所(所)	Basic – Level Service for Legal Advice (unit)	67	66	66	66
配备工作人员(人)	Provide Staff (person)	471	450	427	416
代理讼诉事务（件)	Agent of Litigious Affairs (case)	11464		9228	893
代理非讼诉事务（件)	Agent of Non–Litigious Legal Affairs (case)	439	412	608	206
调解纠纷（件)	Mediating Disputes (case)	169	245	51636	225
担任法律顾问（件)	Taking Legal Advisors (case)	611	821		701
代写法律文书（件)	Legal Document Written on Behalf of Clients (case)	16010	20650	13693	13038
解答法律咨询人次（人次)	Legal Advisory Services (person – times)	16010	20650		
挽回经济损失（万元)	Economic Loss Avoided and Reclaimed (10000 yuan)				
办理法律援助事务（件)	Handling Legal aid Affairs (case)	650	1071	386	243

注：本表数据来自宁波市司法局。2021年指标有所调整，其中司法所工作人员总数、司法所专职人员数和司法所辅助人员数分别对应原司法助理人员数、专职司法助理人员和兼职司法助理人员数，2021年前仍为老指标数据。

Note: Data in this table are obtained from Bureau of Justice of Ningbo Municipality. The indicators were adjusted in 2021, in which the total number of staff, full–time staff and auxiliary staff of the Institute of Justice correspond to the number of original judicial assistants, full–time judicial assistants and part–time judicial assistants respectively, which will remain the old indicators before 2021.

表13－10 续表 Continued

指标	Indicators	2019	2020	2021	2022
参与司法行政工作（人次）	Participating Judicial Administration(person－times)		97		
人民调解工作	**Peoples Mediation**				
人民调解委员会（个）	Peoples Mediation Committees (unit)	3678	3396	3304	3287
调解人员数（人）	Number of Mediators (person)	14352	13615	14593	14523
调解纠纷总件数（件）	Number of Mediating Disputes (case)	91739	71795	97909	115189
调解成功件数（件）	Number of Success (case)	90896	70722	97738	114876
婚姻、继承、赡养抚养（件）	Marrige, Rights of Inheritance,Supporting and Fostering (case)	4628	2601	4781	5328
房屋宅基地（件）	Ground of Building (case)	814	561	612	586
债务（件）	Debt (case)		904	1313	1337
生产经营（件）	Production & Management (case)	417	192	205	224
邻里关系（件）	Relation of Neighborhood (case)	10811	9972	12722	16282
赔偿（件）	Compensation (case)	15766	11376	17108	21355
其他调解（件）	Other Mediating (case)	9742	46189	60997	69764
调解纠纷成功率（%）	Rate of Mediating Success (%)	99.08	98.5	99.83	99.70

表13-11 各区（县、市）火灾情况（2022年）
Basic Statistics on Fires by Region（2022）

指标	单位	Indicators	Unit	全市 Total	市区 Urban District	海曙区 Haishu
火灾起因情况		**Cause of Fire**				
放火	起	Arson	case	3	2	1
电器	起	Electric Appliances	case	1768	1020	243
用火不慎	起	Careless use of fire	case	932	488	117
生产作业	起	Production Operations	case	350	194	40
吸烟	起	Smoking	case	506	281	67
自燃	起	Spontaneous Combustion	case	796	435	41
其他原因	起	Others	case	767	432	33
重大火灾		**Heavy Fire**				
起火	起	Fire	case			
损失	万元	Losses	10000 yuan			
死亡	人	Deaths	person			
损失情况		**Situation of Losses**				
起数	起	Number	case	5122	2855	542
死亡	人	Deaths	person	12	1	1
伤人	人	Injuries	person			
损失	万元	Losses	10000 yuan	5715.00	2625.60	401.40

江北区 Jiangbei	镇海区 Zhenhai	北仑区 Beilun	鄞州区 Yinzhou	奉化区 Fenghua	余姚市 Yuyao	慈溪市 Cixi	宁海县 Ninghai	象山县 Xiangshan
			1			1		
76	123	169	310	99	214	208	159	167
73	63	67	132	36	141	138	95	70
19	17	51	32	35	28	85	26	17
6	30	59	55	64	85	68	33	39
54	31	32	209	68	116	152	66	24
34	65	166	123	11	78	140	5	112
262	329	547	862	313	662	791	384	429
						4	7	
330.40	215.30	631.40	731.40	315.70	677.40	970.50	1065.20	376.00

表13-12 交通事故情况（2022年）
Basic Statistics on Traffic Accident（2022）

指标	Indicators	合计 (Total)			
		事故次数（次）Number of Accident (case)	死亡人数（人）Deaths (person)	受伤人数（人）Injuries (person)	直接损失（万元）Direct Economic Losses (10000 yuan)
总计	**Total**	**1550**	**382**	**1418**	**345.60**
机动车	Motor Vehicles	1188	336	1002	277.70
客运车辆	Passenger Vehicles	27	5	21	3.40
公共汽车	Buses	5	1	4	3.60
一般货运	General Cargos	170	89	101	62.40
企事业单位	Institutions and Enterprises				
军队武警	Armed Forces				
私用轿车	Individuals	404	96	357	92.20
其他	Others	371	109	301	82.40
摩托车	Motorcycles	210	36	217	33.70
拖拉机	Tractors	1		1	0.10
非机动车	Non-motor-driven Vehicles	344	42	399	64.60
其他及行人	Others and Pedestrians	18	4	17	3.30

城市(Urban)				农村 (Rural)			
事故次数（次）Number of Accident (case)	死亡人数（人）Deaths (person)	受伤人数（人）Injuries (person)	直接损失（万元）Direct Economic Losses (10000 yuan)	事故次数（次）Number of Accident (case)	死亡人数（人）Deaths (person)	受伤人数（人）Injuries (person)	直接损失（万元）Direct Economic Losses (10000 yuan)
830	**169**	**792**	**178. 50**	**720**	**213**	**626**	**167. 10**
607	141	531	135. 10	581	195	471	142. 60
20	4	16	2. 50	7	1	5	0. 90
5	1	4	3. 60				
77	36	48	24. 80	93	53	53	37. 60
214	39	197	43. 20	190	57	160	49. 00
186	48	151	42. 40	185	61	150	40. 00
104	13	114	18. 50	106	23	103	15. 20
1		1	0. 10				
214	25	254	41. 20	130	17	145	23. 40
9	3	7	2. 20	9	1	10	1. 10

表13-13 部分年份律师、公证工作基本情况
Basic Statistics on Lawyers and Notarization in Partial Years

指标	Indicators	2019	2020	2021	2022
律师工作情况	**Lawyers**				
律师事务所(个)	Number of Law Offices(unit)	176	178	181	183
个人律师事务所(个)	Personal Law Office(unit)	40	37	35	33
合伙制律师事务所(个)	Law Offices in Partnership(unit)	136	141	104	101
律师数(人)	Number of Lawyers (person)	3629	3764	4314	5097
#专职律师(人)	Full－time Lawyers (person)	2659	2958	3227	3623
聘请担任常年法律顾问单位(家)	Number of Units with Permanent Legal Advisors(unit)	8996	9843	11430	16012
民事案件代理(件)	Agent of Civil Cases (case)	61528	64807	82634	91786
刑事辩护和代理(件)	Agent of Criminal Defense (case)	8748	6129	7089	4860
非诉讼法律事务(件)	Agent of Non−Litigious Legal Affairs (case)	4912	24645	23077	23564
行政案件代理(件)	Agent of Administrative Action (case)	2378	1805	2349	2367
涉外及港澳台法律事务(件)	Legal Affairs With Foreign, HongKong, Macao, Taiwan(case)	194	141	725	1028
解答法律文书(件)	Legal Advisory Services (case)	12876	8879	4720	2477
代写法律文书(件)	Legal Document Written on Behalf of Clients(case)	1715	2025	2263	2743
公证工作情况	**Notarization**				
公证处(个)	Notary Offices (unit)	11	8	8	9
#办理涉外公证(人)	Registered Foreign Affairs (person)	44	52	51	57
公证人员人数(人)	Notarial Personnel (person)	191	208	141	154
#公证员(人)	Notaries(person)	64	64	60	78
办理公证事项(件)	Notarized Documents (case)	75814	52776	55689	14007
国内经济公证(件)	Domestic Economic Affairs(case)	52100	41507	43663	9122
涉外及港澳台公证(件)	Documents on Foreign, HongKong, Macao, Taiwan(case)	23714	11269	12026	226

表13-14 人民法院及检察院补充信息(2022年)
Added Information of People's Court and Procurator's Offices（2022）

指标	单位	Indicators	Unit	总计 Total
人民法院		**People's Court**		
办结申诉申请再审案件	件	Appeal and Applying for Review Closed	case	650
处理群众来信	件次	Deal with Letter from People	case－times	3263
群众来访人数	人次	People Come to Appeal for Help	person－times	
判决被告人	人	Adjudge defendant	person	12278
判处罪犯	人	Sentence Criminals	person	12748
宣告无罪	人	Declare Innocent	person	
五年以上有期徒刑直到无期徒刑	人	Fixed－term Imprisonment of More than 5 years until Life Imprisonment	person	841
不满五年有期徒刑	人	Fixed－term Imprisonment of Below 5 years	person	4396
缓刑	人	Probation	person	6223
免于刑事处分	人	Avoid Criminal Sanction	person	5
其他处理	人	Others	person	1298
#18–25周岁罪犯	人	Between 18 until 25 Years Old	person	
#少年犯	人	Juvenile Criminal	person	168
#女性犯罪	人	Female Criminal	person	
一审民商案件涉案标的	亿元	Case－involving Amount of Bid for Civil & Economic Case in First Instance	100 million yuan	517. 35
执行案件实际到位金额	亿元	The received Amount of Money in Carry out Case	100 million yuan	122. 30
办结申请公示催告和支付令的案	件	Closed Apply to Show the Demand Commonly & Indemnity	case	264
标的	万元	Total Amount of Money	10000 yuan	
检察机关		**Procurator's Offices**		
批捕各类犯罪嫌疑人	人	Approve to Arrest Crime Suspects	person	3281
起诉各类犯罪被告人	人	Accuse Crime Suspects	person	18976
受理群众来信来访	件	Accept Public Report, Accuse Crime and Visit	case	8461
举报	件	Reporting of the Offence	case	453
控告	件	Accuse	case	2456
申诉	件	Appeal	case	5552
提出民事行政抗诉	件	Submit Civil and Administrative Counterappeal.	case	96

表13-15 全市档案人员及馆藏和编研情况（2022年）
Conditions of Files Stored and Used in the Archives（2022）

指标	单位	Indicators	Unit	全市 Total	其中 of Which 市局馆 Municipal	市区合计 Urban District	县市合计 County
机构数		**Number of Institutions**					
档案行政管理机构	个	Administrative Department of Archives	unit	11	1	6	4
国家综合档案馆	个	National Comprehensive Archives	unit	11	1	6	4
现有工作人员数		**Number of Staff and Workers**					
档案行政管理机构	人	Administrative Department of Archives	person	34	12	13	9
国家综合档案馆	人	National Comprehensive Archives	person	164	20	79	65
馆藏档案		**Archives Stored**					
全宗	个	Whole Volume	unit	2930	540	1162	1228
案卷	卷	Files	volume	2966618	509041	936936	1520641
以件为保管单位档案	件	Archives Which Regard a Storage Unit by Files	pieces	3009103	368217	2108272	532614
录音、录像影片档案	盘	Records, Films on Videotape	copy	3889	897	1397	1595
照片档案	张	Pictures	pieces	478400	91752	203592	183056
实物档案	件	Physical Archives	pieces	20251	5105	7627	7519
馆藏资料	册	Number of Material Stored	volume	189821	53000	82957	53864
档案馆总建筑面积	平方米	Floor Space of Archives	sq.m	119345	14527	44326	60492
档案库房建筑面积	平方米	Floor Space of Storerooms	sq.m	33021	5353	12884	14784
本年档案资料利用		**Use of Material in This Year**					
利用档案	人次	Number of Persons Using Material	times	49238	3027	21936	24275
利用档案	卷次	Number of Archives Used	volume	108639	15244	24790	68605
利用资料	人次	Number of Archives Used	times	637	434	69	134
利用资料	册次	Number of Material Used	times	4996	4529	154	313
本年编研档案资料内部参考	万字	Compiling and Researching Material Restricted	10000 words	237.6	21.9	197.7	18.0
本年编研档案资料公开出版物	万字	Public Press Compiling and Researching Material	10000 words	301.8	31.0	240.2	30.6

主要统计指标解释

【全年供水总量】指公用自来水厂和自备水源的社会单位全年的供水总量，包括有效供水量及损失水量。

【城市人口用水普及率】指城市用水的非农业人口数（不包括临时人口和流动人口）与城市非农业人口总数的比例。计算公式：

用水普及率=(城市用水的非农业人口数÷城市非农业人口数)×100%

【公共绿地】指供游览休息的各种公园、动物园、植物园、陵园以及花园、游园和供旅游休息用的林荫道绿地、广场绿地。不包括一般栽植的行道树及林荫道的面积。

【废水排放总量】包括生产废水和生活污水。生产废水指企、事业单位在生产、科研过程中向外排放的所有排放口的废水量总和。生活污水指城镇居民区和企、事业单位职工集中居住区排放的污水量。

【工业废水排放量】指经过企业厂区所有排放口排到企业外部的工业废水量 。包括生产废水、外排的直接冷却水、超标排放的矿井地下水和与工业废水混排的厂区生活污水，不包括外排的间接冷却水（清污不分流的间接冷却水应计算在内）。

【工业废气排放量】指企业厂区内燃料燃烧和生产工艺过程中产生的各种排入空气的含有污染物的气体的总量，以标准状态(273K,101325Pa)计。

【工业粉尘排放量】指企业在生产工艺过程中排放的颗粒物重量。如钢铁企业的耐火材料粉尘、焦化企业的筛焦系统粉尘、烧结机的粉尘、石灰窑的粉尘、建材企业的水泥粉尘等。不包括电厂排入大气的烟尘。

【工业固体废物产生量】指企业在生产过程中产生的固体状、半固体状和高浓度液体状废弃物的总量，包括危险废物、冶炼废渣、粉煤灰、炉渣、煤矸石、尾矿、放射性 废物和其他废物等；不包括矿山开采的剥离废石和掘进废石（煤矸石和呈酸性或碱性的废石 除外）。酸性或碱性废石是指采掘的废石其流经水、雨淋水的pH值小于 4 或pH值大于10.5者 。

【社会福利事业单位】指集中收养社会孤老,残,幼的机构。包括由民政部门管理的社会福利院、儿童福利院、精神病人福利院和城镇集体办的福利院,以及农村集体举办的敬老院。

Explanatory Notes on Main Statistical Indicators

【Annual Volume of Water Supply】 refers to the total volume of water supplied by the public water–works and those owned by individual enterprises and institutions during the whole year, including both the effective water supply and loss during the water supply.

【Percentage of Urban Population with Access to Tap Water】 refers to the ratio of urban non–agricultural population (excluding temporary and mobile population) with access to tap water to the total urban non–agricultural population. The formula is:

Percentage of Population with Access to Tap Water=(Urban Non–agricultural Population with Access to Tap Water ÷ Urban Non–agricultural Population) 100%

【Public Green Area】 refers to green areas of various parks, zoos, botanical gardens, cemeteries, amusement parks, tree–flanked boulevards, green–land squares for tourism and relaxation. Area with trees planted along–side the streets and boulevards are excluded.

【Total Discharge of Sewage】 includes production sewage and domestic sewage. Production sewage refers to the total discharge by the enterprises and institutions in their production and scientific research. Domestic sewage refers to the discharge by urban and rural residential communities and the residential neighborhoods of the enterprise/institutions staff.

【Volume of Industrial Waste Water Discharged】 refers to the volume of industrial waste water discharged, through all outlets, to the outside of industrial enterprises, including waste water produced, direct cooling water, underground water from mines that does not meet the standard of discharge, and the domestic sewage mixed up with industrial waste water when discharged, but excluding discharged indirect–cooling water.

【Volume of Waste Gas Emission】 refers to waste gas emitted from burning of fuels and from production process in the area of the factory, and is measured by 10000 standard cubic metres each year under normal condition.

【Industrial Dust Discharged】 refers to the total weight of solid dust discharged by industrial enterprises in the production process, such as dust of refractory materials from iron plants, dust from coke–screening system or from sintering machines of coking plants, dust from lime kilns, cement dust from building material enterprises, etc. but excluding smoke and dust discharged by power plants.

【Volume of Industrial Solid Wastes Produced】 refers to the total volume of solid, semi solid or high concentration liquid residue produced by industrial enterprises in their production process, including dangerous wastes, residues from melting, slag, powdered coal ash, gangue, chemical residues, tailings, radioactive residues and other residues, but excluding stripped or dug stones in mining (except gangue and acid or alkali stones which are stones washed or soaked by water with a pH value smaller than 4 or larger than 10.5.)

【Social Welfare Institutions】 refer to institutions taking care of old people without children, handicapped people and orphans. They include social welfare institutions run by civil affairs departments, children's welfare institutions social welfare institutions for mental patients, and collective owned old people's homes in tualareas.